M000198540

Guide to Philippines

Other Bradt guides to Southeast Asia

Guide to Burma Nicholas Greenwood
Guide to Laos and Cambodia John R Jones
Guide to Vietnam John R Jones

Guide to
Philippines

Stephen Mansfield

Bradt Publications, UK
The Globe Pequot Press Inc, USA

Published in 1997 by Bradt Publications,
41 Nortoft Road, Chalfont St Peter, Bucks SL9 0LA, England
Published in the USA by The Globe Pequot Press Inc, 6 Business Park Road,
PO Box 833, Old Saybrook, Connecticut 06475-0833

Copyright © 1997 Stephen Mansfield

The author and publishers have made every effort to ensure the accuracy of the information in
this book at the time of going to press. However, they cannot accept any
responsibility for any loss, injury or inconvenience resulting from
the use of information contained in this guide.

All rights reserved. No part of this publication may be reproduced, stored in a retrieval
system, or transmitted in any form or by any means, electronic, mechanical, photocopying,
recording or otherwise without the prior consent of the publishers.
Requests for permission should be addressed to
Bradt Publications, 41 Nortoft Road, Chalfont St Peter, Bucks SL9 0LA in the UK;
or to The Globe Pequot Press Inc,
6 Business Park Road, PO Box 833, Old Saybrook, Connecticut 06475-0833
in North and South America.

British Library Cataloguing in Publication Data
A catalogue record for this book is available from the British Library
ISBN 1 898323 58 5

Library of Congress Cataloging-in-Publication Data
Mansfield, Stephen
    Guide to Philippines / Stephen Mansfield -- 1st ed.
        p. cm.
    Includes index.
    ISBN 1-898323-58-5
    1. Philippines – Guidebooks. I. Title.
DS654.M24 1997   96-53437
915.9904'48--DC21   CIP

Photographs Stephen Mansfield
Front cover: Terraced rice fields
Back cover: An Ifugao woman at Banaue

Illustrations Rebecca de Mendonça
Maps Steve Munns

Typeset from the author's disc by Wakewing Ltd, High Wycombe HP13 7QA
Printed and bound in Spain by Grafo SA, Bilbao

ABOUT THE AUTHOR

Stephen Mansfield is a British-born writer and photographer who has been based in Tokyo since the mid-1980s. His work has appeared in over 80 magazines and newspapers worldwide. He has also contributed photos for several books on southeast Asia. He is the author of a guidebook on Myanmar and writer and co-photographer of *The Unquiet Earth: Images of Burma*. Two more titles – *Tokyo On The Loop: A Photo Journey Around the Yamanote Line*, and *Culture Shock! Laos* – are due out next year. He has travelled extensively throughout Asia and the Middle East and has lived at various times in London, Barcelona and Cairo. As one of the foremost travel writers on Laos he has published many articles on the people and culture of Indochina, as well as a coffee-table book entitled *Laos A Portrait*. He has visited the Philippines several times since the late eighties, having a special interest in the ethnic people of north Luzon. He now divides his time between projects in Asia and his home in the southwest of France.

CONTENTS

Maps

Introduction

The fortitude of the Filipino people, with their innate cheerfulness and optimism in adversity, is quite remarkable. For almost 400 years they have had to contend with Spanish and American colonisation, succeeded by the long arm of dictatorship. Even their well-earned delivery from the oppression of the Marcos years has been periodically undermined by insurgency and the threat of military coups. If this were not enough, the people of the Philippines have, in the last ten years or more, had to cope with a spate of unprecedented natural calamities – earthquakes, typhoons, volcanic eruptions, massive landslides and flooding – that have been visited upon them with an almost Old Testament prodigality and wrath.

Filipinos have been forced, in a sense, to conquer their own history, climate and geology, or at least to reach an accommodation with them. The publication of this book coincides with an extraordinary, and largely hopeful, phase in Philippine history and life. With the last of the American military bases long gone, and statistics indicating that the country is one of the fastest growing new economies in Southeast Asia, the psychology of dependence is visibly on the wane. The nation which hit the world's headlines in 1987 when Corazon Aquino's People Power movement took to the streets is finally freeing itself from the influences of its former patrons and benefactors and beginning in the process to assert its own values and identity.

Filipinos are a hard people to define: oriental by virtue of geography and their Malayo-Polynesian roots, but with a temperament, outlook on life, and earthy catholicism more suited to the Caribbean or Central America than to the races of Southeast Asia. Filipinos are regarded as one of the most convivial and spontaneous peoples of Asia. Beneath the sudden, sometimes volatile, swings from fatalistic and pensive moods to high spirits, is an underlying warmth, generosity and grace few visitors fail to notice. The *joie de vivre* of the Filipino people, their passion for music and rhythm, is most apparent during their festivals and fiestas. It is hardly surprising that these attractive people and their impartial hospitality should attract not only the serious traveller, but also the dedicated seeker of pleasure.

There could hardly be a better time, in fact, to visit the Philippines. Most of the archipelago remains remarkably untouched by commercial tourism. With the exception of major cities and a handful of well-publicised tourist destinations, untrammelled beaches, coral reefs, ancient rainforests, volcanic peaks, nature reserves, marine fauna, and little-known ethnic minorities invite exploration and discovery. In contrast to its natural beauty and eclectic culture, the country's epicurean nightlife offers a heady blend of music clubs, casinos, discotheques and bars to suit most tastes. Visitors encounter few barriers to communication in a country where English is widely spoken and much store is set on sociability.

Visitors will soon discover that the physical and ethnic diversity of the atoll, and the permutations on travel in a country where any number of itineraries for one destination are possible, are virtually inexhaustible. For travellers whose curiosity is not easily quenched, there is always another island just over the horizon.

Part One

THE ISLANDS

Ifugao elder

Chapter One

Background Information

A SHORT HISTORY

> "This is a land of broken promises"
>
> Cory Aquino

The Philippines did not enter into recorded history until the arrival of the Spaniards in 1521, but earlier accounts by Arab and Chinese traders and a trove of recent archaeological findings have provided clues that have helped to piece together an increasingly more accurate identikit picture of the past. The Negritos, a race of dark-haired, cave-dwelling pygmies, are believed to have infiltrated the islands some 25,000 to 30,000 years ago by walking across land bridges that existed between the archipelago and the Asian mainland. This Stone-Age race of hunter-gatherers and fishermen are the forebears of several tribes such as the Batak, Aeta and Mamanuwa who still inhabit the insalubrious jungles and mountain areas found on some remote islands. The Negritos are usually described as the aborigines of the Philippines. An important archaeological discovery, unearthed in 1962 by Dr Robert B Fox in the Tabon Caves of western Palawan, was a 22,000-year-old skullcap. Rudimentary implements, traces of charcoal and the bones of small mammals were also found on the same dig. Tabon Man is believed to have come to the islands 45,000 to 55,000 years ago. The fossilised bones of rhinoceros, elephants, stegodons, various extinct animals and mammals, and a number of Palaeolithic tools, carbon-dated to as much as 150,000 years ago, have also been discovered in the Cagayan Valley. Efforts are being made to connect these findings with the existence of even earlier inhabitants.

Secondary migrations

As the ice melted the seas rose, covering for ever the convenient land bridges which had provided a relatively easy passage for the original settlers who came to these islands. Future migrations by more sophisticated races would be by sea. Almost certainly, the first to arrive were Indonesians, sailing their outrigger canoes from Indochina in a successive wave of migrations between 5,000 and 500BC. They imported a neolithic culture that included such innovations as pottery, woodcarving, tattooing, new farming methods, the manufacture of polished stone tools and later domestic and agricultural implements and utensils of copper and bronze. It is also possible that they introduced the irrigation techniques necessary for the building of the massive, irrigated rice terraces found in northern Luzon.

Next to arrive were the headhunting, but generally more culturally advanced, Malays somewhere between 300BC and AD100. Exponents of the Iron Age, they were able to introduce copper- and iron-smelting and forging techniques that could produce not only tools but more sophisticated and deadly weaponry. They were also able to initiate developments in the making of textiles through the use of spindles and looms as well as pottery and ornament making from glass beads. Later migrations of Malays to disembark on these shores between the 2nd and 13th centuries arrived in boats called balanghais, bringing with them improved methods of rice cultivation and even their own alphabet. The last, and possibly most culturally significant, group to arrive were the Malays of the 14th and 15th centuries, forebears of the Muslim populations of present-day Sulu and Mindanao.

Other influences

It was inevitable, given the location of the archipelago along the sea lanes between the South China Sea and the Persian Gulf, that the advance guards of other cultures, in the form of trading vessels, would leave their influences and imprint on these shores. Trade between Japan and Arabia was already well established by the 9th century, but there were also Siamese, Chinese and Indian seamen plying these waters, as well as the predictable kind of freebooters (pirates, adventurers, missionaries) drawn to virgin territory like this by the prospect of booty, or the harvesting of souls. As the islands' reputation for natural resources and riches, such as the highly desirable pearls found in the Sulu Archipelago, spread, impromptu commercial entrepots like Buansa (present-day Jolo) were gradually established. Cross-cultural exchanges motivated by trade were not uncommon. There is one account, for example, of an Arab ship carrying Filipino traders from Mindoro to Canton in AD982.

Indian cultural influences made themselves felt between the 7th and early 16th century via traders and immigrants filtering in from Indo-Malay empires based in Sumatra and Java, and other land masses like Siam and Indochina that had fallen under the influence of Indian civilisation. Relics from these civilisations have been found on several islands and indicate that the impact of these Indianised, Hindu-Buddhist empires was limited to trade, social customs, folklore, dress, language and the arts, but did not extend to any form of political hegemony.

Historians have been unable to put a date on the islands' first contact with China, but some scholars have suggested that this took place during the vigorous Zhou Dynasty (1066-221BC). Others have claimed that ties were established during the latter Tang Dynasty (AD618-987) era. What is certain is that by the early years of the Southern Sung Dynasty (AD960-1127) a flourishing trade in such items as gold, amber, pearls, tortoiseshell, rattan, hemp, hardwood, turtle shell and cotton, and edible products such as sea cucumbers, honey, birds' nests and shark fins, was reaching the busy stevedores and merchants of Xiamen. In exchange, the Chinese were able to offer their superior porcelain and ceramic ornamentation and wares, ceremonial fans and umbrellas, silk and brocade textiles, and objects of more practical use like lead sinkers for fishing, and tin and iron eating and cooking utensils. Relations between the two trading partners, spurred on by mutual profit, inter-marriage between Chinese merchants and Filipinas, and the establishment of trading ports at places like Cavite, Laguna and Manila, were amicable and enduring, reaching their peak in the 18th century. Chinese influence is still evident in the social customs, arts and crafts, cooking and aesthetic tastes of the peoples of the Philippines, and even in some of the vocabulary that forms part of the Tagalog language.

Non-Muslim Arabs arrived in the 9th century and the beginning of the 10th, seeking alternative trade routes for obtaining Chinese goods, having been expelled from China's central and southern ports. Northern Luzon, Sulu and Palawan provided convenient stopping-off points on their route to Formosa (Taiwan). By the middle of the 14th century, Islam had spread from Sumatra to the Malay Peninsula. With the influential sultanate of Malacca at its geographical centre, it had grown into a power to be reckoned with. A fiercely evangelical religion, Islam brought with it a highly developed culture and social order and a ready-to-implement political system. Muslims established a thriving trading centre on Jolo and, by the 13th century, missionaries had begun to make significant numbers of converts to the new faith. Abu Bakr, a charismatic adventurer and champion of Islam, declared a Muslim sultanate on Sulu in 1450. At the beginning of the 16th century, Sharif Mohammed Kabungsuwan, a holy man from Johore, converted the tribes of the Cotabato Valley to Islam and established the powerful Maguindanao sultanate there. Marriage alliances, strengthened by commercial ties and a political and religious system of belief, provided an inducement to expand throughout large areas of Sulu, Mindanao, and even beyond to southern Luzon and the outskirts of Manila. But for the Spanish conquest of the Philippines, the entire archipelago could well have become an Islamic republic. The arrival of the Spanish began a process which effectively reversed Islamisation, confining it to the impenetrable jungles and mountain fastnesses of the southern islands.

The sword and the cross

The existence of the Philippines was revealed to Spain and Portugal as a result of their intense rivalry for the fabled riches and spices of the Orient, and the manic greed that spurred them on to acquire new territory for their expanding empires. In a series of papal bulls, culminating in the Treaty of Tordesillas in 1494, the two superpowers had agreed to honour a largely imaginary boundary line which divided the known world into two distinct halves. Lands discovered east of the line would go to the Portuguese, those acquired to the west of the demarcation line could be claimed by Spain.

Ferdinand Magellan, a Portuguese navigator of exceptional skill and in the service of the Spanish king, is credited with being the first Westerner to set foot on the islands. Magellan, whose voyage was undertaken to prove his theory that a western route to the Orient existed, arrived on the uninhabited island of Homonhon on 16 March 1521. He then sailed to the nearby island of Limasawa, where he was well received. The ruler, Rajah Kolambu, and Magellan sealed their friendship by making a pact in which they drank a cup of wine mixed with their respective blood. On Easter Sunday, Kolambu and his wife, along with several hundred of his followers, were converted and baptised, and the country's first Catholic mass held.

A few days later, Magellan planted a large wooden cross by the seashore here, claimed the land for Spain and renamed it the Archipelago of San Lazaro. Magellan then proceeded to the trading port of Zubu (Cebu), where he was again well received by the ruler, the avuncular, heavily tattooed Rajah Humabon, who invited him to make a similar blood pact. This in turn led to the voluntary conversion of Humabon's family and over 800 of his retainers. Fragments of the original cross Magellan planted here can still be seen in Cebu. Only one local leader remained hostile towards Magellan and his men: Chief Lapu Lapu, the ruler of nearby Mactan Island. It has never been established whether Magellan attempted to forcibly convert the recalcitrant Lapu Lapu, or whether he was obliged to take sides in some kind of local dispute, but what is indisputable is that Magellan, along with 60 Spanish soldiers, landed on Mactan on 27 April 1521 to confront a fierce contingent of almost 2,000 natives under Lapu Lapu's command. Here, in the words of the expedition's chronicler, Antonio Pigafetta, Magellan, "our mirror, our light, our comfort, and our true guide", met his fate. Humabon, angered at the casual violation of women on his island by the Spanish and given a devastating recent example of their vulnerability, massacred several more of Magellan's frightened men before the now much depleted crew were able to make their escape to Cebu. This incident, resulting from the tragic collision of two uncomprehending cultures, marks the first native resistance to foreign domination in the Philippines.

Only one of Magellan's five ships, the Victoria, survived the voyage, eventually reaching Spain on 6 September 1522. A mere 18 out of the original 264 crew members were aboard. Despite the heavy toll in lives, the expedition had achieved all of its main objectives and was hailed a success. The Victoria earned the distinction of being the first ship to circumnavigate the world, and the rich cargo of spices which the crew had shrewdly picked up in the Moluccas at the beginning of their homeward voyage fetched a high price: more than enough, in fact, to cover the expense of the voyage and come out with a tidy profit. This fact alone, and the vindication of Magellan's theory that a western route both existed and was a viable commercial passage, encouraged the Spanish to consider acquiring more colonies in the Orient. Several more expeditions were mounted between 1525 and 1542. The last of these, led by Ruy Lopez de Villalobos, saw the naming of the islands of Leyte and Samar Las Islas Filipinas, after Prince Felipe of Asturias who would later become King Philip of Spain. The name was later to serve for the entire archipelago.

The Spanish colonial period

In order to establish a permanent colony in the Philippines, a full-scale expedition was sent from Mexico to subdue the islands and convert the natives to Catholicism. The expedition, under Miguel Lopez de Legaspi and the navigator Fray Andres de Urdaneta, arrived in Cebu in 1565, but owing to the hostility of the Cebuanos they were obliged to explore other islands in the Visayas and Mindanao. After making a blood pact with the chief of Bohol, Rajah Sikatuna, Legaspi decided to make the strategically well-placed settlement of Cebu his base of operations for subduing the whole archipelago. The city was set on fire, and a fortified settlement, destined to become Cebu City, was built. After sporadic resistance from the native population who had fled to the hills to regroup, Humabon's son agreed to recognise the authority of Spain, and yet another pact was sealed with blood. Fray Urdaneta was then instructed to return to Spain, a journey which proved to be of enormous significance as he discovered a route via the Pacific Ocean that soon opened up the way for an economically important galleon route between Acapulco and Manila.

With Legaspi installed as governor-general of the colony, the exploration of other islands began in earnest. Constantly plagued by lack of food, Legaspi was forced to resettle in Panay, where he founded the port of Capiz in 1569. Favourable reports describing Manila, its natural harbour and fertile inland plains, combined with a continuing shortage of food, persuaded Legaspi to send Martin de Goiti and his grandson, Juan de Salcedo, there to conquer what turned out to be the kingdom of Maynilad, a prosperous and well-situated region ruled by the young Rajah Sulayman, a figure who staunchly resisted Spanish suzerainty. A second attempt to take the city succeeded, and the settlement was taken without bloodshed. Manila was declared the capital of the Philippines and the Spanish set about constructing a fortified city, which they called Ciudad Murada, or Intramuros. Legaspi died of a heart attack in 1572 before the completion of the walled city.

The colonisation of the Philippines moved rapidly after the acquisition of Manila. Martin de Goiti and Salcedo, arguably Spain's last great conquistadors, took central Luzon, the Laguna de Bay region, Camarines Norte, and Tayabas (Quezon Province), before proceeding to subdue Zambales, Pangasinan and Ilocos in the north. The Cagayan valley and the area of Bicol were also taken. Within only ten years most of the islands were firmly under Spanish control. King Philip's order that the methods used in Spain's conquest of the Americas should not be repeated in the Philippines, combined with little armed resistance on the part of the majority of Filipinos, had made the pacification of the islands a relatively bloodless affair.

Rule by Church and state

The new Spanish rulers did not limit the influence of the clergy to the spiritual or cultural realm only. The Church played a key role in both economic and political fields and eventually came to symbolise the more pernicious aspects of colonialisation. In one of those curious historical ironies, the native population turned more and more towards a Catholic belief system and outlook, but simultaneously developed a strong anti-clerical aversion.

Although the Muslims of Sulu and Mindanao and some of the pagan hilltribes inhabiting inaccessible parts of the interior were never subdued, the arrival of large numbers of friars saw the country divided into different spheres of religious influence. The powerful and intellectually active Jesuits worked throughout Marinduque, Leyte, Samar, Negros, Bool, Cavite and the parts of Mindanao where they were able to establish a toehold. Augustinians were allotted the Ilocos, Cebu, Panay, Batangas, Bulacan and Pampanga. Tribal and animist beliefs were soon cleverly transformed into the rituals and mystique of Catholicism. Incantation became prayer; magic, a trust in miracles, the propitiation of nature expressed in such events as thanksgiving rituals at harvest time, and full-moon festivals, were gradually replaced with religious fiestas, Christian pageantry and the mass, all of which immensely impressed the humble peasants who were exposed to this overwhelming cultural spectacle.

The Filipinos may have become devout Catholic converts, but there the parity ended. The Spanish were not interested in educating their new subjects and consistently refused to teach them their language, limiting their opportunities for self-improvement to learning the scriptures from obliging priests in the local dialect. Unlike the British or the Dutch, who were primarily concerned with the success of their entrepreneurial activities, and were content to allow local rulers to administer their own indigenous populations and permit them to preserve their own religion, traditions and art forms, Spain's aim was to eradicate the native culture altogether and replace it with a docile, easily manipulated, Christianised population. The Church remains a strong influence today and continues to be a unifying factor in the life of Christianised Filipinos. Many fine churches have survived the Spanish legacy.

The Spanish administrators

The islands were administered by members of a Royal Audencia (Supreme Court) with a governor-general appointed by the king at its head. Enormous power was invested with the governor-general. The islands were divided into plots of land called encomiendas, which were often awarded to people who had served the colony in some way with their loyalty. These encomienderos were granted the right to administer and tax the residents within their territory. Because of widespread abuses and its unpopularity with the Filipino peasants, the system was abolished in 1674 and provinces introduced instead. Until 1813 the islands were governed by the Viceroy of Mexico, or New Spain as it then was. This was the period when the galleon trade was at its height. These ships were vital to the coffers of Manila, and the sinking, or fleecing, of a single galleon by pirates could ruin investors and serve a severe blow to the economy of the capital until the next ship came in. On a successful voyage, spices, pearls, gemstones, porcelain and other coveted goods from the Orient would be exchanged for gold and silver. The galleon trade came to an abrupt end with the Mexican War of Independence, and the subsequent decline of Spain's fortunes. After the war, the Philippines was administered directly from Madrid.

Wars and rebellion

During three and a half centuries of colonial rule, Spain faced frequent challenges to its rule in the islands. Many of these were internal uprisings by Filipinos and Chinese residents protesting against general oppression or against specific issues like forced labour and tribute. Others were demands for land reform or reactions to economic exploitation by a powerful and corrupt clergy. Between 1574, the year of the first Filipino insurrection, and the departure of the Spanish, no less than 200 revolts of one kind or another had taken place. Protests which escalated into violence were swiftly and brutally suppressed. The Spanish were engaged in an ongoing struggle with the Muslims of Mindanao and Sulu, who managed throughout the Spanish period to resist attempts to assimilate them into the colony proper. Expeditions designed to quell the independent-minded Moros, as the Spanish disparagingly referred to them, continued to no avail right up until 1895. Coastal villages and ports were also occasionally harassed by Chinese pirates and warlords. Manila was even attacked on one occasion by the wily Chinese mercenary Limahong, who brought 64 junks and over 3,000 men into the bay before being routed.

Until Portugal was annexed by Spain, the Portuguese, who believed that under the Treaty of Tordesillas the islands were rightfully theirs, made several attempts to invade the colony, frequently targeting coastal ports. The Dutch also made several unsuccessful efforts to invade the islands between 1600 and 1647. The British had more luck and, in 1762, at the height of the Seven Years' War between the two rivals, an expeditionary force dispatched from India under General William Draper succeeded in occupying Manila and the surrounding area for 20 months until the capital was handed back to Spain under the conditions of the Treaty of Paris in 1763.

The seeds of nationalism

The short British occupation of Manila saw the stirrings of an independence movement which gained increasing momentum in the 19th century as more liberal ideas began to filter into the country with the opening up of the economy to foreign businesses and trade. With the opening of the Suez Canal in 1869, many Filipinos were able for the first time to leave their country and study in Spain and other European countries, from where they returned with newly acquired liberal ideas. They were also able to observe at close quarters Spain's weakened and demoralised state as a result of its decaying empire and decline as an international power.

The demand for civil and religious reforms took on a more nationalistic character in 1872 when three Filipino priests, accused on trumped-up charges of inciting a mutiny in Cavite, were summarily executed. The movement for freedom and independence became more determined from this point onwards. The intellectual and spiritual leaders of the new movement for reform and eventual independence included the Filipino patriots Graciano Lopez Jaena, Marcelo H del Pilar and Dr Jose Rizal, a gifted man of letters whose nationalist poems and critical essays inspired many literate Filipinos to join the struggle. Jose Rizal founded the Liga Filipina, a seminal nationalist movement, in 1892, but was arrested and exiled to Dapitan in Mindanao, the Philippine equivalent of Siberia, where he was held on the charge of being a revolutionary agitator.

Other Filipino leaders, like Andres Bonifacio, resorted to violence in order to achieve their ends. Bonifacio founded a revolutionary council and society called Katipunan. When the authorities got wind of its existence, several of its members were arrested, tortured and executed. This led to Bonifacio's famous "Cry of Balintawak" on 26 August 1896, which signalled the beginning of the Philippine Revolution. Emilio Aguinaldo, who was shortly to replace Bonifacio as the leader of the revolution, led the first organised uprising in Cavite. On 30 December 1896, Jose Rizal was executed by a firing squad, on transparently false charges of sedition. To the chagrin of the authorities, this transformed him overnight into a hero and martyr, and the flames of nationalism were fanned even more. On 12 June 1898 Aguinaldo proclaimed Philippine independence.

Cuba and the American period

Far away in the Caribbean, Cuba, another Spanish colony, was fighting its own war of independence. The United States, keen to join the ranks of the world powers and to extend its influence overseas, intervened on the side of the Cubans. With Spain and America at war, Commodore George

Dewey, heading a conveniently placed American squadron in the Asia region when hostilities were announced, was ordered to proceed to the Philippines, where he easily defeated the Spanish fleet. In August 1898, the Americans, with the help of Filipino patriots, captured Manila. Assiduously ignoring the key role played by the Filipinos in this struggle, the islands were ceded to the Americans under the Treaty of Paris on 10 December 1898. The United States agreed to pay Spain the sum of US$20 million as a condolence for the loss of their colony. The people of the Philippines soon found out that they had merely exchanged one colonial power for another, and that American promises were no more reliable than Spanish ones.

An incident in which an American soldier fatally shot a Filipino in Manila sparked off the Philippine-American War on 4 February 1899. The country was ruthlessly pacified at great cost to lives, and even after the capture and imprisonment of Aguinaldo, the campaign limped on until 1903. A civil government was eventually set up with William H Taft as the islands' first governor. Not all of the American public by any means approved of the seizure of the Philippines by their countrymen, and growing opinion at home soon made it clear that the practice of colonialism was not compatible with the political ideology and democratic traditions of Americans. The writer, Mark Twain, in fine satirical form, wrote that "we are as indisputably in possession of a wide-spreading archipelago as if it were our own property; we have pacified some thousands of islanders and buried them; destroyed their fields; burned their villages and turned their widows and orphans out of doors ... and subjugated the remaining millions by Benevolent Assimilation which is the pious new name of the musket."

In order to appease growing resentment at the American presence, the Philippine Bill, outlining the procedure for an elected national assembly, was passed in 1902. Manuel L Quezon and Sergio Osmena were appointed respectively as leader and main speaker of the assembly. Filipinos were given civil service appointments as a run-up to eventual independence and two representatives were sent to serve in the US Congress as resident commissioners. The 1916 Philippine Autonomy Act contained a full bill of rights, and in 1934 a constitution was drawn up. In 1935 the Philippine Commonwealth Government was set up. The Americans promised full independence for the islands after a ten-year transitional period, a pledge that was delayed by one year because of unforeseen world events.

War and independence

Only one day after the attack on Pearl Harbor, the Japanese bombed the Philippines and landed in Luzon, entering Manila on 2 January 1942. Both US and Filipino troops suffered great losses at Corrigidor Island and the Bataan Peninsula which fell to the Japanese on 9 April 1942. In what became known as the "Death March", thousands of prisoners of war were sent to a concentration camp at Capas. Many who had survived the ordeals of the march were to die of disease and starvation. General Douglas MacArthur, head of US forces in the Philippines, left for Australia after the fall of Bataan, with the famous pledge "I shall return". The three-year Japanese occupation was marked by unbelievable, often apparently gratuitous, acts of brutality. As they did elsewhere in Asia, the Japanese set up a puppet government under Jose L Laurel, but by 1944 a well-organised resistance movement had formed. The war of liberation began in earnest in October 1944 when General MacArthur landed on Leyte Gulf and began his northward advance towards Manila. The campaign that ensued was one of the fiercest in the whole of the war. Manila was heavily bombed in February 1945 and the Japanese forces, holed up in Intramuros, were forced to retreat to the north. While the Americans conducted their mopping-up operations all over the archipelago, a hopeless last-ditch stand was being made by the Japanese in the north of Luzon. With the surrender of General Yamashita, the so-called "Tiger of Malaya", at Baguio on 3 September 1945, the war came to an end.

The country lay in ruins, the toll in lives had been formidable and the economy was in a shambles. Manila bore the distinction of being the second most damaged city in the war after Warsaw. The Filipinos still had their promise of Independence to sustain them, and instead of allowing the Americans to linger and repair the damage for them, they proudly insisted that the new occupying force honour its word; on 4 July 1946, in an independence ceremony held in Rizal Park, the Filipino flag was raised for the first time. With this gesture ended what has been colourfully described as "350 years in a convent and 50 years in Hollywood".

Manuel Roxas, president of the new republic, had the daunting task of national reconstruction before him, hampered by the emergence of a new breed of corrupt officials and opportunists. His term of office was short lived, however, and when he died of a heart attack in 1948 his post was taken over by Elpidio Quirino. A further setback occurred when the next president was killed in an aeroplane crash. The following years saw the presidency filled by Carlos Garcia, Diosdado Macapagal and Ferdinand Marcos.

The Marcos era

Marcos, a gifted lawyer and rising congressman, finally made it to the presidency in 1965. Early successes in tackling the country's chronic levels of crime and corruption, problems which had earned the islands the unflattering epithet "the Wild East", helped consolidate Marcos' position and he was elected to a second term in 1969. Flushed with success and pronouncing volubly on his concept of a "New Society", but knowing at the same time that the constitution precluded presidential third terms, Marcos declared martial law in 1972. A communist insurgency, a worsening economy and civil disorder were the reasons put forward to the public as justification.

Crime did indeed decrease during the early months of martial law, especially gun ownership and the incidence of violent crimes. Improvements in public health care were introduced and infrastructure changes made. A revitalised foreign policy, resulting among other things in the Philippines joining the Association of Southeast Asian Nations (ASEAN) and organisations like the Economic and Social Commission for Asia and the Pacific (ESCAP), and its provisional membership of the General Agreement on Tariffs and Trade (GATT), were hailed as promising advances. But as time passed it became evident that the rich were shamelessly lining their own pockets, while the poor, as a result of rising prices and a general deterioration in their quality of life, were progressively getting poorer. The economy, shored up by what came to be dubbed "crony capitalism", was clearly going nowhere. Although initially supported by the majority of Filipinos, martial law gradually became synonymous with the loss or suspension of personal freedoms. Journalists were arrested and many publications closed down. Only a limited number of TV stations favourable to the regime were allowed to operate. Businesses and industries owned by opponents of Marcos' policies were seized and taken over by the government. Communist suspects or sympathisers were rounded up in the middle of the night, and the constitution was abolished. Interrogations and beatings were common.

Armed opposition emerged in the form of the Moro National Liberation Front (MNLF) and the communist New People's Army (NPA). The Communist Party of the Philippines was banned and the two main opposition parties, the Democratic Socialist Party and the Philippine Democratic Party (PDP-Laban), were granted little effective domestic power or influence. Martial law was lifted in 1981 but Marcos was able to continue his repressive style of government through the use of presidential decrees. An election was held in June 1981 but few doubted that the results were fixed, and accusations of vote-rigging drew unfavourable attention to the Marcos government abroad, earning it a bad press. The opposition's only course was to try to gain support and exert influence from outside. When the popular exiled former senator, Benigno Aquino, requested a dialogue with the government, he was warned that, should he return, his safety could not be guaranteed. He decided not to heed what was clearly a threat. Within seconds of his arrival at Manila on 21 August 1983, in what turned out to be a suspiciously well stage-managed assassination, "Ninoy" Aquino was gunned down on the airport tarmac by a lone suspect who was then immediately killed by security guards. It has never been proved that Marcos gave the order for Aquino's death, but few Filipinos doubted who was behind the killing.

The assassination, which shocked the world and rocketed Philippine politics on to the front pages of its newspapers overnight, united the people in a way that none of the repressive measures practised under martial law had. Suddenly the country was galvanised into action, and in the parliamentary elections of 1984 the United Nationalist Democratic

Organisation (UNIDO) won a surprising 63 seats. A snap election planned for 7 February 1986 managed to unite many opposition groups for the first time. Aquino's widow Corazon and her vice-presidential running mate in the PDP, Salvador Laurel, agreed to run against Marcos.

The people, clamouring for change, rallied behind their party in unprecedented numbers. Banks, newspapers and businesses and institutions supporting Marcos were boycotted, peaceful street protests were held, and the first stirrings of "People Power" made themselves felt. A major blow to the Marcos camp occurred when Armed Forces Vice-Chief of Staff, Fidel Ramos, and Defense Minister, Juan Ponce Enrile, defected to the Aquino side along with their military units. Closely watched by the world's press, Marcos was restricted in his ability to manipulate the results of the election, and although, when all the votes were counted, both sides claimed equal victory, there could be no question whom the people had chosen. On 25 February, the same day that Corazon Aquino was sworn in as president, four helicopters airlifted Marcos and his extravagant wife Imelda, with their families and aides, from the Presidential Palace at Malacanang to Clark Air Force Base, from where they were later flown off to a lavish exile in Hawaii. The palace doors were thrown open to the public, and the world's journalists and TV crews were able to relay fascinating images of the Babylonian lifestyle in which the President and his First Lady had basked. Marcos died in Honolulu in September 1989. Shortly afterwards Imelda faced charges of investing in US property with public funds, but was acquitted. Numerous private civil suits against her are still being sorted out.

The Aquino years

Aquino moved quickly to restore the rights of free speech and the press, the Supreme Court and other democratic institutions that had been abrogated. She went on to abolish the national assembly, create a new constitution, replace most of the country's corrupt provincial governors and Marcos supporters with her own men, retire more than half the country's generals and free over 500 political prisoners and detainees.

The Aquino years were not easy, however, and despite the popular support given to her by the voters who had put her into office she was unable to introduce any radical changes that would improve the lives of the average, depressingly impoverished, Filipino. Benefits from the short period of economic expansion in the post-election years from 1987 to 1988 failed to percolate down to the ordinary person in the street, and the military were never really tamed. The long-awaited land reform bill failed to materialise and the government had to deal with increasing internal dissent among its own ranks, a secessionist movement in Mindanao and a series of extraordinarily ferocious natural disasters. Six coup attempts to unseat her failed, but threats of fresh military insurrection dogged the remainder of her presidency.

In gratitude for the support of her Defense Minister, General Fidel Ramos, without whom she might not have survived these coups, she proposed him as her presidential successor. Fair elections and a peaceful transition of power brought Ramos into office on 11 May 1992. The President has set forth an ambitious programme of policies to be completed before the end of his term of office in 1998. So far, laws encouraging foreign investment and a genuine effort to counter corruption within the civil service have achieved some results. A historic agreement was signed on 2 September 1996, between President Ramos and Nur Misuari, the rebel chief of the MNLF, ending a 24-year rebellion on Mindanao. Major problems remain, however, in tackling the crippling foreign debt, creating an energy policy that will eliminate the daily brownouts that plague many major cities, dealing with corruption in the military and coping with the destruction and chaos periodically visited upon the islands by natural disasters like the eruption of Mount Pinatubo. For whoever is in office, governing the Philippines remains an awesome task.

GEOGRAPHY

The 7,107 islands and islets of the Philippine Archipelago form a land mass roughly the same size as Italy (about 300,000km^2), but, because of its sprawling shape, a coastline that extends to some 18,000km and its designation as the world's second biggest island group after Indonesia, it seems considerably larger than it really is. A basic grasp of the straggling geography of these islands is vital for travellers, as itineraries will often be determined by distances, accessibility and physical topography. Only 2,000 of these islands are actually inhabited and many of those included in the above reckoning are little more than a few square metres of rock or sandbank protruding above sea level, requisitioned as buoy stands, depth markers, or for passing flocks of terns. Fewer than 2,000 of the islands are actually inhabited, and almost 3,000 of them are unnamed. The islands stretch 1,850km from north to south and, at their widest point, reach a width of 1,107km. The Bashi Ocean in the north, the Sulu and Celebes seas in the south, the South China Sea in the west and the Pacific Ocean at its eastern extremities mark the archipelago's geographical boundaries.

The three principal island groups in the Philippines are Luzon, the Visayas and Mindanao. The northern island of Luzon, together with Martinduque, Mindoro, Palawan and a number of outlying islands, is the largest of the three, covering a land mass of 141,395km^2. The centrally located Visayan Islands cover 56,000km^2 and include the islands of Cebu, Negros, Bohol, Siquijor, Panay, Samar and Leyte. Mindanao in the south is the second largest island formation at 101,999km^2, and contains the island chains of Basilan, Camiguin and the Sulu Archipelago. The highest mountain in the Philippines, Mount Apo

(2,954m, 9,695ft) is found in Mindanao. The second highest peak, Mount Pulog (2,930m, 9,616ft), lies east of Baguio in northern Luzon. Eighteen of the island's 56 volcanoes are active. Major eruptions by Mount Pinatubo and Mayon Volcano in the last decade caused great loss of life and the destruction of large tracts of arable land. Over 50,000 people lost their homes with the eruption of Mount Pinatubo on 12 June 1991 alone. Earth tremors and quakes are common. A massive earthquake struck Baguio City in July 1990, claiming 650 victims and causing untold municipal damage. Several hot springs, some of which may eventually be turned into resorts, are dotted over the islands, particularly in the north. Typhoons are regular occurrences in the Philippines, bringing with them violent abrupt squalls and torrential rain. They are all-year-round phenomena, but the incidence of typhoons is highest in the rainy season. Technically, winds must exceed 64 knots (118.5km) per hour to qualify as a typhoon. Anything below that will be classified as a tropical storm. Water both divides and unites the people of the Philippines. Natural harbours, scenic bays, gulfs and patches of sandy beaches characterise the islands' coastline, while swift streams, cascades and waterfalls run down its mountains into its valleys and gorges. Its longest rivers are the Cagayan River in Luzon, the Rio Grande, Agno, and the Agusan River in Mindanao.

The Philippines was once part of the Asian and Australasian continents, land bridges connecting northern Luzon with Taiwan, and parts of Palawan, Sulu and Mindanao with Java, Borneo, Celebes and Sumatra. The break-up of the continent may have begun as long ago as the Cretaceous period (135 million to 75 million years ago). Dramatic volcanic activity and tectonic rearrangement created the islands we see today. Glacial periods about 10,000 years ago submerged the last of the land bridges. Shallow waters off western Mindanao and Palawan suggest the existence of a sunken continental shelf, while to the east of Mindanao the sea reaches a depth of 10,670m at the Philippine Trench, the second deepest ocean trench in the world.

Population

In the mid-1990s the population of the Philippines stood at fractionally under 70 million. Although the Catholic Church is opposed on principle to contraception, abortion and sterilisation, birth control policies have been introduced by the government, although with somewhat mixed results among a nation that puts a high value on children and is more inclined to talk about "family planting" than "family planning". The birth rate continues to grow at an annual rate of 2.4%, with the average family consisting of six children. As many as 40% of Filipinos are city dwellers, the rest live in the country. The population of Manila exceeds 10 million and has a population density of 12,315 persons per km^2. In remoter parts of the country, the population density is as low as 62 persons per km^2. Roughly 43% of the population is below the age of 15.

Flora and fauna

The islands' fertile volcanic soil, warm tropical climate and relative isolation have been conducive to the growth of thousands of genera and species of plants. There are over 10,000 species of trees, flowering shrubs, vines and herbs, growing wild in the rainforests, mountains, fertile lowlands and chalky coastal woodland areas. Pine, bamboo and palm are the most common trees encountered. Both rare and common orchids grow in abundance. There are over 10,000 varieties, ranging from vandas to the highly scented sampaguita orchid, the national flower of the Philippines. This is the one you are likely to find in your room if you are staying in a luxury hotel, or to have placed as a garland around your neck as you exit from the arrivals hall at the airport if you are a VIP or esteemed business associate. The butterfly orchid (the *waling-waling*) of Mindanao reaches a span of 12.5cm. Bougainvillea are also common. Much of the flora here is similar to that found in parts of Sumatra, Australia, Borneo and even, in the north of Luzon, the Himalayas.

A relatively low conservation ethic has tolerated the depletion of vast areas of forest which provided the perfect environment for many forms of fauna to thrive in. Roughly half the country's land mass is still covered in a dense canopy of trees, but slash and burn, swidden cultivation and logging have already taken a heavy toll on this Eden, causing soil erosion, dehydration and adverse changes in the climate. The work of the Department of Environment and Natural Resources was given a helping hand by the formation of the Bureau of Forest Development in the 1970s and the more recent involvement of non-government organisations like the Haribon Foundation, as well as the interest of conservation groups and ecologists around the world. Protected areas, wildlife sanctuaries, national parks and game and bird refuges have been set up, but more efforts are needed to save the fragile ecosystems that still exist.

The absence of large-scale predators on the islands has meant that many small animals have been able to evolve and thrive. Among the more interesting species are midget and red deer, the *tamaraw* (a relative of the dwarf water buffalo), anteaters, Palawan bearcats, flying lemurs, clawless otters and an impressive pantheon of reptiles that includes pythons, king cobras, monitor lizards, freshwater crocodiles and iguanas. Queen among the 850 recorded species of butterflies and moths is the *Papilio trojano*, a spectacular green and black creature with a wingspan of 18cm, which is found only in Palawan.

The Philippines remains, despite random and indiscriminate hunting, a haven for the ornithologist. Some 160 of the 560 recorded species of birds in the Philippines are indigenous. Luzon and Mindanao are particularly rich in avifauna, but the island of Palawan is, possibly, the finest single spot in the Philippines to observe bird life. Among birds native to the Philippines are the Great Scops owl, Philippine Cockatoo, Philippine mallard, and the Nutmeg Imperial and Siete Colores pigeons. Grassland, forest and swampland play host to a number of increasingly rare birds, including pygmy falcons, peacock pheasants, parrots and the national bird, the protected Philippine eagle (*pithecophaga jeffreyi*), more commonly referred to as the haribon. The extensive shoreline and mangrove forests are home to many kinds of sea birds, such as terns, white-capped noddies, and dawing birds. These are easily observed when the tide ebbs. Other sand foragers include egrets, herons, sandpipers, whimbrels and dozens of other species who feed off small fish exposed in shallow pools and the various molluscs and crustacea that are beached up each afternoon. There are many places in the Philippines where bird-watchers and nature-lovers can put up overnight. Some of the best-known spots include the St Paul Subterranean River National Park, Mount Kanlaon National Park in Negros, Davao's Mount Apo National Park, the Quezon National Recreation Area, Pacijan Island in Cebu and the Pontong lake area near Santadar.

Marine fauna

Despite the devastation wrought by industrial pollution, commercial fishing and the dynamiting of coral reefs, the waters of the Philippines contain a fascinating spectrum of marine life that represents most of the main forms found in the Indo-Pacific region. Commercial fishing concentrates on netting sardines, mackerel, anchovies, mullet, bream, various kinds of herring and tuna, grouper and other fish of this kind. Mussels, prawns, crab and lobster are also much sought after. Poisonous sea snakes, turtles, loggerhead and hawksbill are commonly found in these waters. Magnificent coral reefs are a feature of the islands and there are hundreds of varieties of shell, particularly in eastern Samar, the Tayabas Bay area and Sorsogan. Natural pearls from the Philippines have long been coveted for their size, quality and lustre.

Climate and when to go

Warm and humid for most of the year, the climate is characterised by two recurring seasonal patterns: the dry and the wet. The annual mean temperature is 26.7°C, but there is considerable climatic variation according to region and altitude. Northern monsoons signal dry warm weather from November to May. The heat peaks in March and April. The southwest monsoon means rain, and this continues, on and off, from June to October, with July and August the wettest months. Humidity on average varies between 71% and 85%. Tropical cyclones occur at this time. Their force and frequency are unpredictable, but weather stations in the Philippines give out clear warnings in the days before a storm approaches. Visitors planning to move around the islands should bear these in mind and be prepared to plan accordingly. Signal No1 warns of a typhoon within 72 hours: Signal No 2 means it will hit within 48 hours, and Signal No 3 within 36 hours.

Such is the geographical diversity of the Philippines that one visitor can be languishing in the sun on a steamy, saltwater island at the same time someone else is slipping on a sweater to cope with the night temperatures in the mountains of northern Luzon. Despite this all-year-round variation, most people agree that the optimum months to visit the Philippines are November and February. This is also a good time to catch some of the major festivals like the Ali-Atihan and Dinagyand, which are celebrated at this time, not to mention Christmas with its candle-lit vigils, nativity cribs and costumed processions. March to May are good months for snorkelling, scuba diving and mountain trekking, although this is the time when most of the Philippines decides to take its holiday as well. There are Easter and harvest festivals worth seeing in this season. The typhoon season can wreak havoc with visitors' itineraries but even in this season it is possible, by keeping an eye on weather forecasts, to give the rain and storms a wide berth. Fortunately, the archipelago is sufficiently large and varied enough to be able to find good weather somewhere all the year round, provided that you have a flexible enough schedule.

ECONOMY

So far the Philippines have not done as well as some of the other founding members of ASEAN. President Ramos vowed that by the end of his term of office in 1998, the Philippines would rank as one of Southeast Asia's "Tiger economies", but the chances of this largely agrarian country ranking with the likes of Taiwan, Hong Kong or Singapore by the end of the century seem optimistic by any reckoning.

The world recession of the early 1980s, the instability and plundering of public funds that characterised the Marcos years, a series of droughts and the energy crisis in the early 1990s, a massive earthquake in northern Luzon, the eruption of Mount Pinatubo in 1991 which destroyed much of the fertile rice and food growing Central Plain (the "bread basket" of the Philippines), the loss of over 60,000 jobs and millions of dollars annually remitted by Filipinos who were working in Kuwait before the Iraqi invasion and subsequent Gulf War, plus a succession of coup attempts during the years of the Aquino administration, are only some of the problems inherited by the present government. Despite an encouraging upsurge in industrial growth throughout the 1990s, the nation's gross national product (GNP) still remains on a par with Asian countries like Afghanistan and Bangladesh. A stabilising of the economy through rural development, job creation, a reduction in foreign debt and inflation, and a cut in interest rates are some of the government's current priorities. Despite attempts to alleviate poverty by schemes such as the Philippine Aid Plan and the so-called "livelihood projects", the bottom line, as far as getting the country's economy back on track is concerned, is improved economic management and more foreign investment. A reputation for corruption and red tape, combined with unpredictable brownouts (power failures), as well as a number of kidnappings of wealthy businessmen over the last few years, have made prospective investors nervous about relocating their industries or opening branch offices here. The Philippines depends heavily on aid, loans and funding from Japan, the US and organisations like the International Monetary Fund and the World Bank. The Asian Development Bank offices are based in Manila. As in some other Southeast Asian economies, the export of primary commodities has been the country's main source of foreign exchange earnings. Fortunately, these remain relatively abundant, although the methods by which they are exploited often leave much to be desired.

Agriculture

Corn, rice and sweet potatoes are the main staple food crops of the Philippines, with root crops like taro, yams and cassava grown as supplements, or even replacements in times of rice and potato shortages. Products like coconut, sugar, tobacco, abaca (hemp), fruit and vegetables are its main domestic and export cash crops. Coconut oil has been an important export in recent years. The area around Quezon-Laguna is the leading producer, but more investment in this sector is being made all over the islands. Sugar is produced largely in Panay, Negros and central Luzon. Tobacco was introduced into the Philippines by the Spanish and continues to be a significant export. The main areas for cultivation are found in the Cagayan valley, the Ilocos and parts of the Central Plain. Philippine fruits are sold all over the world. The country is the world's third largest exporter of bananas. There are vast plantations of bananas and pineapples in Mindanao. Other important cash crops include rubber, cotton, kapok, cacao, coffee, sorghum, ginger and various types of nuts and beans.

Despite the widespread use of outlawed fishing methods like cyanide-dazing and dynamiting, fishing and aquaculture have grown significantly in recent years. This includes the innovative use of ponds and rice-paddy channels and ditches for the raising of milkfish and prawns, and the cultivation of seaweed for export. Meat and milk production still falls well below home demand, though there has been a noticeable increase in the raising of cattle, goats, ducks, chicken and pigs. Water buffalo are valued, not only as working beasts, but for their meat and milk.

Fairly primitive tools like ploughshares may often be encountered in the rice and vegetable fields of these islands, but not so in its forests, where up-to-date mechanised equipment is brought in to fell vast swaths of forest. Topping the list of most valuable trees are the hardwoods such as Philippine mahogany, a type of dipterocarp. Mindanao is a major log producer. Narra, ipil and molave are also much sought after for their attractive grain and durability. A number of secondary products having both practical and economic value include resin, bamboo, rattan, gums, natural dyes and seed oils. A certain amount of wood (generally a sustainable quantity) is used locally for furniture-making, house building, carving and as fuel. Smaller faster-growing trees suitable for paper and pulp processing have been cultivated since 1976, when a ban on exporting logs was introduced. Illegal logging, insufficient reforestation and the effects of shifting cultivation are still taking their toll on wood resources, however.

Industry, energy and tourism

The Philippines have a number of other convertible natural resources which should help to put the economy on a better footing in the future. Mineral resources include gold, silver, copper, nickel, zinc, iron, cobalt, platinum, lead and manganese. There is also an abundance of natural non-metals such as gypsum, barite, marble, silica, sulphur, pyrite, guano, clay, dolomite and various kinds of phosphates. The Philippines is the world's largest handler of refractory chrome. However, large areas of the country have yet to be properly geologically surveyed and it has been estimated that as much as 85% of the nation's mineral resources remain unexploited.

Most of the country's manufacturing industries are based in or around Manila, although development projects have been set up more recently in Leyte, Cebu, Mindanao and elsewhere. Industry is largely geared to manufacturing consumer goods for the local market, and in processing raw materials into export food-and- drink goods. Multinational companies have done much to stimulate local economies in the areas where they have established their factories and plants.

Power shortages have proved a serious setback to the country's economic progress. Over US$2 billion is spent each year importing crude oil. The Philippines lie along a potentially rich oil belt extending from Indonesia to Taiwan but, despite the opening of several small oilfields, the country is trapped in the classic Catch 22 situation of not having enough energy to develop its exploration and extraction of oil. Interestingly, the Philippines is the world's second largest beneficiary of geothermal power. Wells drilled to depths of over 4,000m are able to tap limitless quantities of natural steam formed as a result of continuous volcanic activity below the earth's crust. Over 20% of required energy is now produced geothermally. Hydroelectricity generated from dams and large coal reserves are proving to be increasingly useful alternative sources of energy. Solar energy is also an obvious power source which remains to be explored.

The government is keen to promote the development of local businesses that will help remote or deprived areas achieve a higher level of economic self-sufficiency. Technical assistance and funding for such projects as seaweed farms, piggeries, cannery plants for local foods, horticultural nurseries, and local arts and crafts production like woodcarving, flower pressing and weaving have proved remarkably durable and successful in many areas.

Tourism is considered an important element in the economy. The government welcomes visitors, and few restrictions are placed in the way of tourists who, after all, help to provide much needed foreign exchange and employment. Visitor numbers grew from a paltry 14,000 in 1970 to over one million in just a decade. Political instability brought the numbers crashing down between 1980 and 1986, but throughout the 1990s the annual number of tourists and business people to visit the islands has restored the figure to well over the one million mark. The majority of tourists are from nearby East Asian countries, although Americans are now the number one single-nationality visitors. Increasingly, more people are coming from Australia, Britain, Germany and other Western countries. Manila went through a hotel building boom in the 1970s. This was not matched by similar developments in more provincial areas, although many popular coastal resorts now boast outstanding international-standard hotel facilities. Outside Manila, in fact, the budget traveller has considerably more choice than the more affluent traveller. There is usually something to suit most pockets in the Philippines, and, even in downtown Metro Manila, luxury executive suites are often only a stone's throw away from the humble but friendly guesthouses for the backpacker.

THE FILIPINOS

If a country's wealth is its people, then the Philippines is exceptionally well endowed in this respect. Over a hundred culturally distinct linguistic groups and subgroups co-exist to form an ethnic salad that has been described as a blend of "Malay, Madrid, and Madison Avenue". The majority of "Pinoys", as the Filipinos like to call themselves, are Christians affiliated with one of the main eight lowland groupings that account for some 97% of the entire population: the Tagalogs, Pampanguenos, Ilocanos, Warays, Pangasinenses, Cebuanos, Ilonggos and Bicolanos. The significant two remaining groups are the Muslims and pagan hilltribes. With the exception of the Negritos, members of these groups are largely of Malay-Indonesian extraction, with infusions, in many cases, of Spanish, Chinese, American, South American and European blood.

Ethnic minorities

Classified as National Cultural Minorities, the 100 or so tribes inhabiting the Philippines make up about 4% of the entire population. Most of these minorities are descended from the early settlers on the islands, the migrants who arrived by sea, and the Negritos who made their way here over land bridges from Borneo. With the arrival of the Spanish, many of these groups escaped to the mountains or the remote forested coastal areas in order to avoid being converted to Christianity. Today, the vast majority of hilltribes inhabit the northern mountains of Luzon, Mindanao and a small number of outlying islands. The northern hilltribes include the Bontocs, Ifugaos, Isnegs, Tingguians, Kalingas and Ibalois. Some of the most prominent tribes of Mindanao are the Bukidnon, Mandaya, Tiruray, Ismal, Higaonon, Subanon, Ismal, Bilaan, Tasaday, Manobo and T'boli. The Mangya are a significant group who inhabit parts of Palawan and Mindoro.

The short, dark-skinned Negritos, a race of fishermen, nomadic hunters and food-gatherers, are the oldest ethnic group to have survived in the Philippines. They are also the most geographically widespread of the tribal groups, although large concentrations of Negritos can be found in the forested areas of Luzon. They are thought to be related to similar groups living in New Guinea, Indonesia, the Andaman Islands and the Malay Peninsula. The archipelago's 320,000 Negritos are sub-divided into tribes that go under different names. The best-known include the Attas of Cagayan, Quirino and Isabela, the Agtas from Camarines, the Bataks of Palawan, Atis from Panay and Negros, the Balugas and Aetas of Zambales, and the Dumagats, who mainly inhabit Quezon, Rizal and Aurora. Contact with Christianised lowland Filipinos and the shrinking of their ancestral lands has had severely adverse effects on their culture and lifestyle, which continues to be threatened. Efforts are being made by the government to give them the choice of integrating into mainstream Philippine society, staying as they are, or moving into village reservations where it is hoped they will be able to improve their material lot while at the same time preserve their unique traditions.

Muslims

Slightly over three million Muslims, descendants mostly of converts to Islam before the arrival of the Spanish, have settled in Mindanao and the Sulu Archipelago, the greatest concentrations being in the provinces of Cotabato, Zamboanga del Norte and Lanao. They are divided into four main groups: the Tausugs, Samals, Maguindanaos and Maranaos. The Muslim minorities of the Philippines remain closer to Indonesians, Bruneians and Malaysians in their beliefs, lifestyles, dress codes and manners than to the Christian masses. Tensions have long existed between the two religious groups, and in recent years this has been compounded by the resettlement in Mindanao of large numbers of Christian "outsiders". Strong feelings of being discriminated against and treated as backward or second-class citizens in their own homeland have given rise to a secessionist movement spearheaded by the Moro National Liberation Front (MNLF).

Chinese and mestizos

The number of ethnic Chinese in the Philippines (2.2 million) is relatively small compared to some other countries in Southeast Asia, but their influence on the commercial life and culinary preferences of the islands is considerable. The Chinese, like the Moros, were already trading with the Philippines well before the Spanish arrived. The first Chinese immigrants were mainly working-class males from Fukien province, many of whom ended up marrying local Filipina women. Their commercial activities, and self-appointed role as middlemen forming a comprador class between Western traders and the native population, were welcomed by the Spanish, and by 1603 the number of resident Chinese in Manila had grown to 30,000. Large numbers of Chinese flocked to the islands in the 19th century and immigration continued, more or less unabated, until 1952. The Chinese have always stuck together, more from personal compulsion and choice than anything else, quietly building up their businesses, consolidating their trading networks, sending their children to Chinese schools and staying close to their own customs and culture. This industrious race has been one of the most successful minority groups in the Philippines and some of the wealthiest businessmen and families in Manila are Chinese.

Mixed marriages have long been an accepted feature and practice of Philippine society. Early accounts of the islands mention the wedding of a Greek ship caulker, who had sailed here with the first voyage of Miguel Lopez de Legaspi, to the niece of one Rajah Tupas. Mestizos (mestizas in the case of women) are the somewhat lighter-skinned result of these intermarriages between Filipinos and Caucasians, although these days the term refers to the offspring of Chinese marriages with other nationalities as well, and is also applied to resident Eurasians and Amerasians. Mestizos were and are held in high esteem, having traditionally occupied positions of power and influence in the running of the country and its economy. In the 19th century they acquired large parcels of land and became active in agriculture. They then turned their attention to trade, becoming the leading members of an affluent and well educated merchant class. Jose Rizal and many of the early intellectual leaders of the revolution were mestizos. A large percentage of the political and economic oligarchy of the present-day Philippines come from the ranks of the mestizo clans and their foreign-educated children. Former President Aquino was a member of this influential class. It is said that the lion's share of the Philippine economy is run by about 60 mestizo families. Although numerically they represent a mere 2% of the population, over 50% of the total personal GNP of the Philippines is earned by this powerful group.

RELIGION

Christianity

The Spanish friars and missionaries were highly effective in converting the indigenous population to their faith, and today over 90% of Filipinos are Christians. Over 80% are Catholics and roughly 6% Protestants. The Philippines is distinguished by being the only Christian country in Asia. During the American colonial period, missionaries of Lutheran, Methodist and other persuasions were highly active in the islands. The gospels continue to be preached today by the fervent, evangelical missions of the Mormon, Baptist and Mennonite churches. Roughly 4% of Filipinos belong to the Philippine Independent Church, also known as the Aglipay, an early 20th-century sect that is quite closely affiliated, as the name suggests, with the Anglican and Episcopalian churches. About 3% of the population belong to the Protestant Iglesia ni Cristo. The Philippines is fertile ground for numerous religious sects and revivalist movements that have come, in some cases, to resemble personality cults more than religions. The so-called Iglesia Watawat ng Lahi ("Flag of the Race"), for example, appears to be a neo-nationalist movement based on the conviction that Jose Rizal was the direct reincarnation of Christ, and that he will return one day to save the faithful from poverty and suffering. The cult, which is based in Calamba, claims a staggering 250,000 adherents.

The more orthodox Catholic Church has a deep influence not only on the lives of the ordinary Filipinos and on the spiritual and moral values of the society, but also on politics. The clergy have given consistent support to social change and the fight to eliminate poverty. The Church played a key role in the downfall of the Marcos regime.

Islam

About 5% of the population are Muslims. Muslims visited parts of the Sulu Archipelago as long ago as the 13th and 14th centuries, successfully combining trade with conversion to Islam. Two men were particularly influential in disseminating the faith: Sharif Abu Bakr, an Arab from Mecca who introduced the Shari'a (Islamic law) and the Arabic script, and Sharif Muhammad Kabungsuwan, a former soldier of fortune and trader who took up missionary work and eventually founded an Islamic sultanate in Cotabato in 1475. Over 1,000 madrasas, or private religious schools, usually affiliated with the local mosque and partly funded by wealthy Muslim countries abroad, teach the principles of Islam and run courses in reading the Koran in Arabic. Problems have risen from time to time in trying to reconcile some of the more anachronistic aspects of Islamic law with modern civil law and the requirements of the national education system.

Other religions

The skyline of spires and minarets occasionally makes room for the towers and decorative roofs of Buddhist and Taoist temples. Manila and Cebu have significant numbers of devotees to these influential moral philosophies. Elements of Catholicism have been adopted by Filipino Buddhists for extra "insurance", a good example being the number of Virgin Mary statues standing alongside images of Buddhas "Calling to Alms", or in the lotus position, that can be seen in the private mausoleums at the famous Chinese Cemetery in Manila.

Animist beliefs are still held by many of the cultural minorities and hilltribes of the Philippines. The customs and practices of these ethnic groups revolve around ancestor worship, a belief in friendly and malevolent spirits, daily propitiations and offerings to a complex pantheon of nature gods, and rituals, feasting and animal sacrifices conducted by the local shaman or village priest. Many hilltribe minorities, with the exception of the most remote among them, have succumbed to the teachings of the powerful missionaries. Beneath the veneer of Christianity, however, strong animist beliefs and customs often continue to lurk.

LANGUAGE *(see also Appendix One page 301)*

The Philippines' 100 or more ethnic groups speak a total of 70 languages. Eight major languages, along with their respective dialects, are spoken by about 90% of the population. The two major tongues, favoured by a good half of the population, are Tagalog, which is mostly spoken in Manila and central Luzon, and Cebuanao, used in Cebu, much of Mindanao, the eastern Negros and Bohol. Ilonggo, or Hiligaynon, is spoken in Negros Occidental and Panay, Bicol is the dialect of southern Luzon, while Ilocano is the main language of northern Luzon. Other important languages and dialects are Pampango, Waray-Waray and Pangasinan. While English and Filipino, the national language based on Tagalog, are the two official languages of the Philippines, most people use their own dialects.

All the languages and dialects spoken in the Philippines derive from the same proto-root, called Original Indonesian, and can be classified into the Malay-Polynesian family of languages. The evolution of dialects in the Philippines came about partly as a result of the dispersal of early migrants to far-flung and isolated pockets of the islands, where dialects were allowed to erode and be replaced by newer more localised forms. Words were added as contact with foreign traders grew. Many of the major languages in particular, like Tagalog, contain loan words from Spanish, Arabic, Chinese and even Sanskrit sources.

Almost three and a half centuries of Spanish rule have left relatively little imprint on the languages spoken in the Philippines. Spanish was abolished as a compulsory subject in high schools in 1968, but continues to exert some influence, particularly in the area of numbers, time and some cooking terms. It does however, constitute the mother tongue of the Spanish-Filipino mestizos, and other members of this élite upper class.

Since the American era, English has had an enormous influence on modes of communication in the Philippines. It remains the lingua franca of commerce and politics; many publications, including newspapers and magazines, are written in English and the majority of TV and radio programmes are in either English or Tagalog, sometimes a mixture of the two. Filipinos appear to have a natural gift for languages, and it is not uncommon to meet with people who can switch between two or three different tongues with ease. It would be a mistake, however, to think that all Filipinos can speak English, and, even among those who do, it is sometimes quite difficult for visitors to access exactly how much English someone actually knows. The Ramos government is keen to replace English as the medium of instruction in schools with Tagalog. While the idea makes perfect enough sense viewed in the cultural context, in terms of using the language as a negotiating tool in the field of trade and commerce the Philippines do have a tremendous linguistic head start over other, more developed, Asian countries who are struggling at present to learn English. Demoting the language to second place may only succeed in further consigning the Philippines to the back row of Southeast Asian nations.

Chapter Two

Art and Culture

The Philippines has a lively and well supported artistic and cultural life. The arts and crafts of the Christianised lowlands reflect Spanish, Chinese and American influences, while the the south's cultural heritage owes more to the conservative Islamic styles found in Malaysia and Indonesia. The concept of the New Society, promoted by the Marcos administration in the 1970s, brought about a revitalisation of the country's cultural heritage and a new pride in its arts, crafts and folk traditions. There are regular presentations of plays and drama in Filipino and English, concerts and recitals, lectures, film festivals, exhibitions, workshops and dance performances. The National Museum and National Library are the official custodians of the nation's cultural heritage and contain large permanent collections. Nationwide events, displays and performances are organised by the Cultural Centre of the Philippines based in Manila. The complex also includes the Folk Arts Theatre, a Main Theatre, the Manila Film Centre, a library, museum and several small art galleries. The impulse to create finds expression not only in high art, but in the exceptionally visual and decorative folk art forms found in dozens of different kinds of handicrafts, and in the wall murals and colourful designs and motifs used to decorate the island's ubiquitous tricycles and passenger jeepneys. Apart from a healthy level of indigenous support for the arts, an increase in visitor numbers has meant that tourists are, unwittingly, becoming the new patrons of the Philippine arts.

MUSIC

The Philippines is unquestionably one of the most musical nations in the world. Music, like the Catholic mass or confessional, nurtures the soul of the Filipino and is a feature of their daily life. Wherever you go you will be followed by the crackle and vibration of radios, jukeboxes, cassettes, laser-disks and karaoke sets, the voices of Filipino songwriters and crooners, the blast of '"Pinoy rock" and the strains of plaintive Tagalog love songs. Concerts by the Philippine Philharmonic Orchestra, the Philippine Madrigal Singers and other internationally respected groups and visiting orchestras, ensembles and popular artists are held at the Cultural Centre in Manila and at similar venues in other large cities. You will find music bars and clubs in the most unexpected places, including some of the country's most remote islands. Free performances take place regularly at Fort Santiago in the capital, and there are Sunday concerts at Paco and Rizal Park every week.

Some of the most popular Filipino musical forms are the *dallot* of the Ilocanos, the *Kundiman* of the Tagalogs, and the *balitaw* which comes from the Visayans. These are melodic, sometimes sentimental songs strongly influenced by Spanish music, and which are usually accompanied by a guitar. The archipelago's many ethnic minorities have evolved their own music which is often played on exotic instruments like bamboo nose flutes, gongs and metallaphones. The *hagalong* is a two-stringed lute played by the T'boli; the *git-git*, a violin whose strings are made from human hair, is used by the Mangyan, and the *kulintang* is a set of pitched bronze or brass gongs hung from a wooden frame which are played by the southern Muslims at their festivals and weddings.

DANCE

Where there is music there is dance. Every imaginable dance form, from classical ballet and folk varieties to contemporary, jazz and disco, can be found in the Philippines. Internationally well known troupes include the Filipinescas Dance Company, and the Bayanihan Dance Company. Although the Philippines has never developed a recognisable classical dance tradition akin to those found in countries like Cambodia, Bali and Thailand, a multitude of different ethnic dance styles have evolved over the centuries. Two researchers and choreographers of note, Leonor Orosa Goquingco and Francisca Reyes, have done much to bring traditional folk dance on to the stage. The Ballet Philippines, the creation of Alice Reyes, one of the country's most innovative contemporary dancers and choreographers, blends traditional Philippine themes with modern, occasionally political dance performances. "Itim-Asu" is a ballet that deals with the assassination by Spanish friars of a Manila governor-general; "La Lampara", another work with political overtones, is a ballet based on Jose Rizal's final hours of confinement before his execution at Fort Santiago. Several ballet dancers from the Philippines have made a name for themselves as members of European and American dance companies.

THEATRE

There are many opportunities to watch theatrical performances in the Philippines, either at local repertory theatres, during festivals and fiestas, or at large-capacity venues such as the Manila Theatre Guild and the

Metropolitan Theatre. The *carillo*, a show performed with papier-mâché figures which is related to the Indonesian *wayang kulit* or "shadow play", is one of the oldest forms of theatre in the Philippines. *Moro-moros* were comedies depicting the struggles between Muslims and Christians, written in vernacular verse and often performed to the accompaniment of a brass band in front of gaudy, painted backdrops depicting medieval palaces and castles. Performances can occasionally be caught at Paramnaque in Manila, Angeles City in Pampanga and at Bayombong's August fiesta in Nueva Vizcaya. Performances of *yawa-yawa*, vernacular plays in song and dance that portray the life of San Miguel the Archangel, can be seen at Iligan City's fiesta in Lanao del Norte every September. The *zarzuela*, light romantic operettas introduced by the Spanish in the 19th century, had become thoroughly Filipinised by the 1920s, and native playwrights, several of whom were jailed by the Spanish and American authorities, used the form as a satirical vehicle to criticise their colonial masters. Performances can sometimes be seen at the Metropolitan Theatre in Manila.

Plays written for the conventional stage by authors as far ranging as Webster, Molière and Tom Stoppard are regular features on the cultural calendars of the larger cities. Groups like the Teatro Pilipino, Dulaang UP and Repertory Philippines present modern plays in both Filipino and English. The Philippine Educational Theatre Association (PETA) has done much to attract and develop local acting talent. Nick Joaquin, the author of *Portrait of the Artist as a Filipino*, is one of the country's best-known contemporary playwrights. Wilfredo M Guerrero's *Women are Extraordinary*, and Severino Montano's *Lonely in My Garden*, are also well-known works that have received critical acclaim abroad.

CINEMA AND FILM

The Philippine cinema has a mass following, a hard core of fans who turn out regularly for a typical fare of violence, horror and sexually exploitive low-brow films, romantic comedies and low budget musicals. Among the plethora of mediocre and formulaic melodramas, a thoughtful, well directed film occasionally sees the light of day. One such film was *Mababangong Bangungot* by Kidlat Tahimik, a serious socio-political work which was shown abroad under the title *The Perfumed Nightmare*. Ishmael Bernal, Celso Castillo and Gerry de Leon, who has made film adaptations of Jose Rizal's novels, are other notable directors. Lino Brocka, a prolific director of more than 50 films, was the first Filipino to have his work represented at the Cannes Film Festival. An international film festival was hosted at one time at the Manila Film Centre, but plans to make the festival an annual event have not matured. Several excellent foreign films, including *Apocalypse Now*, *Platoon* and Peter Weir's *The Year of Living Dangerously*, were filmed in the Philippines. American, British and Australian films are popular, and films in various European languages are also shown at fringe cinemas, although they may not always be subtitled. There are over 1,000 cinemas in the Philippines. Modern cinemas in some parts of Manila, such as Quezon City, Greenhills and Makati, can be extremely spacious and comfortable. They usually open at about 09.00, the last show going on at 21.00. Cinemas are not expensive.

LITERATURE

Like many tribal societies, the ancient Filipinos had a strong oral tradition that included the reciting and passing on from one generation to the next of songs, poems, riddles, creation myths, legends, fables and lengthy folk epics. Memory and recitation were important for social events and religious rituals. The Ifugao *Hudhud* and *Alim*, the *Lam-ang* of the Ilocanoa and the Bicolano *Ibalon* are among some of the epics that have survived. The *Tarsilas* are genealogical lists that trace the descent of the sultans of Mindanao back to the prophet Muhammed. Precious little remains of the written literature of the pre-Hispanic period as works were inscribed on perishable materials like tree bark and bamboo tubes. Spanish friars, eager to erase all evidence of a written culture pre-dating their arrival, were zealous in their destruction of any form of literature they came across. Some Spanish scholars, however, defied the friars and translated some examples of literature and folk epics, such as *The Code of Kalantiaw*, an epic poem written in Panay in 1433.

The Spanish period saw very little native, non-secular work produced, as the friars censored works that dealt with anything other than religious themes. The best-known figure from this period was Francisco Baltazar (1789–1862), a writer from Bulacan who chose to use his native name, Balagtas. His *Florante at Laura*, an allegorical poem in Tagalog that deals with the Christian conquest of the Moors, contains a subtly disguised protest against Spanish rule. With the rise of a more educated native middle class towards the end of the 19th century, writers like the satirist M H del Pilar, who published under the pen name Plaridel, were able to arouse the national consciousness and help to bring it to the brink of revolution. The greatest Filipino novelist of this period, Jose Rizal, played an immense role in inciting criticism of Spanish misrule with his novel *Noli Me Tangere* and its sequel *El Filibusterisimo*, both of which were translated into Spanish. Rizal's books are widely available in English and still make an excellent read. There are many gifted Filipino writers today who publish their works in English, Filipino and several of the regional languages. Lope K Santos is considered to be one of the finest writers in Tagalog. Manuel Arguilla was a contemporary writer who wrote in English and in his native Ilocano. Nick Joaquin is probably the best-known living writer in the Philippines.

PAINTING AND SCULPTURE

Works by early Filipino painters tend to be mostly religious in nature as they were steered by the all-powerful hands of the friars, but elements of native art, mostly derived from the decorative themes found in weaving and woodcarving, often surface in the portrayal of events from the life of Christ or the saints. Damian Domingo, a mestizo, was the first Filipino to gain recognition for painting non-religious themes. He even rose to the post of professor of the Academy of Drawing in 1821. The Academy produced a number of painters who were to gain renown abroad, including Antonio Malantik, Juan Arceo, Juan Luna and Jose Lozano. Juan Luna and Felix Resurrection Hidalgo won first and second prizes at the prestigious National Exposition of Fine Arts in Madrid in 1884. Their success was hailed as a step towards social equality by Rizal and his compatriots. Some of Luna's best-known works, including the winning entry in Madrid, *The Spolarium*, the *Battle of Lepanto*, *People and Kings* and *The Death of Cleopatra*, are exhibited in the Hall of Masters in the National Museum in Manila. Other paintings by Luna and Hidalgo can be seen at the Museo ng Malacang and in the Lopez Memorial Museum in Pasay City. Growing nationalistic sentiments began to appear in late 19th century stylised genre paintings of landscapes, pastoral life and rural figures.

Fernando Amorsolo (1892–1972), an artist known for his exuberant, tropical colours and lively pastoral scenes, is probably the most celebrated Filipino artist of this century. The Philippines today continues to produce artists of world renown working in a number of different mediums, such as Oscar Zalameda, Arturo Luz, Cesar Legaspi, Anita Magsaysay and Romeo Tabuena. Renato Rocha, Napoleon Abueva and Solomon Saprid are well-known sculptors. Saprid's *Three Priests* stands just in front of Manila Cathedral. *The Cry of Balintawak*, and *The Oblation*, symbolic works of freedom in impressive bronze by the late Guillermo Tolentino, can be seen at the entrance to the University of the Philippines in Quezon City.

The Metropolitan Museum of Manila and the Cultural Centre complex, both on Roxas Boulevard, the National Museum on Burgos Street, the Luz Gallery in the LV Locsin Building in Makati, and the centrally located Museum of Philippine Art are excellent places to view permanent and changing exhibitions of traditional and contemporary art. Tourist publications and newspapers are good sources for information on cultural events in general.

FOREIGN CULTURAL CENTRES

Alliance Française, 2nd Fl, Keystone Bldg, 220 Sen Gil J Puyat Ave, Makati. Tel. 880 402.

British Council, 7 Third St, New Manila, Quezon City, Tel: 721 1981.

Goethe Institute, 687 Aurora Blvd, Quezon City. Tel: 722 467173.

Thomas Jefferson Cultural Center, 395 Sen Gil J Puyat Ave, Extension, Makati. Tel: 818 5484.

HANDICRAFTS

Every region of the Philippines produces its own handicraft products, and although many of these articles are now little more than tawdry knick-knacks churned out for the tourist market, a little patience and a few local enquiries can unearth plenty of high-quality work. Most native craftsmen have workshops or small studios attached to their own homes. Discovering these people and their work places adds extra interest to any trip around the islands, an experience far more rewarding than conventional shopping.

Basketry and canework

Southern Luzon is famous for its abaca products. This tough fibre comes from a relative of the banana tree and is made into dozens of useful items from mats and rope to baskets. Ethnic minorities in Mountain Province and Bohol produce attractive and long-lasting baskets from pandanus, cane, rattan, bamboo and buri. Baskets in other parts of the island are also made from reeds, nipa, wicker, various roots, coconut fibre and vines. Pangasinan is one of the best places to find high quality basketry and cane-work as several minorities here take pride in specialising in their own styles. Ox-carts, laden with baskets of every conceivable shape and size, are a common sight on the road from Pangasinan to Manila. Mindoro and Bohol are also noted centres for basketry.

Weaving

The weaving of cotton textiles pre-dates the arrival of the Spanish by several centuries. This ancient craft is usually done at home, but some villages have pooled their resources and set up workshops which also double as showrooms for visitors interested in buying samples of weaving, or just watching their production. The production of woven textiles remains largely the domain of the country's various cultural minorities, each producing and employing different styles, symbols and designs.

The tribeswomen of Ifugao, Kalinga, Igorot and Bontoc are renowned for their fetching cotton fabrics, especially *lepanto*, a refined cloth that features a number of complex Igorot patterns and motifs. The southern Yakan, Maranao and Maguindanao produce superb, vibrantly coloured skirts and other designs, unmatched in the region except, perhaps, for the exquisite *dagmay* cloth, painstakingly woven by Mandaya-Mansaka women and sold in Davao City. Many of the designs are considered to have beneficial spiritual properties like the cloth made by the T'boli who produce complex tie-dye clothes and blankets. Several minorities embellish their work with beads, brocade and appliqué. *Pina*, a high-quality fabric woven from the fibre of pineapple leaves, is used to make *barong tagalog*, the cool, finely embroidered shirts which are the Filipino male's national dress. The style – loose, buttoned to the neck and worn outside the trousers – became a potent symbol of nationalism after the Spanish introduced a decree forbidding natives to wear ties or tuck their shirts in.

Woodcarving

Items produced in wood can be broadly classified as either tourist kitsch, functional or sacred. Some of the best woodcarvers in the Philippines can be found in the area of Ifugao in northern Luzon, where the tribals keep sacred rice idols called *bulol*. These gifted carvers have also turned their skills towards producing more consumer-oriented goods like salad bowls, giant wooden spoons and forks, and cheese boards, which are nevertheless of quite reasonable quality. Animal and human wood sculptures can be found in abundance in the small woodcarving town of Paete in Laguna. Some of the villages in Palawan and Mindanao are also noted for their woodcarving. Travellers should look out for the statues known as *likhas* (pagan deities) and *santos* (saints). Genuine examples fetch a high price. So too do the convincing fakes that are frequently passed off on unsuspecting tourists.

Metalwork

Ifugao blacksmiths and the silversmiths of Baguio produce quantities of attractive jewellery, but the region most associated with metalwork is the Muslim south. This is where the famous Maranao craftsmen turn out a wide range of interesting bronze and brassware goods that include gongs, shields, betel nut boxes, animal motifs and ceremonial urns. Tausug smiths forge gold jewellery and finely tempered weapons.

Other crafts

Other handicraft items produced in the archipelago include finely embroidered and crocheted table linen and clothing, wind chimes, rattan furniture, shellcraft, leatherware, horn carvings, dolls and papier-mâché horses. Marble eggs and other stone items are associated with Romblon, good quality porcelain comes from Bacolod City, and the country's best guitars are made on Mactan Island in Cebu. Some of the cheaper variety of guitars, like lacquerware, may not be able to withstand less humid climates than the tropical Philippines.

FOOD

Visitors arriving in the Philippines from places like Singapore, Indonesia and Thailand often comment on the blandness and monotony of the Philippine cuisine which, at least initially, appears to consist of little more than plates of steaming rice topped with a strip of salt fish and a garnishing of shrimp or meat paste. The chronically impoverished Filipino people make do with simple, affordable ingredients. This morning's breakfast often turns out to be last night's rice and assorted leftovers, cleverly re-invented by frying with a little garlic and adding a touch of ginger. It may even reappear at *meriendas*, the traditional afternoon snack time, in the form of rice cakes.

Filipino cooks, however, have devised low-cost ways of creating tasty dishes with the use of ingredients like coconut milk, bay leaf, acidic fruits, and a number of vinegar-and-soy-based sauce dips called sawsawan, which are improved with a squeeze of calamansi, a touch of chilli, minced garlic or mustard. Dishes are rarely smothered in sauces, condiments and spices: these are generally used to enhance tastes, not dictate them. One unusual feature of the Filipino kitchen is the combining of two primary ingredients in one dish, such as pork with fish or chicken fried with shrimps.

Philippine cuisine, in fact, is a *mélange* of many indigenous and foreign influences. The Filipina author Monina A Mercado writes that the archipelago's food was "prepared by Malay settlers, spiced by commercial relations with Chinese traders, stewed in 300 years of Spanish rule, and hamburgered by American influences". The strongest of these influences was unquestionably the Spanish one. As many as 80% of Philippine dishes are said to be of Spanish origin. The Spanish preferred their own regional dishes like *paella, arroz valenciana* and *caldereta* to the Indian dishes found in their colonies in the New World. *Adobo,* generally considered the national dish of the Philippines, is a pork and chicken stew flavoured with vinegar, soy sauce, garlic, bits of liver, peppercorns and avocado, that combines regional, Spanish and Mexican influences. Many local dishes, like *kari-kari,* reflect the Spanish taste for thick meat and vegetable plates. *Pochero,* now regarded as a native dish, is a weighty pork and beef dish, flavoured with Bilbao sausages and vegetables. Many dishes adopted in the past by wealthy or middle-class Filipinos were either pure or Spanish-inspired preparations. Many of the recipes served at weddings, fiestas and on other special occasions carry names like *callos, morcon* and *embutido,* that any Spaniard would recognise.

Even some of the country's Chinese dishes bear Hispanised names, like *camaron rebozado,* shrimp fried in batter, and *torta de cangrejo,* a crab omelette. The popularity of Chinese food is quite disproportionate to the relatively small number of ethnic Chinese living in the Philippines. Noodle dishes are known by the general name *pancit. Pancit Canton,* served with *lumpia Shanghai* (spring rolls stuffed with minced meat and dipped into a sweet soy sauce), is a favourite among Filipinos and can be found just about anywhere on the islands. *Pancit palabok, pancit luglog,* and *pancit malabob* are all readily available and popular varieties of noodles. *Pancit Molo,* a tasty version of wanton soup, is a regional speciality from the town of Molo in Iloilo. *Arroz caldo,* sometimes called *lugaw,* is a kind of Chinese congee, a rice porridge served with slices of pork and chopped spring onions. *Siopao,* steamed meat buns, are popular snacks which are often eaten with noodles and soup preparations. Many of these dishes are available at noodle restaurants called *panciterias,* or fast-food joints that go by the name of *carinderias.* Both are popular with budget travellers.

Filipinos enjoy their fish, a taste readily fed by the archipelago's bountiful marine harvests. Seafood is often eaten uncooked, or lightly garnished with soy-and-vinegar-based sauces. Fish stuffed with onions, or grilled, barbecued or steamed in banana leaf, are popular preparations. So too are crab, lobster, crayfish and prawn dishes. *Sinigang*, a kind of Filipino bouillabaisse, is a mouth-watering slightly sour fish broth visitors should try at least once. *Lapu-lapu*, a kind of garoupa, *tanguigue*, a blue marlin, and milkfish bred in ponds are Filipino favourites. Whole animals, usually pig (*lechon*), are roasted and basted at festivals and large private gatherings. The leftovers from *lechon* are turned into *paksiw*, a sugar and vinegar preparation that is added to the dishes served on the following day of the fiesta.

There is plenty of scope for vegetarians in the Philippines, as vegetables and fruit are readily available. *Dinengdeng* and *pinakbet* are good, sustaining dishes that contain aubergine, squash and various green leaves. Strict vegetarians can order this dish without the usual garnishing of *bagoong*, a slightly spicy sauce made from shrimps and tiny fish fermented in brine.

Unlike the Thais or Malays, Filipinos do not coat their food in spicy chillies and coconut milk preparations. There are exceptions, however. The region of Bihol is well known for its fiery dishes like *Bihol express,* a spicy mixture of pork sautéed in garlic, red peppers, diced chillies, ginger, turmeric, onions and coconut cream. Food from the Muslim south remains much closer to its Malay origins, and uses a great number of spices flavoured in coconut milk and served with cassava and rice. Their spicy seafood dishes are well worth acquainting yourself with.

Unlike main dishes, Philippine desserts are similar to those found in other Southeast Asian countries. Sugar, rice flour and coconut are the main ingredients for popular glutinous rice cakes, wrapped in pandan or banana leaves, and for *bukayo*, a sweet made from grated coconut cooked in molasses and then compacted into crunchy bars. *Leche flan* is a Spanish sweet egg custard, or cream caramel, that has survived more regional competition along with *churros y chocolate*, sugared pastries that are dunked in hot chocolate drinks. Bulacan and Pampanga in Central Luzon are the sweet and cake centres of the Philippines. Bakeries selling European-style cakes, biscuits and pastries, *ensaymadas*, a cheese-flavoured bread, and the hard breakfast rolls called *pan de sal*, can be found all over the islands. Chemical- and additive-free ice creams are excellent in the Philippines, their flavours drawing from a wide selection of available tropical fruits that include guavas, durians, mangoes, rambutans, duhot, jackfruit, custard apple, papayas, bananas and *macapuno*, a kind of coconut. *Halo-halo*, a dessert made from preserved fruits, gelatine, caramel custard, ice-cream, shaved ice and myriad other ingredients, is a rich concoction that is enjoyed by those with particularly sweet teeth and stomachs that travel well.

A plentiful supply of tropical fruits means that there are several healthy and thirst-quenching alternatives to drinking 7-Up and Pepsi. Many of the more upmarket hotels and bars specialise in creating their own fruit cocktails, but even roadside stalls and the most humble eateries sell excellent fruit drinks made from pineapple, green mango, coconut and calamansi. Drinks like *tuba* and *buri* are fermented from coconut sap and nipa palms. Rice and sugarcane wines are common, and layaw is a powerful brew made from maize spirit. Matured rums like Tanduay have a good name, although locally produced gin and whisky are best avoided. The excellent and surprisingly cheap San Miguel beer is one of the country's best-known exports. Coffee, with the exception of Batangas *barako*, a native blend, is usually instant, but in the Muslim south, coffee houses serving ground and roasted coffee can be found in most towns.

Eating out used to be the prerogative of wealthy families who would typically repair *en masse* to an expensive Chinese restaurant to celebrate a birthday, engagement or the clinching of some business deal. These days many Filipinos who can afford to eat out with friends and family. Two of the best kinds of eateries where Philippine cuisine is available are the *turo-turo* and *kamayan*. The first are the Philippine version of fast-food restaurants, with all the dishes set out in stainless steel tureens that you point to once you have made your choice. No menus and no fuss here, just good hot freshly cooked and inexpensive dishes. *Kamayan* restaurants, where you eat with your hands from banana leaves, have become quite trendy in recent years with Filipinos eager to make contact with their native or provincial roots. An upsurge in the number of foreign visitors to the Philippines has led to an increase in the number of international restaurants found in Manila and other big cities. Restaurants, bistros and cafés serving Thai, Japanese, Spanish, Indian, Mexican, Korean, German, Italian, French and other cuisines, as well as the ubiquitous pizza parlours, and American chains like McDonald's, Kentucky Fried Chicken and Dunkin Doughnuts, are easily sought out. Many resort areas like Cebu, El Nido and Boracay Island cater specifically for Western and Japanese tastes, a reflection of the kind of tourists who are visiting the archipelago. Small general stores called *sari-sari*, and larger supermarkets, are well stocked with all the basic food necessities visitors might wish to buy for long journeys or self-catering.

FESTIVALS AND HOLIDAYS

Most towns in the Philippines have their own annual festivals and fiestas, sometimes several. Add to this countless native festivals and the fact that all religious holidays and many saints' days are inevitably accompanied by elaborate festivities, and it doesn't take much to see that there are celebrations and pageants every month of the year, and that wherever you go in the Philippines you will never be far from one of these colourful events. History, religion and folklore are the basis for most of these festivals, which are characterised by parades, rituals, music, dancing, the imbibing of large quantities of alcohol, cornucopic amounts of food and all-round high spirits. Foreigners are most welcome to attend these events. At smaller, more local festivals, visitors are routinely pressed to eat and drink as much as they can, before being given royal send-offs. The complete number of festivals held in the Philippines is far too exhaustive to list here. The following is a breakdown of the more interesting and noteworthy ones.

January

1 January: **New Year's Day.** Family gatherings to celebrate *media noche* (a traditional midnight repast), loud explosions of fireworks, and midnight mass for the more devout.

First Sunday in January: **Three Kings' Day.** The Feast of the Epiphany which marks the end of Christmas. Children receive gifts and star-shaped lanterns are hung in doorways and windows to symbolise the guiding star of the story. Santa Cruz and Gasan on Marinduque have special parades on this day.

9 January: **Feast of The Black Nazarene.** A lifesize image of Christ is dragged through the streets of Quiapo in Manila by a barefoot penitent. The procession culminates with a mass at Quiapo Church. The event is attended by in excess of 100,000 people, many of whom try, in an act of ritual cleansing, to touch the image with a handkerchief or piece of cloth.

Third weekend: **Ati-Atihan.** Held in Kalibo on Panay Island, this festival is one of the largest and most exuberant fanfares of colour, music, dance, costume and masks found anywhere on the islands. Often compared to the carnival in Rio de Janeiro, the Ati-Atihan combines the atmosphere and energy of a Mardi Gras with the stunning visuals of an Italian carnivale. Try to book a room from Manila before turning up.

Third weekend: **Feast of the Santo Nino.** Tondo (Manila) and Cebu are good places to be for this event, which marks the feast day of the Holy Infant. This also denotes the end of the week-long Pasundayag sa Sinulog, a festival that is also celebrated in Kabankalan on Negros. Families take small Santo Nino statuettes to their churches to be blessed, and there are performances of the sululog dance.

Fourth weekend: **The Ibayay Ati-Atihan.** A second Ati-Atihan festival takes place 30 kilometres northwest of Kalibo on the weekend after the main event. The festival here is simpler and, perhaps, more authentic than the Kalibo version.

January/February: **Chinese New Year.** Chinatown in Manila is the place to be to catch the firecrackers and dragon dances that announce the Chinese New Year celebrations. These can take place any time between 21 January and 19 February, depending upon the ebb and flow of the lunar calendar.

February

2 February: **Feast of Our Lady of Cadelaria.** A festival that honours the patron saint of Jaro, a suburb in the city of Iloilo. It is said to be the largest religious festival held in the western Visayas.

11 February: **Feast of Our Lady of Lourdes.** Held in Kanlaon Street, Quezon City, this feast, which also takes place in San Juan del Monte in Bulacan Province, celebrates the appearance of the Virgin Mary in Lourdes, France.

14 February: **St Valentine's Day.** The romantic Filipinos set much stock by this day. Presents and cards are sent, and restaurants, discos and cinemas enjoy a brisk business.

22-25 February: **People Power Days.** Nobody, quite rightly, wishes to forget those memorable few days which brought down the Marcos administration and saw the restoration of democracy. The 25th is an official holiday.

26 February: **Dia de Zamboanga.** This is a celebration of Muslim and Christian culture accompanied by religious rituals, regattas and cultural displays.

March/April

Holy Week: **Moriones Festival.** Easter time sees the performance of many passion plays throughout the Philippines. The most renowned is the Moriones Festival in Marinduque. Many ceremonies and rituals lead up to the main event which begins on Good Friday and climaxes on Easter Sunday, when a one-eyed Longinus is chased, and finally beheaded, by masked centurions.

9 April: **Bataan Day.** This is a day of remembrance for the battle which led to the fall of Bataan in 1942, the capture of many soldiers by the Japanese and the infamous Death March. Ceremonies are held at the Mount Samat Shrine in Bataan and at Capas in Tarlac.

14-15 April: **Lami-Lamihan Festival.** An interesting local festival held in Basilan in which local cultural minorities, dressed in their best costumes, join in parades, dances and horse races.

27 April: **Bahug-Bahugan sa Mactan.** A beach on Mactan Island is the annual scene of the landing and death of Magellan. Mock battles are fought early in the morning (usually between 8am and 10am) in the shallow sea where the hapless navigator met his end.

April (May or June): **Turrumba Festival.** An image of Our Lady of Sorrows of Turrumba was found floating in Laguna Lake in 1778, and ever since then a festival has been held in honour of this talismanic figure believed to possess mysterious healing powers.

May

1-30 May: **Santacruzan.** Celebrated all over the islands. A novena precedes this pageant in which the prettiest girls from each village are assigned biblical roles and paraded under floral arches in flower tiaras and *ternos*, traditional butterfly-sleeved dresses. Floral floats, brass bands and candle-lit parades are held in some towns and cities.

1 May: **Labor Day.** A public holiday. In Manila there is a parade in Rizal Park.

3 May: **Carabao Carroza.** Pavia, a town to the north of Iloilo City in Panay, plays host to a number of water buffalo races in which 18 different districts, or *barrios*, compete with each other. A fiesta takes place the next day.

6 May: **Araw ng Kagitingan.** This day pays tribute to Filipinos who have shown exceptional courage in the service of their country.

14-15 May: **Carabao Festival.** This festival is held to honour San Isidro, patron saint of farmers. Water buffaloes are led to the local church square where they are ritually blessed. Water buffalo races are held on the following day. The main venues for this festival are San Isidro (Nueva Ecija Province), Pulilan (Bulacan Province) and Angono (Rizal Province).

June

12 June: **Independence Day.** Church bells ring early in the morning in thanksgiving for the founding of the First Philippine Republic in 1898. There are huge military parades, concerts, speeches and fireworks.

19 June: **Birthday of Jose Rizal.** Holiday and tribute to the Philippines' foremost national hero.

22-25 June: **Halaran Festival.** Roxas City's version of the Ati-Atihan Festival.

24 June: **Feast of San Juan Bautista.** A re-enactment of the life and deeds of St. John the Baptist. Like the Songkran Festival in Thailand, water is liberally thrown not only over the devout, but over anyone else who happens to be passing by.

24 June: **Manila Day.** A film festival and parade mark the anniversary of Manila's declaration as a city in 1571.

28-30 June: **Feast of the Saints Peter and Paul.** The people of Apalit in Pampanga hold boat parades over these days.

July
4 July: **Filipino-American Friendship Day.** Historical ties and pledges of friendship are made at the US Embassy, wreath laying ceremonies take place, and in Rizal Park there is an evening concert.

29 July: **Pateros River Fiesta.** In the duck-breeding suburb of Pateros, a curious festival is held in which the hunting and killing of a crocodile that had threatened the livelihood of the farmers here is re-enacted.

August
Kadayawan sa Dabaw. A two-week-long Orchid Festival held in Davao, on Mindanao. There is also a Food and Drink Festival and a Tribal Festival.

26 August: **Cry of Balintawak.** A number of festivities take place on the actual spot where Bonifacio made his historic call for armed struggle against the Spanish.

September
Third Weekend: **Penafrancia Festival.** The beauty of this river festival, culminating in a graceful boat parade on the Naga River, attracts many tourists.

29 September: **Ang Sinulog.** A major week-long festival held in Iligan City.

October
10-12 October: **Zamboanga Hermosa.** Dedicated to the patron saint of the city, Nuestra Senora del Pilar, this festival includes many religious ceremonies, cultural presentations, and the electing of a Miss Zamboanga.

Second Sunday: **La Naval de Manila.** An evening candle-lit procession from St Domingo Church honours Our Lady of the Holy Rosary, whose intercession is credited with being the cause of a number of naval victories over the Dutch in 1646.

19 October: **MassKara Festival.** Smiling masks are the symbols of this festival, the biggest on Negros. The festival lasts for one week, climaxing in a colourful street parade.

November
1 November: **All Saints' Day.** A national holiday to commemorate the dead. Families gather at cemeteries and often stay overnight, keeping an

impressive candle-lit vigil over their lost ones. The Chinese, who have a special reverence for their ancestors, turn out in droves for this remembrance event. The Chinese Cemetery in Manila is an interesting place to visit at this time.

23 November: **Feast of San Clemente.** San Clemente is the patron saint of fishermen. The grateful community of Angono in Rizal Province turn out to offer thanks and take part in a boat parade.

30 November: **Bonifacio Day.** Also called National Heroes' Day, ceremonies take place all over the country to honour the birthday of the revolutionary leader Andres Bonifacio.

November/December: **Grand Canao.** This festival is a celebration of the cultures of the ethnic minorities of Baguio in northern Luzon. There are opportunities to see tribal rituals and dances and to observe animal sacrifices.

December

8 December: **Feast of Our Lady of the Immaculate Conception.** Held in many cities throughout the Philippines. The boat procession held at night on Malabon River and Manila Bay is particularly worth seeing.

16-24 December: **Simbang Gabi.** The official start of Christmas in the Philippines with many people attending simbang gabi (night masses).

24 December: **Giant Lantern Festival.** A charming lantern parade and contest held in San Fernando, Pampanga Province. The winning lantern is displayed after midnight mass.

25 December: **Christmas.** A family day, much the same as it is in other Christian countries, a movable feast of food and drink and merriment. Children go from one relative to another receiving blessings and gifts.

28 December: **Holy Innocents' Day.** Just the same as April Fools' Day in the West. Filipinos enjoy playing practical jokes on the unsuspecting.

30 December: **Rizal Day.** Annual commemoration of the day on which the Filipino national hero, Jose Rizal, was executed by the Spanish.

31 December: **New Year's Eve.** All the usual party-going, food, drink and bombast associated with these last hours of the year. At the Binalbal Festival of Tudela in Misamis Occidental, people dressed up as witches and ghosts take to the streets in a parade designed to banish evil spirits.

Islamic holidays

There are several times of the year which have special significance to Muslims. Visitors may come across some of the events associated with these dates. The Islamic calendar is lunar, meaning that it is 11 days shorter than the Gregorian one. The dates for cultural and religious events, therefore, change every year.

The First Day of Muharram. This is when Muslims visit the mosque and listen to readings from the Koran.

Ashura. On the tenth day of Muharram, pious Muslims spend the day fasting.

Maulidu'n-Nabi. The birthday of the prophet Muhammed is celebrated on the twelfth day of the third month of the Islamic calendar.

Lailatu'l-Miraj. Verses from the Koran are chanted in celebration of Muhammed's ascent to heaven on the back of a winged white horse.

Ramadan. This is the most important religious period for Muslims. Fasting is obligatory from dawn to sunset but, as in many other Muslim countries, the amount eaten between these hours is often considerably more than is consumed during normal months. In practice, most Filipino Muslims only observe two or three token days of fasting at the beginning and end of Ramadan. The more devout visit their local mosque at intervals throughout the day to chant and recite verses from the Koran.

Lailatu'l-Qadr. Mosques, private houses and streets in the Muslim south are decorated to commemorate the descent of the Archangel Gabriel.

Hariraya Puasa. The official end of Ramadan is marked by a number of religious processions, musical and literary events and feasting.

Hari-Raya Hadji. This is another feast day, this time to celebrate the pilgrimage to Mecca, a journey which many Muslim Filipinos try to do once in their life. The day is passed in visiting mosques and eating in the homes of relatives and friends.

Chapter Three

Recreation and Activities

The Philippines, with its topographical diversity, excellent climate and wide-ranging recreational facilities, is well placed to provide most visitors with what they are looking for. With a coastline longer than that of the United States, its leisure resorts and watersports rank as some of the best and most extensive in Asia. Regattas, sea fairs and the biennial South China Sea Race between Hong Kong and the Philippines are major aquatic spectacles. The Philippines is considered one of the top diving spots in the world, but there are also plenty of opportunities for golfers, mountain climbers, amateur vulcanologists, and for those interested in pot holing, trekking and gold panning, or for the romantically inclined who may wish to go in search of deserted islands, sunken galleons and rare orchids.

WATERSPORTS

Many diving companies have come into existence in the last few years as a result of the growing reputation of the Philippines as a mecca for watersports. A comprehensive programme of diving options has developed to cater for all needs and budgets. The archipelago's beaches and coral reefs are its greatest assets and the recreational potential of the islands has only just begun to be exploited. Upmarket tourists can find first-class hotels and beach clubs at resorts on the islands of Bohol, Palawan and Cebu, while budget travellers will do well at places like Boracay Island, Camiguin and Port Barton. Windsurfing, sailing, game fishing, scuba diving, snorkelling, body-boarding and even parasailing are popular recreational pursuits in the Philippines. The staff of even the humblest beach cottage or bungalow will know somebody who can help organise one of these activities for you.

The best diving spots are usually found away from the more popular coastal resorts, settlements and large fishing communities, where the reef is likely to have been damaged by dynamiting or drainage. The Apo Reef, just east of the tiny island of Apo in the Mindoro Strait, and Tubbataha Reef in the Sulu Sea, are considered to be the finest diving spots in the archipelago, but because of relatively difficult access and the cost involved in reaching them, few visitors go there. The Quiniluban group of islands is another superb but remote diving area whose reputation precedes it. There is no shortage of excellent coastal-based diving areas nearer to small-scale beach accommodation, however. Highly recommended by diving *aficionados* are the islands of north Palawan, Lamon Bay, Sicogon Island, Dapitan, Puerto Princesa, the Sulu Archipelago, Panglao Island, Davao City, the Ten Knots dive resort near El Nido, and the dozens of islands that lie between Cebu and Bohol. Moalboal is said to be the cheapest area in the country to dive. As the potential for diving in the Philippines is almost limitless, many new resorts are likely to be developed in the coming years. One of the cheapest ways to dive is to go through one of the many dive shops that have sprung up in the islands. These provide a complete service that includes hire of all the necessary equipment, boats and, if required, diving instructors. They are almost always located near reasonably cheap accommodation and often have branches in the big cities through which bookings can be made. Inexpensive dive camps, especially those located in Moalboal (Mactan Island), Oslob (Cebu) and Anilao (Batangas), offer a complete package that includes accommodation, food and unlimited diving. For those who can afford it, the ultimate way to dive in the Philippines is to join a dive-boat cruise. These boats have overnight facilities and are equipped to reach the most far-flung and unspoilt reefs in the archipelago. Dive-boats can also be chartered by groups.

The Philippines is one of the best, and cheapest, places in the world to learn scuba diving through an accredited diving course. Many resorts, dive shops and dive camps offer instruction, from intensive four- or five-day courses for beginners to the internationally recognised qualifications issued by the Professional Association of Dive Instructors (PADI) and the National Association of Underwater Instructors (NAUI). Visitors who prefer to buy their own equipment can find a good selection at Dive Mate and Aquaventure Philippines, two shops located on Pasong Tamo Street in Makati, Manila. A useful guide called *Discover the Philippines through Scuba Diving* is available free from the Department of Tourism. *The Diver's Guide to the Philippines* (Unicorn Books, Hong Kong, 1982), by David Smith and Michael Westlake, is available in Manila and makes a helpful and companionable read.

CLIMBING, HIKING AND CAVING

There are no ski resorts in the Philippines but mountain ridges, peaks and the cones of extinct volcanoes provide plenty of scope for the climber. Although many of the slopes are covered in near impenetrable jungle growth, most of the major summits can be reached by hiking trails. When the weather is good, climbers are rewarded with heart-stopping views of the surrounding terrain and coastlines. The best views generally require the most effort, however, and to reach these isolated peaks two to four days are usually necessary.

Mount Apo (2,953m) is the country's highest summit. Other expeditional peaks, requiring careful planning and the services of a local guide, are Mount Pulog (2,930m), Mayon Volcano (2,462m), Kanlaon Volcano (2,460m), and Mount Banahaw (2,177m). Mount Hibok-Hibok (1322m) and Mount Makiling (1144m) are good mountains to practise on before taking on the real behemoths of the Philippines. Some volcanoes may still be active, or showing signs of imminent activity. A visit to the Commission on Vulcanology in Manila, the centre which monitors the archipelago's seismic life, will provide you with all the most recently available data on which areas to avoid. Their centre is in the Philippine Institute of Vulcanology in the Hizon Building, 29 Quezon Avenue, Quezon City. The PAL Mountaineering Club (tel: 815 7205) organises a regular programme of treks and climbs to remote peaks and wildernesses. The area around Batad, Sagada and Banaue in northern Luzon is particularly enjoyable for hiking. There are many trekking clubs in the Philippines. Addresses and events programmes can be obtained from regional tourist offices. The best weather for climbing or trekking is from February to April, but there are so many climatic variants that opportunities for all-year-round activities of this kind exist.

There are thousands of unexplored caves in the archipelago, many of which, because they were used as burial sites, remain unappealing to many of the more superstitious Filipinos. Many still contain skeletons and skull fragments. In some areas like Sagada, trekking companies can organise guides to take you into some of the deeper subterranean caves. Caves are said to have been ideal for the Japanese military to conceal large quantities of booty, very little of which has ever been discovered.

GAMES AND SPECTATOR SPORTS

There is a large sports following among Filipinos. Basketball is the most popular game with the big leagues competing at the Rizal Memorial Stadium and at the Araneta Coliseum. Boxing is another favourite sport. Filipino boxers have won gold medals at the Asian Games, and the famous world heavy-weight boxing championship between Joe Frazier and Mohammed Ali was fought in Manila in 1975. Chess has a large following and there are several international grandmasters who hail from the Philippines, including Rosendo Balinas Jr and Eugenio Torre. Baguio was the venue for the World Chess Championship between Anatoly Karpov and Viktor Korchnoi in 1978. Badminton, tennis, volleyball, pelota, horse, bicycle and motor racing, polo, bowling and pool are also popular. Interesting minor events in the sporting calendar include bullfighting, horse fighting and the carabao races.

Filipino games include *sipa*, in which players use their feet, knees and legs to keep a hollow rattan ball in the air, and *arnis de mano*, an ancient martial art somewhat similar to kendo, in which thrusts and parries using a hardwood stick are employed to defend and engage an opponent. Filipinos also enjoy playing the Chinese game mahjong. *Sungka* is an indigenous game played by two people who move small stones or seashells across an indented board. *Dama* is a Filipino version of draughts which you can often see being played in open doorways, in cafés and on street corners. Any games involving betting are usually well supported. Important cockfights are called stag derbies, and thousands of pesos can change hands during one of these events. "The passion for cock-fighting" Fedor Jagor wrote in his *Travels in the Philippines* in 1873, "can well be termed a national vice." Despite attempts by the Spanish to stamp the practice out, cockfighting remains enormously popular. Sundays and public holidays are the best times to see this blood sport.

PORTABLE MOSQUITO NETS

We specialize in high quality insect nets that provide the ultimate in protection against Mosquitos, Bed-bugs, Fleas and other biting insects.

- A CHOICE OF SIZES AND MODELS TO SUIT YOUR SPECIFIC NEEDS.
- USE ANYWHERE, NO STRINGS NEEDED.
- SURPRIZINGLY LIGHT-WEIGHT.
- PRICES FROM $39 TO $99.
- ORDERS SHIPPED SAME DAY.

FREE BROCHURES 1-800-359-6040
or visit our website http:www.longroad.com

LONG ROAD
TRAVEL SUPPLIES

111 Avenida Drive
Berkeley, CA 94708 U.S.A.
Tel(510) 540-4763
Fax(510) 540-0652

Chapter Four

Practical Information

VISAS

Tourist and business visas valid for 21 days are issued free of charge on arrival at Ninoy Aquino Airport in Manila or at Mactan International Airport on Cebu. There may be some visa exceptions according to nationality, so, if in doubt, check. Your passport must be valid for six months from the date the visa expires. If you do arrive with a visa issued at a Philippine embassy or consulate abroad, it is wise to alert the immigration officer to the fact. This will avoid them issuing you with a standard 21-day visa. If you wish to stay longer than 21 days you should apply for a 59-day visa from the Philippine embassy or consulate in your country before leaving. Applicants must enter the Philippines within three months of the visa being granted.

Extending visas

It is usually no problem extending a visa. Visitors must apply at the Commission for Immigration and Deportation (CID) at Magallanes Drive, Intramuros, Manila. Some hotels and travel agencies will handle your visa extension for you for a small fee. If you are in a hurry to process your visa, it can be obtained within 24 hours by the payment of an "'express fee". If you intend to extend your stay beyond 21 days, you will incur a number of extra fees for visa extensions of 38 days upwards. Anyone wishing to stay beyond six months must pay a fee for a Certificate of Temporary Residence and an Emigration Clearance Certificate. A travel tax is incurred at the airport on departure by visitors who have stayed for a full year or longer. All your documents must be in order before departing the country.

PHILIPPINE EMBASSIES AND CONSULATES

Argentina, ACT Tower, 6th Fl, 135 Sen Gil J Puyat Ave, Makati. Tel: 875655.

Australia, 16th Fl, BPI Bldg, Ayala Ave and Paseo de Roxas, Makati. Tel: 817 7911.

Austria, 4th Fl, Prince Bldg, 117 Rada St, Legaspi Village, Makati. Tel: 817 9191.

Bangladesh, JEG Bldg,150 Legaspi Villlage, Makati. Tel: 817 5001.

Belgium, 6th Fl, Don Jacinto Bldg, de la Rosa and Salcedo St, Legaspi Village, Makati. Tel: 876571.

Bolivia, Pacific Banking Corp Bldg, Makati. Tel: 886948.

Brazil, 6th Fl, RCI Bldg, 105 Rada St, Legaspi Village, Makati. Tel: 888181.

Brunei, 11th Fl, BPI Bldg, Ayala Ave, Makati Tel: 816 2836.

Canada, 9th Fl, Allied Bank Center, 6754 Ayala Ave, Makati. Tel: 815 9536.

Chile, 2nd Fl, Gammon Center, 126 Alfaro St, Salcedo Village, Makati. Tel: 816 0395.

China, 4896 Pasay Rd, Dasmarinas Village, Makati. Tel: 853148.

Colombia, 18th Fl, Aurora Tower, Araneta Center, Aurora Bldg, Cubao, Quezon City. Tel: 921 2701.

Cuba, 51 Paseo de Roxas, Urdaneta Village, Makati. Tel: 817 1284

Denmark, 10th Fl, Citibank Centre, 8741 Paseo de Roxas, Makati. Tel: 819 1906.

Dominican Republic, 312 Shaw Blvd, Mandaluyong. Tel: 797887.

Egypt, 2229 Paraiso, Banyan St, and Dasmarinas Village, Makati. Tel: 880396.

Finland, 14th Fl, BPI Bldg, Ayala Ave, Paseo de Roxas. Tel: 989934.

France, 2nd Fl, Filipinas Life Assurance Bldg, 6786 Ayala Ave, Makati. Tel: 810 1981.

Germany, 6th Fl, Solidbank Bldg, Paseo de Roxas, Makati. Tel: 810 4701.

Greece, Dona Narcisa Bldg, Makati. Tel: 816 2309.

India, 2190 Paraiso St, Dasmarinas Village, Makati. Tel: 872445.

Indonesia, Indonesian Embassy Bldg, 185 Salcedo St, Legaspi Village, Makati. Tel: 855 061.

Iran, 4th Fl, Don Jacinto Bldg, Salcedo and de la Roasa St, Legaspi Village, Makati. Tel: 871561/63.

Iraq, 1368 Caballero St, Makati. Tel: 817 9242.

Israel, 5th Fl, Rm 538 Philippine Savings Bank Bldg, 6813 Ayala Ave, Makati. Tel: 885329.

Italy, 6th Fl, Zta II Bldg, 191 Salcedo St, Legaspi Village, Makati. Tel: 874531.

Japan, L C Bldg, 375 Sen Gil J Puyat Ave, Makati. Tel: 818 9011.

Jordan, 3502 Golden Rock Bldg, 168 Salcedo St, Legaspi Village, Makati. Tel: 817 7494.

Korea, 3rd Fl, ALPAP I Bldg, 140 Alfaro St, Salcedo Village, Makati. Tel: 817 5704.

Libya, 2276 Magnolia and Paraiso St, Dasmarinas Village, Makati. Tel: 817 3461.

Malaysia, 107 Tordesillas St, Salcedo Village, Makati. Tel: 817 4581-85.

Mexico, Adamson Centre Bldg, 121 Alfaro St, Salcedo Village, Makati. Tel: 815 2566.

Netherlands, 9th Fl, King's Court Bldg, 2129 Pasong Tamo St, Makati. Tel: 851 561.

New Zealand, 3rd Fl, Gammon Centre, 126 Alfaro St, Salcedo Village, Makati. Tel: 818 0916.

Nauru, Pacific Star Bldg, Makati Ave, and Sen Gil Puyat Ave. Tel: 818 3580.

Nigeria, 2211 Paraiso St, Dasmarinas Village, Makati. Tel: 817 3836.

Norway, Erechem Bldg, Salcedo St Herrera St and Legaspi Village, Makati. Tel: 881 111.

Pakistan, Alexander House, Makati. Tel: 817 2776.

Panama, Victoria Bldg, Rm 501, 429 UN Ave, Manila. Tel: 583277.

Papua New Guinea, 2224 Paraiso St, Dasmarinas Village, Makati. Tel: 880 386.

Peru, 3rd Fl, Prince Bldg, 117 Rada St, Legaspi Village, Makati. Tel:818 7209.

Romania, 1216 Acacia Rd, Dasmarinas Village, Makati. Tel: 817 9171.

Saudi Arabia, 8th Fl, Insular Life Bldg, Ayala Ave, Makati. Tel: 8173371.

Singapore, 6th Fl, ODC International Plaza, 217 Salcedo St, Legaspi Village, Makati. Tel: 816 1764.

Soviet Union, 656 Vito Cruz, Manila. Tel: 595 639.

Spain, 5th Fl, ACT Tower, 135 Sen Gil J Puyat Ave, Makati. Tel: 818 3561.

Sri Lanka, 5th Fl, Gammon Center, 126 Alfaro St, Salcedo Village, Makati. Tel: 815 1483.

Sweden, 15th Fl, Citibank Center, 8741 Paseo de Roxas, Makati. Tel: 819 1951.

Switzerland, 5th Fl, V Esguerra Bldg, 140 Amorsolo St, Legaspi Village, Makati. Tel: 819 0202.

Thailand, 107 Rada St, Legaspi Village, Makati. Tel: 815 4219.

United Kingdom, Electra House, 115 Esteban St, Legaspi Village, Makati. Tel: 853 002.

United States of America, 1201 Roxas Blvd, Ermita, Manila. Tel: 521 7116.

Vatican, 2140 Taft Ave, Metro Manila. Tel: 583072.

Vietnam, 554 Vito Cruz, Manila. Tel: 508101.

GETTING THERE

Manila is the main port of entry for travellers to the Philippines, followed by Cebu. There are also flights from Borneo and Indonesia which come into Davao Airport on Mindanao. Apart from Philippines Airlines (PAL), the nation's flag carrier, the archipelago is served by scheduled flights from various parts of Europe, North America, Africa and the Middle East, as well as Australia and New Zealand. PAL is the oldest airline in Asia. Pacific crossings and flights to Shanghai and Hong Kong were made as early as 1946. PAL are adding new destinations all the time, particularly in the economically ascendant Southeast Asia region. Other air companies offering regular flights to the Philippines include British Airways, Air France, KLM, Lufthansa, United Airlines, Northwest, Quantas, Swissair, Thai International, Gulf Air, Saudi Arabia Airlines, Pakistan International Airlines, Japan Airlines, Royal Brunei, Egyptair, Air Naura, Air Niugini, Continental Airways/Air Micronesia, Hang Khong Vietnam, China Airlines, CAAC (Air China), Malaysian Airlines System, Korean Airlines and Singapore Airlines.

From the UK

British Airways, PAL and several European airlines fly to Manila from London, so it is worth shopping around for the best, or most seasonal, deal. Vicious competition on the busy London to Hong Kong route offers an alternative way of flying to the Philippines. Hong Kong, like London, is an excellent point from which to shop around for ongoing tickets to practically anywhere else in the world. London is probably the bucket shop emporium of the world. Bucket shops, for those who are not familiar with the expression, are travel agencies that offer discounted tickets released by airlines eager to fill seats even if it means at a reduced profit. Thus, the discount prices are not always so attractive during peak periods. Advertisements for bucket shops, as well as specialist tours and expeditions to Southeast Asia, regularly appear in magazines like *Time Out*, *City Limits*, *LAM*, *Trailfinder*, *Australasian Express*, a number of Sunday supplements and specialist magazines like *The Geographical Magazine*, *Traveller*, *Wanderlust* and *Business Traveller*. Some well-established and reputable agencies in London include:

Trailfinders Travel Centre, 46 Earls Court Road.
Student Travel Association, 86 Old Brompton Road, South Kensington.
Wexas International, 45-49 Brompton Road, Knightsbridge.
Reho Travel, Commonwealth House, 15 New Oxford Street.
Far East Travel Centre, 32 Shaftesbury Avenue.
Flight Deck, 181 Earls Court Road.
All Points Travel, Michele House, 45/46 Berners Street.

Frankfurt, Brussels, Amsterdam and Zürich are also good places to obtain cut-price tickets and regular schedules to the Philippines.

From America and Canada

There are a number of ways to fly to the Philippines from the United States. The best deals are generally from the West Coast. Over a million and a half Filipinos live in the USA. Cities that have large Filipino populations like San Francisco, Los Angeles, Honolulu and Daly City, have Filipino-owned travel agencies offering competitive fares. PAL has offices in Washington DC, New York, Honolulu, Dallas, San Francisco, San Diego, Florida, Los Angeles and Chicago. PAL frequently offer promotional fares. An update on these and other information can be had by calling their toll-free number: (800) 435 9725. Other Asian airlines with Manila routes include Cathay Pacific, China Air and Korean Airlines. Flights with courier airlines like DHL, Federal Express, Skypack and TNT Courier are becoming increasingly more popular ways of travelling to Eastern destinations like Manila and Hong Kong. Publications like *Travel Unlimited, New York Times, San Francisco Examiner* and the *Los Angeles Times* regularly carry advertising on discount air fares to the East.

PAL has Canadian offices in Vancouver and Toronto, and Cathay Pacific do regular flights between Vancouver and Manila, with a stopover in Hong Kong. Kowloon Travel, 425 Abbot Street; Ed Polanin, 2065 West Fourth Avenue; and Wetcan Treks, 3415 West Broadway, are all good Vancouver-based agencies. Travel Cuts is a nationwide discount student bureau with branches in most large Canadian cities.

From Asia

With larger numbers of affluent Asians on the move, discount air fare centres have sprung up all over the East. Bangkok used to be the premier Asian capital for cut-price tickets but, at least for the time being, Hong Kong seems to have taken the lead. Singapore and Penang are also excellent places to obtain onward tickets to the Philippines and other Asian destinations.

Via Bangkok

Sukhumvit Road and the area known as Soi Ngam Duphli are the best bets for discount agencies in Bangkok. Areas where budget travellers congregate, like Banglamphu, are good places to pick up information. The staff at STA Travel, located in the Thai Hotel, at 78 Prachatipatai Road, are helpful and well informed. Trad Travel Service in the Viengtai Hotel, 42 Tanee Road, is also recommended.

From Hong Kong

The sheer number of discount and other travel agencies in Hong Kong, and the options on offer, can leave visitors reeling. Try to select four or five of the most tried and tested agencies and compare their prices and itineraries. The classified sections of the *Hongkong Standard, The Eastern Express* and the *South China Morning Post* all carry advertisements for discount agencies. The Hong Kong based magazine *Business Traveller* often does cost analysis and price breakdowns on countries like the Philippines. Some of the agencies most favoured by old Asia hands are Phoenix Services, Room B, 6th Floor, Milton Mansions, 96 Nathan Road; Morning Star, 1529-32, Star House, Salisbury Road;

Banca Travel Services, 3rd Floor, Shun On Commercial Building, 112-114 Des Voeux Road; Hong Kong Student Travel Bureau, Room 1021, 10th Floor, Star House; and Shoestring Travel, Flat A, 4th Floor, Alpha House, 17-33 Nathan Road.

Via Malaysia
Penang, with its busy little international airport, is a surprisingly good place to find discount tickets. Most of the agencies are located within walking distance of each other in the centre of Georgetown. Try MSL Travel in the Hotel Merlin, 25A Leboh Farquhar, International Tourist Promotion, 53 Kampong Malabar, and Tropical Tours and Travel and Silver Travel Service, both located in the China Hotel.

Via Singapore
Singapore is a major transfer point and R&R spot for travellers flying into or around the East. Classified adverts appear regularly in the *Straits Times* and there are travel bulletins, updates and articles on the region in magazines like *Outbound* and *Vacation*. Compare prices at student Travel Australia (STA), Orchard Parade Hotel; Holiday Tour and Travels, 12 Mezzanine Floor, Ming Court Hotel, Tanglin Road; Airmaster Travel, 36 Selegie Road; and MAS Travel, 633 Tanglin Shopping Centre.

Other Asian options
India is a good place to find tickets for the Philippines with flights departing from Delhi and Bombay. Delhi has the most discount shops. Japan, with its large expatriate population, is a surprisingly cheap travel discount centre these days, although the best deals are reserved for return fares. The Philippines is an increasingly popular destination as it often costs less to fly to Manila from Tokyo or Osaka than it does to somewhere like Okinawa. See advertisements in the *Tokyo Journal* and newspapers like the *Japan Times* and the *Daily Yomiuri*. Seoul and Taipei aren't as competitive as Tokyo but there are occasionally good deals on offer. Jakarta is a small but growing centre for discount fares in Indonesia. Borneo, if you happen to find yourself in that neck of the woods, offers a fascinating route to Manila or Davao from Kota Kinabalu or Brunei. Travellers passing through the scattered islands of the South Pacific and Micronesia, particularly devotees of watersports and the world-class diving offered in this region, may wish to take advantage of an excellent infrastructure of inter-island routes that take in the Philippines. The best fares are offered by Air Naura who fly to Manley via Guam, Naura and Koror in Palau. Continental Airlines also do Manila runs from Guam, Rota, Saipan and Koror.

From Australia and New Zealand
Australia is not a particularly cheap country to fly from but can work out reasonably economical if you add Manila as a stopover to other European, North American or Asian destinations. Return and one-way APEX tickets

are available and some agencies offer discounted return excursion fares. PAL and Quantas fly from Melbourne, Adelaide, Brisbane and Sydney. Air Niugini fly to Manila with a stopover in Port Moresby. Air Nauru also do a Melbourne-Nauru-Manila flight. STA are one of the best discount agencies, with offices in Sydney, Perth, Melbourne, Adelaide, Canberra, Brisbane and Hobart.

Because there are no direct flights from New Zealand to Manila, there are few bargains. Thai International, via Bangkok, offer the cheapest flights. Small student discounts may be available through New Zealand Student Travel Services, Courtenay Place, Wellington.

Round-the-world tickets

RTW tickets have become very popular in recent years, and make perfect sense for long-haul travellers with time on their hands. There are dozens of itineraries and possible combinations. The most comprehensive, and costly, options are full-service, full-fare tickets which allow you to go virtually anywhere you wish on a large number of different airlines. A far cheaper but more prohibitive alternative is to get a RTW package offered by three or four air companies that have combined their services. These allow for unlimited stopovers within the destinations covered by these airlines, and tickets typically of between 120 days and one year duration. Backtracking is not allowed and routes via the Southern Hemisphere tend to be more expensive than their northern counter-routes.

Circle Pacific fares

Certain airlines have combined to offer tickets that circle the globe and that either originate from or take in the Philippines en route. PAL, Quantas and American Airlines have come up with a ticket valid for up to six months that allows you to combine the United States, New Zealand, Australia, Asia and the Philippines in one glorious loop with as many stopovers as you can fit in. PAL and Continental Airlines offer a similar itinerary incorporating Southeast Asia and Japan.

Sea routes

Despite the fact that Manila is a major seaport, there are very few ways of getting there by ship. Some cargo-passenger lines operate irregular services dropping off at Manila, but need to be booked months in advance. They also tend to end up costing far more than flying. Passengers arriving in Manila by ship must have a valid outward bound air ticket. There are occasionally passenger-carrying freighters leaving from Singapore and Hong Kong for the Philippines, but the increase in container shipping has reduced this possibility even further in recent years. There are routes operating between Borneo and Mindanao but, as these sea lanes are frequently infested with pirates, this route is not recommended.

Customs

Visitors are allowed to bring in most standard personal effects such as jewellery and perfume, though receipts may be required for large quantities of camera, video or portable stereo equipment. You are allowed to bring in two litres of alcohol, plus 400 cigarettes and two tins of tobacco. Currency amounting to over US$3,000 must be declared on arrival at the Central Bank counter. You are not officially allowed to leave the country with more than P1,000 in Philippine currency. Security is tight and regular baggage checks for firearms, drugs, pornography and the like are made.

Departure tax

All visitors must pay a departure tax of P500 at the bank counter in the exit hall at Manila Airport. Unless you wish to buy duty-free goods inside the airport or get rid of your pesos in one of the cafés or snack bars there, it is advisable to change all your remaining cash into better-known currencies like dollars, as the overseas rate for pesos can be dismal.

Manila airline offices

Aerolift, Philippine Corp, 2nd Fl, Chemphil Bldg, 851 Pasay Road, Legaspi Village, Makati. Tel: 817 2369.

Air Canada, Asian Plaza Bldg, Tordesillas St, Makati. Tel: 810 4461.

Air France, 7th Floor, Century Tower, 100 Tordesila St, Salcedo Village, Makati. Tel: 815 6963.

Air India, Gammon Centre, 126 Alfaro St, Salcedo Village, Makati. Tel: 815 1280.

Air Nauru, Pacific Star Bldg, Makati Ave, corner Senator Gil J Puyat Ave, Makati. Tel: 819 7241.

Air Niugini, Pacific Bank Bldg, 6776 Ayala Ave, Makati. Tel: 819 0206.

Alitalia, M-3 Gallery Bldg, Amorsolo St, Legaspi Village, Makati. Tel: 850265.

American Airlines, Olympia Bldg, Makati Av, Makati. Tel: 817 8645.

Bourag Airlines, Quirino Ave, Paranaque. Tel: 833 2902.

British Airlines, Ground Floor, Filipino Merchant Bldg, Legaspi St. Tel: 817 0361.

Canadian Airlines, Allied Bank Bldg, 6754 Ayala Ave, Makati. Tel: 810 2656.

Cathay Pacific Airways, Ermita Centre Bldg, 1350 Roxas Blvd, Ermita, Manila. Tel: (598) 06165.

China Airlines, 2nd Floor, Manilla Pavilion Hotel, UN Ave, Ermita, Manila. Tel: 599460.

Continental/Air Micronesia, 6760 Ayala Ave, SGV Bldg, Makati. Tel: 818 8701.

Delta Airlines, Makati Stock Exchange Bldg, Ayala Ave, Makati. Tel: 859215.

Eastern Airlines, Manila Peninsula Hotel, Ayala Ave, Makati. Tel: 872971.

Emirates Airlines, Country Space 1 Bldg, Gil Puyat Ave, Salcedo Village, Makati. Tel: 816 0809.

Finnair, Pacific Bank Bldg, Ayala Ave, Makati. Tel: 818 2601.

Garuda Indonesia Airlines, Ground Floor, Manila Peninsula Hotel, Makati Ave, Makati. Tel: 862458.

Gulf Air, Fortune Bldg, Legaspi St, Legaspi Village, Makati. Tel: 819 0327.

Japan Airlines, Hotel Nikko Manila Garden, Makati. Tel: (810) 977680.

KLM Royal Dutch Airlines, 160 Alfaro St, Salcedo Village, Makati. Tel: 815 4790.

Korean Airlines, Ground Floor, LPL Plaza, 124 Alfaro St, Salcedo Village, Makati. Tel: 815 8911.

Kuwait Airlines, Ground Floor, JEG Bldg, 150 Legaspi St, Legaspi Village, Makati. Tel: 817 2778.

Lufthansa German Airlines, Vernida V Bldg, Legaspi Alvarado St, Makati. Tel: 810 5018.

Malaysian Airways System, Legaspi Towers, 300 Roxas Blvd, Manila. Tel: 575 76166.

Northwest Orient Airlines, Atheneum Bldg, 160 Alfaro St, Salcedo Village, Makati. Tel: 819 7341.

Pacific Airways, Athenaeum Bldg, Alfaro St, Makati. Tel: 819 7341.

Pakistan International Airways, 4th Floor, ADC Bldg, 6805 Ayala Ave, Makati. Tel: 818 3711.

Philippine Airlines, PAL Bldg, Legaspi St, Makati. Tel: 816 6691.

Quantas Airlines, Ground Floor, China Bank Bldg, 8745 Paseo de Roxas, Makati. Tel: 815 9491.

Royal Brunei Airlines, Saville Bldg, Paseo de Roxas, Makati. Tel: 817 163134.

Royal Jordanian Airlines, Ground Floor, Golden Rock Bldg, 168 Salcedo St., Legaspi Village, Makati. Tel: 818 5901.

Saudi Arabian Airlines, Cougar Bldg, Herrera St, Salcedo Village, Makati. Tel: 818 7866.

Sabena Airlines, 2nd Floor, Manila Pavilion Hotel, United Nations Ave, Ermita, Manila. Tel: 508636.

Scandinavian Airlines System, Ground Floor, F&M Bldg, 144 Legaspi St, Legaspi Village, Makati. Tel: 887239.

Singapore Airlines, 138 HV de la Costa St, Salcedo Village, Makati. Tel: 810 4960.

Swissair, 2nd Floor, Country Space 1 Bldg, Senator Gil J Puyat Ave, Makati. Tel: 818 8521.

Thai Airways International, 2nd Floor, Country Space 1 Bldg, Senator Gil J Puyat Ave, Makati. Tel: 815 842131.

United Airlines, Ground and 48th Floors, Pacific Star Bldg, Makati. Tel: 818 5421.

Vietnam Airlines, Anson Arcade, Pasay Rd, Makati. Tel: 874878.

ACCOMMODATION

The Philippines offers a wide, though unevenly spread, range of accommodation to suit most pockets. The largest choice by far is found in Manila, with its five-star hotel and convention facilities and modestly priced guesthouses. First class accommodation is also available in cities like Baguio, Davao and Cebu, and at some upmarket beach resorts. On average, prices in Manila are significantly higher than in the provinces. Popular tourist destinations like Boracay, Puerto Galera and Banaue, where visitors can shop around and compare prices before deciding on a room, generally offer the best deals. Depending on their size and repute, beach locations may offer anything from fully equipped club resorts to nipa huts for the shoestring traveller.

Standards vary enormously, even within one price range. At their best, budget inns and lodging houses provide clean, spacious rooms, a friendly atmosphere and the possibility of facilities like kitchens, hot water for tea and coffee, and laundry services. At their worst, under objective scrutiny, some boarding houses reveal windowless rooms, grubby bedcovers, defective plumbing and long-stay rodents. Many of the seedier hotels cater for "short-time" customers and their hospitality girls; two- or three-hour room rates posted up in the lobby area are a telltale sign. Have a good look at a room before you commit yourself, and always check available exits as fires are commonplace in the Philippines. Expect to pay an additional 25% in tax and service charges on top of your bill at hotels and guesthouses.

The price differential between a shared dormitory in a youth hostel and a guesthouse is often minimal. For visitors planning to extend their stay in the country, apartment hotels, sometimes advertised as "apartels", can be very economical, particularly if shared with one or two other people. Apartments usually come with spacious, air-conditioned rooms, television, refrigerator and cooking facilities. In Manila, where most of these are found, the rents are much more competitive outside of the tourist centres of Makati and Ermita.

In many country towns, villages, and islands off the beaten track, there may be little or no conventional accommodation at all. In such cases, regional tourist offices may be able to put you in touch with a homestay family. Otherwise, the local mayors or village headmen, the *barangay* captains as they are known, are usually extremely helpful in finding temporary accommodation in private homes, school buildings and so on. Camping on the Philippines, unless as part of an organised trek, is generally not a viable option as campsites are few and far between.

MONEY

The unit of currency in the Philippines is the *peso*, which is divided into 100 *centavos*. Banknote denominations are P2, 5, 10, 20, 50, 100, 500 and 1,000. There are one-, two- and five-peso coins and smaller units of 5, 10, 25 and 50 centavos.

Exchanging money

The US dollar is the favoured currency here, generally followed by Japanese yen and the German mark. US dollars usually yield a better rate, especially larger bills like $50 and $100. There are exchange facilities in the airport. Cash and travellers cheques can also be exchanged at commercial banks, hotels, restaurants, souvenir shops and large department stores. Authorised foreign exchange dealers offer a good rate. Their service is also faster than the banks. A large number of these moneychangers can be found along Mabini Street and Padre Faura Street in Manila. You will need to produce your passport for all money transactions. If you are handing over travellers cheques, you will have to show the receipts you obtained when you first bought them. Keep all your Central Bank receipts as you will need to produce these if you wish to reconvert pesos before leaving the country. Large cities like Cebu and Baguio have facilities of this sort but it is wise when travelling in the provinces to carry local currency with a small supplement in US dollars, and the rest ideally in travellers cheques. Major credit cards such as Master and Visa, Diners and American Express are accepted by major hotels, upmarket restaurants and shops. Banks open from Monday to Friday from 09.00 to 15.00 or 15.30, and on Saturdays from 09.00 until 12.00.

Bank accounts

Travellers who are intending to stay several months in the Philippines might consider the idea of opening a bank account here. You can earn a little bit of interest and save yourself the trouble of carrying around heaps of cash or travellers cheques. Your money of course, might devaluate against the peso in the meantime. You should also note that banks are not empowered to insure more than P40,000 of your money. This means that in the event of bankruptcy any amount over that figure does not, legally, have to be reimbursed to clients.

The black market

Black market rates are only worth having if you are exchanging US$100 bills. The lower the denomination, the less the benefit. Manila offers the highest rates, with large touristic cities like Cebu and Baguio offering a little less. Fellow travellers are the most up-to-date source on rates. Changing money on the street can be an extremely risky business. Sleight-of-hand con artists who are adept at short-changing clients, as well as outright theft of the snatch-and-run variety, are everyday occurrences. Beware that counterfeit $100 notes are also routinely passed off on easily duped tourists.

Major foreign banks

American Express, 3rd Fl, Corinthian Plaza, 121 Paseo de Roxas, Legaspi Village, Makati. Tel: 818 6731.

Banque Nationale de Paris, Ground Floor, PCIB Tower II, Makati Ave, Makati. Tel: 815 8821.

Chase Manhattan, 15th Floor, Pacific Star Bldg, corner Makati Ave and Sen Gil J Puyat Ave, Makati. Tel: (818) 985160.

Citibank N A, Citibank Center, 8741 Paseo de Roxas, Makati. Tel: 810 4411.

Hongkong and Shanghai Banking Corp, 6780 Ayala Ave, Makati. Tel: 810 1661.

MISCELLANEOUS INFORMATION

Tourist information services

Tourist information centres run by the Philippine Department of Tourism operate in several countries. There is a reception unit at the airport in Manila and at the Nayong Filipino Complex. The main Department of Tourism information centre is on the ground floor of the Tourism Building, Agrifina Circle, Rizal Park. It is open every day from 08.00 to 17.00. They also have a 24-hour phone service: tel 501728, or 501660. There are regional tourist offices throughout the country that can provide more detailed information on their own areas. *The Daily Express* and *The Manila Bulletin* are newspapers that list events and upcoming entertainments. The magazines *Ex-Pat* and *Mabuhay Philippines Journal* are also useful publications. The commendable *What's On* covers Manila, the Visayas and Mindanao.

Maps

A good map of the Philippines is essential to make sense of the complex geographical sweep and interlocking relations of the islands, as well as to negotiate the urban and downtown sprawl of Manila. Decent starter maps of the country and capital can be picked up free at the Department of Tourism Information Centre. Nelles Verlag produce a useful map of the Philippines which includes a Greater Manila city map. Excellent road maps are made by Mobil and Petron. Heinrich Engeler's Metro Manila is probably the single best map available of the capital. Bookmark's series of maps, highlighting interesting city features and street layouts, are also recommended. To date these include *Metro Manila Landmarks*, *Makati Landmarks*, *Baguio Landmarks* and *Cebu*.

Business hours

Most government departments and businesses open from 08.00 to 17.00 and take their lunch breaks anywhere between 11.30 and 13.00. Embassies and consulates are open to the public from 09.00 to 13.00. Airline office hours are normally from 08.30 to 17.00 in the week and from 08.30 to 12.30 on Saturdays. Large department stores tend to open until 19.00. Smaller shops often stay open until 22.00 or beyond.

Weights and measures

Filipinos use the metric system but in rural areas travellers may still come across examples of the old system, like *ganta* (three litres), *cavan* (75 litres), *arroba* (11.5 kilograms) and *pulgada* (2.31 centimetres).

COMMUNICATIONS

Post and telecommunications

The Philippines postal system is a reasonable one, but mail is often subject to delays, sometimes lost and occasionally interfered with. There is not much you can do about lost mail, but if you are in a hurry to send something abroad it is much quicker to take it straight to the distribution centre near the airport. Mail often gets held up for days on end just getting from the post office to the centre. Before and during the Christmas holidays, you should allow plenty of time for mail to reach home. It is advisable to make sure that letters are stamped, weighed and priced in your presence as these often get removed by light-fingered staff. This happens in even some of the large central post offices. It is not advisable to send documents or cash through the post, unless vital, in which case you should always send by registered post. Parcels should be wrapped in brown paper and string and the address clearly marked. Technically, the post office will not handle parcels over 20kg. Parcels sent by surface mail (sea) to Europe or the United States will take from two to four months to arrive. The General Post Office (GPO) and the Mabini Street Post Office are the most frequented in Manila. The Rizal Park Post Office, near the Manila Hotel, is not so busy.

Receiving post

If you are carrying American Express travellers cheques or using their credit card, you can have post sent to their offices in Manila, Makati or Cebu City. Their Manila address is c/o Client Mail Service, American Express, Pilamlife Building, United Nations Avenue. You can phone for information – tel 8159311. Post can also be collected from the poste restante service at the GPO. This opens from 08.00 to 17.00, Monday to Saturday, and from 08.00 to 12.00 on Sundays. Most post offices are closed on Sundays and on all public holidays. There are poste restante facilities in most major towns. The post office and the American Express people will keep your mail for three months. If it is not claimed by then, it will be returned to the sender. It is important that you tell the sender to write your address clearly and to underline your name.

Telephones

The telephone network is run by the Philippine Long Distance Telephone Company (PLDT). In the provinces community telephone networks run the system. It is usually easy enough to find a call box in large towns, but smaller villages may not have any phone facilities, in which case you may have to resort to asking at the local police station. Long-distance overseas calls are surprisingly easy to place in comparison with local and domestic long-distance calls which can often take an eternity to get through. Overseas calls can be made from a number of different places. Calls made from the PLDT offices on Taft Avenue and Escolta Street are fractionally cheaper. Other convenient locations include the airport, Philippine Global Communications office, and most large hotels. It is 25% cheaper to phone on Sundays. Domestic telephone numbers are constantly changing so check with the various telephone directories or yellow pages before placing a call. Otherwise, call directory enquiries (114) for help. When making long-distance domestic calls, dial 0 then the area code; 109 for calls placed through the operator, and 108 for the international operator.

Useful telephone numbers

Direct dialling assistance	112
Directory enquiries	114
Domestic long distance	109
Overseas long distance	108
Emergency	911
Police	166

Fax and telegrams

Faxes are probably the easiest and surest way of sending a message. Most large hotels and businesses have their own machines these days. Private telecommunication companies like Globe-Mackay and Eastern Telecoms charge less than hotels. International telegram services are generally fast and reliable, though domestic telegrams are often subject to delays. There is a seven-word minimum on telegrams. Letter telegrams, with a 22-word minimum, work out cheaper. Other conveniently located companies for sending faxes and telegrams are Philippine Global Communications, RCA Building, 8755 Paseo de Roxas (tel 8162851), and Eastern Telecommunications Phils Inc, Telecoms Plaza Makati (tel 8158921). They also have an office at Electra House, 115 Esteban St, Legaspi Village (tel 8162645).

Time

The Philippines is eight hours ahead of GMT which makes it two hours behind Australian Eastern Standard Time. Possibly because of the Spanish legacy, or just the relaxed tropical climate and way of life in general, time does seem more elastic in the Philippines than it is even in some other Southeast Asian countries. This is especially true in the countryside where often heard spatial-time references such as "in a short while", "after some time" and the particularly vague "by and by" can indicate anything between a few minutes and a couple of hours. Socially, Filipinos usually set appointments well ahead of the actual time they intend to show up or receive guests. If you are lucky enough to be invited to someone's house, arriving punctually is likely to send your hosts into a panic. Turning up an hour after the set time is considered good manners. None of this applies, of course, to business meetings and the departure times for public transport.

Electricity

The standard electric current in the Philippines is 220V AC, 60 cycles. In the countryside in particular, the actual voltage may be lower, depending upon supply and demand. In some parts of the Philippines the standard current is 110V, as in the United States. Adaptors for American or Japanese style two-point plugs can be bought in Manila. Power failures, or blackouts, are very common in the Philippines, even in Manila, and are called "brownouts". Make sure to pack a pocket torch before coming.

MEDIA
The press

Journalists were heavily censored during the Marcos period, but since then there has been a veritable renaissance of the press in the Philippines. Today there are about 360 publications appearing nationwide in English, Filipino and Chinese. Some of the better-known Metro Manila publications include the *Manila Chronicle*, *Philippine Sun*, *Business World*, *Manila Bulletin*, *Philippine Daily Inquirer*, *Philippine Daily Globe*, and the *Manila Times*. *Tempo* and *Peoples* are among the most critically objective papers in English. *Free Press* is one of the best weekly magazines in the Philippines. *Taliba*, *Ang Pilipino Ngayon* and *Balita* are less influential papers that appear in Filipino and Tagalog. The Philippine Press Institute (PPI) was set up to establish professional standards and sponsor research, book fairs, workshops and journalistic conventions. The Philippine Press Council, in tandem with the National Press Club of the Philippines, monitors and revises journalistic codes of ethics. Scant attention is paid to international events in the Philippine press, although it has improved somewhat in recent years. For world and regional coverage, publications like *Newsweek*, *Time*, *Far Eastern Economic Review*, *Asiaweek* and the *International Herald Tribune* are readily available in large hotels and good bookshops. The *Foreign Post* and *Expat* are weekly English language publications for foreign residents and tourists.

Television and radio

The five television networks have a combined number of 22 relay stations. Government Television (Channel 4) is state owned, the rest are independent. Most programmes are broadcast in either English or

Tagalog. A typical evening's fare might include a sports digest, soap opera, MTV excerpts, a variety show and a hard-boiled "guns and goons" serial. The inordinate number of commercial breaks can be exasperating. Those who can afford it sensibly opt for a satellite dish or cable TV.

There are 103 FM and 235 AM radio stations broadcasts from 06.00 to 24.00 in English and Tagalog. Pop and rock programmes are a favourite with the music-loving Filipinos. Short-wave radios can pick up the BBC World Service, Voice of America and Radio Australia.

Film and photography

Print film is readily available in the Philippines but slide film, especially the slow variety like Kodachrom 64, 25 and Fuji Provia, is more difficult to find. Always check the expiry date and be careful buying from shops in the provinces where storage of film material in humid conditions may have adverse effects like discoloration and under-saturation. Always have film developed as soon as possible. If you are using Kodak slide film and are likely to be away for more than a couple of weeks, it might be worth posting them off for processing in prepaid envelopes, giving your home address. High speed prints can be made in one hour. Manila is probably the best place to stock up on film. Mayer Photo, on Carlos Palanca Street, Quiapo, is well thought after. There are a number of other photo shops nearby on Hidalgo Street. Lead-lined bags provide useful but imperfect protection from airport x-ray machines. These usually have "Film Safe" stickers on them, but in the Philippines it is wise to have your film hand-inspected.

There are few equipment bargains in the Philippines. If you are travelling through the area, Singapore and Hong Kong are excellent places to buy lenses, spare bodies and other items. Tokyo is also good value. Shops in Tokyo offer excellent prices on second-hand gear. A UV filter is always useful in tropical countries, not just to counteract harsh light but also to keep lenses clean. Be extremely careful, especially when staying on salt-water tropical islands, that you keep your cameras and lenses mould free. It can be expensive having lenses dismantled and cleaned by a shop. A waterproof bag can help against salt spray and humidity.

Bookshops

Manila has the most bookshops, although there are also good shops to be found in Cebu, Baguio and other large provincial towns. The National Bookstore has branches around the country and one of the best all-round selections. Goodwill Bookstore offers another excellent choice of reading material. They have two shops in Rizal Avenue, and three others in J Vargas Avenue, in the Ayala Centre in Makati and in the shopping complex at Las Pinas. LA Solidaridad Bookstore on Padre Faura, Ermita, and the Casalinda Bookshop, San Antonio Plaza, Forbes Park, Makati, have the best selection of so-called Filipiniana – books on the Philippines. Bookmark are good general stockists, with a branch near La Solidaridad in Mabini. Alemar's have several branches in Manila too. All the major hotels have their own bookshops but their prices are higher and they rarely have clearance sales as the above stores do.

HEALTH AND SAFETY

The Philippines is said to have one of the best tropical climates in the world and a relatively low incidence of illness, and its health care system by Southeast Asian standards is reasonably good. Visitors can go to largely private, general hospitals, or to community, mobile health centres and rural health centres for medical consultation and treatment. They also dispense medicine. Even quite small towns usually have fairly decently stocked pharmacies. Most tourists leave having suffered little more than a touch of sunburn, an upset stomach, a touch of prickly heat or a surface graze from having come into contact with sharp coral, but a little care and prevention will help to minimise the potential number of health problems you could incur in the Philippines.

Preliminary measures
Vaccinations
No immunisations are necessary for the Philippines. Yellow fever vaccinations are only required if you are arriving from an infected area. If you intend to be there for some time, or have plans to get off the beaten track, a few basic vaccinations against diseases you might come into contact with can be both useful and reassuring. Allow yourself plenty of time for inoculations as some may require second shots or may not be taken in conjunction with other jabs. It is a good idea to be inoculated against typhoid and tetanus. It is also wise to have shots for diphtheria, polio, cholera, measles and smallpox. Most people will have been immunised against these in their childhood so it is a good idea to get a booster. A gamma globulin shot against hepatitis A and a vaccine for the more serious hepatitis B, both common in tropical countries, make good sense.

Medical insurance
A good all-round insurance policy that covers theft, illness and serious accidents is highly recommended. There are a number of different high-to-low-risk policies on offer, so check carefully with your local travel agent. It is a good idea to carry a paper listing any medical problems that you have, blood type, emergency contact numbers and details of any prescriptions or special medication that you use regularly.

Medical kits
Some sort of medical kit is a must. Contents should be stored in a light, easily sealed bag that can be taken on planes as hand luggage. A basic kit could include plasters, an antibiotic powder and salve for treating cuts and scratches, a thermometer and tweezers, ear plugs and swabs to reduce risk

of ear infections, aspirin, anti-diarrhoea preparations for stomach problems, malaria pills if you are going into jungle cover or off the beaten track, a calamine lotion to alleviate irritation from stings, rashes and bites, antiseptic and sun-block creams, a rehydration mixture like Lomotil, water purification tablets, a course of anti-malarial tablets, an insect repellent, sunscreen and suntan lotion, and packets of good quality condoms for occasions when temptation may get the upper hand over preventive abstinence. A bottle of Tiger Balm is useful for muscle aches and pains and for bringing relief from insect bites.

Travel care

Most problems can be avoided with a little planning and attention to your health on the trip. You should be in reasonably good shape before you depart, but if you are taking medication, make sure that you have a sufficient supply and take your prescription with you in case you need a top-up. Be sure to take an extra pair of glasses or contact lenses with you as this will save a lot of hassle and expense. A check-up at the dentist, a couple of months before the trip, is a good idea. Dental facilities in the provinces are not, on average, as good as medical ones. Allow yourself a couple of easy days to adjust to a tropical climate and throw off any jet lag you may feel. Any small cuts or grazes should be addressed immediately as they can become septic within a very short period. Most water is potable, but when in doubt use purification tablets or keep a supply of easily available mineral water handy. Ice cubes and salads washed in suspect water are the usual causes of stomach upsets. Watch your diet in general and be aware of unpasteurised dairy foods, unwashed fruit, and inadequately cooked or lukewarm dishes. Fruit that can be peeled, plenty of grains and roughage, and eggs, nuts and beans will help to ensure some regular protein intake. Iron and vitamin pills can help. Drink more than you think you need to avoid dehydration. Extra doses of salt on food are better than taking salt tablets. It is not advisable to walk barefoot or in open thongs in obviously garbage-strewn urban areas. Don't swim in slow-flowing rivers, lakes or ponds as eye and ear infections are easily picked up. This is also a good way of contracting typhoid or parasitic infections like bilharzia. Try to take at least one shower a day, wash hands before meals, brush teeth with purified or mineral water, not straight from the tap, cover yourself sufficiently when there are droves of insects around, stay out of direct sunlight for long periods and avoid extremes of temperature whenever possible.

Health information addresses

Thomas Cook Vaccination Centre, 3-4 Wellington Terrace, Turnpike Lane, London N8 OPX. Tel: 0181 889 7014.

PPP Medical Centre, 99 New Cavendish Street, London WI. Tel: 0171 637 8941.

International Association for Medical Assistance to Travellers (IAMET), 735 Centre Street, Lewiston, NY 14092, USA. Tel: 716 754 4883.

British Airways Vaccination Centre, 9 Little Newport Street, London WC2H 7JJ. Tel: 0171 287 2255/3366.

British Airways Medical Centre, Terminal 3, Heathrow Airport. Tel: 0181 759 7208.

MASTA, Keppel Street, London WCIE 7HT. Tel: 0171 6314408. Give advice on travellers' health and also sell medical kits and supplies.

Useful books on health care
Richard Dawood, *The Traveller's Health*, OUP.
John Hatt, *The Tropical Traveller*, Pan.
Melissa Shales, *The Traveller's Handbook*, WEXAS.
David Werner, *Where There is No Doctor*, Hersperian Foundation.
Dr Antony Turner, *The Traveller's Health Guide*, Roger Lascelles.
Dr Jane Wilson Howarth, *Healthy Travel: bites, bugs and bowels,* Cadogan.
Staying Healthy in Asia, Africa & Latin America, Moon Publications.

Medical problems
Malaria
Unless you are planning to spend time in the remoter parts of Mindanao or Palawan where malaria is most prevalent, it is unlikely that you will contract this illness in the Philippines. Shaking fits, headaches, fever, sweating and chills are the normal symptoms of malaria, which is spread by mosquito bites. It can, in severe cases, be fatal, although this is fairly rare. It is important to take malarial prophylactics if you think you may be entering infected areas, a course of which typically begins two weeks before a trip, and continues for six weeks after. Unfortunately, there are strains of malaria resistant to most prophylactics, but symptoms can be contained and suppressed by their use. Chloroquine is the most common prophylactic. Lariam is considered by some people to be even better. Mosquitos are at their most active at dusk and throughout the evening and night. Prevention, as they say, is always better than cure. Mosquito bites can largely be avoided by using liberal amounts of insect repellent, carrying a mosquito net for rural areas, burning mosquito coils in your room and wearing long-sleeved shirts or blouses and trousers. A burning candle can help to repel mosquitoes. Perfume, eau de toilette, and dark colours are said to attract mosquitoes. Large numbers of mosquitoes mass for the rainy season.

Dengue fever
This mosquito-borne disease resembles malaria but there is no prophylactic available to deal with it. Symptoms include strong headaches and excruciating joint and muscle pains and high fever. Dengue fever only lasts for a few days and is not fatal. Complete rest and a combination of codeine and aspirin is the usual treatment. Some patients are given an intravenous drip to help them from dehydrating.

Hepatitis

Hepatitis A is the most common, and less complicated, form of the disease, which affects the liver and is usually picked up from infected food, contaminated eating utensils and water. It can unfortunately be transmitted from person to person. There are several telltale signs of the disease. Lack of energy is the most common early sign, but this may also be accompanied by fever, loss of appetite and the emission of orange-coloured urine. Your skin and the whites of eyes may take on a yellowish hue. Absolute rest and a simple balanced diet is the best cure. A gamma globulin injection is an excellent preventive measure but as the effect only lasts for about two months, it is wise to leave it to a few days before you depart. If you are a regular traveller to the tropics, three injections of expensive, but effective, Havrix will give you a ten-year immunity.

Hepatitis B, which is contracted congenitally, through sexual contact, or an infected needle, is a more serious illness altogether as people who have this disease remain carriers throughout their life. The symptoms and treatment are almost identical to A, but the gamma globulin shots are not effective for the B strain. A vaccine for hepatitis B does exist but is expensive. Avoid things like having your ears pierced, acupuncture or tattooing if you feel the conditions are not completely sanitary.

Cholera

Fortunately, this disease is not very common in the Philippines, and when there are outbreaks they are generally well publicised in the media, so that travellers will usually know when to avoid an infected area. Vomiting, watery stools, bad diarrhoea and cramp in the muscles and joints, and feeling completely enervated, are some of the obvious symptoms of cholera. Vaccinations against the disease are not particularly effective. Seek medical help as soon as you can and try to treat yourself for dehydration, which can be severe.

Diarrhoea

In most cases, diarrhoea can be classified as more of an irritation and inconvenience than an illness. Dehydration can be a problem, especially for children, so it is necessary to replace fluids with plenty of unappealing beverages like weak tea and diluted soft drinks. Rehydration tablets may be necessary if the body is not replenishing its fluids quickly enough. This should be supplemented with a simple diet. This shouldn't be too difficult in the Philippines. Stomach preparations can help to alleviate the unpleasantness of diarrhoea but not cure it. They are only advisable if you have to travel. More serious bouts of diarrhoea involving vomiting, stomach pains, mild fever and nausea can be successfully treated with an antibiotic like ampicillin, provided that you are not allergic to penicillin.

Dysentery

Severe diarrhoea symptoms can sometimes indicate a case of dysentery. Strong stomach cramps, diarrhoea-consistency faeces and the passing of blood are signs that you probably have dysentery. If clinically confirmed you will need a week-long treatment of something like flagyl, metronidazole or tinidazole. Ciprofloxacin is often taken in the case of bacilliary dysentery. Tetracycline is also prescribed. Be very clear about the different dosages for adults and children when consulting a doctor. Amoebic dysentery is more serious, and if not properly addressed can cause long-term problems. Like standard diarrhoea, dysentery is caused by contaminated food or water, and can be exacerbated by a sudden change to a tropical climate from a temperate one.

Heat and sun problems

When temperatures soar the dangers from over-exposure to the sun are patently obvious, but sunburn and heat exhaustion can also take place when there is plenty of cloud cover. Calamine lotion is handy to alleviate mild sunburn, but as a precaution for more severe exposure a good zinc-based suncream is vital. A broad-brimmed hat, long sleeves if you can stand them in the heat, a lipsalve to prevent chapping, or a barrier cream of some kind for the nose, will protect you from the harmful effects of the sun. Usually these are not much more than an intense rawness of the skin which can be excruciatingly uncomfortable. Other effects include chills, headache, vomiting and nausea. Heat exhaustion is generally caused by dehydration and salt deficiency. This can cause exhaustion, dizziness, muscle cramps and headaches. Salt and fluid replacement and a quiet readjustment spell are the surest cures. Heatstroke is the most extreme form of illness in this category and can be fatal. People who suffer an attack of heatstroke will need to be hospitalised without delay. Heatstroke is caused by a dangerous rise in body temperature caused by over-long exposure to direct sunlight or high temperatures. Like sunburn and heat exhaustion, sunstroke can be avoided with a little common sense. Prickly heat is quite common in all the tropical countries. Prickly heat is caused when perspiration forms under skin whose pores have not sufficiently adjusted to the new rate of sweat. As the name suggests, these itchy rashes on the skin can be very irritating. Taking regular showers, not spending too much time in the humidity, and applying talcum powder can bring relief.

Rabies

This extremely dangerous viral infection is caused by a bite or scratch from an infected animal, usually, but not always, a dog. If you have not had the rabies vaccine before being attacked, it is imperative to act quickly. The bitten area should be scrubbed for about five minutes in running water using soap and an iodine or spirit solution. This is said to reduce the chance of the infection reaching the brain by 90%. Have an anti-rabies injection as soon as you can.

Aids and other STDs

Gonorrhoea and syphilis are the most common sexually transmitted diseases (STDs) found in the Philippines. Antibiotics are used to treat these conditions, but syphilis continues throughout one's life, often leading to serious complications later on. The only real prevention is total sexual abstinence. There is no effective cure at this time for either herpes or HIV/AIDS cases. Condoms are the most effective deterrent but make sure that they are not one of the more inferior brands that exist. Price will usually give you a good idea of quality, although this is not a completely foolproof yardstick. AIDS is also spread by infected needles, a much more risky business since prevention from contamination is sometimes out of the hands of the patient. One possibility if you do need an injection is to buy a supply of new syringes from a pharmacy and get the doctor to use them. The cost of screening blood for transfusions is prohibitively high for most developing countries, a factor that is sure to have an adverse effect on the number of AIDS carriers, as infection is easily spread through contaminated blood. A relatively low consciousness about STDs in general in the Philippines seems likely to result in a steady increase in the number of people affected with these diseases.

Worm infestations

If treated, parasitic invasion of skin or alimentary tracts is not a serious problem. It is, however, a common one in the Philippines. Humid tropical climates are the perfect incubation conditions for the various kinds of worms that can cause harm. The eggs of threadworms hatch in the intestines, and problems relating to infestation can occur if not treated promptly. Roundworms are even known to enter the bloodstream. In most cases you will be able to diagnose your own condition as their presence is visible in faeces. Infestations of this kind can usually be cleared fairly easily by taking mebendazole. Avoid being a host to hookworms, which enter the body through the sole of the feet, by not walking around barefoot except on the most pristine of beaches.

Fungal problems

Anti-fungal creams and powders generally work wonders in combating problems like ringworm, athlete's foot and other infections that thrive between toes, fingers, and in the groin areas and other body crevices. Loose-fitting cotton garments help to reduce body dampness. Communal showers, unwashed towels and bathing areas where the floor is inadequately scrubbed and obviously damp, are classic spots to pick up fungal infections. Plenty of exposure to air and sunlight, along with regular rinses in medicated soap, can help to clear up infected areas.

Stings, bites and cuts

If you are allergic to stings you should bring an antihistamine with you. Most stings are painful but not serious. Calamine lotion will help to bring the swelling down and provide some relief. Otherwise you could try an ice-pack. Beware of fish, water snakes and special kinds of cone shells that may be poisonous. Scorpion stings are very painful and, in some cases, fatal. Always check your bedding, clothing and shoes when in the remoter rural areas. Jellyfish impart a fearsome sting, so be very careful when swimming, especially in the typhoon season. Local fishermen will be able to give you the best advice on which stretches of water to avoid. Antihistamine creams, calamine lotion and analgesics will help to relieve the pain. Stone-fish and scorpion fish can be hazardous so always wear rubber-soled footwear when paddling about in the shallows.

Cuts and scratches should be treated quickly in hot tropical climates, as infection can be rapid. Cuts incurred from coral are some of the worst risks in the Philippines, and usually take longer to heal. Cuts should be cleaned with mercurochrome or an antiseptic solution. There are many species of snake in the Philippines, only a few of which are deadly. If you are unlucky enough to be bitten, wrap the affected limb with a cloth and proceed straight away to the nearest hospital. If you have the offending reptile with you, it can help with identification and the choice of the right serum or antivenin.

Other irritations

If you are staying at the lower end of budget travel accommodation, look out for bedbugs and lice. They are usually found in linen which has not been sufficiently cleaned. Tiny spots of blood on the sheets and walls nearby are giveaway signs. Lice are worse as they like to settle in the scalp, clothing and pubic hair. Lice can be caught from other people but easily treated with plenty of soap and shampoo and regular dousings in water slightly hotter than you are normally used to. Leeches are not generally a problem unless you are planning to do any trekking in damp rainforest areas. Ticks can be persuaded to withdraw with an application of oil, vaseline or alcholol solution to the affected area.

PERSONAL SAFETY

Theft and security

There is no denying the fact that the Philippines has its fair share of crime. Most incidents of theft, extortion and assaults on tourists can probably be avoided with a little common sense and hindsight. Like any other place in the world, traps are lying in wait for the gullible. A spate of violent crimes and kidnappings-for-ransom cases (mainly of Chinese businessmen) in the mid 1990s, and a number of well- publicised corruption cases, have given Manila the reputation for being the most violent city in Asia. Although petty crime is rampant, the chances of you ending up in the casualty ward of a Manila hospital with multiple injuries are minimal. Filipinos are not violent by nature, as anyone who witnessed the almost Gandhi-like People Power movement of 1986 on television will know.

Poverty, however, is the norm rather than the exception. Anyone flaunting large amounts of cash, wearing expensive jewellery in public or leaving their hotel room unlocked, is obviously asking for trouble. Most crimes occur on the street, or in public places like bus depots. Be alert to bag-snatchers who often use razors to prize valuables from the shoulders of the unsuspecting. Cameras should also be kept out of view when not in use. A good way of concealing, while keeping in use, a camera or small shoulder bag is to strap it on your shoulder over a T-shirt but underneath an open-fronted shirt or blouse. Money-belts are best concealed under a T-shirt too. Inside and front trouser pockets are the best places to keep money which can be divided into various compartments. Bags should be kept close to you: never leave them unguarded on a restaurant chair or table-top, or on the floor at your feet as you might do at home. Luggage should always be carefully stowed away in your room and locked if possible. Buses, jeepneys and boats are favourite targets for thieves, so be careful when boarding and alighting, especially if it is crowded, as it almost always is. The Manila to Cebu shipping route has a particularly bad reputation for crime. Never leave personal items unattended in public, even on beaches.

If you are staying in budget accommodation, it is a good idea to run a quick security check on doors and windows to make sure they fasten properly. An extra padlock is useful, particularly if you are staying in beach huts which are notoriously vulnerable. Try not to leave valuables in a room. If you are getting out of a taxi, make sure that all your luggage is out before you pay the driver. Back alleys in cities like Manila, Baguio and Angeles should be avoided late at night, especially if you have been drinking. Drunkenness, in fact, is one of the most common causes of violence between Filipinos and foreigners. Always avoid sitting at a table near a group of Filipinos who are obviously in their cups. It can sometimes turn nasty. And never allow yourself to be persuaded to join a group of card sharks for a round of poker or gin rummy in the Philippines. You will always lose. Trying to withdraw from a game may prove difficult. In the unlikely event that you do get mugged or held up in a bus or jeepney, it is best to hand over your goods. In the Philippines, guns and knives can materialise at an alarming speed. Thieves and muggers are said to be at their most enterprising during the run up to Christmas, the season of goodwill.

Common tricks and scams

As in most Southeast Asian cities, prolific numbers of con artists operate throughout the Philippines. If you stay long enough, identifying their methods and approaches becomes almost second nature. Overtly friendly overtures from strangers encountered on a park bench who ply you with questions about where you come from and which hotel you are staying at, for example, should put you on the alert. Confidence tricksters often use their girlfriends to lure single men to a private house, back street or car, where they are then easily fleeced. Beware of women who invite you back to their homes to meet their parents, or offer to take you sightseeing. Another trick is for someone to claim to have been your driver from the airport, or even the immigration officer who stamped your passport. Con artists are also known to pose as policemen, plain-clothes detectives and customs officers. Never get inside a car if ordered to by someone you suspect. Insist on walking to the nearest police station. Anyone who approaches you to be an investor in a surefire business project is instantly suspect. There have also been several cases of people being drugged on buses and in cafés, and then robbed. Never accept food, drink or cigarettes from strangers. Little of this applies in the provinces where people remain genuinely hospitable and concerned about the welfare of travellers passing through. Generally speaking, the smaller the community, the better the security. These cautionary notes may give the misleading impression that the islands resemble a lawless banana republic, rife with violence and corruption, a view compounded by the bad press the country has been getting abroad in recent years. Most of these fears are unfounded. The fact is that the majority of visitors form a very positive impression about Filipinos as a whole, and leave having had a marvellous time, promising themselves to return at the first available opportunity.

Drugs
It is quite possible that you will be offered drugs in the Philippines. Heavy fines and prison sentences accompany drug dealing and possession of even the smallest quantities of the softest variety. Avoid at all costs.

Prostitution
The Philippines has justifiably earned the reputation for being one of the biggest flesh markets in Asia. Tourism has undoubtedly played a major role in the increase in prostitution. Single men can expect to be importuned at least once during their stay in the Philippines. The euphemistically termed "hospitality sector" is seen by many women as a means of escaping the grinding, demoralising poverty that exists in many rural areas, and an opportunity to provide for their families back home. Prostitution is not only limited to women. So-called "bini boys" hire their services out to women visitors for prices which seem ludicrously low. There are plenty of children who find themselves enslaved in this trade too. A high incidence of mistreatment by pimps, bar owners and other minders of people working in the flesh trade should be sufficient to put most people off. The AIDS virus and other sexually transmitted diseases have increased at an alarming rate among prostitutes. Unlike Thailand, prostitution is illegal in the Philippines and occasional raids on brothels and other kinds of cat houses do occur from time to time.

The police

In a recent survey, seven out of ten Manila residents confessed to a crisis of confidence in their law-enforcement officers, who were variously described as "corrupt", "incompetent" and "lazy". Public verdicts like these are hardly surprising when the newspapers are full of stories in which the police have been accused, among other things, of complicity in bank holdups, extortion, drug trafficking and worse. As one local businessman was quoted in the Manila press as saying, "Before, if you saw a thief, you would shout 'police'. Now, if you see a policeman, you shout 'thief'." An increasing number of "straight" cops – those unprepared to augment their incomes with a little extortion or drug money – are defecting to private security firms where salaries are uniformly higher. All of this has done immeasurable harm to Manila's image overseas. Tourism and investment in the country have suffered as a result. There are still plenty of honest policemen in the Philippines, however, and what corruption and vice does exist in the police force is unlikely to affect the average tourist. Visitors who expect to encounter the local equivalent of Dixon of Dock Green or Robo Cop, though, may be disappointed.

Women travellers

In a country where women were given the vote years before even some of their Western sisters, it comes as no surprise to learn that women, by and large, are held in high esteem in the Philippines. The former president was a woman, and women can be seen holding key positions in business and finance. There are female judges and governors, consuls, ambassadors, members of senate and congress, United Nations commissions and agency workers, and educators.

Women travellers, in general, will find none of the difficulties that exist in other orthodox religious countries, especially Muslim ones. Thankfully, the "mixture of lechery and contempt", as one woman traveller described to me the way the men in Malaysia sized her up, is largely absent in the Philippines. Most women report that they are treated in an extremely polite and engaging manner by Filipino men. The number of cases in which foreign women have been sexually harassed in the Philippines is very low indeed. In the unlikely event that a Filipino is pursuing you rather more forcefully than you would like, the best thing is simply to ignore the person and walk away. If this fails, ask a Filipina woman to help you get rid of the offending person. This usually does the trick.

WHAT TO PACK

The lighter you travel the better. If you intend travelling around a lot in the Philippines you will need a wide range of clothing to cope with sweltering tropical conditions down on the beach areas, to chilly nights in the mountains. Light, washable, cotton clothes are useful. A pair of jeans and cotton trousers or slacks, socks, shorts, T-shirts, a sunhat, swimsuit, cotton underwear and at least one long-sleeved shirt or blouse for mosquito infested areas, and a light sweater or jacket, is about minimum for clothing. Some people recommend a poncho which can also be used as a groundsheet or cover when taking night buses or sleeping on the deck of a boat. Strong but comfortable footwear, and a pair of rubber thongs for hotel showers, beaches and for wading over coral, are ideal. Casual wear is the norm in the Philippines, but if you plan to treat yourself to a few nights in a swish hotel, to do a little business while you are there, or to dine in an upmarket restaurant, plan your clothes accordingly. Note that it is considered rude to wear open sandals in medium-to-good restaurants. Filipino men wear a *barong tagalog*, a thin, nicely embroidered, long-sleeved shirt for formal occasions. If you can see yourself in one of these, there are plenty available off-the-rack, or you can have one tailor-made at reasonable cost. If you are travelling in the rainy season, stow away a folding waterproof raincoat and collapsible umbrella.

Toiletries are easily found in large towns and cities but it is worth taking enough for the first week before you know where best to shop. You will need a small medical kit (see p.63). A list of other possibly useful items might include a pocket torch, small sachets of washing powder, a linen line, travel alarm clock, cosmetics, Swiss army knife, mosquito net, and a snorkel and mask. Convertible backpacks with carrying handles and shoulder straps are the most convenient bags to put your luggage into, although travel packs are just as convenient and smarter looking. Cheap, tubular nylon bags are convenient for carrying extra things that you might buy in the Philippines or for using as an upcountry travel bag while you leave your main carrier with the hotel or guesthouse back in Manila.

BERKELEY TRAVEL CLINIC

VACCINATIONS & FREE TRAVEL HEALTH ADVICE

Mosquito nets, insect repellents, sterile first-aid kits.

Competitively priced vaccines & travel accessories.

32 Berkeley St, London W1X 5FA
Tel: 0171 629 6233
Open: Mon-Fri 9.00-18.00, Sat 10.00-13.00

70 North End Rd, London W14 0SJ
Tel: 0171 371 6570
Open: Mon-Fri 12.00-18.00, Sat 10.00-15.00

Chapter Five

Getting Around

For such a scattered group of islands, the Philippines is incredibly well serviced for transportation of one sort or the other. Perhaps it is because mobility is so important to Southeast Asians in general, or owing to the ingenuity of the Filipinos themselves, but there are very few places that cannot be reached by land, water or air. A transportation network connects Manila with every major town in the archipelago, from which a sub-network of small boats, jeepneys, and local buses extend their tentacles to the island's humblest villages and hamlets. Transportation is modern, cheap and, on the whole, fairly reliable. Visitors may have to resort to some interesting traditional modes of transport like *bancas* and motorised tricycles to complete the last few kilometres of their journey, machines associated with a slower way of life that still exists in much of the Philippines. The number of options makes travelling here a fascinating experience, as you can advance towards the same destination accessing different forms of transport to suit not only your pocket but also your sightseeing needs and personal whims.

AIR

PAL is the main carrier for domestic flights, with almost 200 departures daily, serving 43 airports nationwide. Manila is the transportation hub for mainly north–south routes that fly direct to destinations in Luzon, and central and southern parts of the Philippines. Cebu is the principal airport serving the Visayas and Mindanao. Boeing 737s and A-300s are used for major cities and large towns, smaller Fokker 50 propeller planes for the shorter runs. PAL have got their act down to a fairly fine art, something that cannot always be said for the passengers. When flying PAL it is important to arrive well before the scheduled take-off time. Access to the departure areas is closed 45 minutes before take-off. If you don't show up beforehand, your seat may very well be given to a passenger on the waiting list, even if you reconfirmed your booking. PAL also has the right to fine people who have reconfirmed but not bothered to show up. Flights are usually heavily booked up between 15 December and 4 January. PAL offers good discounts to students under 26 and people over 60. You will need to take your student card and passport to qualify for the former. The PAL office on Roxas Boulevard, will give you a "Domestic Flight Schedule". The schedule can change several times a year so it is worth consulting a current one when you get there. PAL has an around-the-clock information service which can be reached by telephoning 832 3166.

Aerolift have been flying tourists and business commuters to the Visayas, Mindanao and southern Luzon since they were granted national carrier status in 1989. Their aircrafts are small but plucky, flying regular routes to places like Cebu, Ormoc (Leyte), and Tagbilaran (Bohol), as well as destinations not served by other companies, like Boracay, Lubang and Busuanga. There are also other smaller companies such as Pacific Airways Corporation that will get you to more out-of-the-way airstrips all over the archipelago. Companies like Commuter Air Philippines and CM Aero Services offer charter flights if you have a sufficiently large group. Helicopters are also available for renting from Asia Aircraft Overseas Philippines, Airspan Corporation and PAL.

BUSES

Buses are one of the most comfortable ways to travel long distance in the Philippines and, at about P40-P50 per 100km, extraordinarily good value. Rates for routes using unsurfaced, and hence more uncomfortable, roads are, to the chagrin of many overseas travellers, slightly more expensive than asphalted ones. It is possible to travel virtually the whole length of the archipelago by bus, using connecting ferries between the larger islands. Routes on which first-class air-conditioned buses with reclining seats run (as well as ordinary buses) from Manila to cities in Luzon, Samar and Leyte have a frequent service, while secondary routes may only have one bus a day. In such cases it is important to arrive at the bus depot bright and early. With the exception of the Philippine Rabbit and Lawton depots in Santa Cruz, most of the major bus companies have their depots located in the suburbs of Manila so you should allow time to get there. Student discounts of 15% are given by the major companies, but only on their ordinary buses. Long-distance buses make prescribed stops, normally of about 20 minutes. The restaurants at these stopovers are not particularly cheap, and often not that good. Hawkers selling snacks and drinks appear at every stop so it is not really necessary to take your own food on long journeys. Minibuses also ply some of the same roads the larger vehicles take but only for medium distances. One advantage the minibuses have is that they can, speed permitting, be hailed from the roadside.

TRAINS

Philippine National Railways (PNR) have been jinxed with so many problems that their services have steadily declined to the point where there is now only one line in operation – the Manila to Naga (South Luzon) route. The eruption of Mount Pinatubo in 1991 brought about the closure of the last main route through the Central Plain, and plans to reopen the line and regenerate the railway system in general have been shelved for the foreseeable future. Typhoons and other natural disasters routinely wreak havoc with the line, bring down bridges and cause delays to the service. Travelling time is slow and the cost no cheaper than by bus, so it is little wonder that passenger numbers have decreased so dramatically over the past few years. If you are a train buff and would like to experience what could possibly be the twilight years of railways in the Philippines, you can contact the marketing section of PNR for more information.

BOATS

Unlike buses, where conditions are fairly standardised, and you know more or less what you are going to get for your money, boats in the Philippines are far more unpredictable. Conditions vary enormously in terms of service and regularity. This is also the case with comfort, which can range from luxury suites on smart new vessels to a piece of tarpaulin cover or a rickety cot on the lower deck of a tramp steamer, or the rusting hulk of an overworked ferry. Ships, ferries, launches, pump boats and bancas are the main means of inter-island transport. Cebu and Manila are the two main hubs for the country's sea lanes. The best passenger ships connecting these two spots are fast, reliable and usually reasonably comfortable. A typical air-conditioned cabin for four people on the Cebu to Manila run might cost around P575. Upper and lower deck fares are far cheaper. You should ask around from other passengers to find out which boats are good value and safe. Third-class bunk beds on the decks of some of the larger passenger ships, for example, can be considerably more comfortable and spacious than the humid, overcrowded berths below. Passengers must expect bland food (included in the price of the ticket), cramped conditions, truly dreadful toilets, and, at the first sign of inclement seas, vomiting from the vast majority of Asians on board. It's a good idea to bring your own food supplements and plenty to read.

Launches are used for the longer journeys between smaller ports. Schedules are subject to more delays the smaller the boats become, and in the case of launches, the captain may decide to wait for several hours until the boat is full before departing. Medium to large outlying islands often have their own ferry services. These are usually small vessels where people sit out on deckchairs for periods that can range from as little as 30 minutes to 15 hours or more. Pump boats, or outrigger *bancas*, narrow boats with outboard or inboard motors attached, are used for short island crossings or for runs along the coast from port to port. Safety measures and standards on these boats may be virtually non-existent, so keep a fairweather eye open for approaching typhoons and squalls before committing yourself to a voyage.

Although tickets can normally be obtained on the same day as you wish to sail, it is probably a good idea to book at least one day in advance. This particularly applies over the Christmas period when boats can be booked up weeks in advance. Most inter-island ships dock at Manila's North Harbor. The big companies have their offices and agencies in the same area, with branches in Makati, Binondo and Ermita. There is also a whole fleet of decrepit-looking ships moored along the lugubrious north bank of the Pasig River, near the San Miguel brewery. These Conradian hulks are cargo-passenger ships that make trips between small ports whenever work comes their way. It is possible to approach the captain and get yourself included on the passenger list, although you should allow plenty of time for delays en route if you do. Most of the principal sailing schedules are published in the *Manila Bulletin* newspaper. For smaller vessels and more out-of-the-way routes, you will have to go down to the wharves and make your own enquiries.

JEEPNEYS

Jeepneys have become so much a part of the Philippine way of life that they are now an indispensable part of its colourful folk culture. They began life as surplus jeeps released by the US military at the end of the war to help alleviate the chronic shortage of public transport. Enterprising Filipinos extended their bodies to make room for more passengers. What look at first glance like stately Edwardian charabancs turn out on closer inspection to be the very personal creations of exuberantly eclectic minds, what have been described as "pop-art on wheels". Exterior chrome and wood-panelled flanks are decorated in flamboyant colours like gypsy wagons, pennants fly from aerials, interiors are decked out in furbelows and chintzy frills, and bonnets are occasionally, though more rarely as time passes, adorned with trotting silver horses. Messages, proverbs, quotes from the bible and personal counselling are pinned up inside the vehicle, next to lists of destinations and schedules. These days, the decor has been toned down quite a bit but jeepneys are still one of the most eye-catching features of the Philippines. In a fine testament to the place the jeepney has assumed in popular Philippine culture, Emmanuel Torres has written that, "Beneath the visual gush is a way of life of toiling tens of thousands of masses, an index of popular taste, current fads and fashions. The Symbol of Optimism under the pressures of adversity."

The official maximum for a jeepney is ten passengers, but in reality they are usually jammed to the gunwales, especially in rural areas where they shuttle back and forth between one provincial town and another. You can get the best view by occupying one of the two seats next to the driver. Like buses, jeepneys follow a scheduled route within large cities which are divided into zones. You pay for the number of zones crossed. Destinations are displayed on the front of the jeepney and stopping-off points en route on the side of the vehicle. In country areas they often wait near the marketplace for enough passengers before leaving. You can flag down a jeepney even in the centre of Manila, but it may not actually stop, so you have to be prepared to hop on as it slows down for you. When you want to get off, shout "Para!", and knock on the roof for good measure.

METRORAIL

Metrorail, a light rail rapid transit system, is a convenient and efficient way of getting around. At present the train crosses the centre of Manila on elevated tracks between Pasay City and Caloocan City, with several stations between. There are plans to build two more LRTs in the near future.

TAXIS

Taxis are good value providing that the driver is prepared to use his meter or to stick to a fee agreed beforehand. Many taxis in the Metro Manila area are yellow, four-passenger vehicles. Most are not air-conditioned. Those that are may try to charge you a bit extra on top of the set fare. Other drivers may claim that their meters are not working, in which case you should simply find another. Taxi drivers often pretend not to have any small change so it is wise to carry some low denomination coins with you. Tipping is not necessary in the Philippines, but if you do give a deserving driver a little extra, it is much appreciated. Non-metered Public Utility (PU) cars serve as taxis in Cebu City and elsewhere. They charge a flat fare around town. Fares for longer distances have to be negotiated and agreed before boarding.

TRICYCLES

Motorised and pedal tricycles operate in provincial towns, and are familiar sights on many of the rough unmade roads out to villages. They can carry two or three passengers in their sidecars, although one may have to sit on the pillion behind the driver. Drivers will rarely quote you the correct local rate so it is best to check before boarding and then simply hand over the money at the end.

CALESAS

There are very few of these two-wheeled, horse-drawn carriages left in the Philippines but a few operate in Manila's Chinatown and in one or two provincial towns like Vigan and San Fernando. There are also a few, operating under the name *tartanillas*, still running in Cebu. The most romantic route in Manila is along Roxas Boulevard. A trot along here at sunset might cost P10-P15. As always, fares should be agreed before getting on.

RENTAL CARS

Unless you have a specific need for a car, driving yourself around the Philippines is inadvisable. The combination of inherited Latin machismo and Oriental fatalism can be lethal for the uninitiated. If you must drive here, Hertz have car rental offices in Manila, Baguio, Angeles City and Olongapo. Avis have representatives in Manila, Angeles, Cebu and Baguio. There are several smaller local companies as well. Cars can also be rented with drivers, a much better idea if you can afford it. If you rent yourself you must be between the ages of 25 and 65, and have an international or valid foreign licence with you. Payment is usually through credit card. Rates are worked out according to the model, and length of the rental. Check the condition of the car very carefully before signing anything. Check that third-party accident insurance is included in the rental fee.

CYCLING

Serious long-distance cycling is in its infancy in the Philippines, but you might see one or two intrepid pioneers exploring the islands in this fashion. It is easy enough putting a bicycle on a ferry boat to the next island, and finding accommodation in even remote villages is usually no problem providing that you are flexible. As long as you have plenty of stamina and allow yourself enough time, cycling could be an interesting way of getting around the archipelago. With a generally good standard of roads, plenty of food and drink waystations and amenable people to help out when you need a tube repairing or something straightened out, no doubt there will be more people doing this in the near future.

ROAD AND RAIL COMPANIES

Baliwag Transit, 33 EDSA, Cubao, Quezon City. Tel: 999132.

Pantranco North Express Inc, 325 Quezon Ave, Quezon City. Tel: 997091–98.

Philippine Rabbit Bus Lines Inc, 819 Oroquieta St, Sta Cruz, Manila. Tel: 71 5819.

Victory Lines, 561 EDSA, Pasay City, 713 Rizal Ave, Caloocan City. Tel: 833 0293.

Inland Trailways, M Earnshaw, F Cayco and Sampaloc St, Manila. Tel: 617 912.

Philtranco, EDSA, Apelo Cruz St, Pasay City. Tel: 833 5061.

Sunshine Transportation Inc, 359 Don Carlos Revilla St, Pasay City. Tel: 832 3601.

Philippine National Railways. Tel: 206978 (passenger information). Tel: 210011 (other departments).

SHIPPING COMPANIES

Aboitiz Shipping Corp, Pier 4 North Harbor, Tondo, Manila. Tel: 276332. Destinations: Leyte, Mindanao, Panay, Romblon.

Asuncion Shipping Lines, 3038 Jose Abad Santos, or Pier 2, Tondo, Manila. Tel: 711 3743. Destinations: Lubang, Mindoro, Palawan.

Carlos A Gothong Lines, Pier 10, North Harbor, 468 San Fernando, Binondo. Tel: 213 61113. Destinations: Cebu, Leyte, Panay.

F Escano Lines, Pier 16, North Harbor, 409 San Fernando, Binondo. Tel: 211 61112. Destinations: Cebu, Leyte, Masbate, Mindanao.

Negros Navigation Co, Pier 8, North Harbor, Negros Navigation Co Bldg, Amaiz Ave, Makati. Tel: 816 3481. Destinations: Negros, Mindanao, Panay.

Sulpicio Lines, Pier 12, North Harbor, 415 San Fernando, Binondo. Tel: 479 62029. Destinations: Cebu, Bohol, Leyte, Mindanao, Masbate, Negros, Panay, Samar.

Sweet Lines, Pier 6, North Harbor, Arnaiz Ave, Makati. Tel: 263524. Destinations: Cagayan, Cebu, Bohol, Davao, Leyte, Samar, Surigao, Zamboanga.

William Lines, Pier 14, North Harbor, 1508 Rizal Ave Ext, Caloocan. Tel: 219821. Destinations: Davao, Cebu, Bohol, Mindoro, Masbate, Palawan, Negros, Panay, Samar, Romblon.

THE GLOBETROTTERS CLUB

An international club which aims to share information on adventurous budget travel through monthly meetings and *Globe* magazine. Published every two months, *Globe* offers a wealth of information from reports of members' latest adventures to travel bargains and tips, plus the invaluable 'Mutual Aid' column where members can swap a house, sell a camper, find a travel companion or offer information on unusual places or hospitality to visiting members. London meetings are held monthly (Saturdays) and focus on a particular country or continent with illustrated talks.

Enquiries to: Globetrotters Club, BCM/Roving, London WC1N 3XX.

Part Two

THE GUIDE

Dome of Manila Cathedral

Chapter Six

Manila

"If the traveller to that distant city were to brave the directionless tangle of slums on foot … he might win through into this hidden land."

James Hamilton-Paterson, *Ghosts of Manila*

Few people would describe Manila, at least on first contact, as a beautiful city. Its snarling, congested streets, petro-incinerated buildings, overcrowded slums, prowling hookers and greasy pimps evoke comparisons with the lively but festering capitals of Caribbean banana republics. And yet Manila, with a population of almost 12 million, attracts people like no other city in the Philippines. Davao, the country's second largest city, has a population of a mere one million. Manila pulsates with life at all hours, and the city's superb location at the mouth of the Pasig River, between the volcanic farmlands of the southern Tagalog region and the fertile rice granary of the Central Plain, endows its surroundings with an insinuating beauty that is often overlooked by visitors. And for those prepared to eschew shopping excursions to the likes of Makati, or an afternoon of more conventional sightseeing, unique, even bizarre and exotic, locations and experiences are easily sought out.

HISTORY AND ORIENTATION

Trading communities lived on the present site of Manila long before Legaspi landed there in 1571 and proclaimed the modest but strategically well-placed settlement the capital of the Philippines. The value of its crescent-shaped bay and natural harbour was recognised as early as the 5th century. From the end of the 11th century to the 13th a bustling riverine trade appears to have flourished with the annual arrival of merchant ships from Sumatra, Malacca, Java, Siam, India, China, Japan, Arabia and elsewhere. The town was known at that time as Maynilad, a name whose etymological roots would appear to spring from two words: *may*, meaning "There is", and *nilad*, a form of waterlily resembling a mangrove plant, that grew along the banks of the Pasig River and along the nearby coast. More observant travellers than I claim to have seen stalks of the *nilad* plant floating down the Pasig even now.

By the middle of the 16th century, Maynilad had become a 2,000-strong, bamboo-palisaded city-state, ruled by the Muslim warrior Rajah Sulayman and his two uncles, Rajah Matanda and Rajah Lakandula. When Miguel Lopez de Legaspi, the Spanish conquistador, caught wind of the thriving and well-placed town, he set sail, in the wake of his grandson, for Maynilad. After two efforts to subdue the town, the Muslims were finally defeated. With this victory, the Spanish began the construction of Fort Santiago at the mouth of the river. Legaspi also oversaw the building of a fortified medieval town that would become Spain's grandest and most permanent monument in Asia. Apart from serving a military purpose, the walled city of Intramuros ("Between Walls"), as it was called, quickly became the focus of the nation's economic and religious life. Ecclesiastical and civil life, as well as the lucrative galleon trade, were conducted and invasions repulsed from here. The first of these were a series of attacks by pirates, culminating in an invasion by the Chinese warlord Limahong in 1574. With the routing of the Chinese, King Philip II bestowed the town with the name "Distinguished and Ever Loyal City" (*Isigne y Siempre Leal Ciudad*), an epithet whose tedious length never quite managed to usurp the use of Maynilad, especially among the native populace. Intramuros continued to be the seat of the Castilian upper classes, the soldiers, friars, missionaries and privileged mestizos, eventually growing into a district of the city itself. There were four gates connecting Intramuros with a catchment area in which Spanish commoners, Indios (as native Filipinos were referred to by the Spanish), Japanese and even Armenians lived. Government administration was conducted strictly inside the walls. Commerce took place outside, in the swelling suburbs across the river where a growing Chinese community of enterprising traders, middlemen and entrepreneurs were kept under a close and confined scrutiny. It was not possible, however, to contain the industrious and intelligent Chinese in this northern quarter which was known as Parian, an area that was soon superseded by the Christian Chinese business district of Binondo. Other districts like Tondo, San Miguel, Quiapo and Santa Cruz soon began to take shape to the north of the city, while residential districts like Ermita, Malate and Dilao sprang up to the south.

The capital's first two centuries were characterised by alternate periods of turbulence, stability and insularity. Manila weathered several blockades and invasion attempts by the Dutch, sporadic uprisings by the Filipino and Chinese communities and a brief occupation by the British between 1762 and 1764. By the end of the 18th century, with the galleon trade in decline, economic realities forced the Spanish to permit foreign ships and companies a foothold in the capital. Commerce increased, but so too did the trade in more liberal ideas and attitudes from Europe and America, hastening the transformation of Manila into a truly cosmopolitan city.

Manila was the incubator for the revolution which broke out in 1896. By the time the Americans took over the running of the city, the population of Manila had swollen to 200,000. In marked contrast to the increasingly apathetic and money-strapped Spanish, American colonisers enthusiastically set about building roads, installing sewage and drainage systems, and providing the city with electricity, gas and water supplies. The Japanese bombardments of December 1941 brought a hasty end to the city's plans for self-improvement, and the Americans, persuaded that only a retreat from the city would save it from total obliteration, withdrew, leaving Manila to three dire years of oppression and misery. In one of those historical ironies, in which war more than anything else acts as accomplice and catalyst, the Japanese turned the University of Santo Tomas, an enlightened Dominican institution set up for the education of native Filipinos, into a concentration camp for American prisoners. With the advance of the American "liberators", the Japanese destroyed bridges, and razed as many buildings to the ground as they could. As it became more obvious that they were hemmed in by the American forces, the Japanese military went on a senseless rampage of looting, murder, rape and destruction never before witnessed in the city. By the time the Americans were in control, Manila had become the second most devastated city after Warsaw in the Second World War.

Manila's extraordinary rise from the ashes of colonialism and war, and its expansion to become one of the largest capitals in Southeast Asia, have not been without casualties. Patchy urban development, overhasty construction and the dominance of powerful and wealthy interest groups have seen further polarisation between spacious and affluent areas like Makati, Forbes Park and Dasmarinas, and growing slum areas like Tondo, where over one and a half million people dwell, often in the most abject of poverty.

Because Manila is so widespread and sprawling it can be difficult to get one's bearings. In the midst of this apparently shapeless sprawl are clearly defined centres, each with its own identifiable character and designated function. South of the river, the oldest part of Manila, including Intramuros, is where most of the historical and cultural interest lies. The Immigration Office and GPO are also here. Rizal Park, stretching from Taft Avenue down to Roxas Boulevard on the bay, lies a little further south from here in what might be termed the main city centre. Directly south of the park are the tourist centres of Ermita, Malate and Pasay City, with the business centre of Makati off to the southeast. The airport is found in the southern suburbs. Chinatown, the North Harbor wharves, and immensely crowded districts like Tondo, Binondo and Quiapo, all lie north of the river.

ARRIVING

Once you have passed through customs you will find telephones obligingly placed near the luggage carousels. These are free for local calls and give you the chance to book a hotel room while you are waiting for your bags to materialise. Baggage trolleys, on the other hand, are not free. You will have to pay P30, or US$1, a charge that includes a porter, that is, in the unlikely event that you can find one. If you want to reconfirm an onward or return flight at this stage, the major airlines have their counters upstairs on the second floor.

So far so good. For most visitors the hassles most often begin with transport. Despite countless, long forgotten or relegated schemes to improve transit facilities from the airport to the heart of the city, a normally simple enough action like trying to find a taxi charging a reasonable fee can, and usually does, turn into an ordeal, one that many jet-lagged or exhausted travellers are not up to. If you remember that extortion is the norm, and try to keep a cool head, you may be able to haggle a driver down to P150–250 for a trip into somewhere like Ermita or Makati, although even this is well over the odds. Beware of drivers whose meters suddenly stop working, or whose sleight-of-hand deftly adds an extra 20 or 30 pesos to the fare, or people who insist that you have to pay double to cover the return ride to the airport. There are supposed to be standard, authorised taxis operating from the departure level of the airport. Their fares are supposed to be fixed for certain distances and destinations. Many of these drivers, however, are not the unblemished professionals they present themselves to be, so be alert for the same old tricks. On my last trip to the Philippines there was a limousine counter in the airport charging US$20 for most downtown destinations, an expensive but hassle-free option. If you have booked a night or two at a good hotel, you may very well find that a car is included in the deal. This is, without doubt, the best way to arrive in the Philippines. An alternative would be to leave the airport altogether by following the signs to the car park. Proceed from there until you see the road running from the airport. It may take a bit longer but you can flag a taxi down from there. The correct current fare to a hotel on Mabini Street should be around P100. An even cheaper option, if you have the stamina for it after your flight, is to ask directions for Harrison Street (it is about half a kilometre from the airport) where there are buses and jeepneys bound for Taft Avenue and Mabini Street. This is not recommended at night. If you don't have too much luggage and are game for a slightly longer walk, you can continue right from Harrison Street until you reach the South Terminal (Baclaran) of the Metrorail. There are two stops along Taft Avenue, in Ermita: Pedro Gil Station and United Nations Avenue Station.

FACILITIES

Accommodation

You would be surprised how many fabulously rich people there are floating around in developing countries. Whether you are in Bangkok, Saigon or Jakarta, accommodation to rival the most majestic establishments of the colonial past are easily sought out. The age of

A young Filipina out for a spin

An Ifugao elder near the small village of Cambulo

Above: *A traditional headdress of the Ifugao who, until quite recently, were practising headhunters*

Below: *Detail of tribal clothing and weaving*

Above: *A village in the heart of Mindanao*

Below left: *Outside an Igorot house near Baguio*
Below right: *A sunken boat in the swamps of Palawan*

opulence has definitely returned. To be fair, many of these hotels are also used by honeymooners on a once-in-a-lifetime spending binge, company representatives who would never dream of staying in such plush surroundings with their own families, UN staff, visiting academics, convention people and other perfectly mortal visitors. If you do wish to treat yourself to a couple of nights in one of Manila's best, you will find that room rates, by international standards at least, are not too prohibitive. Even in refined and gracious hotels of the calibre of the Manila Hotel and the Mandarin Oriental, rooms can be had for as little as US$140–175. During the off-season between June and September, many of Manila's top hotels offer special discounts of anything between 20–50%, making a stay there almost seem like a bargain. All the hotels in this category have swimming pools, restaurants, coffee shops, bars, business centres, banqueting facilities, function rooms and nightclubs. Some may have health clubs with saunas and gyms, tennis courts, mini-golf courses, and secretarial services. Rooms are equipped with TVs, refrigerators, telephones and faxes. Manila has rooms to suit every kind of traveller from the well-heeled to the shoestring. Whether you want to stay in a dormitory bed, luxury suite or rent your own apartment by the week or month, Manila has it.

Deluxe hotels

Century Park Sheraton, Vito Cruz, Malate. Tel: 522 1011, fax: 521 3413. Conveniently located near the Cultural and Convention Centre and Harrison Plaza. Singles start at US$180, doubles from US$200. Business and family-size suites begin at US$275.

Hotel Inter-Continental Manila, Ayala Ave, Makati. Tel: 815971, fax: 8171330. Singles start at US$200, doubles from US$250. A large business clientele use this hotel which is conveniently located near the large Makati financial district. It has 381 rooms, all the usual amenities and a popular discotheque. Offers an extended stay discount.

Hotel Nikko Manila Garden, 4th Quadrant, Makati Commercial Centre. Tel: 810 4101, fax: 8171862. Singles from US$150, doubles US$180. Suites are from US$250. As the name suggests, this is a Japanese-owned hotel. Many Japanese and Chinese businessmen stay here. Excellent Japanese restaurants, sauna and gym.

Hyatt Regency Manila, 2702 Roxas Blvd, Pasay City. Tel: 831 2611, fax: 833 5913. Singles from US$150, doubles US$170. Located between the Cultural Centre Complex and the airport. A superb health club and good restaurant.

Mandarin Oriental Manila, Makati Ave, Makati. Tel: 8163601, fax: 817 2472. Singles start at US$190, doubles from US$240. Suites begin at US$350. This very refined business hotel has 467 rooms. It offers discounts in the low season.

Manila Hotel, Rizal Park, Manila. Tel: 470011, fax: 471124. Singles from US$125, doubles US$150. General Douglas MacArthur resided here. A wonderfully atmospheric old colonial building with spacious rooms, excellent dining facilities, tip-top service and pleasant secluded grounds. Palm court orchestras sometimes play in the lobby.

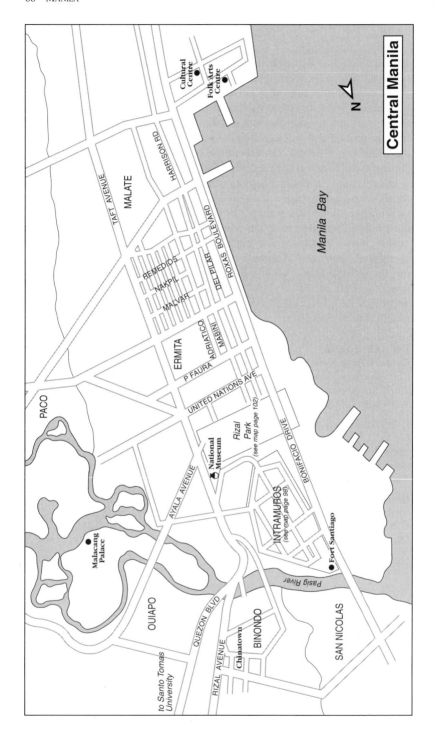

Central Manila

N

Manila Bay

Cultural Centre

Folk Arts Centre

HARRISON RD

TAFT AVENUE

MALATE

ROXAS BOULEVARD

DEL PILAR

MABINI

ADRIATICO

REMEDIOS

NAKPIL

MALVAR

ERMITA

P FAURA

UNITED NATIONS AVE

PACO

National Museum

Rizal Park
(see map page 102)

BONIFACIO DRIVE

AYALA AVENUE

Malacañang Palace

INTRAMUROS
(see map page 98)

Fort Santiago

Pasig River

OUIAPO

QUEZON BLVD

RIZAL AVENUE

Chinatown

BINONDO

SAN NICOLAS

to Santo Tomas University

Manila Peninsula, Ayala Ave, Makati. Tel: 8193456, fax: 815 4825. Singles from US$195, doubles US$275. Suites are over US$400. Located in the business district. The lobby has a friendly happy-hour get together which attracts a large following of business people, tourists and yuppies.

Silahis International Hotel, 1990 Roxas Blvd, Malate. Tel: 573811, fax: 502506. Singles from US$130, doubles US$150. Good location overlooking Manila Bay. There is a casino here too for those so inclined. Enquire about seasonal discounts.

Westin Philippine Plaza, Cultural Centre Complex, Roxas Blvd. Tel: 832 0701, fax: 832 3485. Singles from US$175, and doubles from US$195. Suites start at US$375. Close to the Convention Centre and right on the waterfront, a good location, with an excellent outdoor swimming pool, nine-hole mini golf course and tennis court. It still manages to offer off-peak discounts.

First class hotels

Admiral Hotel, 2139 Roxas Blvd, Malate. Tel: 572081, fax: 522 2018. Singles from US$100, doubles US$125. One of the oldest hotels in Manila. Bags of atmosphere and excellent value.

Ambassador Hotel, 2021 A Mabini St, Malate. Tel: 550 601119, fax: 521 5557. Singles from US$75, doubles US$90. This is the one with the celebrated revolving disco on the 16th floor.

Holiday Inn Manila, 3001 Roxas Blvd, Pasay City. Tel: 597961, fax: 522 3985. Singles begin at US$130, doubles from US$150. Suites from US$240. All the usual facilities associated with this world-renowned chain. The health club is particularly good. Located just in front of the Cultural Centre Complex.

Hotel La Corona, 1166 M H del Pilar. Tel: 502631, fax: 521 3909. Singles from US$75, doubles starting at US$85. Good amenities at a reasonable price. Has an international restaurant and business centre.

Legend Hotel, Madison St, Mandaluyong. Tel: 6331501–12, fax: 6320845. Singles US$99, doubles US$110; with jacuzzi single US$115, double US$125, including breakfast. Located 5km from international and domestic airports.

Manila Midtown Hotel, Pedro Gil, Ermita. Tel: 573911, fax: 522 2629. Singles begin at around US$120, doubles US$130. Good value with sauna, pool, gym and tennis courts. Good location near the tourist nightlife areas.

Manila Pavilion, UN Avenue, Ermita. Tel: 573711, fax: 522 3531. Singles at US$ 130, doubles from US$140. Close to Rizal Park, an ideal location. Has a swimming pool, business centre with convention facilities, and a casino.

Philippine Village Hotel, MIA Avenue, Pasay City. Tel: 831 7011, fax: 833 8248. Singles from US$100, doubles start at US$120. Suites from US$240. This 322-room hotel is conveniently located near the international and domestic airports. Next door to Nayong Philipino.

Standard hotels

Aloha Hotel, 2150 Roxas Boulevard, Malate. Tel: 599061, fax: 521 5328. Standard rooms at P1,500, suites are P2,400. Good location on the waterfront. Korean, Chinese and seafood restaurants. All rooms have air-conditioning and baths. Suites have private terraces overlooking Manila Bay.

City Garden Hotel, 1158 Mabini Street, Ermita. Tel: 5218841, fax: 522 1699. Rooms from P1,300. This well looked-after and run hotel in the tourist centre of Manila is deservedly popular with visitors. It might be worth faxing them with a booking well in advance. Rooms have TV, air-conditioning, refrigerator and bath.

Galleon's Hotel, 1607 J C Bocobo Street, Malate. Tel: 521 2283, fax: 5211072. A wide range of rooms from P1,600 to P2,500, including breakfast. Nicely finished rooms with TV, air-conditioning and bath, in an elegant old town house. Bar, restaurant and airport service.

Hotel Las Palmas, 1616 A Mabini St, Malate. Tel: 506661 69, fax: 522 1699. Rooms from P1,400. A well-established hotel with travellers. Friendly atmosphere. Every room has air-conditioning and bath. Family and executive suites available and special off-season rates. Restaurant and swimming pool.

Hotel Royal Co-Co, 2120 Mabini St, Malate. Tel: 5213911 11, fax: 521 3919. Rooms from P1,190 to P2,400. A nicely decorated hotel that offers refrigerators and jacuzzis in its more expensive rooms. All rooms with TV, air-conditioning and bath.

Lai-Lai International Hotel, corner of Gandara Street and Ongpin Street, Santa Cruz. Tel: 482061, fax: 496110. Rooms from P990, suites for P2,000. Said to be the best accommodation in Chinatown. Comfortable rooms with TVs, air-conditioning, and bath. Restaurant and coffee shop.

Midland Plaza Hotel, M Adriatico, Ermita. Tel: 573011. Rooms from P1,500. A good place if you want to do some self-catering as there are kitchenettes attached. All rooms have TV. Ask for a top-floor room where there are views of Manila Bay. There is a coffee shop, function rooms and secretarial services here for businessmen.

New Solanie Hotel, 1811 Leon Guinto St, Malate. Tel: 508641 45. Singles and doubles in the P1,300–1,600 range, with TV, bath and air-conditioning. The more expensive rooms in this quiet and friendly establishment also have refrigerators and cooking facilities which may be good for families.

Sundowner Hotel, 1430 Mabini St. Tel: 275161 61. Rooms at around P1,700. Rooms have TV. Refurbished with 24-hour coffee shop and airport transfers.

The Swagman Hotel, 411 A Flores St, Ermita. Tel: 599881, fax: 521 9731. Rooms from P1,400. 24-hour restaurant, airport transfers. All rooms have TV, air-conditioning and bath.

Economy accommodation

Birdwatchers Inn, corner of A Flores and Mabini Sts, Ermita. P400 for fan, P575 with air-conditioning, and P850 with air-conditioning and bath. A very comfortable and popular guesthouse.

Commodore Pension House, 422 Arquiza St, Ermita. Tel: 596864. Rooms for P225–275. Clean, no-nonsense accommodation.

Congress Family Hotel, 1433 M H del Pilar. Tel: 595482. Basic but clean rooms for P175–200. Good location, excellent value. A real shoestring guesthouse.

Iseya Hotel, 1241 M H del Pilar St, Ermita. Tel: 592016, fax: 522 4451. Singles and doubles with TV, air-conditioning, bath and refrigerator for P800.

Reasonably comfortable place with a restaurant. Tourist and entertainment area. They have a Sunday barbecue. Avoid rooms that face on to the street.

Mabini Pension, 1337 Mabini St, Ermita. Tel: 598853, fax: 595219. Rooms with fans for P350–400, with fan and bath for P450–550, and with air-conditioning and bath for P650–750. A well-located and popular place, rooms are a bit on the small side and those above the reception counter can be noisy during the night. There are one or two larger rooms which can be rented for up to six people. The helpful and friendly staff can arrange visa extensions and air tickets.

Malate Pension, 1771 M Adriatico, Malate. Tel: 593 3489, fax: 597119. Dormitory beds for just P110, or with air-conditioning for P125, rooms with fan for P325–375, fan and bath for P400–550, and with air-conditioning and bath P550–750. Suites with kitchens and TVs are also available for P975. The choice of rooms, and the central location, make this very popular with tourists. Try not to end up with a room facing the street as these can be quite noisy.

Merchants Hotel, 711 San Bernardo St, Santa Cruz. Rooms with air-conditioning and bath for P450–500. Off the main tourist areas to the north of the capital. It has a restaurant and disco.

Midtown Inn, 551 Padre Faura St, Ermita. Tel: 582882. Rooms with fan and bath start at P450, with TV, air-conditioning and bath for P650–700. Simple but clean and well run. The inn was rebuilt after a fire in the early 1990s. The new rooms are the more expensive ones.

Pension Natividad, 1601 M H del Pilar St, Malate. Tel: 521 0524, fax: 522 3759. Dormitories with fan at P120, rooms with fan for P400–450, fan and bath for P550, air-conditioning and bath for P750. The staff are very obliging here and the ambience feels homely and secure.

Pension Filipina, 572 Arkansas, Ermita. Tel: 521 1448. Standard room for P450 –500. Friendly and secure.

Pius XII Catholic Centre, 1175 UN Ave. Tel: 573806. P150 for dormitory beds, P300 for a room with fan, and P450 with air-conditioniong. A well run and secure place to stay. Has a restaurant, swimming pool, gym, tennis courts and chapel. Good value.

Richmond Pension, 1165 Grey St, Ermita. Tel: 585277. Singles and doubles in the P200–350 range, depending on whether you take a fan or air-conditioned set-up. A small pension down a side street. Good if you want some peace and quiet.

Santos Pension House, 1540 Mabini St, Ermita. Rooms with fan are P300, with fan and bath P350, and with air-conditioning and bath P500. Ask to see a couple of rooms before signing up as there are considerable differences. The pension has a passable restaurant.

Townhouse, at the Villa Carolina Townhouse, 201 Roxas Blvd, Unit 31, Paranaque. Dormitory beds start at P90, singles/doubles with fan are P250–300, rooms with fan and bath go for P350–400, and air-conditioning and bath for P550. Cheaper weekly rates are possible. Run by a friendly couple. Good restaurant and convenient for the airport.

White House Tourist Inn, 465 Pedro Gil St, Ermita. Tel: 522 1535, fax: 522 4451. Rooms with fan for P300–400, with air-conditioning for P500–550. Has a decent restaurant. The Australian management have fixed up a beer garden as well.

Youth hostels
Manila International Youth Hostel, 4227 Tomas, Claudio St, Paranaque. Tel: 832 2112, fax: 818 7948. Members P75, non-members P100. Good laundry facilities and garden. Meals are possible on the premises. Only 2km from the airport.

YMCA, Arrocesros St. Tel: 471461. P150 for a dormitory bed, P350–400 for a very basic but clean room.

YWCA, 880 UN Ave. Tel: 599658. P150. Women only.

Apartments
Casa Blanca 1, 1447 Adriatico St, Ermita. Tel: 596011 18. One-room apartments for only P10,000 monthly. Their two-room apartments are P13,000. They are likely to be booked up well in advance so a call or fax is advisable.

Copacabana Apartment Hotel, 264 Edsa Extension, Pasay City. Tel: 831 8711, fax: 831 4344. P27,000 monthly for one-bedroom, P30,000 for two-bedroom apartments. Has some extras to recommend it like a swimming pool, sauna, coffee shop and restaurant.

Mabini Mansion, 1011 Mabini St, Ermita. Tel: 521 4776. One-room studios cost from P15–22,000 monthly, two-room apartments are P23,000–29,000. Daily rates from P1,100.

Tropicana Apartment Hotel, 1630 Luis M Guerrero St, Malate. Tel: 590061, fax: 522 3208. One-room apartments rent for P30,500 a month, deluxe versions for P35,000, and two-bedroom apartments for P48,500. There is also a deluxe two-bedroom apartment for P55,000. There is a pool and restaurant.

Restaurants
Cosmopolitan Manila caters not only for visitors keen to try the local cuisine, but also for the kind of visitor who refuses to eat the same dish twice. Food fanciers can explore the whole gamut of Philippine food from the aromatic street stalls along Padre Faura and Taft Avenue, simple *carinderias* restaurants in Ermita, and seafood markets where fish is cooked to order, to a buffet or gourmet meal accompanied by live music or a fashion show in one of Manila's top hotels. Eastern, European and American food can be explored in the dense tourist zones of Ermita, Paco and Malate where prices are often as attractive as the dishes. Well- stocked supermarkets, all-night convenience stores, bakeries, delicatessens and wet (meat and fish) markets provide a further option for self-catering. The following are lists of moderate to cheap restaurants mostly within Manila's central tourist belt, or other well-known areas like Makati and Chinatown.

Filipino restaurants
Jumbo Garden and Restaurant, 1193 J Bocobo St.
Galing-Galing, 1133 L Guerrero.
Aida's, on M H del Pilar St, Ermita.
Nielson Tower Club and Restaurant, Ayala Triangle, Makati.
Aling Asiang, Greenbelt Centre, Makati.
Maynila, in the Manila Hotel.

Aristocrat, along Roxas Blvd, San Andres.
Bulwagang Pilipino, corner of Maria Orosa St and Arkansas St, Ermita.
Harbor View, South Blvd, near the end of Rizal Park.
Myrna's, on M H del Pilar St, Ermita.
Savory Restaurant, branches on T M Kalaw and Arquiza.
Guernica, Remedios Circle.
Barrio Fiesta, on J C Bocobo St.
Nandau, corner of Lourdes St and Roxas Blvd, Pasay City.
Tito Rey, Sunvar Plaza, Amorsolo corner of Pasay Rd, Makati.
Kamayan, along Padre Faura.

Chinese restaurants
Pink Patio, Uy Suy Bib Bldg, 531 A Paredes St.
Eva's Garden, Adriatico St, Malate.
Hong Kong Tea House, on M H del Pilar St, Emita.
New Wok Inn, on Remedios Ave, near the Malate Church.
Empress Garden, 1721 M Adriatico.
Maxim's Tea House, corner of Roxas Blvd and T M Kalaw St, Ermita.
Oceanic Restaurant, 777 Ongpin, near the Ongpin North Bridge.
New Carvajal Restaurant, Carvajal Alley, between Nueva St and Quintin Paredes.
Palo Alto, on UN Ave.
Sea Palace, on Mabini St, Malate.
China Park Restaurant, Plaza Nuestra Senora de Guia.
Mrs Wong Tea House, corner of M H del Pilar St and Padre Faura.

Other Asian restaurants
Japanese
Yamato, on Adriatico St, Malate.
Hakata, 1131 M H del Pilar St.
Tempura-Misono, in the Hyatt Regency Hotel, Roxas Blvd.
Fujiyama, 1410 Mabini St.
Kimpura, on Ayala Ave, Makati.
Iseya Restaurant, on Padre Faura, Ermita.

Korean
Korean Garden, Burgos St, Makati.
Korean Village, 1783 M Adriatico, Malate.
Korean Palace, also on Adriatico, Malate.

Thai
77 Cuisine, 1726 M Adriatico. Also serves Singaporean and Taiwanese dishes.
Sukhothai, on Makati Ave, Makati.
Taste of Thailand, inside the Mile Long Arcade, Amorsolo St, Makati.
The Rama, on Kalayaan Ave, Makati.
Flavours & Spices, corner of Greenbelt Drive and Legaspi St.

Indian and Middle Eastern
Green House Middle Eastern Food, corner of Pedro Gil and Adriatico.
Al-Sham's, 1421 A Mabini.
Kashmir Restaurant, on Padre Faura. Another branch on the corner of Guerrero St, Makati and Makati Ave.

European
Swiss Bistro, 494 Soldado, Ermita.
New Swiss Inn, Gen Luna, Paco.
Swiss Hut, M H del Pilar St, Ermita.
Treffpunkt Jedermann, on Jupiter St, Makati.
Edelweiss, 1335 M H del Pilar St, in front of the Fast Food Center.
Munchen Grill Pub, corner of Mabini St and Padre Faura.
La Taverna, on the corner of Pedro Gil and Adriatico St.
Alda's Pizza Kitchen, on Adriatico St, Ermita.
La Gondola Italian Restaurant, on Makati Ave, Makati.
Lafayette Café Restaurant, on M H del Pilar St.
L'Eau Vive, on Paz Mendoza Guazon Ave, Paco.
Au Bon Vivant, 1133 L Guerrero.
L'Orangerie, on Zodiac St, Makati.
Guernica's, M H del Pilar St.
El Comedor, corner of Pedro Gil and Adriatico St.
Muralla, inside the San Luis Complex, General Luna St, Intramuros.

American style
Steak Town and Chronicle Café, 1738 Adriatico St.
New Orleans, on Legaspi St, Makati.
Rosie's Diner, corner of R. Salas and M H del Pilar St.,
Hula Hut, just behind Rosie's Diner.
Tia Maria's, a Mexican restaurant on the corner of Carolina St and Remedios St, Malate.

Fast food
McDonald's branches can be found in Makati, and the Manila Pavilion Hotel. The outlet on United Nations Ave is probably the best.
Big Daddy's Hamburger, on Padre Gil.
Shakey's Pizza, branches on Taft Ave, Mabini St, Remedios St and Makati Ave.
Pizza Hut, several branches throughout central Manila.
Jollibee, a hamburger joint on Padre Faura, Ermita, and other places.
Kentucky Fried Chicken, all over Manila. The branch in Harrison Plaza, Malate, is popular.
Mister Donut, on Mabini St, and elsewhere.

Buffets
Lunch and dinner buffets were originally the preserve of big international hotels, but these days you can find reasonably priced spreads at several restaurants and cafes, although some of the best buffets continue to be served in hotels. You don't have to be a guest to have buffet breakfasts in a hotel.

Zamboanga Restaurant, Adriatico St.
The Revolving Restaurant, in the Manila Royal Hotel, Carlos Palanca Sr St, Santa Cruz.
Café Vienna, in the Holiday Inn, Roxas Blvd, Pasay City.
Pistang Pilipino, on Mabini St.
Bungalow Restaurant, San Marcelino, Escoda, Paco.

The Concourse, in the Hotel Nikko Manila Garden, Fourth Quadrant, Makati Commercial Centre, Makati.

Café Ilang-llang, in the Manila Hotel, Rizal Park, Ermita.

Sabungan Coffee Shop, in the Manila Midtown Hotel, corner of Pedro Gil and Adriatico St.

Vegetarian

Nonesuch Restaurant, 435 Remedios St.

New India House, 1718 M Adriatico.

Quan Yin Chay, on Soler St in Chinatown.

Mother Sachi, on Gil Puyat Ave, between Ayala Ave and Pasong Tamo St.

Pure Vegetarian Food Garden, J Bocobo St, Malvar.

American Health Food Restaurant, in the Hare Krishna temple, 1446 Looban, Paco.

24-hour joints

Most of the round-the-clock restaurants in Manila are concentrated in the nightless tourist area of Ermita. Dunkin Donuts, on Taft Ave and Remedios Avenue, provide the donuts and fresh coffee you need to make it through the Manila nights. Other places that never close are:

Diamond Tea House, 445 United Nations Ave.

BBQ Singapore Restaurant, on Adriatico St.

Maxim's Tea House, 1000 T M Kalaw.

Self-catering

International Supermarket, J C Bocobo, Ermita.

7-Eleven, corner of Adriatico St and Padre Faura, Ermita, and many other locations throughout Manila.

Martin's Products Bakery, M H del Pilar St.

La Tienda Supermarket, on Burgos St, Makati. Sheraton Delicatessen Shop, Vito Cruz, Malate.

San Andres Market in Malate has a wonderful selection of fresh fruit, vegetables, seafood and meat. The easiest place to shop if you are preparing your own meals on a regular basis in your *pension*, guesthouse or apartment.

Nightlife

Despite attempts to tone down the racier aspects of the city's nocturnal life, Manila, in common with Bangkok and Hong Kong, is one of Southeast Asia's finest and gaudiest neon orchids. Once one of Manila Bay's stunning sunsets has signalled the approach of evening, the town seems to experience a veritable quickening of pace, the release of a brash unrehearsed energy. Night conceals the city's imperfections for a few hours and the distressing ugliness of certain parts of Manila achieves a fleeting beauty and promise.

Manila has all the necessary ingredients for a good night on the tiles, being prodigal with good food, drink, live music, cinemas, a full agenda of cultural events and other entertainments. Whether your mood is high-brow or low-brow, there's a forum for most tastes and needs. In spite of a campaign by the mayor's office to "clean-up" the city back in the early and mid 1990s, Manila's irrepressible night-life goes on largely unaffected. The seedier side of Manila entertainment, its girlie bars, massage parlours, hostess bars and cat houses, like prohibition-period drinking dives, don't so much disappear as simply reinvent themselves, and then, after a decent interval, pop up again on different premises.

Happy hours (17.00 to 19.00 in most cases) announce the start of the evening's proceedings. In some of the more upmarket bars and music lounges, drinks at reduced prices are served along with live music in the form of a pianist, female signer and backing band, or an instrumental group. Other places specialise in jazz, rock, pop and folk acts, the sentimental croonings of *kundiman* (love song) balladeers, or the do-it-yourself exhibitionism of karaoke. In the more upmarket nightclubs, the spectacle of lavishly choreographed floor shows, and guitarists and violinists serenading between the tables, is not uncommon. Quezon City is fast becoming a major entertainment centre with most of its clubs, discos and bars concentrated along Quezon Avenue and Tomas Norato Avenue. Non-stop action of a more affordable kind is likely to be found along Manila's so-called Strip, the tourist belt of bars, night cafés, rock video clubs and karaoke lounges associated with the districts known as Ermita and Malate, the honey-pots of Manila. The Filipinos are highly regarded as musicians. Some of the best live music anywhere in Asia is to be found here. Broadly speaking, the demarcation lines of this entertainment and red-light district are the streets that fall between, and liberally spill over from, M H del Pilar and A Mabini streets, from United Nations Avenue to Malate Church, and from M Adriatico to Remedios Circle. All life, as they say, is here.

Useful addresses of bars, pubs and nightclubs
Slouch Hat Pub and Restaurant, 11–12 M H Pilar St.
Lili Marleen, on M H del Pilar St.
Swiss Matterhorn, on M H del Pilar St.
Hideaway Pub, T M Kalaw St.
Birdwatcher's Bar, corner of Mabini and A Flores Streets.
Treasure Island, in the Philippine Plaza Hotel.
Niagara Super Club, on Alhambra St.
The Champagne Room, in the Manila Hotel.
Playhouse, on Burgos St.
Firehouse, in the International Karaoke Complex, Roxas Blvd, Pasay City, along with a number of other bars.
Lovebirds, 1207 H M del Pilar.
Visions, 1313 M H del Pilar.
Jealousy, on Quezon Ave, Quezon City.
Man and Machine, Morato Ave, Quezon City.
Live music

Live music

Hobbit House, Mabini St.
Hard Rock Café, on Adriatico St.
Bistro RJ, in the Olympia Bldg, Makati Ave.
Calesa Bar, in the Hyatt Regency, Roxas Blvd, Pasay City.
Club 21, Mabini St.
Pistang Pilipino, Mabini St Penguin Café, Remedios St.
My Father's Moustache, M H del Pilar St.
Lobby Court, at the Philippine Plaza Hotel, Cultural Centre Complex, Malate.

Discos and dancing

Faces, Makati Ave, Makati.
Limelight Theatre, 1900 M Adriatico, Malate.
Equinox, Pasay Rd, Makati.
Euphoria, Hotel Inter-Continental, Ayala Ave, Makati.
Tito Dance Club, 1900 M Adriatico.
Lost Horizon, Philippine Plaza Hotel, Cultural Centre Complex, Malate.
La Cage, Roxas Blvd, Pasay City.
Valentino, in the Manila Midtown Hotel, corner of Adriatico St and Pedro Gil.
Billboard, on Makati Ave.
Stargazer, in the Silahis Hotel, Roxas Blvd, Malate.
Rumours, Makati Commercial Centre.
Cocoon, on Pasay Road.

Cinemas

The Philippines has a lively, though decidedly low-brow, film industry of its own. The lavish Manila Film Centre, the costly brainchild of Imelda Marcos, never achieved its purpose of becoming regular host venue to the Manila International Film Festival, an event that was supposed to rival its Cannes, Vienna and Tokyo prototypes. When 40 construction workers were killed in an accident precipitated by the rush to complete the building for the opening of the 1982 festival, Imelda had concrete poured over the bodies in order not to delay the construction further by having to spend time removing the bodies. The First Lady is said to have ordered an exorcism later on to expel ghosts from the site. Needless to say, the festival never got off the ground and the centre today remains largely unused.

Home-produced and foreign films are shown all over the city, but the best cinemas are located in showcase areas like the Makati Commercial Center and the Araneta Center in Harrison Plaza. There are also cinema belts in Santa Cruz, Quezon City and along Claro M Recto Avenue and Rizal Avenue.

Concerts and theatre

A regular programme of classical and other concerts are held at the Cultural Centre of the Philippines (CCP) on Roxas Boulevard. Every Sunday, free, televised live concerts of pop and rock music are held in

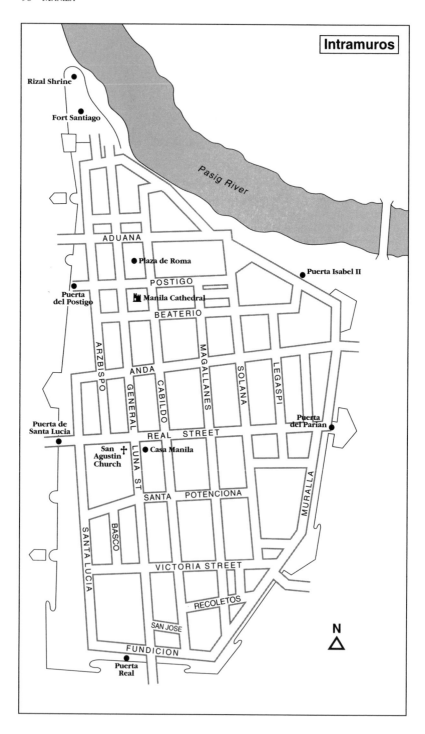

Rizal Park from 17.00. Free concerts of chamber music are held in Paco Park every Friday (weather permitting) at 18.00. There are also the open-air Puerta Real Evenings held inside the walled city every Saturday from November to May, from 18.00. The main venues for theatrical performances are the Cultural Center of the Philippines, the Meralco Theatre, Rajah Sulayman Theatre, Insular Life Theatre and the Folk Arts Theatre. See the arts and entertainment section of daily newspapers or "what's on" magazines for listings of performances.

CENTRAL MANILA
Intramuros
If you have a good pair of legs most of Central Manila is easily negotiated on foot, allowing, that is, for food and drink stops along the way. The walled city of Intramuros was the nucleus of the old Spanish city. Improvements in the construction of its walls, which were made of earth, tufa and brick, spanned a period of 251 years. Seven gates led to the inner city through walls which at some points reached a base width of 14 metres. Its drawbridges were lowered at 4am and raised at 11pm. Only the elite Spanish community and Spanish mestizos were allowed to reside here. In its heyday the walled city contained government buildings, the residences of the archbishop and governor-general, churches, monasteries, the houses of religious orders, military barracks, an arsenal, schools, colleges, a university, hostels, a printing press and the homes of the privileged Castilian upper classes. Most of Intramuros was destroyed during fighting in the Second World War, but concerned civic groups and the efforts of the Intramuros Administration have done much to restore the city to its former glory. This is where Manila's history as a capital began, so it is fitting to start an exploration of the city here.

Fort Santiago
The unevenly shaped wedge of Intramuros is dominated by Fort Santiago, which occupies the old city's most strategic site overlooking the Pasig River and Manila Bay. Rajah Sulayman's original bamboo-palisaded stockade was located here. Construction of the stone fortifications under the guidance of a Jesuit engineer began in 1584. The tone of the Spanish administration is set by a relief carving visitors can glimpse at the entrance to the fort, which depicts St James, the patron saint of Spain, slaying the Moors. The site has been witness to some key moments in Philippine history. The British made this their base during their brief occupation of the city in 1762–64, and the native Tayabas regiment staged a mutiny here in 1843. Dr Jose Rizal was incarcerated in the fort for two months before his execution. HIs final poem, *Mi Ultimo Adios* ("My Last Farewell"), was written and smuggled out from here. Countless numbers of Filipinos were imprisoned in the fort's infamous dungeons and cells over the centuries, and during the Japanese occupation the Bastion of San

Lorenzo, a storage area for munitions and artillery, was used as a torture chamber. Many prisoners met their end by drowning during this period, after being thrown into dungeons built below the river's high tide mark. The fort has been successfully renovated and the surrounding gardens pleasantly landscaped. Several memorials in Fort Santiago testify to its past. The Rizal Museum, a two-storey building housing his memorabilia, is open to the public from 09.00 to 12.00 and from 13.00 to 17.00. You can buy Rizal's two influential novels, *El Filibusterismo*, and *Noli Me Tangere*, both banned by the Spanish, in English editions here at the little bookshop in the museum. A memorial park called the Shrine of Freedom has been laid out here and is popular with local people. Near the western ramparts there is a collection of stately old cars used by former presidents and people like General MacArthur. The Rajah Sulayman Theatre is also found here on the former site of the old military barracks. Plays in Filipino are sometimes put on in its open-air auditorium. Admission to the fort is P10.

Plaza de Roma

Known as Plaza Mayor during the Spanish period, this imposing square, just a few minutes' walk from Fort Santiago, was the core of the old Spanish city, surrounded by the Ayumtamiento (Town Hall), the Palacio Real and Manila Cathedral. Until its conversion into a garden in 1797, it was the scene of important public events, religious festivals, processions and even bullfights. The palace was destroyed by an earthquake in 1863 and newer buildings constructed on the site are used as government offices and by the Intramuros Administration. The imposing Romanesque hulk of Manila Cathedral, which is now the main feature of the plaza, was completely reconstructed in 1958 with financial help from the Vatican. The present cathedral is the sixth construction erected on the site since the original wooden building put up in 1581. The Cathedral is the most important religious structure in the Philippines and attracts a steady stream of devotees as well as tourists. The Cathedral is noted for its octagonal dome, mosaics, bronze statue of the Virgin Mary, vivid stained-glass windows and one of the largest organs in Asia, a whopping-great Dutch model with 4,500 pipes.

San Agustin Church

Perhaps it was thanks to the building's sturdy 1.5m-thick walls, or the fortuitous granite lions donated by Chinese converts that grace the entrance to the building, but miraculously San Agustin Church is the only one out of seven such churches built within Intramuros that has survived intact the collective onslaught of fires, earthquakes and war. Completed in 1607, the interior has various later stylistic accretions such as its painted *trompe l'oeil* finishing, choir stalls inlaid with ivory, baroque pulpit, 18th-century organ and French chandeliers. The remains of several of the last great conquistadors, including Juan de Salcedo and Martin de Goti, are buried here along with the tomb and effigy of Legaspi. The church is a popular spot for weddings. There is an interesting monastery-museum adjoining the church which houses an important collection of manuscripts, rare books and religious art and artifacts. The museum also has a small but interesting collection of photographs showing images of 19th century Manila. The museum is open every day 08.30–12.00, 13.00–17.00. Admission is P10.

Casa Manila

Not far from the San Agustin Church there is a group of reconstructed period houses well worth seeing. Designs for the reconstruction of one of them, the Casa Manila, were based on 19th-century photographs, more recent aerial shots and original materials such as balustrades, adobe stones and timber taken from other houses of the same epoch. Oriental and European furnishings and decor blend well with embroidered Philippine bed-hangings, woodcarvings and centrepanes, and beautiful hardwood floors that get a regular polishing with banana leaves said to increase their lustre. The Casa Manila is open 09.00–14.00, 13.00–18.00 from Tuesday to Friday. On Saturday and Sunday the closing time is 19.00, and it is closed on Mondays. Admission P15 for adults, P5 for students and children under 12.

Gates and walls

You can do a circuit of the walls, gates and bastions of Intramuros by continuing south along General Luna Street until you come to the Puerta Real. Formerly used for religious processions and formal state occasions, the interior of the Royal Gate holds a collection of church silver. Spiral staircases lead up to the ramparts. If you follow Muralla Street northwards towards the City Hall, you will soon see another gate, the Puerta del Parian. A little further on, Puerta Isabel II on Magallanes Drive is the newest gate, opened in 1862, not for purposes of defence, but to alleviate the increasing flow of traffic between Intramuros and Binondo. Isabel's statue stands in front of the gate which is flanked by small offices and refreshment parlours. Postigo del Palacio, the next gate you reach, faces Manila Bay. Jose Rizal was led through here on his way to an untimely execution at Bagumbayan Field, now renamed Rizal Park. The 18th-century Santa Lucia Gate is the last breach in the walls before you find yourself on Bonifacio Drive, within view of the Manila Hotel and the Intramuros Golf Course. Continue south from here, cross the intersection at Burgos Street, and Luneta, or Rizal Park, is facing you on the left.

Rizal Park

One of Manila's much needed lungs and a genuine sanctuary in the centre of the city, Rizal Park was named after the nationalist hero who was brought here for execution at dawn on 30 December 1898. The spot where he died is marked by a bronze statue inscribed with his last poem. A

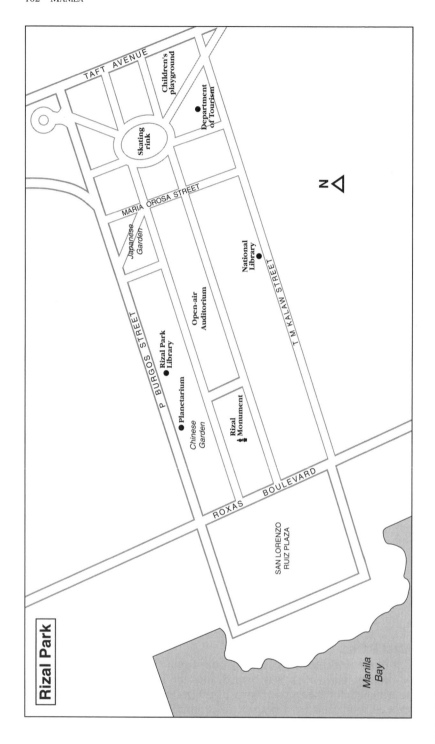

Rizal Park

lightshow recreating the events leading up to the execution is shown here every day. The English version of the soundtrack comes on at 19.30. Tickets cost P20. The Rizal Fountain, a well from which Rizal is said to have drunk during his student days in Heidelberg, is not far from here, having been brought over from Wilhelmsfeld, a village in Germany. The park starts to come alive in the early hours of the morning as elderly Chinese people gather for sessions of *tai chi chuan*. Rizal Park is the scene of family picnics, presidential inaugurations, free Sunday concerts, parades and Independence and New Year's Day celebrations. It was here that almost a million people gathered to show support for Corazon Aquino back in 1986. The central section of the park has a number of attractions including a Japanese Garden with little rainbow bridges and stone lanterns, an open-air auditorium, planetarium and a Chinese Garden replete with a scaled-down relic of the Summer Palace in Beijing. The eastern section of the park abutting Taft Avenue has a skating rink, a garden full of tropical plants and a splendid children's playground, a veritable Jurassic Park of petrified stone dinosaurs and monsters painted in lurid colours.

The National Museum

A short walk from here along Burgos Street takes you to the National Museum, the official home to the country's cultural heritage. Admission to the museum is free. Here you will find works of art (including Juan Luna's key masterwork, Spolarium), natural history, archaeological and ethnological exhibits, including a section of the fossilised skullcap of Tabon Man, a prehistoric find from Tabon Cave, Palawan. There is also an interesting display in the museum's Maritime Heritage Gallery of seven native boats, carbon dated to between 890 and 710BC. The museum opens Monday to Saturday 08.30 to 12.00, and 13.00 to 17.00.

NORTH OF THE PASIG

Crossing the Pasig River, the crowds seem to get thicker, the traffic slows to a crawl and the buildings seem to squeeze in a little closer to the kerb. Poorer people shoehorned into less space characterises the areas of Quiapo, Santa Cruz, Escolta and Chinatown, but so too does local colour, lively communities and several points of real interest to the visitor. These include, among other things, Malacanan Palace, the extraordinary Chinese Cemetery, the University of Santo Tomas and the important shopping centre of Santa Cruz. A constant stream of jeepneys link Quiapo and Santa Cruz with Mabini Street and Taft Avenue.

Quiapo and Santa Cruz

Quiapo's main attraction for foreigners and visiting Filipinos is its church, founded in 1586. The current structure, built in 1935, houses the talismanic Shrine of the Black Nazarene, a lifelike image of Christ carved by Mexican Indians in black wood and brought to the Philippines in the 17th century. Quiapo Church is a magnet for the devout as well as the slightly superstitious, and is surrounded by a fascinating collection of stalls selling rosaries, medallions of the saints, candles, prayer books, amulets and all manner of religious artefacts. Fridays and Holy Week are particularly interesting as these attract large crowds of worshippers, some of whom can be seen making their way from the entrance to the the church of the Narareno on their knees. Every January Quiapo's Feast of the Black Nazarene draws large crowds of people who come to see the statue carried through the streets in an evening procession. During the festival, the Plaza Miranda is the scene of concerts and other entertainments. At other times the square is often co-opted as a platform for electoral campaigns and political rallies.

Quiapo is also worth visiting for its lively secular markets. Many of these are found in the backstreets and alleys to the west of the church, where the ambience of a bazaar crammed with all sorts of merchandise attracts large numbers of shoppers, as well as pickpockets. Running parallel with Quezon Boulevard, the main thoroughfare that bisects Quiapo and Santa Cruz, right under Quezon Bridge itself, is a tremendous handicraft market known locally as "llalim ng Tulay", meaning, quite literally, "under-the-bridge-market". Quinta Market is not far from here as well, and slightly to the east lies Manila's main Muslim area, easily discerned from the large gold dome and crescent moon of the mosque that dominates the skyline of Quiapo and Santa Cruz.

Malacanang Palace
Northeast of Quiapo, by the Pasig River, Malacanang Palace was, for a long time, the official residence of Philippine presidents. Corazon Aquino refused to live there, turning it instead into a people's museum. Today, the Museo ng Malacanag, as it is known, continues to operate as a public museum but also serves as a venue for cabinet meetings, official visits and state functions.

The name Malacanang may derive from the Tagalog, *may lakan diyan* (the place of nobles). Built as a private residence in the late 18th century, rich traders, high-ranking members of the Spanish military, American and Japanese administrators, governor-generals and a line of presidents ending with the twenty-year residence of the Marcoses, have all added to or diminished the grandeur of the palace. During the American period, the original wooden structure was replaced with concrete, though the exterior was left unchanged.

Malacanang was methodically stripped of much of its character during the time the Marcoses lived there. The old palace was hastily demolished and replaced with a larger new one, many of the original furnishings were swept away and even the beautifully wrought ironwork which stood at the entrance to the Executive Building, and was such a distinctive feature of the building, was relegated, quite literally, to the scrap heap, from which it was later, affectionately, retrieved. Two hours after helicopters removed the remaining members of the Marcos dynasty from the palace, thousands of euphoric Filipinos swarmed through its gates, discovering within the evidence of a wealth and extravagance even they were unaware of. In the basement storage room, now known as "Imelda's department store", packing cases full of electronic equipment, evening gowns, designer clothes with the price tags still on them and, most puzzling of all to the thunderstruck poor who walked around the rooms in those first hours, the 1,220 pairs of shoes that have come, along with the gallon bottles of custom-made French perfume discovered in the Marcos' bathroom, to symbolise, more than anything else, the narcissism and excesses of the former First Lady.

The palace is open from 09.00 to 12.00, and from 13.00 to 15.00 on Monday and Tuesday for an admission cost of P200. On Thursday and Friday it opens from 13.00 to 15.00 for guided tours for only P20. The palace may occasionally be closed for official visits and other special occasions, so it is better to check in advance. Tel. 588946 for information.

University of Santo Tomas

If you are in the vicinity of the palace it is worth visiting the nearby University of Santo Tomas on Espana Street. Founded by Dominican friars in 1611, this is the oldest institute of its kind in the Philippines. The university was relocated to its present site in 1927 after the destruction of the original building. The former entrance, however, the "Arch of the Centuries", a stone gate decorated with the figures of saints, has been kept as it was. Among some of the notable alumni of this prestigious university can be counted Emilio Aguinaldo, Jose Rizal, M H del Pilar, A Mabini and four Philippine presidents. The university library boasts an excellent collection of rare manuscripts and books, medals and coins, and the oldest printing press in the country. Its Museum of Natural Science, on the second floor, is well worth looking at. There is also an exhibition of religious art in the gallery there. The university is open Monday to Saturday, from 08.00 to 12.00, and from 14.00 to 17.00 during term time.

Chinatown

The roots of Manila's Chinese community go back almost as far as the suspicious Spanish friars and administrators who allowed these Oriental merchants and artisans to settle north of the river in the area which is now Binondo, providing that they stayed well within canon-firing distance of the ramparts of Intramuros. Today's Chinatown, instantly recognisable from its restaurants, mah-jongg clubs, small tea houses, cubby-hole shops, kung-fu schools, ornamental arches, "heavenly gates" and acupuncture clinics, occupies parts not only of Binondo but of the districts of Santa Cruz and San Nicolas. Chinatown proper can be found in the gridlock of crowded streets defined by Nueva, Ongpin, Quintin Paredes, Gandara and Pinpin Streets. The area is always lively, particularly at night and on

Sundays when its restaurants come into their own, but seethes with even more activity during the Chinese New Year (between 21 Jan and 19 Feb) and the Moon Festival (between Aug and Sept) when the tiresome traffic comes to a halt and pedestrians take over.

Follow any of the small, winding streets at the heart of Chinatown and you will eventually come to Binondo Church, an impressively large building dedicated to Our Lady of the Rosary, situated in a small tree-lined plaza. The church was built in 1596 for the community of Chinese converts. After the war it was repaired, but the bell tower and its western facade are original. Ongpin Street leads to yet another place of worship, the Santa Cruz Church, the Shrine of Our Lady of the Pillar, built by Jesuits in 1608 to serve the Chinese community.

The Chinese Cemetery

One of the most unmissable sights on any visitor's itinerary of Manila is unquestionably the Chinese Cemetery in the north of Santa Cruz, in the area aptly named Monumento. Here among some of the most grandiose tombs in the world, a whole city of the dead has been laid out, replete with streets, back alleys, small plazas and houses. A fascinating blend of Buddhist, Catholic and Taoist architectural elements prevails, with plaster-cast Virgin Marys placed beside writhing serpents and dragons of decidedly Chinese provenance. Many of the wealthier deceased occupy two-storey mausoleums equipped with refrigerators, bathrooms, marble floors, air-conditioning and even mailboxes. A lot of these mansions for the dead are a good deal more prosperous-looking and spacious than those of the living. If that sounds like exaggeration, glance over any one of the cemetery's boundary walls. Caskets have been set in the wall embrasures of the cemetery, while indeterminate numbers of squatter families have created vast and hellish slum settlements of their own on the other side.

On Sundays and at special times of the year like All Saints' Day, the cemetery is crowded with visiting Chinese families, but at other times the deserted streets and empty squares revert to an eerie silence. The cemetery opens daily from 08.00 to 17.00. Jeepneys marked "Monumento" come here from Mabini Street, Taft Avenue, Rizal Avenue, and Santa Cruz. You can also catch the Metrorail to Abad Santos Station and walk or tricycle the remaining 600 or so metres. Guides are highly recommended as they have some fascinating tales to tell about the area, and also provide a useful security escort on quieter days when there may not be many people around.

SOUTHERN MANILA

Ermita and Malate

Most visitors end up sooner or later spending time in these two districts, if they are not staying in one of them already. The one-time residential area of Manila's middle and upper classes, they now constitute Manila's main tourist belt. Here is the centre of Manila's effervescent nightlife, jam packed with bars, restaurants, nightclubs, antique and souvenir shops, travel agencies, coffee houses and a whole host of hotels, guesthouses and *pensions*, a fascinating mixture of tourist sleeze and Oriental Bohemia.

Like everywhere in Manila, Ermita and Malate have their fair share of churches to serve the spiritual needs of its resident community. A statue of Nuestra Senora de Guia, the city's patroness of galleons, is enshrined in Ermita Church, situated in a small, shady plaza of the same name. Set back from Rozas Boulevard and backing on to Mabini Street is Malate Church, dedicated to Nuestra Senora de Remedios, protector of women in childbirth. The church is busy on her feast day (26 Nov) when mothers bring their newly born to offer thanks. Less than one block from here is the Carfel Seashell Museum, an interesting introduction to the countless forms of shell and coral found in the waters of these islands. The extensive San Andres Market is also near by. Manila Zoo and the Botanical Garden lie south of here and can be reached by following Adriatico Street.

Roxas Boulevard

This is one of Manila's most spacious avenues, running a north–south route along Manila Bay. Before the Second World War this was one of the most fashionable boulevards in the city, its white, sea-facing mansions and manicured gardens home to foreign diplomats and wealthy businessmen, before they moved out to the likes of Dasmarinas and Forbes Park. Vestiges of its affluent and expansive past are still found in the presence of the Manila Yacht Club, the American Embassy, Central Bank and its numerous art galleries. The Central Bank houses both the Metropolitan Museum with its regular exhibitions of international and local art, and the Money Museum, with its permanent collection of pre-Hispanic coins, foreign banknotes and gold artifacts.

The Cultural Centre Complex, Imelda Marcos's costly and controversial pet project, lies on reclaimed land extending from Roxas Boulevard into the bay. The main building houses a 2,000-seat concert hall, a 400-seat theatre, archaeological museum, a library and the Contemporary Art Museum. The complex also houses a spacious Design Centre, a Convention Centre, the Philippine Centre for International Trade and Exhibitions, the Film Centre, Westin Philippine Plaza Hotel and various amusement areas and fast-food chains. The Folk Arts Theatre, which is often used as a venue for trade fairs and rock concerts, is also here. One of the more architecturally interesting buildings in the complex is the Coconut Palace, designed by Francisco Manosa, one of the Philippines' most daring architects. The palace is a showcase for Philippine design. All the building materials are indigenous to the Philippines, 70% deriving from the island's "tree of life", the coconut. Its soaring hexagonal pavilions and trapezoidal layout house seven private and function rooms, each decorated and furnished with arts and crafts representing different regions of the Philippines. It is a good, although somewhat contrived, introduction to areas that you might be interested in visiting later in your stay.

Pasay City and Paranaque

The boundary between Manila and Pasay City is marked by Buendia Avenue. South of the Philippine Centre for International Trade and Exhibitions, at 10 Lancaster Street, behind the Hyatt Regency Hotel, is the superb Lopez Memorial Museum, not to be missed by anyone interested in Filipiniana. The museum's collection includes some of Jose Rizal's diaries and letters, old travel literature and prints, paintings by Hidalgo and Luna, and rare books and maps.

Continue south along Roxas Boulevard and you soon reach the old salt-making town of Paranaque, which is also well known for its embroidery. Balaran is a district within Paranaque that is noted for its church, also known as the Church of Our Lady of Perpetual Help. This Redemptorist Church is most interesting on Wednesdays when the weekly novena takes place, and a whole host of food and merchandise stalls spring up around the site.

A little distance from here, towards the international airport, you will find a telescoped version of the Philippines, carefully laid out in a theme park at the Nayong Pilipino, "Philippine Village". Theme parks have gained quite a lot of credibility in Asia in recent years and have even won over some of the hardest cynics. The thing to remember is that, generally, theme parks, in this part of the world at least, don't make any claims to be the real thing. They ask you to exult in the quality of the replica and to admire it as a good reproduction of the authentic article, rather than suspend your disbelief and pretend that you are actually being fêted by Ifugao headhunters in the fastnesses of northern Luzon or whatever. Theme parks in Asia are about fun, and the Nayong Pilipino is certainly that, as well as a reasonable digest of what you might expect as you travel around the islands. Tours show you locations like Bicol, the Visayas, Mindanao and Sulu, the Cordilleras and Ilocos, and southern and central Luzon in detailed microcosms. You'll also see highlights of the country's history and culture, such as Magellan's Cross in Cebu, houses on stilts from Samal, the Cagsawa ruins in Bicolandia and Bohol's Chocolate Hills. Other attractions are the Museum of Philippine and International Dolls, the Philippine Museum of Ethnology, an excellent aviary, and a garden featuring bougainvillea, cactus, herbal plants, hibiscus and palms. There is also a children's playground, a restaurant serving real Philippine food and several shops selling regional handicrafts. There are regular folk dance performances staged throughout the day. The village is open from Monday to Saturday, 09.00–19.00, and on Saturday and Sunday, 09.00–20.00. Admission is P85. Buses pass by the village from Taft Avenue. Jeepneys run from Baclaran.

Makati

Makati is an oasis of modernity and conspicuous affluence set down in a seething Third World city. It is the capital's main showcase, the country's financial and commercial hub, surrounded by residential sectors where wealthy Filipinos and large numbers of foreign residents make their home. Built on swampland owned by the influential Ayala-Zobel family, Makati began to be developed in the 1950s, when it was divided into commercial and economic zones and residential villages like Dasmarinas and Forbes Park. Here, Manila's elite live in opulent mansions and luxurious town houses so removed from the lives of ordinary Filipinos that the private streets of many of these privileged ghettos are cordoned off with gates and patrolled by a private police force.

Makati proper is recognisable from its office blocks, high-rise condominiums, shopping and commercial complexes, department stores, designer boutiques, elegant air-conditioned shopping malls, upmarket restaurants, art galleries, nightclubs and plush hotels. It is also the location for many embassies, consulates, airline offices, golf and polo clubs.

If you do venture into this costly area of Manila, spare time for the Ayala Museum on Makati Avenue. This contains a remarkable display of over 60 revolving, three-dimensional dioramas that cleverly depict highlights from Philippine history. There are also archaeological and ethnographic exhibits, models of ships and boats, religious artifacts, works of art and ethnic handicrafts on display. The museum is open from Tuesday to Sunday, 09.00 to 19.00 and charges P20 for admission. The interesting Ayala Museum Aviary, an attractive 20m-high walkway containing some 200 different species of birds from the Philippines, is just behind the main museum. There is also an orchidarium in the same complex.

About 10km from Manila, at Fort Bonifacio, the American Military Cemetery and War Memorial contains 17,206 identified graves of American and Allied servicemen who were killed in action during the Second World War. The grounds also contain a monument to over 36,000 servicemen whose remains were never recovered. The beautifully tended grounds, carefully planted with trees, shrubs and bushes and well laid-out lawns, attract a steady stream of visitors from all over the world who come here to pay quiet homage to these war dead.

CATCHMENT MANILA

Quezon City

Named after its founder, President Manuel Quezon, this former capital of the Philippines is four times larger than Manila and has a population of well over one million. The area was built with the intention of creating massive housing projects with all the modern amenities for low salaried workers. When the Pope was driven here to celebrate mass before a vast crowd in 1970, thousands of slum homes en route to this worker's utopia were masked off by wooden construction-site walls, hastily erected to keep reality well away from from the papal gaze.

Quezon City today has many elegant homes and gardens within its so-called "housing projects", spacious boulevards, several government offices, the main campus of the University of the Philippines, hospitals, television stations, a golf course, and many good restaurants along Tomas Morato Street, Quezon Avenue, Cubao and West Avenue. The Quezon Memorial Circle, with its mausoleum and monument, City Museum and Art Gallery, marks the centre of the city. Another campus, the University of Ateneo, with its Ateneo Art Gallery, can be found in Loyola Heights. Near to the highly respected Philippine Heart Centre for Asia, the Museo ng Buhay (Museum of Filipino Life), part of the Central Bank building, is located on East Avenue. The museum depicts the lifestyles of lowland Filipinos, including the well-to-do land owning classes, in the last century, and contains all sorts of curious domestic items, utensils and antique furnishings.

The city's commercial centre is Cubao, a large shopping and entertainment area noted for its department stores, cinemas, restaurants and its large Farmer's Market and Seafood Market. The gigantic Araneta Coliseum is a world venue for sporting events, championship fights, stag derbies, ice shows, pop concerts and circuses. The annual La Naval procession, held to commemorate Spanish naval victories over the Dutch, is held around the Santo Domingo Church on Quezon Avenue every October.

Caloocan City and beyond

To the north of Manila, the industrial city of Caloocan is best known for its monument to the revolutionary hero, Andres Bonifacio, who signalled the start of the revolt against the Spanish here in 1896. A little further up the coast from here is the country's biggest fishing port at Navotas. Malabon, another fishing port famous for its fish noodle dish called *Pancit Malabon*, is near by. The scene changes dramatically every year on Good Friday when Malabon is witness to a gruesome parade of masked flagellates. Not far from Caloocan, the eastern suburb of Pateros is famous for its duck breeding and egg industry. Marikina and San Juan are other eastern suburbs of note, the former for its high quality shoe industry, the latter for the Alto Crafts Doll Museum at 400 Guevarra Avenue. There are over 2,000 dolls on display here, depicting all walks of Philippine life and history.

Las Pinas

Included among Manila's southern suburbs of Pasay City, Paranaque and Muntinlupa, is the old salt-production town of Las Pinas on the road to Cavite. Visitors generally come here to visit Las Pinas Church, famous for its unique bamboo organ. A Spaniard, Father Diego Cerra, began building the organ in 1816. The 5m-high instrument, comprising some 174 bamboo pipes, was completed in 1822. After years of neglect and damage caused by the effects of earthquakes and typhoons, the organ was eventually sent to Bonn in Germany for restoration. Its unique sound attracts professional players from all over the world, many of whom turn up for the annual Bamboo Organ Festival. Buses marked "Las Pinas/Zapote" leave from the centre of Manila for Las Pinas. South-bound jeepneys can also be taken from Baclaran.

Chapter Seven

Manila Side Trips

There are many rewarding day trips within one to three hours from Manila which visitors can avail themselves of without having to check out of their hotel. Most hotels and guesthouses in Manila, however, are happy to look after your bags while you are away if an overnight stay is more desirable. The four southern and eastern provinces of Cavite, Laguna, Batangas and Rizal, collectively known as CALABAR, are perfect for day trips or short one-nighters. This pleasant area of lakes, rivers, green, pastoral fields, mountains, mineral baths, caves and craggy seashores is soaked in legend and history. The provinces attract visitors in pursuit of watersports, fishing, hiking, golf and relaxation. Its highly regarded artisans and craftsmen, whose work is found in the craft shops of Manila and is also exported abroad, are known for their work as woodcarvers, silversmiths, shipbuilders, embroiderers and weavers. The areas are well served by public transport. The Pantranco South Express Bus Company, and the BLTB Bus Comapany, ply these routes daily. Areas to the north and west of Manila, notably Angeles, San Fernando, Bataan Peninsula and Corregidor Island, offer similarly accessible attractions.

SOUTH OF MANILA
Cavite
Close to Manila, Cavite, the Philippine Navy's main base, is an unremarkable town. Its passable beaches, leisure parks and Aquinaldo House Museum make it an easy and pleasant-enough day trip from the city, however. Cavite Province's five-star Puerto Azul Beach Hotel and resort is the closest deluxe beach hotel to Manila.

Getting there
Cavite is only half an hour by bus from Taft Avenue and Baclaran.

Where to stay
Puerto Azul Beach Resort, Ternate (40km southwest of Cavite City). Tel: 574731 40. From simple rooms with fan and shower for P1,600 to suites at P5,500. Good facilities for watersports and relaxation.

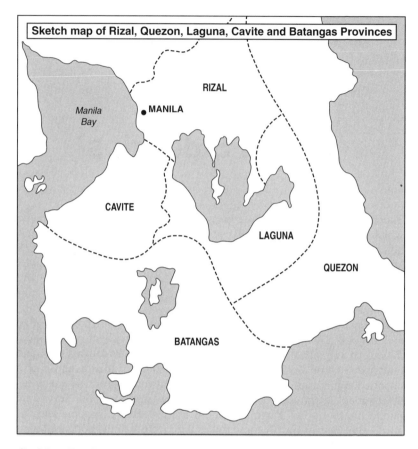

Sketch map of Rizal, Quezon, Laguna, Cavite and Batangas Provinces

Caylabne Bay Resort, same location as above. Tel: 8188385. Perfectly good rooms with air-conditioning and bath for P2,000–2500. Has a swimming pool, golf course, tennis court and nice restaurant. Watersports equipment can be hired at reasonable cost.

Naic

Quite a bit further down the coast from Cavite, keen fishermen can have a good day out at Naic, well known for papacol, or triggerfish. Boats can be hired at the Seaside Beach Resort for trips to the fishing grounds around Fraile and Carabao Islands. The best months are from June to September, although fishing can be done all year round.

Tagaytay Ridge and volcano

Tagaytay Ridge, with its magnificent views of Taal Lake and the volcanic island at its centre, is one of the best day trips that can be undertaken from Manila. Difficult to believe though it is, this diminutive volcano is one of the deadliest in the archipelago. Tagaytay is a popular summer resort for the Manila rich, many of whom have second homes located here in the cooler climate that goes with an altitude of 600m or more. When the weather is clear, excellent views of the crater lake can be had from the town. You can arrange for a guide to ferry you across the lake so that you can climb the volcano, but get a proper seismic report first. The Philippine Institute of Vulcanology and Seismology has an old station at Buco, on the edge of the lake. The staff can give you updates and forecasts, as well as show you some of their instruments and equipment. From whichever side you glance down on the volcano, the views are spectacular, but a particularly good perspective can be had from Mount Sungay, 10km east of Tagaytay. You'll also find the disused **Palace in the Sky** near here. The palace was built by Ferdinand Marcos to accommodate the Reagans on their state visit to the Philippines. In *The Snap Revolution*, James Fenton, one of the first persons to set foot in the Marcos' private apartments, just minutes after the palace was opened, recalls that "in every room I saw, practically on every available surface, there was a signed photograph of Nancy Reagan". The Americans must have left a strong impression. Admission to the palace is P5.

Trips to the volcanic island are best made from Talisay, a town located down on the shores of the lake. A boat with guide, return trip, shouldn't cost you more than P600.

Getting there
Take a BLTB bus marked "Lemery" or "Batangas" and go to Tanauan. There are jeepneys from here to Talisay. The distance from Manila is 56km. Buses from Batangas to Tanauan are more comfortable than jeepneys.

Where to stay
In Tagaytay
Taal Vista Hotel, on National Rd. Tel: 224, fax: 225. Manila reservations Tel: 810 2016. Air-conditioned rooms with bath for P2,000. Nice restaurant and good views of the lake. Also puts on folk dance performances.

Villa Adelaida, Foggy Heights. Tel: 267. Manila reservations, Tel: 876031 39. Fan and bathrooms. Good value at P900, but expect increases at the weekend.

In Talisay
International Resort. Rooms with fan and bath for P500. Very basic, and not very "international".

Rosalina's Place. Rooms with fan and bath for P150, without for P70/120. Reasonably comfortable with its own restaurant.

Taal Lake Guest House, in village of Leynes, near Talisay. Basic rooms with fan for P200–300. Has a restaurant.

Batangas
This province is a popular choice for jaded or work-driven Manila folk, keen to get away for a night or two or even an afternoon on the coast. Batangas is the nearest decent diving area from Manila, and a good selection of hotels and guesthouses have sprung up along the area's

attractive cove-and-bay indented coastline. Nasugbu, Matabungkay and the archaeological and colonial town of Calatagan are well-known resorts, while the coral-studded waters around Balayan Bay and Verde Island are perfect for divers and sports fishermen. The diving season here is from November to June, although there are some places like Verde Island and Balayan Bay where it is possible to dive all year round. Batangas, which is famous for its embroidery, is a good base for a two- or three-day exploration of other sights in the area.

Getting there
A BLTB bus leaves Manila every day at 12.30 for Matabungkay, and then goes on to Calatagan. Alight at Lian and then take a jeepney or tricycle the remaining few kilometres. BLTB buses leave every hour for Nasugbu. Jeepneys originating in Batangas can be taken to Lemery. You will have to change then for Balayan and again to Nasugbu. There are plenty of jeepneys connecting Matabungkay and Nasugbu.

Where to stay
Matabungkay and Nasugbu
Matabungkay Beach Club, Manila reservations, tel: 817 6723. Comfortable cottages and hotel rooms in the US$70–100 range. Swimming pool and scuba diving facilities.

Coral Beach Club, Matabungkay. Comfortable and tidy cottages with fan and bath for P700 and air-conditioning and bath for P900.

White Sands Beach Resort, Muntinbuhangin Cove, Nasugbu. P800–1,000. The cottages here have no electricity but storm lamps make for a romantic setting and there is a good restaurant.

Maya-Maya Reef Club, Nasugbu. Tel: 233. Cottages with fan and bath at P1,250–1,400, air-conditioning and bath for P1,800–2,000. Good value as it has excellent facilities – tennis court, restaurant, swimming pool, and nicely laid-out gardens. Their diving shop is well equipped and helpful with advice. Manila reservations, tel: 810 8118, fax: 8159288.

Calatagan
Baluarte Inter-Continental Resort. Manila reservations, tel: 815 9711. Air-conditioned bungalows with baths are good value at US$80–100 for this five-star resort. Excellent watersports facilities, beach access, horse riding, tennis and an 18-hole golf course.

Laguna
Calamba
Many towns in the green, water-fed province of Laguna, between the Central Plain and volcanic mountains of southern Luzon, are located on or near the shores of Laguna de Bay, the biggest freshwater lake in the Philippines. Calamba, the birthplace of Jose Rizal, is one such town. The town takes its name from a giant jar (calamba) inscribed with all the

names of the local villages, or barangays. Jose Rizal's house, opposite the Municipal Hall, is now a national shrine, open from Tuesday to Sunday, 08.00 to 12.00, 13.00 to 17.00. The area from Calamba to Los Banos is prodigal with hot springs. There are many thermal resorts on the road between the two.

Getting there
It is about an hour by BLTB bus from Manila to Calamba. Look out for buses marked "Santa Cruz". Many of the buses going to Manila from Santa Cruz and Pagsanjan pass through Calamba.

Where to stay
Crystal Springs, Bagong Kalsaga. Tel: 545 2496. Several spacious rooms with air-conditioning and bath for P950. Excellent value as each room has its own personal mini-pool.

Cora Villa, Bagong Kalsaga. Tel: 545 1277. A cheap place to stay with fan and bathrooms for P250–400.

Los Banos
As the name suggests, Los Banos is a hot spring resort, the thermal centre of the Philippines. Franciscans built a hospital here in 1602 on the strength of the waters' reputation for having curative properties. Many resorts here have their own access to the sulphur pools that flow down from Mount Makiling. Apart from finding different ways to wrinkle your skin, visitors to Los Banos can also pop into the International Rice Research Institute. Rice specialists from many countries come to this non-profit organisation to study and train. The institute was set up in the early 1960s by the Rockefeller and Ford foundations. A short walk from here, the College of Agriculture and Forestry has a beautifully planted campus, and several picnic areas commanding good views of the area nearby. The upper slopes of Mount Makiling, which looms conspicuously behind the campus, is now a national park with heaps of fauna and wildlife. The volcano is said to be inhabited by a goddess, Mariang Makiling. If you take a jeepney the short distance up to the Philippine Art Center, you will get a splendid view of Laguna de Bay.

Where to stay
City of Springs Resort Hotel, N Villegas St. Tel: 50137, fax: 50731. Fan and bathrooms from P350, air-conditioning and bath from P500–1,000. The more expensive rooms have whirlpool baths. Restaurant and several pools.

Lakeview Resort Hotel, 728 Lopez St. Tel: 50101. Spacious and comfortable rooms with fan and bath going for P500, air-conditioning and bath P600. Several pools and a restaurant.

Benido's Dormitory, junction of Mayondon and Dangka streets. Only P150. Very basic.

Makiling Lodge, near the City of Springs Resort. Another cheap option at P150–200 for simple but private rooms.

Alaminos

Despite the exorbitant rates charged to enter Alaminos, or "Hidden Valley Springs", a secluded and private resort retreat located in a jungle setting of ancient trees and superlatively sized plants, the place is highly recommended. The beauty of the location in any case soon overcomes the sensation of being ripped off, and the entrance fee, a stiff P1,140 on weekdays and P1,425 at weekends (expect, as with all figures quoted in this book, to make an annual price adjustment), does include a welcome cocktail, buffet lunch, afternoon snack and unlimited use of all hot springs and changing rooms. The springs are located in a 90m crater on the side of Mount Makiling. No wonder it attracts so many photographers. If you can walk the relatively short distance from Alaminos to the main entrance gate, all the better. Rapacious tricycle drivers will try to demand an outrageous P100–150 for the ride. Visitors who wish to stay overnight can find accommodation here.

Getting there

Considering what a magnificent hideaway this is, it is surprisingly easy to get to. Buses marked "Santa Cruz" leave the BLTB Terminal every day, passing through Alaminos on their way to Los Banos. It is about a 90-minute journey.

Where to stay

Hidden Valley Springs. Manila reservations, tel: 509903. Singles with air-conditioning and bath go for P2,800, doubles with air-conditioning from P4,700–5,000. The price includes breakfast and admission fee for the resort, although not the buffet lunch. There are also cottages, nipa huts and tents for rent from the same people. Cottages cost P5,300 a night, the tents P1,000 per person.

San Pablo

San Pablo City was founded in 1678 and rose to be a major copra centre, although these days it is best known as an important transportation nucleus, linking Quezon, Rizal and Batangas. Despite its commercial eminence it is a wonderfully bucolic area, renowned for its seven lakes, and an ideal place for hikers and mountain climbers. The 1,144m (3,754ft) Mount Makiling can be safely, though arduously, tackled from this side. The more convenient, though higher, climb is Mount Banahaw, at 2,199m (7,217ft). Its mist-shrouded slopes, springs and waterfalls suggest a mystical setting, which is exactly how the Filipinos think of this mountain. During Easter many devotees come here, tracing their animist roots no doubt, to pray, meditate and sip from the holy springs of Mount Makiling.

Ten kilometres south of San Pedro, near the border with Quezon on the road to Tiaong, is the 25-hectare Escudero Estate and Villa, a huge Spanish-style coconut plantation. The estate and villa are open to the public and well worth seeing. It is also possible to stay overnight in the grounds of the villa. After paying your P80 admission fee you will be received with a welcome drink of *buko* (fresh young coconut juice), and be taken on a ride through the estate on a *carabao*. The museum here has an unusual collection of items on display (religious reliquaries, stuffed animals, icons, the costumes of former local beauty queens) that appear to have come from frequent raids on the villa's attic.

Where to stay

The Villa Escudero, Tiaong. Tel: 2379. Well-decorated and comfortable cottages with bath from P800. There is a restaurant. Manila reservations, tel: 593698.

San Rafael Swimming Pool Resort, on the road to Alaminos. Cheap cottages with bath for P350–500. There are actually two pools here.

Sampaloc Lake Youth Hostel, in Efarca Village. A very cheap option. You get your own room for P75–100.

Pagsanjan

If the scenery around Pagsanjan and its emerald green gorge looks familiar it is probably because you have seen one of the movies *Apocalypse Now* or *Platoon*, important shots from which were taken here. Those who have seen the documentary *Hearts of Darkness*, made by Francis Ford Coppola's wife, will know how an idyllic spot of location work in the Philippines quickly turned into a nightmare for the director and his foreign cast.

Apart from the stunning beauty of the area, many people come here to have themselves paddled up the Pagsanjan River and gorge in a *banca*. It is a very inflexible tour but worth joining in as it is really the only way to do it. The 7km trip up river, usually with two rowers or *banqueros*, takes about an hour. There is then a short photo break, swim and optional extra raft ride into a cave set back behind the spectacular falls here. The thrills and spills come when you have to shoot the 14 small rapids downstream. The best time to do this is in August and September, during the rainy season, when the river is at its highest. You will need a good sunhat and covering for legs and arms if you are not to be sunburnt on the trip. Take something like a plastic bag or special waterproof protection for your camera and film as well. Many travellers have complained that the banqueros have tried to squeeze extortionate tips from tourists on the understanding that if they don't pay up, they are likely to have a bumpy ride back. Resist all such pressures, and once on terra firma make a point of complaining to the tourist authorities.

Getting there

The easiest way to Pagsanjan is to take one of the daily BLTB buses from Manila to the rather nondescript town of Santa Cruz. From there it is a short jeepney ride. If you are hoping to get to Pagsanjan from Tagaytay without going all the way back to Manila, you can take a bus to Zapote, transfer on to an Alabang-bound jeepney, and then bus to Santa Cruz before hopping on to another jeepney for Pagsanjan. It sounds like a lot of work but is actually quicker and less time-consuming.

Where to stay
Pagsanjan Village Hotel, Garcia St. Decent singles and doubles with air-conditioning and bath for P250–350.

Camino Real Hotel, 39 Rizal St. Tel: 2086. Nice-looking and spacious rooms with fan and bath for P500, and with air-conditioning and bath for P650–750. A good restaurant.

Wily Flores Lodge, on Garcia St. Rooms without fans for only P75, with fans for P100–150.

Pagsanjan Youth Hostel, 237 General Luna St. Charges P75 per person.

Where to eat
The Duraafe Restaurant, on General Jaina St. Recommended. Closes early at 20.30.

D'Plaza Folkhouse and Restaurant. Good pizzas, other food and live music.

Rizal
A great deal of the flatlands on the western side of Rizal Province have been eaten up by the urban sprawl from Manila, but as you travel towards the foothills of the Sierra Madre it becomes wilder, more configurated and rugged. Rizal's cultural and scenic assets include some noteworthy churches in the municipalities of Baras and Morong; Cardona, which is the centre of the milkfish industry; the lively market town of Binangonan; and Jalajal, which contains the remains of a *hacienda* built by Paul de la Gironier, a French doctor who lived in the Philippines at the beginning of the 19th century. Two places with considerable visitor interest, however, are the towns of Angono and Antipolo.

Angono
A mere 29km from Manila, the artist colony of Angono, with its lovely setting amidst the Rizal Hills, feels light years away. Artists are still working in Angono, and visitors who go there can watch them at work. The Balaw Balaw Restaurant, run by the artist Perdigon N Vocalan, doubles as a gallery. The town is best known, however, for its colourful and energetic Carabao Festival, held in May on the Feast of San Isidro de Labrador, patron saint of farmers. The town's own fiesta in honour of San Clemente is an equally lively event in which the whole town joins. The highlight of this November event is a parade of *higantes*, papier-mâché giants who are marched through the town on stilts, dressed in Philippine costumes.

Antipolo
With its cooler, fresher airs, Antipolo was a fashionable summer resort during the Spanish period. The renown of the town was also attributable to the presence of Our Lady of Peace and Good Voyage (Nuestra Senora de la Paz y Buen Viaje), a statue that was brought from Mexico in 1626 and left in the custody of Antipolo's resident Jesuits. Believed to have

mysterious powers, it was made patron saint of the galleons. Between 1641 and 1748 it was allegedly responsible for ensuring the safe passage of eight crews who sailed to Acapulco and back. The icon is still revered by the faithful who come during its four daily unveilings, to touch and offer prayers for safe journeys and the fulfilment of other personal wishes. To celebrate the Virgin's last voyage a serenade was held in Antipolo, a custom that has since been revived and expanded into a May pilgrimage and festival. Picnics are eaten and dance performances take place on a stage set up in front of the waterfalls at Hinulung Taktak. On the eve of 1 May, pilgrims set out from Manila to walk the 29km to Antipolo, arriving at dawn for a special mass held at the shrine. The town has a similarly spirited event, the Feast of Our Lady of the Immaculate Conception, every 8 December.

Where to stay
Most people trundle back to Manila after visiting Antipolo but, if you would like to stay over, there are a couple of reasonable options.

Villa Cristina Resort, on Taktak Rd. A friendly, small-scale operation with rooms for P350–400.

Las Brisas Resort, just off Provincial Road. A similar deal, with smallish but clean rooms for P300–350.

NORTH OF MANILA

Bataan
Bataan Peninsula was one of the first regions of the Philippines to be subjugated by the Spanish. Dominican friars first established missions here in 1572. Located southwest of Pampanga, the peninsula has a wild natural interior, with craggy buffs and headlands in the west, and developed coastal towns and small resorts to the east. Strategically well placed at the entrance to Manila Bay and with commanding views of the South China Sea, Bataan has played an important role in the history of the nation. It is best remembered as the scene of fierce resistance by Filipino-American forces to the Japanese in the Second World War. It was on the way from Mariveles on the southern tip of Bataan that thousands of emaciated prisoners of war died from malnutrition, disease and the brutality of their captors while being force-marched up the peninsula to the Japanese concentration camp at Capas, Tarlac. "No soil on earth," General MacArthur was later to remark, "is more deeply consecrated to the cause of human liberty than that on the island of Corregidor and the adjacent Bataan peninsula." At the summit of Mount Samat, the Dambana ng Kagitingan (Altar of Valour) honours those who fell during the war. There is an observation gallery located in the arms of the cross, from where it is possible to gain a complete view of the surrounding sea and land. Large areas to the south of Balanga, the provincial capital, are industrialised. An oil refinery, chemical complex,

shipyards, electronic assembly plants and an export processing zone are all located here. Bataan is also a major supplier of fruit to Manila. Some parts of the coastline, particularly the stretch between Olongapo and Bagac, are closed because of operations by the Philippine Navy. The Vietnamese Refugee Processing Centre, where English and other basic adjustment skills are taught to refugees, is located along this forbidden coastline at the town of Morong.

Starting in the northeast, there is a game refuge, the Roosevelt National Park, located near the town of Hermosa. A little further east the fishing town of Orani is the site for one of the Philippines' annual "crucifixions", on Good Friday. On a similar theme, a passion play is held in nearby Samal, a town also noted for its high quality embroidery work. Several pleasant, though unremarkable, beach resorts dot the coast between Balanga and Mariveles. At Calcaben guests can enjoy the excellent amenities of the Villa Carmen Resort and also hire bancas for the trip to Corregidor Island. Although the area around Mariveles is primarily an industrial zone, there are also several resorts, an Aeta minority settlement and several hot springs.

Getting there
Many Philippine Rabbit Company buses undertake the daily run from Manila to Balanga, Mariveles and Morong. Victory Liner buses ply the one-hour Olongapo to Balanga route.

Olongapo
Olongapo, where the US Navy was stationed until 1991, is a reasonably good base from which to explore the peninsula, the Mount Pinatubo area to the north and points further on such as the Zambales coastline. Most of the facilities associated with the entertainment industry that sprang up overnight to cater for American servicemen (rock clubs, girlie bars, nightclubs, brothels and hamburger joints) have now closed down. Four-minute boat rides can be taken from Olongapo to the former R&R resort of Grande Island, however, at the entrance to Subic Bay. An all-inclusive day trip there costs P875. Boats leave three times a day and can be booked through the Grande Island Office, Triple Crown Hotel, 1270 Rizal Ave, in Olongapo.

Where to stay
Manila Champion Hotel, on Rizal Ave. Decent rooms with air-conditioning and bath for P300–400. In the heart of the former, now struggling, red-light bar area.

Diamond Lodge, on Rizal Ave. Among the best cheap accommodation in town, with rooms for P200.

Moonstone Apartments, 2132–2148 Rizal Ave. Tel: 5301. Very good value with double rooms with air-conditioning and bath for P600–675. The hotel has a swimming pool, coffee shop and restaurant.

Mount Pinatubo

After possibly the most violent volcanic eruption of the century, the cost to human life and property caused by Mount Pinatubo's devastating discharge of lava, ash and other detritus is only now being reckoned. What is for certain is that the eruption that began on 15 June 1991 and continued until the start of September, caused almost 900 fatalities, over 1,000 hectares of arable farmland to be wasted, over 40,000 homes to be destroyed and a further 250,000 people to be left homeless. The ingenuity and optimism of the people affected by the eruption, their admirable gift for turning a calamity into an asset, is evident in the way the area has been developed into a major, and very successful, tourist attraction. No sooner had the ash and sand from the eruption cooled than it became apparent that an extraordinary other-worldly landscape had formed over the area: coagulations of up to 25m and strange ravines and escarpments that could be safely explored on foot or by jeep.

Touring Pinatubo

Hiking is an ideal way to see the bizarre formations that lie to the southwest of Angeles City, although you will only be able to cover a small section of this vast area this way. The ravines here are a confusing labyrinth of deceptive pathways and sometimes disorienting trails and sights, so it is not recommended to hike through this area alone. Jeepneys should be taken from the village of Sapang Bato to Pinatubo Trail, where you can then arrange to be picked up three or four hours later at the same point. If you want to see more of this spectacular landscape you can hire a car in Angeles and head southwest towards Porac and the Sacabia Lake Resort area. A photo exhibition based on the eruption can be seen at Paskuhan Village, one of the stops on the road to San Fernando. Motorised trips of the area for groups or individuals can also be arranged. Contact the staff at Clarkton Hotel, Don Juico Ave, or Island Tours, Captain Cook Hotel, Plaridel Rd, Plaridel I, both in Clarkview. The best overview of Pinatubo and its weird ash-heaps is afforded from the sky. This is a must for keen photographers and can work out to be a relatively inexpensive excursion. The Angeles City Flying Club (ACFC) has a large number of two-seater planes that will give you a one-hour tour for P500. Contact the ACFC, c/o Woodland Park Hotel, Lizares St, Dau. Charter flights for up to five passengers are possible from Manila but they are more expensive. For more information contact Interisland Travel & Tours, at 1322 Roxas Blvd, Ermita, Manila. Tel: 522 4748, fax: 522 5795.

Angeles

Like Olongopo, Angeles benefited economically from its proximity to an American military installation, in this case Clark Air Base. The withdrawal of the free-spending Americans, combined with the mess caused by the eruption of Pinatubo, had dire economic results for the city. The year 1991 was a truly dreadful one for this region of the Philippines but, like Olongapo, Angeles has pulled itself together admirably and the cut-price rates offered by its hotels, many of whom offer Pinatubo tours, have attracted a steady stream of visitors to the city. This has also brought new customers to its bars, nightclubs, restaurants and shops: A trade fair and carnival held here in February, and a religious festival in October to mark a Spanish naval victory over the Dutch, have helped to keep the visitor momentum going. The recovery is going to take a long time though.

Getting there
It takes 90 minutes by Philippine Rabbit bus from Manila. There are several daily. You can pick up a Manila-bound bus from Dau, a suburb of Angeles, or go to the terminal. There is also a special air-conditioned bus called the "Fly the Bus", which departs daily from the Swagman Hotel on Flores St, Ermita, at 10.30. There are several other bus arrangements like this leaving from other Manila hotels and well-known tourist venues like the Sundowner Hotel and the Birdwatcher's Inn, and from the Munchen Grill on Mabini St, Ermita.

Where to stay
Marlim Mansions, on MacArthur Highway, Balibago. Tel: 22002. Comfortable rooms with TV, air-conditioning, bath and plenty of elbow room for P700–850, suites from P1,500. There is a restaurant, swimming pool and tennis court.

Oasis Hotel, Clarkville Compound. Tel: 202 5847. Lives up to its name – quiet and friendly. Singles with air-conditioning and bath for P450–550, doubles with the same for P700.

Orchid Inn, 109 Raymond St, Balibago. Tel: 602 0370, fax: 888 2708. Neat, well appointed rooms with refrigerator, TV, air-conditioning and bath from P450–500. There is also a restaurant and swimming pool.

New Liberty Inn, on MacArthur Highway. Tel: 4588. Excellent value. Fan and bathrooms for only P200, air-conditioning and bathrooms at P250–400. Restaurant, swimming pool and garden. Friendly people running the inn.

Where to eat
The Manhattan Transfer Restaurant, on MacArthur Highway. A good place for steaks and other American dishes.

Thai Canteen, on Field Av. Spicy Thai dishes at reasonable prices.

Maranao Grill Restaurant, in the Oasis Hotel. One of the best spots in town for steak dishes.

The Sixties, on Don Juico Ave. Singaporean and Malaysian dishes are the speciality here. Also some German food available.

Peking House Restaurant, on MacArthur Highway. Good economical Chinese food.

Nightlife

La Copacabana, on MacArthur Highway, has a fixed-price happy hour from 17.00 to 18.00 in which you are invited to "drink as much as you can".

Hotsie Totsie, a disco on the ground floor of the Chicago Park Hotel.

The Music Box, one of the town's most popular discos is next door.

Margaritaville, an atmospheric hang-out for those nightbirds looking for a late night drink.

Studio I, on MacArthur Highway, has lively, slightly risque floor shows on Wed, Fri and Sat, from 21.00.

San Fernando

The capital of Pampanga province is best known for its realistic re-enactments of the Crucifixion, in which religious enthusiasts are nailed to wooden crosses on the outskirts of the city during the Good Friday celebrations. December is a festive month in San Fernando. A Giant Lantern Festival is held here, the province celebrates its Foundation Day on 11 December, and the town's increasingly well-supported Christmas Village is in full swing. This is one of the largest tourist draws the city has. The Christmas Village, located at Paskuhan Village, just outside San Fernando, is a permanent display of the traditions and customs associated with the festive season, and includes large arts and crafts displays, Christmas food, other novelties and the inevitable souvenir shops. The Pinatubo Museum and the tourist office are also located here.

Getting there

Several Victory Liner and Philippine Rabbit buses leave Manila each day for San Fernando. Olongapo-bound buses usually stop off at San Fernando on their way. There are also several Victory buses running through San Fernando from Baguio to Olongapo which often stop here as well.

Where to stay

Pampanga Lodge, in the plaza opposite the town's main church. Has comfortable singles and doubles with fan and bath for P150–250. These are the 24hr rates. Check for 12hr prices.

CORREGIDOR ISLAND

Not strictly part of Bataan Peninsula but commanding excellent views of it across Manila Bay, Corregidor Island's 6.5km length and tadpole-shaped outline belie its historical importance. The island bore witness to the comings and goings of pirates from Sulu and China and naval battles between the Spanish and the Dutch. Under the Spanish, bonfires were lit on the island to announce the approach of the long-awaited galleons, as well as hostile ships. A lighthouse was later erected there to guide ships along the coastline. Corregidor is best remembered as the spot where Filipino and American soldiers made their last stand against the Japanese in 1942. Corregidor was heavily bombed, obliging its defenders to retreat further into the island's labyrinth of tunnels. A shortage of ammunition, food and water, rather than courage, forced them to eventually surrender to the Japanese. May 6 is observed as Araw ng Kagitingan, "Day of Valour", and is a national holiday in the Philippines.

The island is divided into five geographical sectors: Topside, Middleside, Bottomside, Malinta Tunnel and the so-called Tail. Much of the island can be negotiated fairly effortlessly on foot, but sightseeing bus tours, which include the boat trip from Manila, can be booked from virtually any travel agent in the capital. There is also a light and sound show depicting the history of the island which visitors can pay extra to see. Visitors who wish to stay overnight can put up at the Corregidor Inn, a graceful old hotel that charges P1,700–2,000 for its nicely furnished rooms, and P4,000 for suites.

Getting there

It takes 70 minutes to cover the 48km by boat from Manila. The MV Island Cruiser leaves from the ferry terminal near the Cultural Centre Mon–Fri, at 09.00, doing the return trip at 15.00 Sat–Sun, at 07.30 and 13.30, returning at 12.30 and 17.30. The Villa Carmen Beach Resort near Mariveles also arranges day trips to Corregidor if you happen to be in the Bataan Peninsula rather than Manila.

Are you **suffering** from

Wanderlust ?

then subscribe to the only
magazine that guarantees **no cure** !
Wanderlust is *the* magazine for the independent-
minded traveller, covering destinations near and far,
plus features on health & safety, news & events,
book & product reviews, ...and a great deal more!
Available on subscription worldwide, with a money-back guarantee
– for details phone or FAX at anytime on
(01753) 620426, or write to
Wanderlust(BP), PO Box 1832, Windsor, Berks. SL4 5YG, U.K.

Chapter Eight

Zambales

THE WEST COAST

Extending from the Bataan Peninsula up to its northern tip at Cape Bolinao in Pangasinan, Zambales Province is divided from the central Luzon by the Western Cordillera, or Zambales Mountain Range. Its rugged topography takes its character from these chromite-rich mountains, and most of its towns are located along the narrow and much-indented strip of coast that runs the length of the province. Apart from mineral deposits, Zambales is known for its salt production, pottery, shell craft, rope-making, mangoes and production of the pungent bagoong, a fermented fish sauce. Mount Pinatubo is part of its mountain range and, until they were displaced by its eruption, the Aeta minority, some of the aboriginal inhabitants of this region, could still be found in parts of Zambales. There is good snorkelling along the length of this coast with beautiful coral reefs and sheer drop-offs for those with deep-sea equipment. Many of the beaches north of Santa Cruz are sufficiently off the beaten track to have remained relatively unspoilt. The area came under Spanish rule early on in their colonisation of the islands, and settlements at Iba, the provincial capital, Masinloc and Santa Cruz date back to the early 17th century.

FROM SUBIC BAY TO SAN FERNANDO (LA UNION)

North of Subic Bay, the highway soon reaches Castellejos, scene of the annual much-photographed Balaybay Calvary which takes place, as other re-runs of the crucifixion in the Philippines do, on Good Friday. Penitents, followed by flagellantes, lug their wooden crosses to a hilltop for a spectacle which may be altogether too realistic for some tourists. Unless you are interested in the BCI-Dizon Copper Ore project at San Marcelino, Pundaquit and San Miguel are the next points of interest on this route.

Pundaquit and San Miguel

Twice daily jeepneys connect San Antonio, an agreeable market town on the highway from Subic, with the quiet and unassuming fishing village of Pundaquit. The village has a good beach in its own right but a lot of people opt to spend their few hours or overnight stop in Pandaquit, exploring the area's craggy offshore islands, inlets and coves. Boats can be hired for about P500 a day to visit Capones Island and Camera Island, both of which have virtually unblemished beaches set between their rocky headlands, and interiors of bracken, stone and palm. You can walk along the sands at Pundaquit, cross a shallow river and soon reach San Miguel, the former site of an important US Naval Communications Centre.

Where to stay
Pundaquit
Capones Beach Resort. Tel: 632 7495, fax: 631 7989. The best place to stay here, with comfortable, well-kept rooms with fan and bath for P550, air-conditioning, bath and refrigerator for P750. Located on the beach with its own restaurant.

San Miguel
San Miguel Hotel. Rooms with fan and bath for P175, air-conditioning and bath for P300.

Big Foot Resthouse. Similar prices to above. Rooms with TV are P400.

Where to eat
San Miguel Restaurant. Has fine Filipino food and live music.

The Meathouse Carlsberg Garden Restaurant. Sounds faintly Teutonic. No surprises then to find that it serves hearty German dishes along with its Filipino choices.

North to Iba
There are quite a few more guesthouses in San Antonio and on the highway north of the town. The road continues through La Paz to the pottery town of San Felipe. There are some superb, little-known beaches 7 or 8 kilometres north of this town. If you have your own transport or can arrange for a jeepney to take you there and pick you up at an agreed time, a good day's swimming and snorkelling can be had here. There are more good beaches north of Cawayankling Bridge and Cabangan. You may catch glimpses of salt-beds as you drive towards Botolan as this is a large salt-production area. Shortly before arriving in Botolan, close to the Porac, you pass by the Villa Loreto Beach Resort, where you can rent cottages.

Botolan
Botolan used to be a good place for people interested in ethnic minorities, as the Negroto of the Zambales Mountains (Zambals), and other minorities like the Aeta and Aburlin, inhabited the nearby interior. It might be worthwhile enquiring whether the dispersal caused by Mount Pinatubo blowing its top has settled down by now and brought some of these tribes back to their ancestral birthplaces. On my last visit this was not the case.

Iba

"Provincial capital" is rather a grand build-up for what is in fact, a rather quiet market town of 27,000 inhabitants, but Iba has some good, though increasingly degraded, beaches, ranged to north and south of the town. These, and the popular Kalighawan Festival in March, are the town's main draw cards. Sand Valley is possibly the area's best beach. The restaurants here are worth sampling too.

Getting there

There are several Victory Liner buses daily to Iba from Manila via Olongapo, a journey of about five and a half hours. Buses also run from Olongapo to Iba.

Where to stay

Sand Valley Beach Resort, 1km north of Iba. Tel: 911 1739. Not as good as it used to be. A big difference in room rates between fan and bath ones for P350, and rooms with air-conditioning and bath with an asking price of P850.

Rama International Beach Resort, in Bangantalinga, roughly 4km from Iba. Fan and bath rooms for P600/800, air-conditioning and bath for P850–1,200. Well maintained with restaurant. They can arrange diving trips.

Vicar Beach Resort. Tel: 711 4252. The attraction here is its location along a pleasant, palm-fringed bay. Cottages with fan and bath for P450–600. Good value and restful.

Masinloc

The main road north of Iba passes Palauig Bay with its lighthouse and then proceeds to Masinloc, the former capital before Iba eclipsed the town. There are several offshore islands in this area which divers will want to check out. On one of them, San Salvador, it is possible to stay overnight, although the accommodation there may look less appealing when the sun goes down. A little further south, Magalawa Island is said to be excellent for snorkelling. Boats can be hired in Masinloc for the round trip crossings to islands of your choice, or by the day.

Getting there

It takes about six hours by Victory Liner bus from Manila to Masinloc, via Olongapo. There are also plenty of buses originating from Olongapo, which, like the Manila buses, will be going on to Santa Cruz and Alaminos.

Where to stay

Little Hamburg. Tel: 931 1089. Cheap and cheerful with rooms for P200–250 with fan and bath, or air-conditioning as an extra for P350–450. Good restaurant with Filipino and some European dishes, and German specialities. The disco could be a bit noisy. Cottages also at the Little Hamburg Seaside.

Puerto Asinan Lodge, at Kahawangan. Peace and quiet and a friendly atmosphere. P200 for rooms with fan only, P300 with bath. There is one spacious cottage for rent at P600.

The Hundred Islands

Located off the southern shores of the Lingayen Gulf in Pangasinan province, the Hundred Islands National Park, run by the Department of Tourism, is an interesting concentration of coral islands, a relaxing place to cruise around on a *banca* in search of that tiny white beach where you can play Robinson Crusoe for the afternoon. Divers will be less enamoured of the islands, though, as senseless dynamite fishing has clouded the waters of the area and caused severe damage to much of its underwater coral.

Lucap and Alaminos

Lucap and Alaminos are the main gateways to the Hundred Islands. Lucap has many hotels and guesthouses all competing for the custom of new arrivees, so it is sometimes possible to haggle down the price of a room. These two resorts can be itchy with people over the Easter and Christmas holidays, when prices soar. Bolinao, a little town a few kilometres to the north, is a good alternative during these peak times. Bereft of beaches but within access of the Hundred Islands, Bolinao has yet to be inundated with tourists. Alaminos, with its salt-making plant, is a good place from which to visit the Umbrella Rocks on Sabangan Beach and the subterranean river at Nalsoc Caves.

Bancas for the islands can be boarded at the pier in Lucap where you will have to buy a ticket for the park. The fare has been fixed at P250 per boat, but the bancas are allowed to take up to six people. From the park you can arrange your own transport for whatever period suits you. Most people find five or six hours about maximum. People usually end up on Quezon Island, as it has a drink and snack stand. If you are spending the whole day here it would be wise to take your own picnic. A good hat is advisable too as the island's low shrub and bracken affords little shade. The best diving is said to be off Lopez, Children's, Clave and Devils islands. You can rent snorkelling gear and fishing rods at Gloria's Cottages or Maxime by the Sea, in Lucap.

Getting there

There are hourly Pantranco North and Dagupan buses leaving Manila for Alaminos. All of these buses go via Angeles. It may be necessary to change at Lingayen. The journey takes about five hours. There are also Victory Lines buses going from Olongapo to Alaminos. There are some Baguio–Alaminos connections as well, run by the Pantranco North company.

Facilities
Lucap
Last Resort. P250 and P350 respectively for singles and doubles with air-conditioning and baths.

Maxime by the Sea. P300 for a room with fan, P450 with fan and bath, and P550 for rooms with air-conditioning. A well-established place with helpful staff who can advise on trips to the islands and snorkelling or diving gear. Nice terrace and restaurant.

Kilometer One Tourist Lodge and Youth Hostel. 1km from the pier head. Very cheap and clean place with dormitory beds for P100. Rooms with fan for P130.

Gloria's Cottages. Large rooms with fan for just P200.

Paradise Island Resort. On Cabarruyan Island, near Lucap. Fan and bath rooms for P450. Well run and friendly. Can arrange diving and boat trips around the islands.

Alaminos
Alaminos Hotel, on Quezon Ave. Tel: 552 7241. Singles with fan for P150, doubles with fan and bath for P200, and with air-conditioning and bath for P450. Well organised and clean.

Where to eat
Most of the hotels and guesthouses have their own restaurants. Guests very often end up eating there. This is the norm in most small towns in the Philippines. The pier area has a number of so-called "canteens" which have cheap food. The **Plaza Restaurant** in Alaminos serves Filipino food and often has a folk singer. The **Imperial Restaurant** is also not bad. The **Ocean View Restaurant** serves tasty dishes and is cheap.

Lingayen
Lingayen, the capital of Pangasinan province, is situated on an island in the Agno delta. It is really two cities, at least architecturally: the old Spanish section and the American one. The town's beach stretches for an impressive 11.5km along the gulf. The area around here is littered with the detritus of the American landing, and if you nose around you may come across the remains of mouldering US tanks, and at least one Japanese fighter plane.

Getting there
There are several Dagupan and Pantranco North buses leaving from Manila every day, via Angeles. There are also regular buses heading for Alaminos and Dagupan which pass through Lingayen.

Where to stay
Lingayen Resort Hotel. Rooms for P400 with air-conditioning and bath. Has a swimming pool.

Viscount Hotel, on Maramba Blvd. Tel: 137. P250 for rooms with fan and bath, P400 with air-conditioning and bath. Has a good restaurant.

The Lion's Den Resort, on Lingayen Beach. Tel: 198. Rooms with fan and bath for P400. Has a restaurant.

Dagupan

This minor port and market town is attractively situated on the Dagupan River and is bisected by waterways, each spanned by bridges. The town was founded by Augustinian missionaries in 1590. The 120,000-strong city has a university and a modern cathedral. There are some good beaches within a few kilometres of the town. Pugaro-Suit Island Beach, a little north of the city, has a 2km stretch of beach and dunes. Dagupan is a good place to sample seafood and the local delicacy, *cayo*, coconut candy.

Where to stay

Mc-Adore International Palace Hotel, on Galvan St. Rooms with air-conditioning and bath for P400. Has a swimming pool.

Boulevard Hotel, on Arellano St. Simple rooms with fans for P200.

Tondaligan Fiesta Cottages, in Bonuan, on Blue Beach. About 3km outside town. Tel: 2593. Recommended. Has good rooms with air-conditioning and bath for P600–750. Has a very nice seafood restaurant attached.

Hotel Mil Excel, on A B Fernandez Ave. Tel: 4463. Basic but comfortable rooms with fan and bath for P300, air-conditioning and bath P400. Has a restaurant.

Where to eat

Most of the best restaurants, especially Dagupan's well-regarded seafood ones, are located along A B Fernandez Avenue. These include the **De Lux Panciteria**, the excellent **Dagupena Restaurant**, and **King Wanton House**. There is a **Shakey's Pizza Parlor** along here too.

San Fabian

Everyone who comes to the little coastal town of San Fabian remarks on how friendly the people are. The town is strongly associated with faith-healing, a practice that has a strong following in the Philippines. White Beach stretches from Nibaliw West to Bolasi and has a few resort places nearby. The beach is more buff-grey than white. Bolasi and Alacan, 4km and 5km north of White Beach, have sandy beaches which are quieter and have not been developed for tourism yet.

Getting there

There are a lot of buses and minibuses running daily between Dagupan and San Fabian. If you are coming from Manila or Angeles it is best to get on a bus bound for San Fernando, Vigan or Laoag. You can then alight at Damortis and ride the remaining 15km or so south to San Fabian by minibus via Alacan and Bolasi.

Where to stay

Bremen's Resthouse. As simple and unpretentious as it sounds, with rooms for P100.

Sierra Vista Beach Resort. Tel: 7668, fax: 7532. Quite upmarket for this little place. Has spacious, well-furnished rooms with air-conditioning and bath for P1,200–2,000. It has a swimming pool and restaurant and various watersports amenities are available.

Lazy 'A' Resort. Tel: 4726. Another relatively expensive place. Rooms with air-conditioning and bath for P800–1,800. Two-bedroom cottages with fan and bath are more pricey at P1,700–3,000.

Agoo
You will pass through this town on your way north to Bauang. Few people stay overnight but there are one or two points of interest for travellers with time on their hands. The Spanish constructed a simple bamboo and nipa church here at the end of the 16th century. The building was destroyed in an earthquake in 1892. The church's Image of Our Lady of Charity survived the disaster. This was attributed to divine intervention and, as so often happens in the Philippines, the icon was upgraded to a shrine of its own and rehoused in the huge Agoo Basilica. It is a popular pilgrimage site during Holy Week. Other sights in Agoo include the Museo Iloko which has some interesting items of china, religious reliquaries and antiques. There is also the nearby Imelda Park and, on the road to Baguio near Pago, the former Marcos Park, a resort complex dominated by a massive bust of Marcos cut into the rock, an idea no doubt inspired by the more august presidential faces at Mount Rushmore.

Bauang
Although the beach here is not actually that good, more like a dirty grey tidemark than a dazzling white mirage, Bauang is rated as the most popular sea and sun resort in the whole of northern Luzon. The water, however, is usually clean, the coral reefs are attractive, and the town is noted for its pyrotechnic sunsets. The fishing is said to be good in these waters. *Bancas* with tackle or snorkelling gear can be hired for the day. Ask to be taken to the Poro Peninsula beach and coral garden. Naguilian is a small town about 10km from Bauang which is famous for the production of high quality basic, a drink much favoured by the Ilocanos people. This native wine is made from pounded bark and guava leaves mixed with fermented sugarcane juice, ingredients which give absolutely no clue to the taste of this potent brew. Accommodation in Bauang is extensive. If you cannot find what you are looking for, just go to the next hotel or guesthouse you see.

Getting there
Many Times Transit, Philippine Rabbit, Maria de Leon and Farinas Trans buses run between Manila and Bauang, via Angeles. It is also possible to fly PAL to San Fernando and then take a jeepney for the 8km south to Bauang. There are many other local bus connections linking Bauang with the other coastal towns mentioned before.

Where to stay
The following is a short digest of the accommodation on offer.

Cabana, in Paringao. Clean and tidy rooms from P800 have air-conditioning and bath. Hotel has a swimming pool, restaurant and watersports amenities.

Bali Hai Beach Resort, at Paringao. Tel: 412504, fax: 414496. Appealing and comfortable rooms for P850 with fan and bath, P940 with air-conditioning and bath. Offers a swimming pool, restaurant, windsurfing and the use of Hobie Cats.

Leo Mar Beach Resort, at Baccuit. Simple but pleasant rooms with fan and bath for P400–500.

Southern Palms Beach Resort, at Pagdalagan Sur. Tel: 415384, fax: 415448. Very comfortable rooms with TV, refrigerator, air-conditioning and bath for P650–1,000.

Sunset Palms Beach Resort, at Paringao. Tel: 413708. Rooms with fan and bath for P300–450. Has a restaurant.

Where to eat
Restaurants in some of the resorts and guesthouses are worth checking out. Foremost among these are those found at the **Bali Hai**, **Fisherman's Wharf** and **Villa Estrella**. **The Cabana** has a pretty authentic Mongolian barbecue every Saturday night.

San Fernando
This commercial and provincial capital of La Union Province was named at its founding in 1734, after the Spanish King Ferdinand. Built on seven hills overlooking Poro Point Peninsula, this well-appointed town of 86,000 people has a sizeable Chinese community. The Ma-cho, or "Heavenly Mother", Temple is an interesting *mélange* of Catholic and Chinese symbolism and decor. There is also a Chinese Friendship Pagoda near the Bayview Hotel. During the Feast of the Virgin (12–16 Sept), the Virgin of Caysasay is carried up to the Ma-cho Temple from its shrine in Taal City. Visitors usually try to climb the 153 steps up to Freedom Park for a sweeping view of the town and the South China Sea, although Mirador Hill is actually the highest observation spot. The Museo de la Union, not far from Freedom Park, presents a good introduction to the people and culture of the province. It opens from 09.00 to 17.00 daily. The museum is housed inside the Provincial Capitol Complex which also includes the tourist office. What there is of the city's nightlife is found in and around the central plaza where most of the discos and watering holes are located.

Getting there
PAL flies to San Fernando but the schedule is irregular so you will have to check with them in Manila or wherever your departure point is. The city is well served by Farina Trans, Times Transit, Maria de Leon and Philippine Rabbit buses from Manila. Vigan- and Laoag-bound buses frequently pass through San Fernando. There are also minibuses from

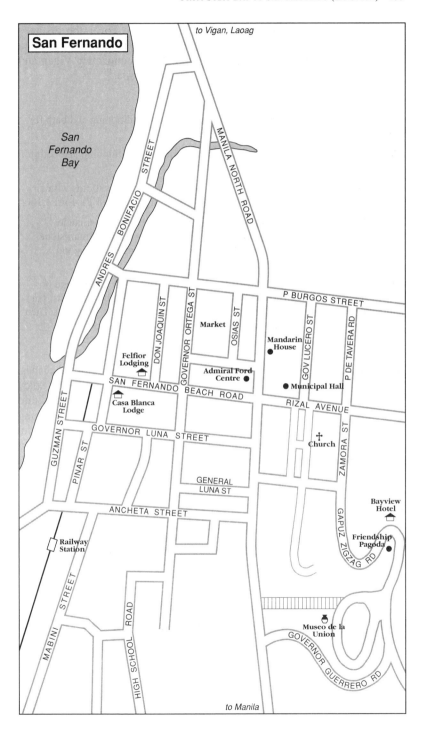

San Fernando

San Fernando Bay

to Vigan, Laoag

MANILA NORTH ROAD

ANDRES BONIFACIO STREET

P BURGOS STREET

DON JOAQUIN ST

GOVERNOR ORTEGA ST

Market

OSIAS ST

GOV LUCERO ST

P DE TAVERA RD

Mandarin House

Felfior Lodging

SAN FERNANDO BEACH ROAD

Admiral Ford Centre

Municipal Hall

RIZAL AVENUE

GUZMAN STREET

Casa Blanca Lodge

GOVERNOR LUNA STREET

ZAMORA ST

Church

PINAR ST

GENERAL LUNA ST

ANCHETA STREET

Bayview Hotel

GAPUZ ZIGZAG RD

Friendship Pagoda

Railway Station

MABINI STREET

HIGH SCHOOL ROAD

Museo de la Union

GOVERNOR GUERRERO RD

to Manila

Dagupan and San Fabian. Buses and jeepneys also cover the distance between San Fernando and Baguio. There are many Times Transit, Farina Trans, Philippine Rabbit and Maria de Leon buses connecting Vigan and Laoag with San Fernando before they go on to Manila.

Where to stay
Bayview Hotel, on Zigzag Rd. Good rooms with air-conditioning and bath for P300.

Plaza Hotel, on Quezon Ave. Standard rooms with air-conditioning and bath for P500.

Sea & Sky Hotel, on Quezon Ave. Tel: 415279. Superbly kept rooms with air-conditioning and bath for P550–750, suites with refrigerator and TV for P1,100.

Sunset Beach Resort, in Montemar Village, 9km north of San Fernando. Tel/Fax: 414719. Worth the inconvenience of being out of town. Small stone cottages in a pleasant garden for P450. Friendly establishment with good Filipino and continental-style food.

Scenic View Tourist Inn, next door to above. Tel: 413901. A good range of accommodation from dormit0ry beds at P100, nice rooms with verandahs, fan and bath for P300–350, and with air-conditioning and bath for P500–550. Their suites go for P850. Pleasant rooftop restaurant and swimming pool.

Where to eat
Nuval's Caranderia, on Don Joaquin St, specialises in regional dishes. Noted for its "jumping shrimp salad", which is made by pouring spicy vinegar and calamansi on to a small bowl of shrimps that are shocked into "jumping", before slipping into a quick marination period prior to being consumed. There are many good Chinese restaurants in San Fernando. Quezon Avenue contains some of the best. **The Bamboo Grill**, **Midtown Food Palace**, **Mandarin Restaurant**, and **Gold City Fastfood** are all good. The **Hongkong Seafood House** on Governor Luna St is also recommended. Cheap Filipino-style lunches can be had at the **Café Esperanza** in the town plaza.

MARCO POLO
TRAVEL ADVISORY SERVICE

Low air fares worldwide • Round the world flights
Unrivalled knowledge and experience

0117 929 4123

24A PARK STREET, BRISTOL BS1 5JA

Handmade festival decoration

Above: *A well-restored corner of Intramuros*

Opposite: *Tricycle drivers waiting for customers outside Manila Cathedral*

The Chinese Cemetery in Manila

Chapter Nine

Ilocos and Abra

The northwest section of Luzon is occupied by the region known as Ilocos, which consists of La Union, Ilocos Sur, Ilocos Norte and, slightly to the east, Abra. For once, the expression "rugged beauty" is more than a travel cliché, aptly describing as it does this narrow, straggling coastal plain with its backdrop of mountains and wild, sea-eroded shore. Vigan, the capital of Ilocos Sur and the *encomienda* of the conquistador Juan de Salcedo, is one of the finest Spanish cities left in the Philippines. There are many impressive Spanish churches in the region, often distinguished by massive stone buttresses that have been built into them as a reinforcement against earthquakes, to which this region is particularly prone. Rugged is a word that also applies to the industrious, resourceful and thrifty people of this region whose character has undoubtably been shaped by their surroundings. The Ilocanos are well regarded for their pottery, weaving and jewellery-making. The region is subject to climatic extremes, being exposed to typhoons from the South China Sea and the southwest monsoons. A great deal of rain can fall between May and October, while November through to April can be dry and parched, with droughts often reported in the far north.

VIGAN

This provincial capital of roughly 38,000 people, built at the confluence of the Mestizo and Govantes rivers, is generally considered to be the best-preserved Spanish town in the Philippines. At least that's what the film crews who regularly repair here to shoot scenes along Mena Crisologo Street, or against the backdrop of massive stone baroque churches, think. Vigan's charming backstreets, a clearly evident colonial heritage, pleasant little plazas and the sound of passing horse-drawn *calesas* evoke a strong sense of history, at least until the crazed motorbike and sidecar combinations that have recently started to plague Vigan's streets appear. The city lends itself to serendipity, especially in the early morning and evening. It may be useful to have a rough idea of the general layout of the city, however.

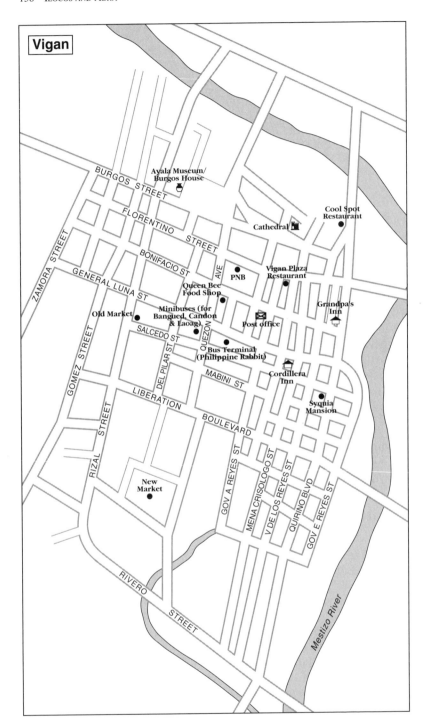

St Paul's Cathedral, first begun in 1574 but not completed in its present form until 1800, is a good starting point. Its bell tower, occupying a separate building, has beaten silver panels around its main altar. Carvings of Fu dogs above the outer doors of the Cathedral hint at the influence of Viga's Chinese community. The Archbishop's Palace, completed in 1783, is next door to the Cathedral. The area south of the Cathedral is especially visitor-worthy as this was the 19th century Chinese mestizo quarter. This wealthy élite built homes which incorporated practical features like solid stone and brick lower walls breached by arched doorways leading to small inner courtyards, with aesthetic touches and designs such as the sliding windows and polished wooden floors of the inner living quarters, tiled patios, balconies with Spanish style grillwork and decorative overhanging eaves. Syquia Mansion on Quirino Boulevard, built for a Chinese merchant in 1830, was the residence of Elpidio Quirino, president of the Philippines from 1948 to 1953, and contains an interesting collection of antique furniture and other personal effects that belonged to Quirino. The elegant Governor's Mansion on Mabini Street is another beautiful period residence.

Vigan is very much a city of plazas, most of which are named after a national hero or statesman and can, like the streets of many Philippine cities, be read as an analogue of the country's history. On the corner of Plaza Burgos for example, Plaza Leona Florentino Plaza is a memorial to one of the Philippines' first noteworthy women poets and playwrights, who was born near here at the Casa Florentino in 1849.

The Ayala Museum and Library on Plaza Singson Encarnacion is housed in an impressive colonial residence which is worth seeing in itself. It contains a good collection of Tingguian and Ilocano belongings, paintings and the personal memorabilia of Father Jose Burgos who lived here. The museum is open Tues–Sun, 09.00 to 12.00, and 14.00 to 17.00. Admission P5.

Much of Vigan's quotidian existence revolves around its two busy markets and Quezon Avenue, its main shopping strip. Vigan is also associated in the mind of Filipinos with its jar factories. Some can be found along Rizal Street. You will see these dark brown containers, called *burnay,* all over the province as they have many practical uses. The smaller jars are popular souvenirs as well.

Getting there

There are plenty of Philippine Rabbit, Farina Trans, Maria de Leon and Times Transit buses every day from Manila to Vigan. San Fernando has its Philippine Rabbit service doing this route and there are also services from Claveria and Aparri. There are several minibuses running between Laoag and Vigan as well as the four bus companies already mentioned who service this route. Some buses stop outside of the town, requiring a P4 tricycle ride into the centre.

Where to stay

The Cordillera Inn, 29 Mena Crislogo St. Tel: 2526, fax: 2840. A good chance to stay in a renovated colonial villa at affordable prices. Comfortable and elegant rooms with fan for P400, fan and bath for P600 and with bath and air-conditioning for P750–900. The restaurant here is also very good.

Aniceto Mansion, on Mena Crisologo St. Claims to be the top hotel in Vigan. Well-cared-for rooms with air-conditioning and bath for P800–950. Has a reasonable restaurant.

Grandpa's Inn, 1 Bonifacio St. Tel: 2118. One of the cheapest, though not necessarily cleanest, options in town. Rooms with fan for P150, fan and bath P240, air-conditioning and bath P380.

Where to eat

The Cordillera Inn. If you are staying here you can sample their breakfasts and judge for yourself. Has a good selection of Filipino and other dishes.

Cool Spot Restaurant. One of the more authentic food options in Vigan. Specialises in Ilocano regional dishes.

Vigan Plaza Restaurant. A good place for sandwiches and other snacks.

Victory Restaurant. Offers a different menu each day.

For fast food and take-away items try **Mr Donut** on Mabini St, or the **Queen Bee Food Shop** on Quezon Ave.

BANGUED

Situated on the Abra River floodplain, Bangued, the capital of Abra Province, dates back to 1598 when Augustinian monks founded it. Essentially the market centre of an agrarian people and province, Abra remains trapped unwillingly in a time-warp, confined by its own lack of development. An excellent view of this little-visited city and its girdle of fields and mountains can be had from Victory Park on Casamata Hill near the town centre. Abra's sights are limited to a small museum, a church that dates back to 1722 and the nearby Consoliman Cool Springs.

Getting there

A limited number of Times Transit buses run between Manila and Abra daily. It is easier from Vigan where there are several minibuses and Times Transit buses running from the terminal.

Where to stay

LAF View Inn, Burgos St. Charges P150 for basic but clean rooms.

Marysol Hotel, on Taft St. Tel: 8260. Rooms with fan for P250, air-conditioning and bath for P450–500. Very plain but said to be the poshest hotel in town.

Abra Diocesan Pastoral Center, in the church complex. Simple rooms with fan and bath for P150–200, with air-conditioning and bath for P300.

Restaurants in Abra

Good eateries are few and far between, but you can try **Syd's Café** close to the Municipal Hall, where they serve tasty chicken and steak barbecued dishes. **Jade's Restaurant** is also quite good. At night around the town square you can eat hot snacks at the street stalls.

LAOAG

Set 8km inland from the sea, Laoag is the capital of Ilocos Norte, one of the most beautiful provinces in Luzon. The city is a good base for forays into the surrounding countryside. For a fine view of the city and the broad Laoag River, climb Ermita Hill. The St William Cathedral of Renaissance, built between 1650 and 1700, with its sinking bell tower and exterior grotto and staircase, are well worth seeing. The Laoag Museum also justifies a visit as it contains a comprehensive collection of traditional costumes. The museum is open every day, 08.00–11.30, 13.00–17.00. Laoag's nightlife is limited to discos, one casino and the occasional Sunday cockfight.

Getting there

PAL flies to Laoag on Mondays, Wednesdays and Fridays from Manila. PAL offices are at the Laoag International Airport (tel: 220537), and along Rizal St. (tel: 220135). You can take a jeepney from the airport at Gabu, which is 14km from the town centre.

There are plenty of Maria de Leon, Farina Trans and Philippine Rabbit buses leaving Manila for the 10hr ride to Laoag every day. Buses go via San Fernando and Vigan. Philippine Rabbit buses leave on the hour from Baguio as well and there are several minibuses every day from Vigan to Laoag. There are regular morning buses for Aparri, Claveria and Tuguegarao. Jeepneys serve nearby *barangays*.

Where to stay

Fort Ilocandia Resort Hotel, near the airport, on Scuba Beach. Tel: 221166-70, fax: 415170. Very swish for these parts, with prices to match. Rooms with air-conditioning and bath go for P2,200–2,400, suites for P3,500. Excellent amenities with swimming pool, casino, disco, restaurant and watersports equipment.

Texicano Hotel, on Rizal St. Entrance on General Hizon St. Tel: 220606. Rooms with fan and bath for P150–200, with air-conditioning and bath in the new wing of the building for P450–570.

Hotel Casa Llanes, on Primo Lazaro Ave. Tel: 221125. Big rooms with fan and bath for P200, with air-conditioning and bath for P300–350. Good value.

Pichay Lodging House, also on Primo Lazaro Ave. Tel: 221267. Comfortable and friendly. Possibly the best value in town. Rooms with fan and bath for P200–250, with air-conditioning and bath for P300–340.

Where to eat

Peppermint Brickside Café, on Don Severo Hernando Ave. The best place in town for Ilocano cuisine. A little pricey. Folk music in the evenings sometimes.

City Lodging House, on General Luna St. Inexpensive Filipino food.

Bunny Food House, on Rizal St. Good affordable Filipino food.

Dohan Food & Bake Shop, also on Rizal St. Cheap and tasty.

Barrio Fiesta, on Nolasco St. Excellent Filipino dishes and others but a little expensive.

Colonel Fast and McBurgee, both on FR Castro Avenue. Fast-food restaurants.

Side trips from Laoag

There are many interesting side trips possible in the vicinity of Laoag. The pretty town of **Sarrat** is the seat of the Marcos family. You can visit the house where the old devil lived. It is now the Marcos Museum, and displays a good deal of Marcos-era memorabilia, starting with an old clock set at the time of his birth. There is a lovely church here founded by Augustinians. It was restored, along with the plaza in which it stands, for the ostentatious wedding of Marcos's daughter Irene in 1983. The elaborate ceremony, to which 5,000 guests were invited, plus the catering bill, is said to have cost the country over US$10 million. To the north of Laoag, **Bacarra** is renowned for its bell tower, visible from a great distance. The dome of the church collapsed after an earthquake in 1930, presenting today's photographer with a spectacular, pell-mell image of destruction and neglect. There are arresting views from the top of the bell tower as well. Bacarra is also renowned for its 17-string wooden harps which are still handmade there. **Seksi Beach**, near the town of Pasuquin, is a wild, windswept stretch of sands where you can see women working with salt pans. A few kilometres south of Laoag you come to **Batac** where there is another memorial to the Marcos dynasty, the Malacanang del Norte, a public museum. **Paoay**, with its famous "earthquake baroque" style fortified church, is close to Batac. **Suba Beach**, where the Fort Ilocandia Resort Hotel is located, is a wonderful fabulist setting of sweeping dunes, woolly hills and high-rising surf. **Suad White Beach** at Pagudpud, situated some 60km north of Laoag on Bangui Bay, is regarded by many seasoned travellers to the Philippines as the most beautiful beach in northern Luzon. The developers obviously agree with them as there is a government resort complex planned for this virgin stretch of coast. Go now while you can.

Chapter Ten

The Cordillera

The Cordillera Central massif, with its three mountain ranges forming a north-to-south extended spine down to the Central Plain, and separating the Cagayan Valley from the Ilocos coast, is a region of outstanding natural beauty. The area consists of the provinces of Benguet, Kalinga-Apayao, Ifugao and Mountain Province. The deservedly famous Banaue rice terraces, one of the world's great agro-engineering feats, are found in the province of Ifugao; Sagada has its hanging coffins and pastoral hiking trails; and Baguio, miraculously restored after a devastating earthquake struck it in 1990, is once again the picturesque and bustling summer capital it has always been. The Cordillera does not appear to have been affected by inflation as much as the lowlands of the Philippines or perhaps they just haven't noticed yet. Either way, many people who wish to extend their stay in the Philippines choose the Cordillera to do it. The region is home to some of the country's most fascinating ethnic groups, including, among others, the Igorots, Bontocs, Ifugaos, Tingguians, Kalingas and the little known Isnegs. In order to get from one town in the Cordillera to the next, you will pass over some of the steepest and most dramatic landscapes in Southeast Asia.

BAGUIO

Often described as the summer capital of the Philippines, this temperate city, the provincial centre of Benguet Province and a major market, transportation and tourist centre, manages to live up to most of the epithets (City of Pines, City of Lovers, etc) that have been applied to it. Burnham Park, located in the centre of the city, with the main commercial centre to one side, is a useful orientation point for visitors. Baguio's impressive main market is another good landmark, as the Dangwa Tranco and Philippine Rabbit bus terminals and many of the city's budget hotels are located in this area. The Victory Liner, Dagupan Bus Line and Pantranco North terminals are off Governor Pack Road, near the museum and tourist office. Baguio is a pleasant city to walk in but is also well served by jeepneys and taxis.

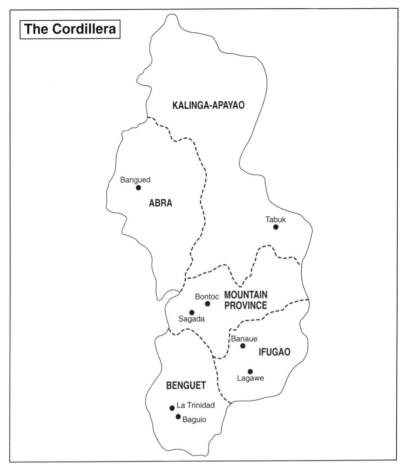

Baguio has a resident population of over 220,000 people but, what with all the business people, students and tourists who make it their temporary base, the city has been known to swell to almost double that number, particularly at special times of the year like Holy Week, when prices and even commodities in the city also become inflated. The city is an important educational centre, with five universities and the Philippine Military Academy. Many of the mountain and hilltribe people from the Cordillera come down to the city to study. Baguio is also a renowned spiritual centre, attracting droves of faith healers and zealous Christian missionaries. In many ways, Baguio is all things to all people. Rich Filipinos build their summer residences here, couples spend their honeymoons at one of its better hotels, and travellers en route to other destinations in the Cordillera linger here for a few days on their way. The city and its rather reserved residents receive mixed reviews from travellers. Some find it a welcome change from the high spirits and hassles of the Third World, while others complain that it wants the normal *joie de vivre* one generally associates with the Philippines. The writer Pico Iyer captured at least one side of the city when he wrote that, "In the mild drizzle of a dark afternoon, the place had a cosy market-town feel of hot cakes and light rain; on a calm Sunday morning, the peal of church bells through the mist took me back to an English village." With some of the heaviest rainfall in the country, an Englishmen might very well feel at home in Baguio.

Markets and shops

Baguio's famous market is a wonderful cornucopia of fruit, meat, fish, vegetables and fresh produce, mostly from nearby La Trinidad, aptly referred to as the "vegetable garden" or "salad bowl" of Luzon. Other parts of the market sell honey, flowers, homemade jam, raw tobacco, hilltribe textiles, woodcarvings and clothing. Strawberries (including strawberry wine) and *kalamay,* a native sweet, are some of the local specialities found here. The market is also a good place to come and eat. Its upstairs section has many *carinderias* and snack stalls offering cheap tasty Filipino food.

The market at Baguio is a good place to explore the handicrafts of this region, but it is also possible to buy direct from the makers at a reduced cost, although you will of course have to make the effort to visit the workshops and studios of these craftsmen. An easy way to sample handmade goods without making journeys into the back-of-beyond is to visit the St Louis Filigree School and the Easter School of Weaving, both in Baguio. The former specialises in silversmithery. You can watch young silversmiths at work in the trade school at St Louis University and buy direct from the St Louis Filigree Shop. Craftsmen at the Easter School of Weaving specialise in making clothes and household items like embroidered napkins and tablecloths. The school is located in the northwestern suburbs of the city and can be reached by jeepney from Kayang and Chungum streets. There are many individual shops as well in Baguio which sell good quality handicrafts at affordable prices. Munsayac Handicrafts on Leonard Wood Road is a good all-round store. Baguio Baboo Handicrafts on Laubach Road specialises in basketry. Baguio Paperworks on Ruiz Castro make paper crafts, and the Phoenix Gallery and Coffee Shop at Rizal Park has a good range of items from the Cordillera as well as old photographs and paintings for sale.

Sights and viewpoints

The parks and promontories of Baguio are good places from which to gain elevated and spacious views of the city. Burnham Park, named after the American who planned the city, is the largest, boasting a number of restaurants, a boating lake and orchidarium. It is not recommended to linger in the park after dark as there have been several cases of tourists being attacked there.

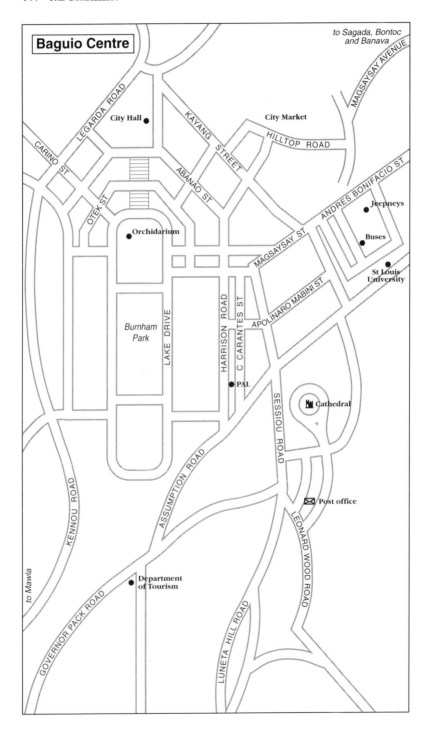

A trip to the Botanical Gardens, a little out of town, can be combined with a visit to Wright's Park and Mines View Park. From here you can get a terrific view of the hills surrounding the city and Benguet's gold and copper mines in the distance. Arguably the best view of Baguio is to be had from Dominican Hill, site of the Diplomat Hotel, a former Dominican seminary. A view almost to match this one is offered by Mirador Hill near by. Jeepneys can be taken from Kayang Street to this area. The 225 steps leading up to the Lourdes Grotto on the hill is a popular climb for pilgrims during Holy Week.

In the northern sector of Baguio, the Bell Church is an interesting excursion if you happen to be going in the direction of La Trinidad. The Bell Church Sect who own the premises somewhat resemble the Cao Daist sect in the southern and delta area of Vietnam, combining as they do the teachings and philosophies of Christianity, Buddhism, Confucianism and Taoism. There must be a touch of superstition thrown in for good measure too, as you can have your fortune told here if you ask. Jeepneys originating in Magsaysay Avenue, pass by the church.

Baguio Mountain Province Museum, on Governor Pack Road, has a very good collection of ethnic items from the Cordilleras, Mindanao and other parts of the Philippines. The museum is open daily from 09.00 to 17.00. The Filipino-Japanese Friendship Garden is near here. There is also a smaller museum devoted to the artifacts of minority groups within the Central Cordillera chain at Camp John Hay. Admission costs P10. The museum is open Tues–Sun, from 09.00 to 12.00, 13.00 to 17.00. Camp John Hay is a former US military recreation camp which is now run by the Department of Tourism who have opened restaurants and accommodation facilities here and created a pleasant landscaped garden area. It is a quiet and relaxing place where visitors can follow hiking trails and enjoy a wide range of sports like golf and badminton, and use the amenities of its gym. Other facilities include souvenir shops, a post office, cafés, a cinema and an ice-cream parlour. In the evening the site becomes the domain of restaurant-goers and film buffs. You can get there by using jeepneys marked "Scout Barrio" which leave from Harrison Road.

Getting there

PAL flies to Baguio every day. Their office in Baguio is on Harrison Road, near the Baguio Park Hotel. Tel: 2628. The airport is at Loakan, 12km from the centre.

Baguio is an important transportation hub so there are numerous buses passing through on their way to Manila, Abra, Vigan, Banaue and many other destinations. Buses start to leave Manila quite early, usually from 05.00, and continue throughout the day. The main buses running the Manila to Baguio route are the Danwa Tranco, Pantranco North, Philippine Rabbit, Dagupan Bus and Victory Liner fleets. You can also board these buses at Angeles as they stop over there. The journey takes about six hours, slightly less on the downhill return to Manila. Many

Philippine Rabbit and Marcitas Liner buses run from San Fernando to Baguio daily, and Pantranco North buses do the Dagupan to Baguio route which takes two hours. From Olongapo, there are Victory Liner buses every hour, passing through Angeles. If you are coming from Banaue, as many travellers will, there is a daily service to Baguio which leaves on the dot at 06.45 and 07.30. There are bus services to Bontoc and Sagada as well, and practically every other direction out of Baguio.

Where to stay
Top end
Baguio Palace Hotel, on Legarda Rd. Tel:7734. Rooms with bath for P1,550, suites for P2,500. Has a Chinese restaurant.

Camp John Hay, off Loakan Rd. Large. 1–4 bedroom suites for P2,400–3,000.

Hotel Supreme, 113 Magsaysay Ave. Tel: 2855. A quiet place just outside town with singles with bath for P1,100, doubles for P1,250, suites at P1,400.

Vacation Hotel Baguio, 45 Leonard Wood Rd. Tel: 3144. Comfortable rooms with bath and TV in nice setting for P1,450–2,000.

Standard
Burnham Hotel, 21 Calderon St. Tel: 2331, fax: 442 8415. Rooms with bath for P650–780. Nicely furnished old house with a Chinese restaurant.

Baden Powell Inn, 26 Governor Pack Rd. Tel: 5836. Good choice of rooms from dormitory beds at P140, singles and doubles with bath for P500–650, and two-bedroom apartment suites with kitchens for P3,200. Price sometimes includes dinner and breakfast (usually what they have left over in the kitchen), but watch out not to order drinks with it for which you will be charged an arm and a leg !

Kisad Pension House, 24 Kisad Rd. Tel: 3507. Good standard rooms with bath for P850–1,100. A good coffee shop here.

FRB Hotel, General Luna St. Rooms with bath for P500–650. Has a restaurant, coffee shop and small shopping centre.

Swagman Attic Inn, 90 Abanao St. Tel: 5139. Well-cared-for rooms with TV for P850–940. Has a restaurant. Like many of the hotels and guesthouses that use the world "Swagman", this one is Australian-run.

Economy
St Mary's Pension House, 11 Manzanillo Subdivision, Easter Rd. P120 for basic but clean rooms. Offers a discount for YHA members.

Casa Vallejo, 111 Session Rd Extension. Tel: 3045. An old colonial house with reasonable rooms at good rates. P250–340 standard, P350–460 with bath. Friendly staff.

Patria de Baguio, 181 Session Rd. Standard rooms with no frills for P350–470. Has a coffee shop.

Cypress Inn, 29 Abanao St. Tel: 2416. A cosy place with rooms for P390–500. Has a restaurant.

Pine City Pension, 21 Ferguson Rd. Very basic but clean and one of the cheaper options in town. Rooms for P150–200.

Where to eat
The Baguio Country Tavern, Abanao St. Very international selection, catering for tastes that range from Japanese to Spanish.

Cook's Inn, 21 Calderon Rd. You choose your own ingredients here and have them cooked for you.

Patria de Baguio, on the corner of Cathedral and Session roads. Good Filipino and other dishes.

Slaughterhouse Restaurants, near the slaughterhouse on Balajadia St. This alarmingly named chain is very popular with Filipinos as the food is, well, fresh! It is also, because it arrives direct from source, very reasonably priced.

Café by the Ruins, 23 Chungtug St. Has an excellent bakery but is best known as one of the finest restaurants in town for native Cordillera cooking. Good atmosphere with ethnic music. Drop into the Phoenix Art Gallery next door to see the work of local artists.

Attic Swagman Inn, on Abanao St. Has good Filipino and English style cooking.

Traveller's Restaurant, on Lakandula St. A good place for a Filipino or American breakfast.

Star Café, on Abanao St. Goes one better and serves Ifigao breakfasts.

Sizzling Plate Baguio, on Session Road. Excellent European-style food. Run by a Frenchman.

Dainty Lunch Restaurant, 56 Session Rd. Cheap breakfasts and lunches. Many local people go here.

Music and live performance
Anyone who thinks Baguio is restrained, a convent town in the hills, obviously hasn't investigated its vibrant live music scene. Baguio's folk music boom may have faded a bit but it has been superseded by several other forms of musical entertainment such as karaoke bars, rock clubs, disco and jazz venues.

Folk houses
Cozy Nook, on Assumption Rd.
Lighthouse, on the main gate of Camp John Hay.
Music Box Pizza House, on Zandueta St.
Cuckoo's Nest, on Bonifacio St.
Fireplace, on Assumption Rd.

Jazz
Songs, upstairs above the Patria de Baguio Restaurant on Session Rd.
Amapole Pub, on Session St. Sophisticated ambience with piano bar.
Café Teria, at the Marhalika Livelihood Centre.

Discos and nightclubs
Rumors, on Session Rd.
Spirits, on Otek St.
Peek a Boo Disco, on Abanao St.
Dream World Disco, out of town on the Marcos Highway.

Others
Baguio Coffee Station. Shows pop and rock videos.
Orange County, on Abanao St. Country and Western and rock music venue.
Joey's Place, on Legarda Rd. Popular karaoke spot.

Side trips from Baguio
There is no shortage of destinations near Baguio for one-day or overnight stopovers. These include Asin Hot Springs, an area of sulphur baths set in lovely green hills; a trip to Sablan, 21km west of Baguio, a small town which produces pineapples, coffee and the famous Baguio brooms called *boyboy* ; La Trinidad, the tiny capital of Banguet Province and a major fruit and vegetable growing area, and Crystal Caves, 5km from Baguio, a series of subterranean chambers believed to have been a former Igorot burial site.

INTO THE MOUNTAINS
Baguio to Kabayan
The 82km road trip from Baguio to Kabayan is not only spectacular, crisscrossing imposing dams, reservoirs, the meandering Agno River and the mountain rims and crests of the Cordillera proper, but is a spectacular journey back in time. Kabayan is one of the oldest towns in Banguet Province. The 10,000 or so Ibaloi who live here are known for their production of red rice and Arabian coffee, but Kabayan's real fame stems from its extensive burial caves and mummies. In 1977 helicopters landed one night near some of the man-made pits outside the town, and fled with a number of stolen mummies, a theft later blamed on foreign anthropologists. Several of the more important caves are now locked. It is still possible to see Kabayan's extraordinary mummies by undertaking treks of two to four hours with an experienced guide. So far, 21 of the burial caves have been mapped, but it is reckoned that there may be as many as 200 yet to be excavated. There is a museum in the municipal hall where you can also see mummies. It opens from 08.00 to 17.00.

Getting there
A Dangwa Tranco bus leaves Baguio for Kabayan at 09.30 every morning for the six and a half hour ride.

Bontoc
An ordinary-looking city in a spectacular location, Bontoc is the capital and main transport hub of Mountain Province. The 30,000-strong city is the cultural centre of the Bontoc Igorot, but there are also Kalinga and

Ifugao tribes living in some of the outlying villages. Bontoc's sights can be seen quite comfortably in two or three hours.

Bontoc on foot

Bontoc is right in the heart of the Cordillera, so visitors might like to pay a tribute to its colourful minorities and gain an introduction to their culture by visiting the very well laid-out Bontoc Museum. The museum was first started by Belgian missionaries who had been working in the area for many years. Its four rooms contain a number of interesting items including old photos, traditional houses and a number of artifacts associated with headhunting. Open from 08.00 to 12.00, 13.00 to 17.00. Admission P20. The All Saints Mission Weaving School is a good place to go and watch craftsmen at work making shoulder bags, clothing and other textiles. The Hiding Place Canteen, on the main street, sells a number of Igorot handicrafts as well. Zania's Store, near the museum, is another good place to find more Igorot artefacts. The Massage Centre of Bontoc is a good place to go for a professional massage treatment after long treks through the surrounding mountains.

Getting there

Bontoc is well served by buses and jeepneys. Several Dangwa Tranco buses run daily from Baguio starting at 06.00. There are also buses from La Trinidad. There is one early-morning jeepney from Banaue to Bontoc which people start to board around 06.30. It may leave as late as 07.30 depending on how quickly it fills. There is a later bus leaving between 10.00 and 11.00. There are several jeepneys doing the one-hour Bontoc to Sagada route every day.

Where to stay

Vista Pension, behind the municipal hall. Rooms for P90–150, doubles with bath for P450. A quiet back-street location with a nice coffee shop.

Village Inn. Clean and comfortable singles for P90, doubles at P120.

Bontoc Hotel. Tidy and cosy rooms for P60–120. This hotel has a restaurant.

Happy Home Inn. Tel: 3021. Singles for P60–120, doubles with bath for P180.

Where to eat

The choice is mostly limited to hotels that have restaurants. The best are the **Pines Kitchenette and Inn**, and the **Mountain** and **Bontoc** hotels.

Side trips from Bontoc
Rice Terraces at Maligcong

Unless you are in a rush to proceed to Sagada or Banaue, the rice terraces at Maligcong are an essential stopover for any traveller to this region. They are regarded as some of the most intact examples in the Cordillera. You will have to make a strenuous three-hour trek to reach the village and its two spectacular amphitheatres of green billowing rice. There are no real facilities here for travelers to stay, and it is advisable to take some food provisions with you. There are no direct jeepneys to the terraces but you might be able to catch one to Guinaang which would cut your walk down to two hours. The village of Maligcong is a further 2km hike up a trail which you will see just before you reach Guinaang. Ask to confirm the direction if you are not sure. While you are in this vicinity you may have time to drop in on Mainit where there are a number of hot sulphur springs. Mainit can be reached on foot from Guinaang by taking the road downhill. It is also possible to go directly from Maligcong but you would probably be better off asking a guide to lead you down this path as it can be quite convoluted even for people with a well-developed sense of direction.

SAGADA

For backpackers, budget travellers and those who appreciate the pleasures of nature, Sagada is the Philippines' alternative summer capital. People often end up staying far longer than they originally set out to, seduced by the town's agreeable climate, friendly residents, excellent guesthouses and tasty food, the area's full complement of cultural assets and its reputation as a meeting place for travellers. Sagada is a well kept little place, more village than town, set in a beautiful landscape with fine hiking trails that lead through cool pine woods, past stone-walled terraces and the area's famous "hanging coffins", and out to limestone pinnacles and burial caves. Sagada gets its fair share of rain, particularly from June to September, but it can rain at any time. The months from December to February are often blessed with clear blue skies, but the nights can be cold, so take a light sweater or jacket and a folding waterproof raincoat just in case. You may have to ask your guesthouse for an extra blanket at night.

A walking tour

Stop off first at the Masferre Inn where you can buy a good map of the area and its hiking trails for P5. A close-up view of some of Sagada's hanging coffins can be had by walking past the church opposite the St Joseph Resthouse, until you reach the graveyard on the hill above it. Drop down into the gorge behind and you will see a faint trail leading left towards a rock face. It only takes about ten or fifteen minutes from the main road, but very few people go there. The coffins are suspended on the rock (an old Igorot burial custom) and are made of pine. If you look carefully you will see chairs set under the coffins which have been placed there for the spirits to rest on.

It is advisable to hire a guide or join one of the morning or afternoon group treks that get organised most days if you wish to see some of the many burial caves which are located around the town. Most of the guesthouses in Sagada can easily arrange a tour of this kind. Several of the caves near town, like Lumiang and Sugong caves, can be easily explored

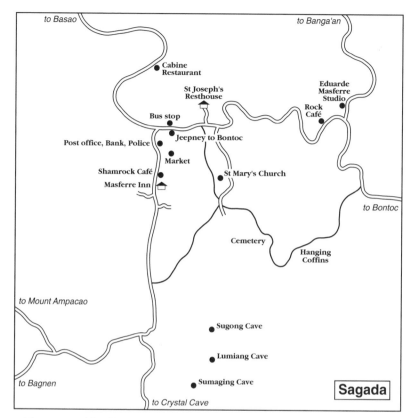

to Basao

to Banga'an

Cabine
Restaurant

Eduarde
Masferre
Studio

St Joseph's
Resthouse

Rock
Café

Bus stop

Post office, Bank, Police

Jeepney to Bontoc

Market

St Mary's Church

Shamrock Café

Masferre Inn

to Bontoc

Cemetery

Hanging
Coffins

to Mount Ampacao

Sugong Cave

Lumiang Cave

to Bagnen

Sumaging Cave

to Crystal Cave

Sagada

without a guide. Kerosene lamps are usually taken on more extensive forays to Crystal and Sumaging caves, as torches are not strong enough to penetrate the gloom. You will need a good pair of shoes or boots as well. Many of the caverns and chambers are wet and slippery. Visitors bent on penetrating into the deepest reaches of these caves, an exploration that could take several hours, should be prepared to paddle, or even wade at points through cool water with low overhangs. This is definitely not an option for claustrophobes.

A master photographer

A little under 1km out of town on the road to Bontoc, visitors should make a point of dropping into the Eduardo Masferre Studio. Masferre was a gifted photographer who set himself the task of recording the vanishing culture of the region's ethnic minorities, particularly the Igorots and Ifugao for whom he virtually became their official self-appointed photographer. Masferre's atmospheric images, printed in grainy, high contrast monochrome, span a period from the 1930s up to the late 1950s and are probably the best photographic record left of this era. Masferre's work has been published in a book which can be bought either at the studio or in the Masferre Inn which is run by the late photographer's family. You can also buy postcards and prints of his work. A revival of interest in Masferre's images is apparent as you travel around the Cordillera, where you will frequently come across his work gracing the walls of museums, hotels and cafés.

Getting there

The Baguio to Sagada route is well serviced by Skyland Express, Dangwa Tranco and Lizardo Trans buses. Buses leave early at 06.00, 07.00 and 07.30 daily. There are also buses from La Trinidad. Catching a jeepney there before departure will guarantee you a better chance of a good seat. The Sagada to Baguio run can leave any time between 05.30 am and 06.30. There are sometimes buses at 09.00 but the last two times I waited here for one to turn up, nothing happened. My alternative was to take the first available jeepney to Bontoc and then change on to a Baguio-bound bus. If you are going on to Banaue you will have to hop on a jeepney heading for Bontoc and then catch another bus or, more likely if it is later in the morning, a jeepney for the rest of the way.

Where to stay

Masferre Inn. This is highly recommended as it is a popular place for travellers to meet up, has a pleasant, tastefully decorated ambience and a good restaurant hung with large blowups of Eduardo Masferre's photos. Spacious rooms for P75–120.

Ruby's. Friendly and clean. Excellent rooms for P75–130.

Saint Joseph's Rest House. Set in a pleasant landscaped garden. A friendly place with helpful staff. Small but adequate rooms for P50–75. Shared bathroom and sinks for washing your own laundry. Tall people may find some of the hardboard beds a little short.

Pines View Inn. Warm atmosphere in this family-run guesthouse, but unfortunately only two rooms to rent. Good value if you can get in, as the rooms are spacious and have their own kitchens. Not bad for P70–120.

Olahbinan Resthouse. Cosy rooms with bath for P450, without for P100–250. There is also a suite at P1,000. Good restaurant here.

Rocky Valley Inn. A clean and convivial guesthouse with rooms for P75–130.

Where to eat

Moonhouse Café. Good food in an almost trendy setting.

Cabine Restaurant. Reservations are necessary for this superb little restaurant serving regional and Filipino dishes.

Masferre Café. In the guesthouse. Good simple food. Huge quantities. An excellent place to have breakfast before catching a long-distance bus.

Shamrock Café. Small place that does good lunches and early dinners. Banana cake and yogurt with mountain honey, two Sagada specialities, are usually available here.

Rock Café. A pub-grotto that stays open a little longer than the usual 21.00 closing time observed by everyone else in Sagada. A cosy place near the Underground River.

Side trips from Sagada

A pleasant, undemanding walk of one hour or less can be taken from Sagada to the small town of **Banga'an** where there are a few original Igorot houses still left. Watch out for backyard dogs if you step off the main road to explore the pathways connecting private houses on Banga'an's slopes, though. A slightly longer hike will get you to **Mount Ampacao** where you will be rewarded with a fine overview of Sagada and its surrounding countryside. If you can find it, **Bokong Waterfall**, directly north of town, is a pleasant place to have a swim in the natural cistern that forms beneath the cascade. Theoretically, it should take about 30 minutes to get to. It took me about an hour and a half after enquiring the way of several people I met en route there.

BANAUE
Guardians of the Terraces

Few ethnic minorities in the Philippines have attracted as much attention and interest as the Ifugao. Inhabiting some of the more insalubrious parts of the Cordillera, the Ifugao, with their centuries-old beliefs and practices have, at least until recent developments in communications and roads, managed to preserve their traditional culture and to resist the more radical forms of change other tribes have succumbed to.

It is not their tribal customs or ceremonial dress, still occasionally worn by village elders in remoter areas, that the Ifugao are celebrated for, however. Ifugao Province is renowned for its matchless rice terraces, the most spectacular being found in and around the town of Banaue. Believed to date back some 2,000 years or more, these masterpieces of agricultural engineering have been described, not without some justification, as the eighth wonder of the world. Starting at the bottom of river valleys, they rise, tier upon tier, to heights of over 1,000m in some cases. Impressive though these working rice fields are, with boundary walls that are said to reach a total length of 20,000km, visitors to the Ifugao terraces are even more astonished to discover that this giant reclamation task was achieved with primitive tools such as wooden shovels, spades and sharpened and scalloped stones. With no plains suitable for rice cultivation, the Ifugao were obliged to create fields by carving shelves from the mountainsides, each paddy carefully shaped to fit the contour of the slopes. Some of these mountains must have sorely tested the endurance of the Ifugao, but these tribespeople managed to transform even the steepest slopes into giant gardens of fantastic beauty, each terrace carefully irrigated by a skilfully designed system of water channels that run from upper to lower paddies. The walls of the terraces are made from stones taken from riverbeds and

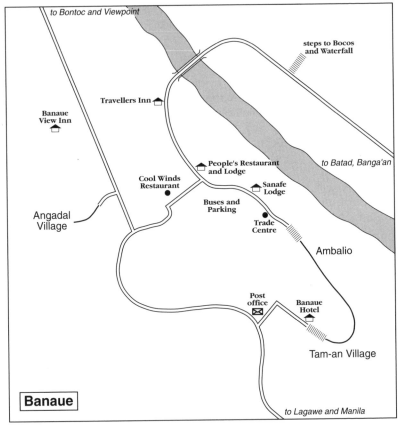

to Bontoc and Viewpoint

steps to Bocos
and Waterfall

Travellers Inn

Banaue
View Inn

to Batad, Banga'an

People's Restaurant
and Lodge

Cool Winds
Restaurant

Sanafe
Lodge

Buses and
Parking

Angadal
Village

Trade
Centre

Ambalio

Post
office

Banaue
Hotel

Tam-an Village

Banaue

to Lagawe and Manila

sealed together with clay. The Ifugao terraces are often compared to other man-made wonders like the pyramids at Giza or the Great Wall of China, but while these monuments were built by slaves, coolies or other forms of forced or bonded labour, the terraces at Banaue appear to be the result of a voluntary and co-operative effort by a people united in their will to survive and sustained by a trust in their gods.

Conquistadors and headhunters

The Ifugao were first "discovered" by the Spanish in the 16th century, but throughout the colonial period strongly resisted them. When the Spanish left in 1898, most of the Ifugao region remained virtually unexplored. Belgian missionaries began harvesting souls in this region during the 18th century, a task later taken over by Dominicans from the lowlands. The result has been a sizeable flock of Christianised Ifugao.

Nature worshippers and animists by inclination, the Ifugao were, until quite recently, known to be practising headhunters. War dances took place on the rice terraces themselves, one man being elected to extract revenge against a member of a rival group. As recently as the 1980s, occasional, though increasingly rare, cases of headhunting were reported in the area. In the last few years many young Ifugao have left their ancestral homes in search of jobs in cities and towns or in the tourist industry. Other tribe members have abandoned their fields to work in the goldmines in the neighbouring provinces of Nueva Vizcaya and Benguet. In Banaue and other parts of the Cordillera one can see terraces that are overgrown with weeds and others that have dried up because irrigation channels have not been properly worked or maintained. The disappearance of forest cover due to illegal logging, which appears to be rampant in the area, has also had an adverse effect on the supply of water to the terraces.

The town

Banaue itself is fast becoming a casualty of tourist, or at least promotion, overkill. This does not detract from the beauty of its terraces, but it might do in the near future. Spurred by the growing number of visitors arriving on the daily bus from Manila, the town appears to be sprawling unchecked over its once productive fields. A preference for corrugated metal homes over the traditional houses on stilts, with their thatched, pyramid-shaped roofs, has turned a charming, though no doubt harsh, pastoral village in the mountains into an urban eyesore. In an irony that is becoming all too common throughout the developing world, the triumph of prefabricated homes, honking jeepneys and rotting heaps of garbage sited in rivers, where only a decade ago the Ifugao fished with nets for mountain carp and trout, threatens to undermine the very environment that attracts people here in the first place.

That said, Banaue still occupies a magnificent, though degraded, setting and one that no visitor to the north can afford to miss. The town reaches an elevation of 1,300 metres. The area where buses and jeepneys park and where there is a lively Saturday morning market could be designated the centre of Banaue. The town's one bank is near here, and the Trade Centre, rebuilt a few years ago after being destroyed by fire, is a reasonable place to look for regional crafts. Most visitors, rain permitting, spend their days in Banaue wandering over the paths that thread across the terraces, visiting Ifugao villages, or walking up to Banaue View Point, a spot at the top of town from where there are magnificent views across the terraces.

Getting there

There is only one bus a day from Manila, a Dangwa Tranco vehicle which leaves between 07.00 and 07.30 and takes a good nine hours to get to Banaue. If this one is full you could try taking a bus heading in the direction of Llagan, Tuguegarao and Aparri. Alight at Solano and then take a jeepney to Lagawe and another one to Banaue from there. There is no accommodation in Lagawe so you should not arrive there too late if possible. There are also a couple of Dangwa Tranco buses every morning from Baguio to Banaue. These leave at 06.45 and 07.30. In the reverse direction, the Dangwa Tranco buses depart from Banaue to Baguio at exactly the same time. The key Banaue to Manila bus leaves between 07.00 and 07.30.

Where to stay
Banaue Hotel. Tel: 4087, fax: 4048. The most exclusive accommodation in town, and the only one with a fax machine. Singles and doubles with bath for P1,900 and P2,300. Unquestionably the most comfortable place in town with an excellent restaurant, bar and swimming pool.

Banaue View Inn, on the Bontoc Rd. Tel: 4078. Dormitory beds for P100, rooms with bath for P440–550. Many of the rooms have an excellent view of town.

Sanafe Lodge. Tel: 4085. Dormitory beds for P100, singles and doubles with bath for P550 and P700. Quite comfortable rooms, though sometimes noisy as the hotel is located in front of the bus rotary. Has a restaurant and a lovely observation gallery overlooking part of the town.

Green View Lodge. Tel: 4021. A humble but clean and tidy place with dormitory beds for P100, and rooms with bath for P400–500.

Traveller's Inn. Tel: 4020. Basic but clean and very cheap for Banaue. Rooms for P120–150.

People's Lodge. Tel: 4014. Simple but cosy rooms for P120–190, P450 with bath. Has a good bakery and restaurant.

Where to eat
Cool Winds. A snug little place built on a rock bluff near the market. Favoured by locals. Basic Filipino food at lower than average prices.

Banaue Hotel. More upmarket but offers set meals for tourists which sometimes include Ifugao dancing.

Stairway Lodge. A popular meeting place for travellers and an evening dinner venue. Cheap and cheerful.

Halfway Lodge. Everything said about the aforementioned applies here. You will see the same backpacker crowd at one or the other of these two popular places.

Las Vegas Restaurant. Offers similar food to all the other restaurants in Banaue but may be a little cheaper than average.

Side trips from Banaue
The picturesque village of **Poitan** can be reached in 30 minutes from Banaue, making it one of the shortest hikes outside of town. Despite its proximity to Banaue it retains some interesting vestiges of local culture, among which is a sacred stone post, protective stone walls which completely surround the village and a pit at the centre of the settlement where village elders gather as they have done for centuries, to discuss the affairs of this tiny community. There are active woodcarvers and weavers here too. Poitan is not without its commercial side, though, and if you ask

to see the village's collection of *bulol*, Ifugao rice god statues, you will soon enough be asked for a fee to photograph them.

Despite its inconvenient location, **Batad** has become quite well known in the last few years. You should be in fairly good shape to hike for two or three hours uphill to reach this secluded village, but it is obviously worth the effort as several people do it every day. Batad has one of the most beautifully maintained rice terraces in the Cordillera, and its relative isolation, culturally speaking, has been a blessing, helping the village to avoid some of the negative aspects of tourism Banaue is now facing. Batad is certainly worth an overnight stay, as it is possible to walk from here to an inviting natural swimming pool an hour or so away, and also combine your visit with a two-hour trek the next day to **Cabulo**, a hamlet set right in the middle of rice terraces that seems to embody the ideal of an Ifugao village even more than Batad does. The super fit can walk a further three hours beyond Cabulo to **Pula**, an even remoter, less spoilt Ifugao village.

Getting there

It is an arduous but straightforward enough procedure getting to Batad and then on to Cabulo. A jeepney will take you the first 12km on a normal paved road, and then drop you off at the trail for Batad. You should try to prearrange a time for returning to Batad with the driver, either the same day or for the following one unless, that is, you are prepared to walk back to Banaue. If you decide to do this and then change your mind, you might be lucky and see a jeepney going your way. They are always prepared to stop and pick up another passenger, even if it seems a physical impossibility squeezing in another person.

Where to stay

All the accommodation in Batad is much of a muchness: peaceful, basic rooms, simple food, but always friendly and helpful. Nobody will rush you here. You may wish to take some food or drink supplements with you, although you can usually get the essentials here, including bottles of San Miguel. All the inns charge the same sort of fee – something in the vicinity of P75. A stay in Batad or Cabulo is definitely not going to break the bank. In Batad you can stay at the **Foreigner's Inn** near the church, the **Welcome Inn**, near the main viewpoint, **Romeo's Inn**, which overlooks the village, the **Hillside Inn**, which probably has the most commanding view, or at a handful of other cosy, perfectly adequate little places. Accommodation in Cabulo, at least at the time of writing, is limited to Lydia Domanglig's place. Lydia, the owner, gives visitors a warm welcome, and is in charge of everything right down to the cooking. She charges a modest P50 for a night's accommodation.

Chapter Eleven

The Far North and East

A large chunk of the northeast of Luzon is occupied by the Cagayan River valley, a large, fairly populated land tract that absorbs parts of the provinces of Cagayan, Nueva Viscaya, Quirino and Isabela, and a number of little-visited offshore islands like the Batan Islands. Beyond the populous valley, vast areas of Cagayan province in particular remain only sparsely settled, forest covering at least half the region, with swamps, grassland and sudden patches of arable land accounting for the rest. Cagayan and Isabela boast some of the most beautiful and untamed stretches of coastline in Luzon, the potential of which is only just being realised. The Cagayan Valley itself has been inhabited since ancient times and has provided archaeologists and anthropologists with finds that have been dated back to 8030BC. Before the Spanish arrived, the Japanese and Chinese appear to have traded with the inhabitants of this area. The Spaniards founded missions wherever they found settlements, and giant fortified churches were erected by the Dominicans. The valley became the seat of the Diocese of Nueva Segovia from 1594 until 1755, conferring on the area a temporary importance it sadly no longer retains. One feels the presence of these long-gone intruders through their remains. A combination of geography, the harsh unpredictable northern elements, lack of funds and the relative obscurity of the area have conspired to keep this region at the periphery of tourism. Undeveloped, but full of scenic attractions, visitors to this wild part of the Philippines may have to rough it at times, but the rewards for those willing to put up with the inconveniences more than repay the effort.

BATAN ISLANDS

The most important islands, both economically and geographically, are Sabtang, Ibayat and Batan. The northernmost of the small chain, called Y'ami Island, is far closer to Taiwan than it is to Manila. The climate of the Batan Islands, also known as the Batanes, is severe and unpredictable, as a result of their position, making flights to the little grass strip there subject to frequent delays and cancellations. The islands are also exceptionally typhoon prone, especially between June and September, while the months from October to early March can be very wet. In practical terms, this limits most visits to April and May, not much of a tourist season.

The inhabitants of the Batanes are mostly native Ivatans. Life is not easy here and the main food staple in a bad year may be little more than a monotonous round of root crops supplemented with vegetables stored from the last harvest and a generous haul of fish, weather permitting that is. One of the Ivatans' main preoccupations is ensuring that the walls and roofs of their houses are sufficiently insulated for the family to hunker down during a strong typhoon. Squat cottages with tiny doors and windows, built in sheltered areas, with lime and stone walls of up to 1m thick and with heavily laden roofs of *cogon* grass, tightly bound with rattan and sticks, are the archetypical Ivatan homes which seem so cosy and picturesque to visitors.

Getting there

The most practical way to get there is by flying, although there are boats from Manila to Basco on Batan Island, but only four a year! PAL flies three times a week from Manila to Basco. It also lays on two extra flights via Tuguegarao and another two via Laoag. Inter-island boat services are good when the weather co-operates, but even in what appear to be fairly clement conditions the swell can be alarming.

TUGUEGARAO

The capital of Cagayan Province was severely damaged by US bombing in the Second World War. The old colonial part of town and the cathedral have been repaired since then, though rather unimaginatively. The city is situated on a bend of the Cagayan River. Its main features are its large market and the provincial capital complex which is located a few kilometres outside of town. The building houses the important Cagayan Provincial Museum with its interesting and eclectic assortment of religious artifacts, Chinese porcelain, antique furniture, fossilized teeth and the skeletons of stegodons and other creatures that inhabited the valley over half a million years ago.

Getting there

PAL flies return to Tuguegarao every Monday, Wednesday, Friday and Sunday from Manila. The PAL offices are at the airport and on Rizal Street (tel: 446120).

Pantranco North buses leave on the hour for the nine-hour drive to Tuguegarao, going via Santa Fe, Cagayan and Ilagan. There is one bus a day from Bontoc which goes via Banaue. Roxas- and Aparri-bound buses from Manila stop off at Tuguegarao. You can also catch jeepneys from places like Tabuk and Tinglayan.

Where to stay

Hotel Delfino, on Gonzaga St. Simple, clean accommodation for P200–250.

Pension Abraham, on Bonifacio St. Tel: 1793. Rooms with fan for P150–200, with bath for P240–270, and with air-conditioning and bath for P300–375.

Hotel Leonor, on Rizal St. Tel: 1806. Basic rooms for P100–160, better rooms with fan or air-conditioning for P120–200 and P240–300. Quite comfortable with a popular restaurant.

Pensione Roma, on Luna and Bonifacio Sts. Tel: 1057. Rooms with fan and bath for P240, air-conditioning and bath for P550–600. Well organised and friendly place with its own restaurant.

Olympia Hotel, on Washington St. Tel: 1805. Rooms with fan and bath for P160–200, air-conditioning and bath for P 260–320. Clean and simple place with restaurant.

Where to eat

The **Apollo Restaurant** near the bus terminal is popular for its cheap *ihaw ihaw* food. The **Pampanguena Restaurant** has a good selection of dishes, pastries and cakes. Hotels and inns serve fairly standard Filipino food, the best among them being found in the restaurants at the **LB Lodging House**, **Georgies Inn** and the **Hotel Delfino**.

Side trips from Tuguegarao

The main focus of interest in this area, and the reason why many people make Tuguegarao their base for a day or two, is the **Callao Caves National Park**. The caves are located about 25km east of Tuguegarao and can be reached by jeepney or tricycle from nearby Penablanca. Only seven out of an estimated 100 chambers have been excavated. The caverns are large, with well-preserved stalactites and stalagmites, coloured walls and, in some cases, natural skylights. The first chamber, reached after climbing 206 steps up a cliff face, contains a chapel with pews, a stone altar and a recreation of the grotto at Lourdes. Visitors who wish to stay overnight can put up at the Callao Caves Resort.

To the north of Tuguegarao, near **Iguig**, there is a curious 11ha field called "Calvary", in which lifelike concrete statues depicting the Stations of the Cross have been placed. This is an important pilgrimage spot during Holy Week. Near Gattaran, some 40km east of Tuguegarao, are the impressive 100m-high **Tanlagan Waterfalls**. Not far from here are the **Mapaso Hot Springs**. Also to the north, ornithologists will appreciate the **Magapit Game Refuge and Bird Sanctuary**.

APARRI

Apparri, a fishing and trading port as well as oil depot, is the most important settlement on Luzon's northern coast. There is a good beach to the east of town with excellent surf. Aparri is a big producer of *bagoong,* a strong shrimp sauce. Most people who stay in Aparri have come for the sports fishing. Hemingway would have liked nearby Point Escarpada, the best piece of marlin fishing to be had in the Philippines. You can hire boats at San Vicente for big game fishing trips of this kind.

Getting there
Daily Pantranco buses from Manila to Aparri go via Ilagan, Tuguegarao and Gattaran. It is a long 11hr haul. There are also buses from Laoag and Vigan, and one bus a day from Claveria.

Where to stay
Pipo Hotel, 137 Macanaya St. Tel: 22122. Reasonable rooms for P120–180.

Victoria Hotel, on De Riviera St. Decent rooms for P180–240.

Ryan Mall Hotel, on Rizal St. Tel: 22369. Quite good rooms in a hotel with the best restaurant in town. A little overpriced for this area though. Rooms with fan and bath for P280, air-conditioning and bath for P380–575.

CAPE ENGANO

"Cape of Enchantment", as it translates, is an unusually beautiful stretch of headland, with an old Spanish lighthouse perched above a picture-perfect bay replete with a curving white beach and well-preserved coral. The only way to reach the bay is by chartered *banca*, which no doubt explains its pristine state. This can only be done in good weather, when it takes about one hour. The cape forms part of Palaui Island, with its small community of Dumagat Negritos. Its possible to stay overnight in the schoolhouse in the settlement or at the lighthouse. If you opt for the latter you should take enough food and drink to share with the keepers there, a nice way of repaying them for their hospitality. Don't forget to arrange for the *banca* to come and pick you up.

CLAVERIA

Claveria is another beauty spot in the far north which is worth visiting if you are in the area. The tiny offshore islands of Punta Lakay-Lakay and Baket-Baket can be reached from here. There is not much accommodation in or around Claveria but visitors can try asking at the **Traveller's Inn** on the road to Taggat, or at the home of the family who ran the Sun Beach Cottages before the complex was swept away in a typhoon.

THE BABUYAN ISLANDS

Separated from mainland Luzon by the treacherous waters of the Babuyan Channel, this group consists of five main islands and a number of smaller, uninhabited islets. Chinese and other Oriental seafaring races appear to have passed by the islands well before the Spanish set foot here. Japanese burial jars have been found on the main islands. If you would like to see isolated fishing and agricultural communities that have remained virtually unchanged, this is the place to go. A passenger boat leaves once a week for Calayan Island. From there it is possible to find boats heading for the Babuyan Islands. Fuga Island is the closest to Claveria and can be reached in under three hours. Beaches, scuba diving and game fishing are said to be excellent on and around its shores. There is an old Spanish church on this island. Fuga is known for its crayfish and wild honey. You will have to get permission to visit the island as it is owned by Alfonso Lim, owner of Taggat Industries near Claveria. You can approach him in person or his manager for the necessary permit. Accommodation on these islands is limited to personal appeals to the village heads for a floor to sleep on, or, in the case of larger settlements and villages, a knock on the door of the local mayor or priest. Small gifts as expressions of gratitude, and enough food and drink supplies to be self-sufficient, are essential.

Getting there
Take one of the Vigan- and Laoang-bound buses from Aparri to Claveria. There is also one Vigan-bound bus going from Tuguegarao to Claveria. A Pantranco North bus leaves Claveria for Manila, via Tuguegarao, every morning at 10.00. It is a long 14hr ride to Manila.

ISABELA PROVINCE

Few visitors linger for long on the rugged and isolated coast of Isabela Province, preferring to stick to the main towns with their pleasant provincial pace of life. North of Santiago, the main National Highway through the Cagayan Valley reaches the bustling little town of **Cauayan**, which is noted for its church, a vigorous market, and a disproportionately high number of good restaurants. Cauayan is at the centre of a major rice-growing area. PAL flies to Cauayan twice weekly from Manila and there are a number of Pantranco North buses daily from Manila. **Roxas** is about 20km northeast of here and popular with travellers who wish to sample the life of an authentic rural town, almost completely untouched by mainstream tourism. **Ramon**, site of the huge Magat High Dam and reservoir, the old town of **Reina Mercedes** and **Ilagan**, the provincial capital and largest town in the region, are all found within the populous Cagayan Valley belt. The **Santa Victoria Caves** lie a few kilometres north of Ilagan in the foothills of the Sierra Madre mountains. The friendly town of **Palanan** is really the only noteworthy settlement of any kind along Isabela's wild, elemental coast. Logging and subsistence farming keep its local economy going. There are no roads north or west of Palanan so you would have to take a boat from San Vicente or hike over a very rough series of mountain trails to reach the town. **Baler** is actually in Aurora Province, just over the border from Isabela, but worth mentioning on account of its good surf, snorkelling and hiking trails. You can also hire boats for fishing excursions here.

Chapter Twelve

South Luzon

The narrow, attenuated province of Aurora continues south from Baler until, almost unnoticed, it blends into Quezon Province. The two administrative regions were created by the Spanish in 1591 and called Kalilaya, after Juan de Salcedo had settled the area. Quezon's coastal communities seem to have suffered periodic attacks from Muslim pirates over the years. In 1841 the town of Tayabas was the scene of a major rebellion against Spanish rule, led by Hermano Pule, the founder of a breakaway religious brotherhood. The southern portion of the province was renamed Quezon in 1946 after Manuel Quezon, the revolutionary hero and president of the Philippine Commonwealth. Aurora was named after his wife. The densely forested Sierra Madre, inaccessible mountain spurs north of Mauban, non-existent coastal roads and unprotected harbours have conspired to hold back Quezon's development. Few visitors, with the exception of a trickle of hardy surfers, get to these prohibitively difficult coastal areas. Mount Banahaw (2,177m, 7,144ft), the scene of a curious religious homage during Holy Week, is the highest peak in the region, sitting astride Quezon and Laguna provinces. The more populous Tayabas Isthmus connects central Luzon with the Bicol Peninsula. Low coastal plains replace the wooded interior and Quezon's major product, copra, comes into its own as coconut plantations stretching all the way to Camarines Norte appear beside the north–south highway.

The southeastern stretch of Luzon consists of the provinces of Camarines Norte, Camarines Sur, Albay, Sorsogon and Catanduanes. The area, collectively known as Bicolandia, forms a land bridge between the Tagalog and Visayan cultures. Bicol is known for its excellent beaches, caves and lakes which offer all sorts of recreational possibilities for stressed-out Manila residents on long weekends. The fertile volcanic soil of this region has given birth to a rich belt of hot springs, perfect for soothing out the pressures of city life Filipino-style. The culinary equivalent of these bubbling sulphur pools, the fiery spicy cuisine of Bicol, which makes liberal use of coconut milk and red-hot chillies, makes a nice change from the standard Filipino fare.

THE ROAD SOUTH

Sariaya

Quezon City's main southbound highway passes the interesting town of Sariaya, where there are a number of well-preserved colonial houses in the backstreets near the old church. Anyone looking for high quality souvenirs to take home will find Sariaya a godsend. The local aristocracy of land and plantation owners have provided a steady stream of authentic antiques for the shops here. The Sina-Una Antique Shop near the market is one of the most reputable places to buy genuine verified antiques in Sariaya. You will also find several shops selling more affordable souvenirs made from rattan. The town is noted for its turtle-shaped bread called *pinagong* and its Pahiyas harvest festival in the middle of May, an event which attracts people from all over the region.

Lucban

A little north of here in the foothills of the Sierra Madre, the old Franciscan settlement of Lucban is a quiet country town with a number of old colonial houses and a pleasant shady plaza that sees little outside life for most of the year. In May it bursts into unaccustomed activity, however, with its own Pahiyas Festival, one of the best of its kind in the province. The whole town is beautifully decorated, each doorway and window carefully hung with dyed rice wafers, straw dummies, local sweets and coconut fronds, symbols of the harvest thanksgiving. A solemn commemoration service to San Isidrio Labrador, patron saint of farmers, is held in the church, followed by an animated afternoon procession in which fruit, sweets and vegetables are thrown from windows to the passing crowd. In June Lucban's papier-mâché dummies are dusted off and paraded through the streets in the colourful Gigantes Festival.

Lucban is also one of the starting points for the northeast ascent of Mount Banahaw. This is particularly interesting over Holy Week. Native people have long considered the area a "mountain of many cathedrals", and, in the observances of an esoteric cult that has existed here for centuries, homage is paid to the mountain in the belief that, according to local legend, Calvary was magically transported to Mount Banahaw. During Holy Week, devotees of the sect gather on the mountain, bathe in its holy springs and make the pilgrimage to the cavernous Kuweba ng Dios Ama, the Cave of God the Father.

Lucena

Lucena City, named after a tiny village in Andalusia, is the provincial capital and a key commercial and transportation hub on the southern highway. Nearby Dalahican and Cotta Port are also convenient places from which to catch boats bound for Romblon and Marinduque. There isn't a great deal to see in Lucena itself, apart from its 19th-century domed cathedral, one decent park, and nearby copra-processing plants. It is, however, a good base for visits to the Quezon National Park. It is about 30km to the park. You will have to hop off the bus about 5km east of the turn-off for Padre Burgos (all the drivers know the spot) and then hike up the road to the park. It takes a little under two hours to hike from the entrance to its highest point, the summit of Mount Mirador, from where the views are superlative. The trail cuts through an unspoilt rainforest, studded with limestone caves, waterfalls and a dense tropical vegetation, home to a veritable aviary of squawking birds and teeming wildlife. Visitors are allowed to pitch their tents at Camp Training, but most people come here as a day trip from Lucena. There is a drinks stall in the park but it is wise to bring enough food for the excursion.

Getting there
The 3hr trip from Manila is served by Superlines, BLTB and Philtranco buses. Buses also leave Santa Cruz for Lucena, and there are any number of jeepneys from places like San Pablo and Los Banos.

Where to stay
Lucena Fresh Air Resort, in Isabang District. Tel: 712424. Singles and doubles with fan for P160–200, fan and bath from P240–300, and with air-conditioning and bath for P440–550. This is good value with spacious rooms, a nice garden, restaurant and a swimming pool.

Viscount Hotel, on Gomez St. Centrally located with simple, clean rooms for P200–250.

Hotel Halina, 104 Gomez St. Tel: 712902. Decent rooms with fan and bath for P200–250, with air-conditioning and bath for P320–400.

Travel Lodge Chain Motel, in Isabang District. Tel: 714489. Clean and well organised. Single and double rooms with fan and bath in the P220–300 range, with air-conditioning and bath for P340–500. The suites here are P750.

The Pagbilao Islands
One of the best-kept secrets in this part of the Philippines, the twin islands of Pagbilao Chico and Pagbilao Grande, are found to the east of Lucena. They are joined by a sandy isthmus, raised for about half a kilometre above the sea. The islets surrounding them are blessed with pristine white beaches of the sort you often see on postcards but seldom find easy to locate. The two islands are distinguished by cliffs, coves and a hilly interior with clumps of giant yuccas and small, emerald forests. Needless to say, the swimming and snorkelling in these coral islands is superb. The main settlement is Tulaybuhangin, meaning "sand bridge". The islands can easily be reached by *banca* from the nearby mainland port of Padre Burgos, a charming fishing village itself worthy of a look. Most people visit the islands as a day trip but the few foreigners who have been there agree that it justifies a longer stay-over. Some enterprising local person may very well open a guesthouse here in the near future. Until then, you

will have to either camp there, ask the mayor if any of Tulaybuhangin's residents would be willing to put you up for the night, or stay at a hotel on the mainland. The Cala de Oro Beach Resort near Pagbilao town has rooms for P220–300.

Lamon Bay to Naga

The Maharlika Highway drops to the Pacific coast at Atimonan and follows the coconut-fringed fields and rice paddies of Lamon Bay before rising up the peninsula to Camarines Norte. Atimonan and the next town of note, Gumaca, are the only places offering accommodation along this stretch of the coast before reaching Daet, so if you are planning to stay overnight somewhere, these would be the places to do it.

Where to stay

Victoria Beach Resort, on the highway at Atimonan. Tel: 965. Simple accommodation for P140, P240–320 with fan and bath, and P440 for a double with air-conditioning and bath.

Pinky's Lodge and Restaurant, in Gumaca. P70–120 for rooms with a fan, P140–180 with a bath, and P220–300 with air-conditioning and bath. A comfortable and friendly place.

Rosarian Pension House, in Gumaca. Very plain and simple but clean. Small rooms for P80–120.

Daet and Mercedes

Daet and the vicinity around the town offer slightly better accommodation options than Atimonan and Gumaca if you want to rest up or break your journey before pressing on to places like San Miguel Bay and Naga. A busy trading centre lying on a fertile plain, Daet is the provincial capital of Camarines Norte. Bagasbas Beach, a 4km tricycle ride from here, is one of the best sandy stretches on this part of the coast, and excursions can also be made to the lively fishing village of Mercedes which has a colourful early morning market. You can take a boat to Apuao Grande Island from there, a lovely place with fine white beaches. Those ubiquitous Australians, the Swagman Travel company, have a beach resort there.

Getting there

Pacific Airways runs flights between Daet and Manila every Monday and Friday. There are plenty of buses from Manila every day bound for Daet or Naga and Legaspi. Superline, BLTB, Philtranco and JB Bicol Express Line are the main carriers. There are also buses coming the other way from Legaspi and Naga, and a regular minibus service from Naga. Mercedes is best reached by jeepney, although you could do it by tricycle just as easily.

Where to stay
Daet
Daet Tourist Inn, on Pimentel St. Spacious and clean rooms for P220–300.

Hotel Alegre, on Lukban St. Clean and reasonably priced rooms with fan and bath for P180–220, air-conditioning and bath for P300–360.

Karilagan Hotel, on Moreno St. Tel: 2265. Rooms with fan and bath for P150–200, air-conditioning and bath for P320–400. Suites go for P450–500. A good location but because it is so central, and has banqueting and conference facilities, it can be a trifle noisy at times.

Apuao Island
Apuao Grande Island Resort Hotel. Very pleasant cottages with fan and bath for P750. The resort has an excellent range of amenities, including a swimming pool, golf course, restaurant, tennis court, and facilities for windsurfing, sailing, diving and hiring Hobie Cats. Reservations can be made through the Swagman Hotel in Manila.

Where to eat in Daet
New Grandeur Restaurant, on Lukban St. Reasonably priced Filipino and other food.

King's Tea and Noodles and the Mandarin Restaurant, both on Lukban St, have good, inexpensive Chinese food.

Sampaguita Restaurant, in the Sampaguita Department store. Good, wholesome food at affordable prices.

Serrano's Snack House, on Vincents Ave, near the market. A handy 24-hour joint.

Naga City
Surrounded by the lush ricelands of the Bicol Plain, Naga is not only the region's main commercial and transportation centre, but also its religious, educational and cultural hub. Situated between the imposing cone of Mount Isarog and San Miguel Bay a few kilometres away, this lively and appealing city boasts a number of cultural assets that include the University of Nueva Caceres, with its seminaries and private museum, one of the largest cathedrals in the country, and the shrine of Our Lady of Penafrancia which contains a small statue of the Virgin Mary, the palladium of the city, to which the people of Naga are immensely attached. The Franciscans chose Naga for the site of the San Francisco Church, completed in 1578 and one of the oldest in the Bicol region.

Naga is well known for its festival in honour of the Virgin of Penafrancia which is held every September. At this time the city fills with visitors and good accommodation can be difficult to find. The massive market is well stocked with regional products including handicrafts made from abaca and *buri,* and the local speciality, *pili* nuts.

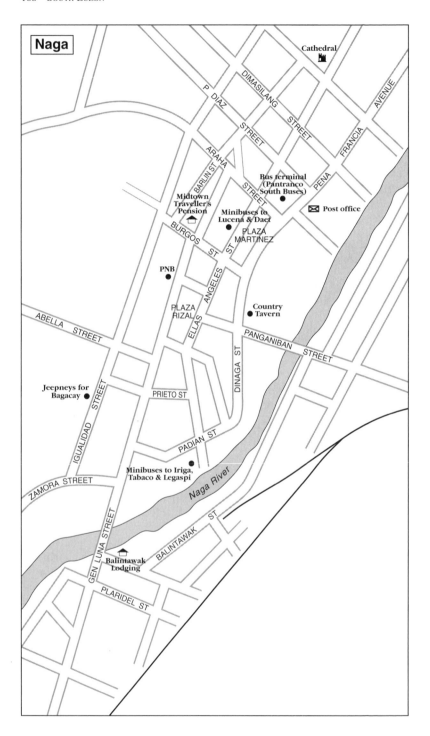

Getting there

PAL has a daily return flight between Naga and Manila. One PAL office is at Pili Airport, the other on Elias St. (tel: 2574). The airport is about 12km from the downtown area. If you want to get to town by jeepney you will have to walk to the main road to catch one. Otherwise you can give the Aristocrat Hotel a ring and they will give you a lift for P200, even if you are not one of their guests. There are also tricycles to the town centre.

There are plenty of buses running between Manila and Naga. The main companies are the J B Express Line, BLTB, and the Philtranco Company. There are two daily Sunshine Run buses from Tramo St in Pasay City, Manila, at 08.00 and 19.00. You can book through their office on M H del Pilar, Ermita (tel: 506601-06). There are many Philtranco, BLTB and J B Bicol Express Line buses every day from Daet. Some may also be going on to Legaspi.

Where to stay

Mini Hotel, near the railway station. Very reasonable, clean rooms for P170–240.

Aristocrat Hotel, along Elias Angeles St. Tel: 215230. Claims to be the best hotel in Naga. Rooms with fan for P270, with fan and bath for P350–400, and with air-conditioning and bath for P470–590. Their suites are P1,250. It has a restaurant and a disco. Hotels with discos in the Philippines, like the Costa Brava, can be a mixed blessing.

Balintawak Lodging, near the railway station. A friendly little place offering clean, adequate rooms for P170–240.

Moraville Hotel, on Dinaga St. Tel: 33584. Excellent value. All rooms have TV and are tastefully furnished, clean and quiet.

Fiesta Hotel, on Padian St. Tel: 212760. Very clean and tidy place with good-sized rooms with fan for P200–240, air-con and bath for P300–390, and suites for P470–590. There is a restaurant and disco.

Midtown Traveller's Pension, on General Luna St. Tel: 212474. A friendly and agreeable place with good-sized rooms for P190–220, with fan and bath P240–280, and P320–400 with air-conditioning and bath. Suites are from P470–590.

Where to eat

New China Restaurant, on General Luna St. Good-value Chinese food with a different menu each day.

Ming Chun Foodhouse, on Penafrancia Ave. Good standard Chinese and Filipino dishes. They can recommend mixtures of the two.

Carl's Diner, in the Plaza Real. A retro-style American restaurant with a good selection of Filipino and fast-food dishes.

Another fast-food place with echoes of Americana, is the **Graceland Fast Food**, also in the Plaza Real. **Shakey's Pizza** at the Aristocrat Hotel continues the tradition. The **Country Tavern** usually has live music.

IRIGA TO THE SOUTHERN TIP
Iriga and Lake Buhi
Iriga City is a pleasant enough town to stroll around but, apart from its twin-towered cathedral and the Bicol Folkloric Museum, the main reason travellers stay here is to visit nearby Lake Buhi and Mount Iriga. The lake is 16km from Iriga City and is easy enough to get to by jeepney. Most leave from Felix Alfelor Street, near the Bayanihan Hotel. One of the attractions of the lake used to be its curious 3mm-long fish called sinarapan, which were present in great abundance until Buhi's short-sighted fishermen depleted the lake's stock by overfishing and introducing larger predatory fish who, naturally, set about exterminating the smaller ones. The Bureau of Fisheries and Aquatic Resources have done a lot to save and restore the lake's stock in recent years. You can see examples of this fish at the aquarium in the Municipal Building or, if you prefer them on your plate, at the Hotel Ibalon, where they serve their renowned "Thousand Fish Omelette".

You can hire a *banca* to cross the lake, but it's cheaper to just take the ferry as most of the locals do. Mount Iriga can be climbed from Buhi or from its north side. You should start fairly early as the ascent takes about four hours and there is no accommodation in the vicinity. You might also think about hiring a local guide which makes the climb much easier. Some of the Agtas tribals who live in this area make excellent guides.

Where to stay
Ibalon Hotel, on San Francisco St. Tel: 352. Definitely the best accommodation in town, this graceful little hotel also has one of its best restaurants. Elegant rooms for P420–500. Great value.

Ibalon Village Resort, 1km from town. A restful location with accommodation in the P400–500 range. Has a pool and restaurant.

Lemar's Place, on San Nicolas St. Tel: 594. Basic but very agreeable guesthouse with rooms with fan for P90–120, with fan and bath for P140–180, and with air-conditioning and bath for P240.

Bayanihan Hotel, on Governor Felix Alfelor St. Tel: 556. Comfortable rooms at economic rates. Fan rooms for P90, singles and doubles with fan and bath for P190–240.

Legaspi
Legaspi is the capital of Albay Province, a busy university town with a lively port area but few real sights for the visitor. The market is worth a look as there are a number of handicraft stalls there. St Raphael Church is interesting in that it has an altar made from volcanic rock taken from Mount Mayon. Near the main wharf there is a curious headless statue. This is apparently in memory of a Filipino resistance fighter who was beheaded by the Japanese. Legaspi's tourist office on the north side of Penaranda Park is said to be one of the best in the country. The helpful

staff here will give you armfuls of maps and other information about the area. Most visitors to Legaspi are here for more attractive sights outside of town, foremost of which is the formidable Mayon Volcano.

Getting there

PAL has daily flights between Manila and Legaspi. There are also flights from here to Cebu. The PAL offices are in the airport (tel: 5247), and in the Chinese Chamber of Commerce Building, on Rizal Street. The airport is only 2.5km out of town.

There are no shortages of Inland Trailways, J B Bicol Express Line and BLTB buses from Manila to Legaspi. Philtraco buses also pass through Legaspi on their way to Matnog at the tip of the peninsula and further on to Tacloban and Davao. You can also catch air-conditioned Legaspi-bound buses through Sarkies Tours. Their Manila daily departure leaves at 19.00 from Indiana St, Ermita. This is a popular way of doing it so you should book a seat in advance (tel: 508959). There are several Philtranco, BLTB, and J B Bicol Express Line buses daily from Naga to Legaspi.

Where to stay

Catalina's Boarding House, 96 Penaranda St. A small and cosy guesthouse with rooms with fan and bath for P220.

Tanchuling International House, on Jasmin St, Imperial Subdivision. Tel: 2788. A little bit out of town but worth the slight inconvenience. Peaceful location and friendly staff. Excellent value with singles and doubles with fan going for P220, and with air-conditioning and bath for P490. Has a pretty roof garden.

Mayon Hotel, on Penaranda St. Spacious and quiet rooms with fan and bath for P250–300.

Hotel La Trinidad, on Rizal St. Tel: 2951-55. Probably the most upmarket accommodation in Legaspi. Has a swimming pool, restaurant, coffee shop, and a small cinema in the same building. Singles and doubles with air-conditioning and bath for P640 and P950. Their suites are P1,450. If you book in with them they will pick you up from the airport.

Victoria Hotel, also on Rizal St. Tel: 22101-04, Fax: 23439. Extremely comfortable setting. All rooms have TV. Singles and doubles with air-conditioning and bath for P490 and P700–780. Airport service and restaurant.

Where to eat

Wayway Restaurant, on Penaranda St. Excellent Filipino food, including all the fiery Bicol specialities. Many people consider this to be the best eatery in Legaspi. Judge for yourself.

Four Seasons, on Magallenes St. Inexpensive Chinese food.

Golden Dragon, on Rizal St. Another cheap Chinese place with good food

New Legaspi Restaurant, on Lapu-Lapu St. Good range of Filipino food at economical rates.

South Ocean Villa Chinese Restaurant, in the market square. Popular with the local Chinese community so it must be reasonably good.

Magic Pan, on Rizal St. Rather expensive but delicious food.

Quick n' Hearty Fast Food, on Rizal St. Lives up to its name.

There are many cheap food stalls in and around the market area.

Side trips from Legaspi
Mayon Volcano

This very active volcano is unquestionably the main attraction for most visitors to the region. Of the Philippines' 21 active cones, this is one of the most feared. Since the records were first kept in 1616, this ill-tempered volcano has erupted almost 50 times, the last occasion being in 1993 when 30 people, including a group of American vulcanologists, were killed. A sulphureous plume rises continuously from Mayon, reminding residents and visitors alike that its fury can be unleashed at any time. Mayon's name derives from the Bicol word magayon, signifying "beauty". The mountain and the surrounding 55km² national park are certainly that, but Mayon's sinister side gives the whole area another complexion. Any treks up the slopes of the mountain should only proceed after consulting the tourist office, who can also organise hiking tours there with a much-needed professional guide. Even this may not be totally safe. Remember that the 1993 eruption occurred without the slightest warning. Tours are also the best way up as you will have to spend the night on the slopes, probably at Camp 1 or Camp 2, necessitating a tent, sleeping bags and enough provisions to last you the course. Take a sweater or light jacket as well. Night temperatures drop at these higher altitudes even in the south.

Daraga and Camalig

These two spots are easy to reach from Legaspi and can be combined in a one-day excursion. Daraga has a splendid Franciscan church built in baroque style. The church, which dates back to 1773 and stands on a clearing at the top of a hill above the town, affords a great view of Mayon. Daraga's night market is a bustling affair with some wonderfully aromatic food offerings spicing the air as you walk around under storm lamps and flash strips thick with mosquitoes.

Camalig is where people go to see the famous Hoyop-Hoyopan limestone caves at Cotman, 8km to the south. The caves are quite extensive so it is just as well to have a guide. Ask around Camalig for one to take you to Calabidogan or Pariaan caves, the most interesting sites. Here you will see some fabulous caverns with stalactites and natural pools. You can take a jeepney to Camalig from the market at Legaspi. There are also buses heading towards the town which can be boarded at the terminus. Tricycles are the best way of getting to the caves. There is a small admission price to enter.

Bacacay and Cagraray Island

Proceeding north from Legaspi through the disappointing beach resort of Santo Domingo (erroneously called the capital of the "Mayon Riviera"), the road passes by the Santa Misericordia Volcano Observatory on its way to Bacacay, a small fishing village with a ruined Spanish watchtower. Visitors sometimes take *bancas* across from here to Cagraray Island and its surrounding, mostly uninhabited, islets. There are no roads on the island but you can find your way to its best stretch of sand, the one called Masibis Beach, by following a series of footpaths. The white sands here lend themselves perfectly to playing the sandpiper for an afternoon. If you really like the place and are not put off by the locals' insistence on the presence of evil spirits on the island, you could stay at the Sacred Heart Mission in Cabasan.

Malilipot

North of Bacacay, still circling the toes of Mayon, the Busay Falls at Malilipot are a good destination for a picnic and swim. The cascades here fall from a height of about 250m into a series of seven pools, each one perfect for bathing in. You shouldn't need a guide to get on to the footpath that leads to the base of the falls. Just take the path that ascends from the left of the village church. It is about 1.5km from there. When you reach the bottom of the falls you will see a path to the right. Take this to reach the upper falls. While you are in Malilipot, have a look around. Like many villages in this area, it is a centre for abaca. You can buy sturdily made bags, slippers and other items here. If you go in July and August you can buy exceptionally good pineapples and avocados while they are in season.

Tiwi hot springs

The coast road from the uninteresting market town and port of Tabaco leads to Tiwi, an insignificant place but for its proximity to the renowned hot springs. Because of the building of a number of geothermal power stations, the springs are sadly much depleted. Most of the boiling springs that have not dried up are found near the youth hostel. The locals still boil their eggs in some of the pools here, as they do in parts of other countries like Japan and Indonesia.

Where to stay

The Youth Hostel. This is a very cheap place and good for meeting other travellers. You only pay P70 per person for a double cottage. You can pay a bit more and have a private room with a private bath, and a small surcharge for use of the pools. Day visitors are also welcome to use the pools for a small admission fee.

Manantial de Tiwi Resort. Next to the hostel. A bit more upmarket with air-conditioned rooms with their own private pools for P440. Food is served both here and at the hostel.

Sorsogon

Sorsogon is the capital of Sorsogon Province which lies at the southeastern extremity of Luzon. It is the region's main commercial and cultural centre. Located at the head of a sheltered bay, Sorsogon was almost completely destroyed by an earthquake in 1840. It is well known as a port for the shipment of abaca and as a convenient base to explore this southern tip. Rizal Beach near the town of Gubat is not far from Sorsogon and can be easily reached by jeepney. Rizal Beach is expansive and largely unspoilt and makes a pleasant place to spend a day or two away from it all.

Getting there

J B Bicol Express Line buses run almost every half-hour from Legaspi to Sorsogon. There may be Philtranco buses going through Sorsogon en route from Manila to Matnog, but don't count on getting on, as all the seats may be prebooked.

Where to stay
Sorsogon

Mercedes Country Lodge, on Peralta St. Well-liked budget hotel. Rooms with fan for P240.

M A Bistro Lodging House, on Peralta St. Another cheap alternative with a small restaurant attached. P180 for a small room with fan.

Dalisay Lodge, also on Peralta St. Clean and straightforward guesthouse with rooms for P90–120 with fans, and P120–150 with fan and bath.

Gubat

Meliza Lodging House. P200 for a room with fan and bath. It is much better to try and stay on Rizal Beach itself, preferably at the Rizal Beach Resort. It's a bit run-down looking but the location is fine. Rooms have views of the beach. Dormitory beds for P100, rooms with fan and bath for P240–350, and rooms with air-conditioning and bath for P450.

Lake Bulusan and Irosin

Mount Bulusan and nearby Bulusan Lake are at the very centre of the last bulbous spur of land that completes Luzon. The lake is surrounded by dense forest full of wild flowers, orchids and other colourful flora. The lake is small and can be walked around in a circuit of under 2km. If you descend along the main road from the lake you can stop off at Masacrot Soda Spring for a swim or soak before pressing on for Irosin. The town is unusual as it is located in a sunken crater, surrounded by arable farm land. About 3km north of Irosin is the Mateo Hot and Cold Springs Resort, a relaxing place where there are three pools of different temperatures to be sampled. Mapaso and Bulus springs are not far from here if you enjoy taking the waters.

Getting there
There are plenty of J B Bicol Express Line buses every day from Legaspi to Irosin and Bulun. The Manila to Tacloban buses are usually full. A few jeepneys run between Irosin and Bulusan.

Where to stay
Bulusan
Villa Luisa Celeste Resort, in Dancalan. Good-sized rooms in a clean and friendly place. Fan and bath for P300–370, with air-conditioning and bath for P500.

Bulusan Lodging House, near the municipal hall. Rooms with fan for P90–150. Cosy place run by a friendly local teacher.

Irosin
Mateo Hot and Cold Springs Resort, San Benon, Monbon. See above comment. Rooms with fan are P130–250, with fan and bath P270. Cottages with fan, bath and kitchenette are only P270.

Lena's Lodging House. Plain and simple rooms in a friendly guesthouse. Rooms with fan for P70–120.

Matnog
Although Matnog Bay is quite scenic, the only reason most travellers consider spending time in this quiet fishing port is because it happens to be the ferry terminal for boats operating between Allen and the port of San Isidro on Samar. Cardinal Ferry and San Pablo Lines are the companies operating these routes. If you do get stuck waiting for a boat in Matnog, try staying at **Villa's Inn**, the **Seaside Eatery**, or at **Mely's Snack House** near the dock.

Getting there
There are several jeepneys every day running from both Legaspi and Irosin to Matnog. There are also buses coming from various other starting points in Luzon that will be boarding the ferries at Magnog. You can sometimes get a seat in Legaspi if you are lucky, but don't rely on it.

Chapter Thirteen

Five Islands

CATANDUANES

Separated from southern Luzon by the Lagonoy Gulf and the Maqueda Channel, Catanduanes Province, the 12th largest island in the Philippines, and its neighbouring island, Panay, face out on to the Pacific Ocean, a source of frequent typhoons that have earned the island the name "Land of the Howling Winds". Rainfall reaches its maximum between October and December, but it can rain throughout the year. The summer months from April to June are the driest. A combination of bad storms and a lack of employment have resulted in a slow exodus of migrants to the mainland, leaving Catanduanes with a falling population density, one that is already well below the national average. A restricted number of coastal plains, a mountainous and hilly central massif rising to just over 700m, and an interior that remains, even now, practically unexplored, have driven most people to settle in the southern part of the island where there is a proper infrastructure of roads. The 190,000 Bicolanos who live here are known for their strong religious leanings. English is widely spoken and understood but a heavily accented Bicolano, the language of southern Luzon, is the preferred tongue. Although Catanduanes gives the impression of being off the beaten track, it is easy enough to get from Luzon to Virag, the provincial capital and main port of entry. The island offers not only the promise of a secluded hideaway, but friendly people, attractive villages, picturesque landscapes and excellent beaches. So why the absence of visitors? Overcoming the mental barrier of yet another sea crossing? Scepticism at the enthusiastic reports of other travellers just back from the island? Probably a bit of both, plus some very real obstacles to an extended stay. The main one is accommodation. Outside of Virac and Puraran there are almost no lodging houses of any kind, leaving visitors largely dependent upon the goodwill of local mayors or village chiefs to sort out a bed for the night on their behalf. That said, many people are content to stay in Catanduanes' relaxed capital and enjoy day trips to the more far-flung beaches.

Virac

More small town than provincial capital, Virac is a pleasant, homely place which can be easily negotiated on foot. There are no real sights as such, but excellent beaches and waterfalls are within easy reach. Popular side trips include the waterfalls at Binanuahan, Paday and Macutal, jeepney rides around the island, chartering boats for a day's coastal cruise, or a trip to nearby Panay Island. There are also, of course, all of those marvellous stretches of sand found at places like Igang, Talisay, Marilima and Magnesia Beach.

Getting there and around the island

PAL has flights to Catanduanes from Legaspi on Monday, Wednesday and Friday, and from Manila to Virac every day. The airport is 4km southwest of Virac. The PAL office is in the Airport (tel: 260). Tricycles can be taken from the airport to town. The ride should not cost more than P10.

Ferries can be taken to Catanduanes from Manila, Legaspi and Tabaco. Jeepneys are the best way to get around the island, although the service is limited. There are three daily return runs from the market in Virac to Pandan in the north. The first jeepney leaves at 07.00, stopping for breakfast at San Andres. There is also a jeepney that goes from Virac to Viga and Tambugnon, and another two that run from Virac to Puraran and Gigmoto. Baras is well served, with a regular number of buses and jeepneys. Hiking roads, as opposed to trails, are interesting, particularly on the unmade route from Bato to Viga which passes through little-visited villages and forests.

Where to stay

L&H Resthouse, near the Magnolia ice-cream parlour. Popular with budget travellers. Simple rooms with fan for P140.

Sandy's Pension House, near the pier. Tel: 617. Small rooms with fan for P100–150. Has a restaurant and terrace area.

Christopher Restaurant, on the main street. Simple rooms for P180–240.

Catanduanes Hotel, on San Jose St. Tel: 280. Reasonably comfortable rooms with fan and bath for P240–290. Has its own restaurant

Cherry Don Resthouse, on San Pedro St. Tel: 516. Plain and simple but clean rooms for P80–120 with fan. Popular with backpackers.

Bosdok Beach Resort, on Magnesia Beach, 12km southwest of Virac. The resort is set in a lovely location with a fine beach. Spacious well-built cottages with fan and bath for P275 and P400. Has a swimming pool and restaurant. Excellent value.

Twin Rock Beach Resort, on Igang Beach, 8km southwest of Virac. A well organised and comfortable place. Cottages with fan and bath for P270, and with fan and bath for P400. Comfortably furnished rooms with fan and bath for P500, air-conditioning and bath for P740.

Where to eat

Chicken House, near the roundabout. Has tasty fried chicken and other dishes. Popular with locals as it is not so expensive.

Sultida's Inn, on San Pedro St. Very cheap Filipino and Bicol food.

Café de Paul, on A Surtida and San Jose Sts. A good range of meat and seafood dishes.

Catanduanes Hotel Restaurant. Up on the roof of this hotel. Very good inexpensive Filipino dishes.

The area around the market, as in most towns in the Philippines, has a good selection of food stalls.

Puraran

This exquisite beach spot is worth a special mention. One of the finest beaches in Catanduanes, Puraran is a tiny resort located about 30km northeast of Virac in a beautiful setting along this largely undeveloped coastline. The resort is especially popular with serious surfers, the ones who like to take on the big November to January breakers. The surf is good from the end of July but you should be a strong swimmer if you intend going out over the reef or in some of the swirls nearer the beach itself where there can be powerful undercurrents. For normal holidaymakers, the ideal time to visit this resort is from March until the end of June.

Getting there

Catch one of the two Gigmoto-bound jeepneys that leave from the market in Virac at 09.00 and 10.00 every day. They stop off at Puraran on the way. You can ask them to drop you near the resort of your choice. You can go all the way by tricycle which is great fun but more expensive.

Where to stay

Puraran Beach Resort. Pleasant cottages for between P300 and P550. A well-appointed restaurant. Standards are high here as it is run by a Japanese-Philippine group.

Pacific View Beach Resort. Simple cottages popular with budget travellers. P300 includes two meals. Very friendly and good value.

MINDORO ISLAND

A formidable mountain spine and dense virtually unexplored forests separate the two halves of Mindoro, dividing it into the twin but quite distinct provinces of Occidental Mindoro in the west and Oriental Mindoro to the east. Few roads penetrate the interior, and Mindoro's only highway forms a loop around the island. The interior of the island is the almost exclusive domain of the native Mangyans. The geology, plant and wildlife of the island is closer to Borneo and the southwestern island of

Palawan than to the Philippines. Mount Halcon (2,586m, 8,487ft) and Mount Baco are the island's highest peaks. Sharp ridges and deep valleys covered in dense rainforest and secondary woodland on the lower slopes give way to marshland, mangrove swamps and limestone cliffs and buffs as the land descends towards cliff and beach. The Spanish, who found small Muslim settlements here when they first arrived, named the island from a contraction of "mina de oro" (goldmine), after finding small traces of gold on the island. Muslim raids on the Mindoro coastline continued right up to the 19th century. During both the Philippine-American war and the Second World War, Mindoro was the scene of some fierce fighting. In 1980 Fumio Nakahara, a captain in Japan's Imperial Army, was discovered living on the slopes of Mount Halcon, in the heartland of Mondoro's interior. Another Japanese soldier who went native and lived to tell the tale was the extraordinary Lt Hiroo Onoda, who stepped out of the forests of nearby Lubang Island in 1974 after spending the intervening years waiting for military dispatches from Tokyo. Onoda made a remarkable readaptation to the changes of post-war Japan. I used to see him making guest appearances on Japanese television. He was also well known for running Duke of Edinburgh style survival courses for young people and company recruits, and for having published a very readable book, *No Surrender: My Thirty Year War*.

For most foreign visitors, however, Mindoro means Puerto Galera. This resort in the north of Oriental Mindoro is fast becoming the focus of conflicting interests between locals who see tourism as a goldpot that should be developed at all costs, and the environmental lobby who are concerned not only for the already embattled ecology of the area, but also for the degrading effect of too many visitors on the lifestyle, customs and morals of the young people in the region. The advent of loud discos, fast-food outlets, tacky souvenir shops, prostitution, available drugs, and a militant brand of nudism practised by some tourists, has fascinated some local people, while outraging others. If the commercial development of this coast is allowed to continue at the present pace, tourism could become a divisive force in the local community.

Getting to and around Mindoro

There are Pacific Airways flights from Manila to Calapan on Monday, Wednesday and Friday. The same schedule applies with their Mamburao to Manila flights. PAL flies from Mamburao to Manila on Fridays and Sundays and from San Jose to Manila daily, except for Wednesdays and Fridays.

It is possible to buy combined bus and ferry tickets from Guerta Galera to Manila that go via Batangas. There are several boats sailing from Puerta Galera to Batangas every day, with extra services laid on for the weekends. Normal costs for a one-way ticket are between P50 and P70. There are also three or four boats every day from Calapan to Batangas. The boats from Sablayan and San Jose are less frequent. You can also check out boats from Mindoro to Marinduque and Panay islands. There are ways and means of getting to Romblon Island by large outriggers from Pinamalayan and Bongabong, and to Tablas Island from Roxas.

Jeepneys are the logical and most enjoyable way of getting around the island as you can break your journey at several staging posts, or link up with tricycles if it suits. There are many jeepneys running between San Jose in the south and Guerta Galera in the north. There are also plenty from Calapan to Puerto Galera and places between. There are fewer serving the Mamburao to Abra de Llog route. The one statutory jeepney that does undertake this journey starts out at 06.00 from Mamburao. If you have the time and are prepared to be flexible, you can also take outriggers along the coast, linking up with jeepneys and tricycles at will.

Oriental Mindoro
Puerta Galera

Puerta Galera's rise to near international resort level was inevitable considering its fabulous harbour, its superb series of connecting beaches, and its backdrop of green, forest-smothered mountains. The town stretches for about 10km either side of the commercial, tourist and transportation hub of Poblacion where the docks are and most of the downtown hotels and guesthouses are located. Poblacion is a friendly town with a number of good shops, a bank, post office and good views of the harbour and its yachts. There is a lively festival called the Feast of Our Lady of Fatima held on 13 May, and a fiesta on 7 December which falls at the same time as the town's Feast of the Immaculate Conception. Day trips inland to places like the waterfalls at Tamaraw, Mount Malisimbo or one of the local marble quarries can also be made. Most people come here for the beach life, and are not usually disappointed. Each beach attracts its own followers and most resorts are able to offer accommodation to suit everyone's budgets. Amenities and ambience change from beach to beach. Some, like Sabang, are highly developed, offering a good choice of restaurants, discos and opportunities for watersports; others are secluded and undeveloped. Some fall between these two categories. Room rates at these beach resorts are at their highest between November and May, dropping during the off season months. Note that the dock area and ferries coming into the port are full of touts who will offer to introduce you to a cottage or lodging house. While this might save time, and most of these people are not particularly unscrupulous, they will be getting a commission for every person they bring, one that will surely be reflected in the price of your accommodation. You can do better on your own or by talking to other travellers. Even at the peak of the tourist season there are plenty of places available.

Underwater Mindoro

Generally speaking, the waters around Puerta Galera are clear, the sands white and coral gardens easily reached. Diving and snorkelling

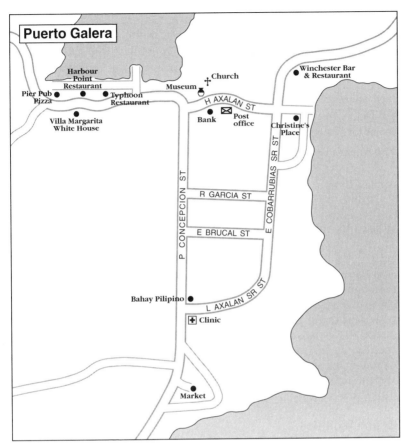

Puerto Galera

Harbour Point Restaurant

Pier Pub Pizza

Typhoon Restaurant

Villa Margarita White House

Church

Museum

Winchester Bar & Restaurant

H AXALAN ST

Bank

Post office

Christine's Place

E COBARRUBIAS SR ST

P CONCEPCION ST

R GARCIA ST

E BRUCAL ST

Bahay Pilipino

L AXALAN SR ST

Clinic

Market

are major activities in this area. As these activities can, weather permitting, be done all the year round, there are no shortage of equipment shops, clubs and diving schools. Some of the best shops can be found on Sabang, Big Lalaguna and Small Lalaguna beaches. Capt'n Greggs on Sabang Beach run intensive courses of between three and five days that can lead to international qualifications if required. The courses are excellent value for US$250. Galleon Dive Shop in Small La Laguna and Asia Diversion in Big La Laguna rent scuba-diving gear and can arrange for boat hires and tuition as well. One of the best diving areas is below Escarceo Point, where there is plenty of coral and many species of fish. The undertows can be quite perilous here for inexperienced divers. Snorkelling in shallower water can be done at Big and Small La Laguna beaches. If you can get together a small group of divers or snorkellers and rent a *banca* for the day, it can be quite economical at around P600 all told. More ambitious diving trips, organised by dive shops, can be taken to Apo Reef and Busuanga from February until May.

Where to stay in and around Puerto Galera

Bahay Pilipino Hotel and Restaurant, near the market. Central with the added advantage of a decent restaurant. Clean rooms with fan for P220.

Villa Margarita White House. Basic but clean rooms with fan for P300–380.

Holiday Garden Apartelle. Under the same management as the above. A little more upmarket with fan and bath for P400, and nice little apartments for P840.

Christine's Place, on the outskirts of town. A friendly place to stay with fan rooms for P180–220.

Fisherman's Cove Beach Resort, 1km from town. Rooms with fan and bath for P360. Has an Italian restaurant.

Apple's Huts, on the road to Sabang. A popular place with budget travellers. Very basic cottages for P120–140. Good atmosphere.

Where to eat

There is an astonishing range of restaurants in and around Poblacion, catering for international travellers, most of whom who sooner or later come here to eat. European and Filipino dishes are normally served in the restaurants here. The **Veradero Restaurant** is good for Filipino food at cheap to medium rates. The **Harbour Point Bar and Restaurant** is in the same league but has more drinks on offer. The **Bahay Pilipino** in the market serves mostly European dishes aimed at foreigners. Other places specialising in familiar home-from-home dishes are the Australian-run **Cloud 9**, **Fe's Place** and the **Winchester Pub and Restaurant**. The Winchester shows films most nights. The **Typhoon Restaurant** and **Pier Pub Pizza** are also good.

Beach facilities
Big La Laguna Beach

Possibly the best area for snorkelling. Also a good beach here.

Rosita's Inn and Restaurant. Clean rooms for P240–440.

El Oro Restaurant and Resort. Very good rooms with fan and bath for P280–450.

La Laguna Beach Club. Expensive rooms with fan and bath for P880, with bath and air-conditioning for P1,240. It does have a swimming pool, floating restaurant ("Who cares?" I hear you shout), a good restaurant and facilities for windsurfing and diving.

Small La Laguna Beach

This beach attracts a lot of backpackers and other budget travellers who like to stay a long time on Mindoro.

Havana Moon Beach Resort. Clean and tidy rooms with fan and bath for P180.

Nick and Sonia's Cottages. Nice friendly set-up with cottages with fan and bath for P300 and P480. There is a restaurant here, but the pricier cottages have refrigerators and small kitchens suitable for self-catering.

VILLAGE LIFE

Above: *An Igorot house in the hills near Baguio*

Below: *A village built on the slopes near Bontoc*

MARKET PRODUCE

Above left: *Rice is an important staple, along with potatoes*

Above right: *Cinnamon sticks for sale in Bohol street market*

Above: *Fresh farm produce for sale in a street market in Davao*
Below left: *Red hot chillies are a feature of Bohol dishes, but are not typical of Philippine cuisine in general*
Below right: *Garlic in a market in the Visayas*

TOURIST LIFE
Above left: *Fruit cut into flower shapes at a top hotel restaurant in Manila*
Above right: *Some of nature's succulent harvest*
Below: *Tourist bungalows on Puerto Galera*

Carlo's Inn. The cheaper rooms here with fan and bath go for P280–390, small apartments with kitchen and fridge for P380 and P600. The more expensive rooms overlooking the beach have TVs, refrigerators, air-conditioning and bath but cost a princely P1,600. A good base, as there is a restaurant and a telephone available for making overseas calls.

Sabang Beach

Not the best beach in Puerta Galera by any means, but certainly the most developed one: some would say adversely developed. Still, if you like life with a big 'L' (discos, sleazy bars and the noise from portable stereos), this is the place to stay.

Travellers Station. Bungalows for just P200. Popular hang-out for budget travellers.

Capt'n Gregg's Divers Lodge. Popular with divers as it has the gear shop attached. Good rooms with fan and bath for P350

Terraces Garden Resort. Tel: 912-3080136. Nice rooms and a good ambience. Rooms with fan and bath for P450–500.

White Beach

You will come across a lot of "white beaches" in the Philippines. This one actually is white, and immensely popular too.

White Beach Nipa Hut. Many small cottages with fan and bath for P300–350. There is also a restaurant.

Delgado's Cottages. Spacious cottages with fan and bath for P350.

Summer Connection. Cottages with fan and bath for P450. Quiet and well appointed at the western end of the beach.

Aninuan and Talipanan Beaches

Possibly the two quietest beaches in Puerta Galera. Recommended if you like to be on the periphery of things with a view of what's going on nearer the centre of town.

Tamaraw Beach Resort. Tel: 912 3066388. A popular place to stay as you can choose from a number of differently sized cottages. All with bath and fan for P380–590.

Aninuan Lodge. A smaller place but with a nice shady location on the beach. Cotttages with bath for P280 and P390.

Mountain Beach Resort. Located at the foot of Mount Malasimbo. Spacious rooms with fan and bath for P540–650. There is a restaurant.

Calapan

Like Puerta Galera, there isn't much to do or see in Calapan, the provincial capital of Mindoro Oriental, at least in the way of sightseeing. It is a pleasant enough place with a small museum and the Sanduguan Festival, which features a re-enactment of the first encounter between native Mangyans and Chinese traders (21 May). There are some quite good beaches near by, the best being Balete, Aganhao (black sand) and Silonay. There are also some Mangyan villages in the vicinity, like Tarogin and Paitan, which can be visited. You can get to Calapan easily enough by taking a jeepney from the docks at Puerta Galera. They leave regularly from 07.00 onwards. There are also minibuses from Roxas.

Where to stay
There are a number of small-scale lodging houses in the P180–250 price range which include the **Casa Blanca Annex**, **Eric Hotel**, **Riceland Inn** and **Queen Rose Lodge**. The **Traveller's Inn** on Leuterio Street can be recommended. It has basic, clean rooms with fan for P100–120, and with air-conditioning and bath for P380.

Pinamalayan
The island of Marinduque is visible from this coconut-growing area, some 60km southeast of Calapan. People come here to catch boats bound for Marinduque, and the two islands of Maestro de Campo and Banton, both in Romblon Province.

Roxas
Not so many people stay at Roxas either, unless they are looking for a boat to take them on to Tablas Island, or the ever-popular Boracay. There are some small lodging houses in this quiet little town and Melco Beach is near by.

Mansalay
This is a good place for people interested in anthropology, or those who are concerned about the fate of vanishing cultures, as Mansalay is a base for visiting Mangyan minority villages. A Dutch priest, a Father Postma, has lived in this area for a number of years and is quite an authority on this ethnic group. Don't waste his time though, unless you have good reason to look him up. He doesn't take kindly to playing the role of tour guide to groups of wide-eyed visitors looking for the exotic. If you are seriously interested in this field, however, he and fellow volunteers can be contacted through the mission here.

San Jose
San Jose is the province's main industrial centre and the only reason most visitors put time in here is to visit nearby Mangyan villages, or as a jumping-off point for the Apo Reef or Palawan. There are not many attractive places to stay in San Jose and the town is not noted for its restaurants. There are one or two beaches nearby, like Aroma and Babog, but they do not match up to those at Puerta Galera and elsewhere.

Getting there

PAL has flights linking Manila and San Jose four times a week. The airport is about 5km northwest of town. There are RCG Liner and Ramadel Express buses every morning between Calapan and San Jose. There are also several jeepneys from Mamburao and Bulalacao.

Where to stay

Big Newk Hotel, Airport Rd. Clean rooms near the airport for P130–180.

Kapit Bahay Mini Hotel, on Rizal St. Simple but clean rooms for P180–220.

Sikatuna Town Hotel, on Sikatuna St. Tel: 697.

Seafront Hotel, on Airport Rd. Small, simple rooms from P150–180 with fan and bath, P440 with air-conditioning and bath. Has a rather basic restaurant.

Apo Reef

Tiny Apo Island is dwarfed by its own reef, a massive National Marine Park of 34km^2. The reef is home to an immense wealth of marine life and other features that include over 300 species of fish, stunning coral, world-class dive sites with sudden spectacular drop-offs, and sunken wrecks. Apo Island is wooded with a small lighthouse and is fringed with white sands. It is possible to camp here overnight but you would need to take your own equipment, food and plenty of water. At twilight, pestilential numbers of mosquitoes and sandflies appear on the island, so make sure you are safely fastened into your tent by then. The reef is seventh heaven for divers but is also a spectacular area for snorkelling. There are no regular boat services out to Apo Reef so you have to make your own arrangements. You could either hire a small *banca* from Sablayan for a 3hr circuit of the reef and island, or charter a larger *banca* with some other people for a whole day. This should not cost more that P3000. Serious divers should join a properly organised dive-boat tour.

Pandan Bay

Another genuinely unspoilt pocket of the Philippines well worth exploring from Sablayan is North Pandan Island in Pandan Bay. More attractive than its southern twin island, North Pandan's main beach is a study in picture postcard clichés – copra-white palm-fringed sands, aquamarine water and the odd colourful *banca* or skip placed just at the right photogenic angle on the shoreline. The northern section of the island is covered in dense jungle right down to its beach.

Where to stay

The **Pandan Island Resort** offers the only accommodation on the island. A very friendly and relaxed set-up run by French people. Rooms with fan and bath for P240, spacious cottages using solar energy for P400. There is also a house for rent at P900. It can accommodate up to four people. The resort has its own boat which departs for the island every day at around 10.00 from the landing pier at Sablayan.

Mamburao

As the provincial capital of Mindoro Occidental, Mamburao deserves a mention. There are no sights worth noting here however. Fish farming in ponds and boat building are the town's main occupations. There is a good beach 3km from here at Tayamaan.

Where to stay

Traveller's Lodge. Basic rooms with fan for P100–180, fan and bath for P190–280, and with air-conditioning and bath for P520–850. Not a bad restaurant.

Tayamaan Palm Beach Club. 4km northwest of town. Cottages with fan and bath for P480. This is a better place to stay than the town as the setting of cottages sitting under palm trees on a pretty, sandy bay is very pleasant.

THE LUBANG ISLANDS

Lubang Island and its neighbours in the same group (Ambil, Golo and Cabra), are located west of the Batangas coast and north of Mindoro. One of the main sources of income for the islanders is the sale of garlic. The waters around the islands are popular with sports fishermen and also provide a wealth of shells. Lubang Island has some good beaches, sheltered coves and bays. The north section of the island is the most populated, although the south, with its rugged coastline and several secluded beaches, is arguably the most attractive. Binacas on the south coast is very good for snorkelling. There is also a good beach at Tagbac, west of Lubang. The north is known to have the best surf, though, and the fishing here (lobsters, crab and coral fish) is better. The island's main settlement is at Lubang, although Tilik is where most of the boats dock. The wreck of a famous Spanish galleon, the San Jose, was found in shallow waters off the shore of Labang a few years ago. Some interesting pieces of earthenware and Ming porcelain have been retrieved, though quite what happened to its wealth of gold bullion nobody seems quite sure about.

Getting there and around

Pacific Airways has a daily flight to Lubang from Manila. There are boats to Lubang from Mindoro, Luzon and Palawan throughout the week. Jeepneys run between Talik and Lubang town. There are also occasional, horse-drawn *carretelas* between the two towns. You can charter your own boat if you wish to visit nearby islands like Ambil and Cabra.

Where to stay

There is only one place to stay on Lubang at the present time, the **Mina de Oro Beach Resort** in Lubang. They have mediocre-to-fair rooms for P250–440. There is a small restaurant there. Otherwise, you will have to ask around for a private house willing to take in visitors.

MARINDUQUE ISLAND

Lying between southern Luzon and Mindoro, Marinduque Island is a circular land mass of wooded hills and craggy coves and bluffs. The island is surrounded by extensive coral reefs. Marinduque in the 17th century was an important dry dock for the building of galleons. The island is best known for the Moriones Festival, a major event in the year's cultural calendar (see Festivals and Holidays in *Chapter Three*). This is held over Holy Week, usually in March or April. The island's seminal tourist industry gets a kickstart over this period with people arriving from all over the Philippines. Once the festival is over, the island slips back into low gear for the rest of the year. Coconuts are the island's main cash crop. Rice is grown for domestic use and herds of cattle are also raised on the island's grassy slopes. Marinduque has some important mineral deposits, including copper and iron. Mining is the main industry on the island and two companies are licensed to operate here now. The cottage industries of the Tagalog-speaking Marinduquenos are textile weaving (from abaca), basketry and the making of items like bags and mats from *buri*.

Getting there and around

There are daily PAL flights from Manila to Boac. The airport is 13km from Boac. You can catch a boat from Cotta, near Lucena City (Quezon) every morning at 10.00. There are also twice-weekly departures from Pinamalayan and Balanacan in Mindoro. There are many jeepneys connecting the main coastal towns of the island and many of its inland villages.

Boac

Located slightly inland on the Boac River, the provincial capital of Marinduque is a bustling market town. Its main sight is its solid-looking church, built in 1792 to honour the Lady of Biglang-Awa, to whom deliverance from an attack by Moro pirates is ascribed. There are a few quite good beaches within reach of Boac, the best being Tabing Dagat, Lupac, Laylay, Balogo and Sun-Raft.

Where to stay in and around Boac

Expect prices to double during the Moriones Festival.

Susanna Inn. Tel: 1997. Good rooms with fan for P220–280, fan and bath for P300–380, and air-conditioning and bath for P440–650. Has a restaurant and is friendly.

Cely's Lodging House, on de Octobre St. Popular with budget travellers. Small, clean rooms with fan for P180. Has a restaurant.

Cassandra Beach Resort, in Caganhao. Good rooms with fan for P180, and cottages with fan and bath for P220. There is a restaurant.

Pyramid Beach Resort, in Caganhao. Tel: 1493. Friendly and helpful staff. Rooms for P170–220, with fan for P240–300.

Aussie-Pom Guest House, in Caganhao. Nicely kept and spacious rooms for P240. There is a restaurant and kitchen that can be used by guests. They also hire out snorkelling equipment.

Southern Marinduque

There are several short excursions which can be made from **Buenavista**. The town itself has an interesting market which attracts ethnic minorities from the surrounding mountains. The market is at its liveliest at the weekend. **Mount Malindig** (1,157m, 3,797ft) is accessible from here. So too are the **Malbog Sulfur Springs**, at about 3km from town. **Elefante Island**, which has the extraordinary Fantasy Elephant Club, a very upmarket beach resort built with Japanese money, can be reached by boat from Lipata. **White Beach** at Poctoy, near Torrijos, is said to be the best beach on Marinduque. *Bancas* can be hired from here for snorkelling expeditions over the reef.

Tres Reyes Islands

It only takes 30 minutes from Buenavista to the "Three Kings Islands", named, naturally, after Balthazar, Gaspar and Melchior. The islands are renowned for their good diving and snorkelling, particularly Balthazar Island. The marine life is also extensive around these islands. Watch out for the hammerhead sharks, though. There are also quite strong currents and tides between the islands, which are inhabited by fishermen. There are no real facilities for staying overnight here. You should take your own food and plenty of drinking water with you for an excursion here. *Bancas* for sailing around the Tres Reyes can be hired from the village of Pingan on the southwest coast of Marinduque.

Santa Cruz and area

Santa Cruz is Marinduque's largest settlement. There is also a port at Buyabod, 4km from the town centre. Like Boac, it has an imposing, fortress-like church, this one built in 1714. It has some quite impressive statues and paintings worth looking at. There is not a great deal to do in the town itself but it is a good place to be based for side trips in the region or out to the **Santa Cruz Islands**. There are good beaches on these shores and very few visitors. The finest for swimming and snorkelling is probably the long beach on **Maniuayan Island**. You can reach the island by boat from Batik. They usually leave around 07.00. Tricycles can be hired for the 10km ride out to **Bathala Caves**. These are on the private property of the Mendoza family, from whom you will have to buy a ticket to enter the four fully excavated caves.

Getting there

There are boats from Lucena on Luzon to Santa Cruz. Regular jeepneys connect Santa Cruz and Boac. They all go via Mogpog.

Where to stay

Rico's Inn, just in front of the school. Friendly place with fan rooms for P180–220.

Park View Lodge, near the town hall. Simple rooms for P240 with fans.

Joville Resort Hotel, 4km from town. Basic rooms with fan and bath for P340–390.

MASBATE ISLAND

Masbate Island, province and town (they all bear the same name) is an interesting halfway house between the cultures of Bicol and the Visayas. Masbate enjoys good beaches, green, hilly landscapes, highland ranges where cattle are grazed and friendly islanders who are always happy to see a stranger. Fishing, cattle farming and small-scale gold mining provide the main source of employment. Tourism as yet plays very little role in the economy of the island. Masbate remains relatively dry from January to June, with wet months for the remainder of the year. The Spanish settled the island at the end of the 16th century. Masbate's hardwood forests persuaded them to build shipyards here where galleons could be constructed.

Getting to and around the Island

PAL has daily flights from Masbate to Manila, and Monday, Wednesday and Saturday runs from Masbate to Legaspi. Masbate Airport is 1.5km south of town. Sulpicio and Madrigal lines have weekly schedules to Masbate, and William Lines has a Manila–Odiongan (on Romblon) route once a week. Sulpicio Lines also has a two-way, Cebu–Masbate route leaving Masbate on Saturday morning. Lapu-Lapu Shipping Lines also offer a weekly voyage to Cebu City from Cataingan. There are alternative routes to Samar and Romblon as well. Ask around for other, less known, shipping companies and their schedules. There are several daily jeepneys to Mandaon, where people can visit the Kalanay Cave, and to other smaller settlements on the island. *Bancas* can also be arranged for point-to-point sailing around the rocky coast. Boats can also be chartered to visit Ticao Island, facing Masbate town. Visitors can stay at the **Delavin Lodging House** in San Fernando, Ticao's main settlement.

Masbate town

The provincial capital is also the main port of entry to the island. Masbate has little to offer the visitor in the way of *divertissement* but is the best base for exploring the island and finding transport to outlying villages and unspoilt rural spots. Tramping vessels occasionally make unscheduled stops at Masbate. They are usually prepared to take more passengers on if their destinations suit you.

Where to stay/eat

Crown Hotel, on Zurilio St. Very basic rooms with fan for P220.

St Antony Hotel, on Quezon St. Tel: 180. Clean rooms with fan for P130–180, with fan and bath for P220–280, and with air-conditioning and bath for P340–400.

The food in Masbate, like the accommodation, is not stunning. You could try **Paola's Restaurant** for Filipino and European, or the **Peking House Restaurant** for Chinese food. There is also **Maxim**, and **Jona's Snackhouse**. The **Petit Restaurant**, on Quezon Street, is one of the best eateries in town.

Outrigger boat or banca *on Boracay Island*

Chapter Fourteen

The Central Visayas

The closely knit group of islands lying between Luzon and Mindanao are called the Visayas. The six largest islands in this set comprise the largest of the 11 main islands in the Philippines. The larger islands are characterised by dry, mountainous interiors, and a shortage of arable land and coastal plains. Many of the inhabitants of the Visayas have been forced to migrate to Luzon and Mindanao or even overseas in order to find work. The central Visayas is where Spanish colonisation began, quickly fanning out north to Luzon and finally to the Muslim-held areas of Mindanao and beyond. The three main cultural and linguistic groups of these islands are the Cebuanos, Ilonggos and Warays. The central Visayas comprise the islands of Cebu, Negros Oriental, Bohol and Siquidor. The coastal area of these islands are well known to tourists, especially Cebu, which offers world-class diving spots and international beach resorts. The coral and marine life of this region is exceptional. Cebu is the repository of much of the early colonial history as well as an important catalyst of Catholicism in the Philippines. The western Visayas include the islands of Panay and Negros Occidental, the home of the Ilonggos. The principal cities of this area are Iloilo and Bacolod. Iloilo is an important cultural centre and the province has a large number of remnants from the Spanish era. The city is well known for its annual Masskara Festival. Panay Island hosts one of the best-known events in the country, the Ati-Atilan Festival, the Philippines' very own Mardi Gras. Samar and Leyte are the homelands of the Warays. Samar Island is divided into three provinces and Leyte into two. Samar's best-known attractions are the Sohoton National Park and Underground Caves. Leyte is associated in many people's minds with General MacArthur's return and liberation of the Philippines. These remain some of the most underdeveloped islands in the Visayas, their economies hindered partly by their susceptibility to strong, havoc-wreaking typhoons.

CEBU ISLAND

Cebu Island, province and city occupy a key position in the country's cultural and economic life. Its geographical position at the navel of the

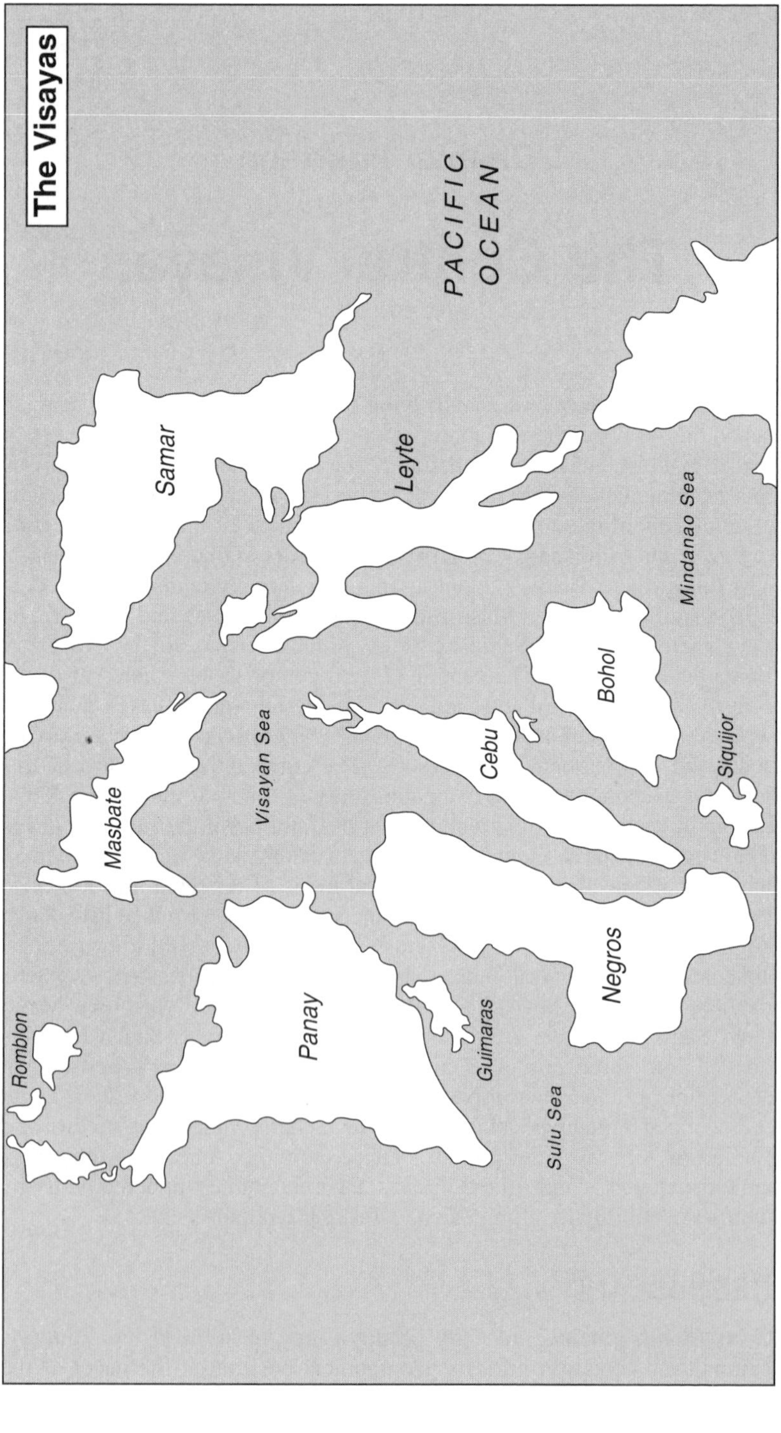

The Visayas

PACIFIC OCEAN

Samar

Leyte

Mindanao Sea

Bohol

Visayan Sea

Cebu

Siquijor

Masbate

Negros

Romblon

Panay

Guimaras

Sulu Sea

archipelago makes it the nation's main shipping crossroads. The island's excellent beaches, diving spots, and historical heritage continue to attract not only foreigners but also Filipino tourists who come in a steady stream all the year round. Both the people and the language are known as Cebuano. Zubu, or Sugbo, the original name for the kingdom of Cebu, was a prosperous entrepôt even before the arrival of the Spanish. Magellan's chronicler, Antonio Pigafetta, observed in 1521 that there were traders from Arabia, China, Japan and Siam already well established on the island, and that the local people had their own laws, industry, commerce and forms of dance and music. Gold ornaments and jewellery, he noted with satisfaction, were worn by even quite ordinary people.

Cebu Province consists of 167 islands and islets, the largest being Cebu Island, Mactan, Daanbantayan, Bantayan and the Camotes Islands. The island is flanked to the west by Negros and to the east by Bohol. Its five main cities are Cebu, Lapu-Lapu, Danao, Mandaue and Toledo. Almost all the main settlements are located along the island's narrow coastal strip. Cebu sits on the edge of the area's typhoon belt, but the southern part of the island is partly sheltered from the southwestern monsoons by the land mass of Negros. Generally speaking, central and southern Cebu are fairly dry from January to May, and somewhat wet from June to October. The driest months are February to April.

"Cebu c'est boom" has been the catchphrase used for several years to describe the mood and progressive economy of an island which has the highest per capita income and population growth in the country. With limited natural resources, industry and trade have become the mainstay of the economy, along with tourism and shipping. Its existing arable land has been put to good use, however, and as you tour the province you will see fields cultivated with rice, coconut, sugarcane, kapok, tobacco and all manner of vegetables and root crops. Corn is the food staple of the Cebuanos, much but not all of which is grown here. Grapes, mangoes and roses are important products for commercial export. Coal is a major earner with over 60% of the country's supply coming from Cebu. Visitors will note that Cebu is a major shell and coral centre. Other handicrafts apart from shellcraft include cloth weaving from fruit fibres, the production of bamboo and rattan objects, pottery and guitar making. The island has been promoted in tourist literature all over the world, and has been phenomenally successful in attracting the international traveller. Like Bali Island, the accommodation on Cebu ranges from humble bamboo and nipa huts favoured by backpackers and shoestring travellers, to the luxury five-star hotels and other complexes built in places like Nivel Hills and Mactan Island.

Getting to and around the island

Apart from over 20 daily PAL flights to Cebu, there are direct flights to the airport on Mactan Island from Hong Kong, Japan and Taiwan. There are several foreign airline offices located in Cebu. PAL's offices are at

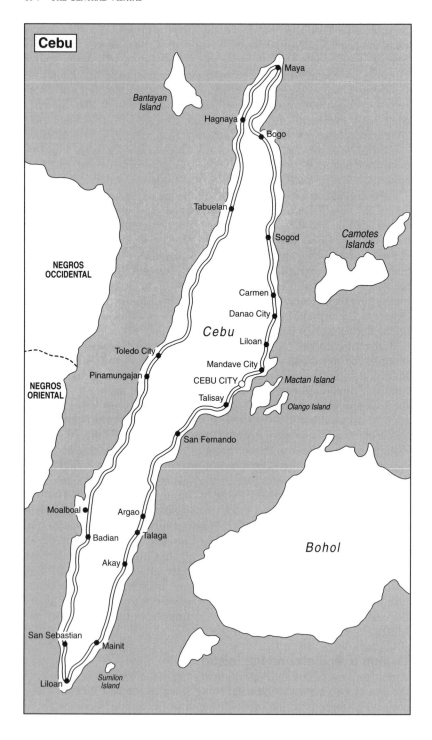

Cebu

Bantayan
Island

Maya

Hagnaya

Bogo

Tabuelan

Sogod

Camotes
Islands

NEGROS
OCCIDENTAL

Carmen

Danao City

Cebu

Liloan

Toledo City

Mandave City

Pinamungajan

CEBU CITY

Mactan Island

NEGROS
ORIENTAL

Talisay

Olango Island

San Fernando

Moalboal

Argao

Badian

Talaga

Akay

Bohol

San Sebastian

Mainit

Liloan

*Sumilon
Island*

Mactan International Airport (tel: 88435), on Escario Street (tel: 52736), and on General Maxilom Avenue (tel: 79154). The airport is 13km from the downtown area. Shuttle buses and limousines are available from the airport to the city centre. Daily sea links between Cebu, Manila and major ports within the Visayas and Mindanao are well developed. The Cebu to Bohol trip is particularly popular with visitors as it only takes about four hours. Check the shipping line notices and announcements in the local press or visit their offices directly to buy tickets and confirm schedules. These can sometimes change without warning. Buses and minibuses link all the major towns on the island. Where they don't go, jeepneys will. Taxis with and without air-conditioning are supposed to be metered, but make sure they are running before you set off. An agreed fare can be negotiated for longer journeys. Hertz have an office on General Maxilom Avenue (tel: 91143) if you would like to explore the province by car.

Cebu City

Founded in 1565, Cebu City is the oldest city in the Philippines. It is the third most populous too, after Manila and Davao, home to over 650,000 people. Its large Chinese population are mostly engaged in commerce and it also has a large body of students who come from other parts of the Visayas or Mindanao to study at its universities or colleges. For many Filipinos Cebu, with its pleasant streets, historical buildings, cheerful Cebuanos, thriving economy and apparent civic order, represents a much more congenial place to live than Manila. A lot of travellers tend to agree with this verdict, many of them deciding shortly after arrival that this is the place they will stay for the remainder of their trip. "The Queen of the South", as this likeable city is known, is not difficult to get to know even on foot. Cebu's historical monuments and fascinating backstreets are located in the old downtown area north of the port. The oldest street in the Philippines, Colon Street, named after Columbus, is located here in what used to be the old Parian District, a Chinese ghetto. It is a rather run-down and grubby-looking street these days, and doesn't seem to have kept pace with the economic development evident in Cebu's so-called "Uptown" area of smart restaurants, cafés, sports clubs, department stores and boutiques. There is a tourist information desk in Mactan International Airport but to get more detailed information, city maps and so on, go to the main tourist office in the GMC Building on Plaza Independencia near the port and Fort San Pedro area (tel: 91503).

Cebu's main sights
Magellan's Cross
This is a good place to begin a tour of the city. Magellan held the island's first Catholic Mass on Cebu on 14 April 1521, planting a cross on the spot to mark the conversion of Rajah Humabon, his family and about 800 of his

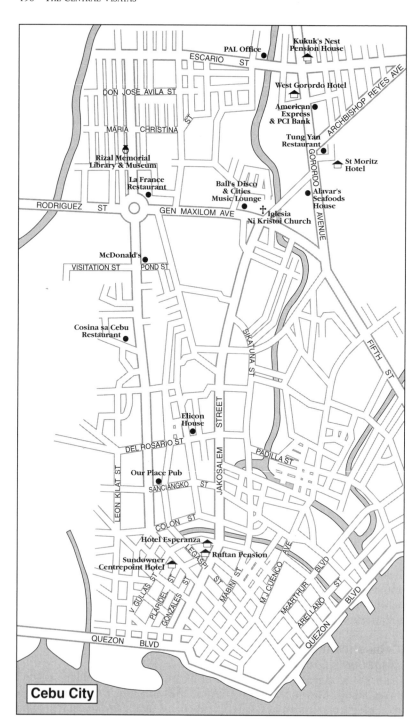

Cebu City

followers. Believing the cross to possess miraculous powers, locals took small chips from it over the centuries. To avoid it being completely whittled away, a pavilion was built near the City Hall and the remains of the original incorporated into a new cross. You can see the events of Magellan's landing and the famous mass depicted in paintings on the ceiling of the building housing the encased cross.

Fort San Pedro

Legaspi ordered the building of what is the oldest fort in the Philippines in 1565, as a defence against sea and land attacks on the settlement. The first defences were made of bamboo but were later replaced by a sturdier stone construction. Like Intramuros, Fort San Pedro, named after Legaspi's flagship, formed the nucleus of a Spanish military and clerical elite. The fort has served a number of different purposes during its chequered history: as a Spanish bastion, American military barracks, schoolhouse, Japanese prisoner-of-war camp, hospital for injured liberation troops, and now, as an innocuous garden and zoo. The fort was restored in 1968, including its roof observatory and towers. The inner court now has an open-air theatre and a café where visitors can sit in a walled garden. Admission for foreigners is P7.50.

Basilica Minore del Santo Nino

The former San Agustin Church is the only basilica in the Far East. It takes its name from the Santo Nino statue given by Magellan as a baptismal gift to Rajah Humabol's wife, Queen Juana. When Legaspi landed in Cebu after a fire had swept the city in 1565, the statue was discovered unharmed, providing yet another source of veneration for the devout Philippine people. The present Basilic Minore is built on the site where the relic was found. The diminutive, 30cm-high image is an object of great pride not only to Cebuanos but to Filipinos in general, and the January feast celebrated in Cebu in honour of the saint is echoed in smaller festivals all over the country.

Casa Gorordo Museum

Located in the main street of the old Chinese Quarter, later to become the abode of the well-to-do merchant and professional classes, the Casa Gorordo is a beautifully restored 19th-century house once owned by several generations of the influential Gorordo family. The house was opened to the public after being acquired by the Aboitiz Foundation in 1980. Paintings by Cebuano artists are exhibited on the ground floor. The upper storey contains a dining room, an office decorated in period furniture, a master bedroom, a *sala*, or living room, and a library with old photographs and books, including some faded copies of Jose Rizal's novels. The museum is open every day except Sunday, from 09.00 to 12.00, and 14.00 to 18.00. The admission price of P10 includes an interesting and informal guided tour.

Carbon Market

This market, which takes its name from an area near by, where coal used to be dumped, is the city's main central market. It is always lively and, although the wet market section may not interest visitors that much, there is a large section set aside for local handicrafts. They also display arts and craft objects from the Bohol region. There are many guitar shops in nearby Lincoln Street. It's a colourful market that attracts not only tourists but a number of pickpockets and bag-snatchers as well.

Museums and private collections

The **University of San Carlos Museum** has the most important collection of historical items in Cebu. The displays comprise a number of Spanish period objects and religious relics, and older items of ethnographic interest like burial jars and pre-Hispanic jewellery. There is also an excellent natural history section. The University of the Southern Philippines has a small exhibition area called the **Rizaliana Museum**, containing some of Rizal's writings, letters, drawings and personal effects. There are a number of private collections in the city which can be visited by arranging appointments through the tourist office. These include the **Arcenas Collection** of ceramics, the **Don Victoriano Reynes** stamp collection and the **Jumalon's Lepido Mosaic Art Gallery**, a fascinating but rather bizarre collection of mosaics made from hundreds of butterfly wings.

Taoist temples

In the millionaire ghetto of Beverley Hills to the northeast of the city centre is a large Taoist temple, evidence of the continued presence of a Chinese community on Cebu. There is a fine view of the city from the temple precincts. Slightly to the left of this temple there is another Taoist building, the Heavenly Temple of Charity, also perched at the top of a hill. This is a more interesting temple than the first one with an impressive central altar decked out with a host of favourite deities. You can get here by taking a jeepney marked "Lahug" from Jakosalem Street, or Osmena Boulevard. A taxi will take you there directly for P30–40, though they may ask for more.

Where to stay
First class

Cebu Plaza Hotel, Nivel Hills, Lahug. Tel: 311231, fax: 312069. Rooms with air-conditioning and bath from P3,000–5,800. Suites here are from P800–3,000. Five-star rating. Has a swimming pool, tennis court, coffee shop, restaurant, disco. Fine views over the city and beyond.

St Moritz Hotel, on Gorordo Ave. Tel: 74371-74, fax: 312485. Good value for this level with well decorated rooms with air-conditioning and bath for P1,540–1,680. Suites are excellent value at P2,340.

West Gorordo Hotel, on Gorordo Ave. Tel: 314347, fax: 311158. Very tastefully decorated and well run establishment. Rooms with TV, air-conditioning and bath for P1,430, and suites for P2,800. A restaurant, gym and sauna.

Montebello Villa Hotel, in Banilad. Tel: 313681, fax: 314455. On the edge of town, so quiet and with a lovely garden. Coffee shop, restaurant and swimming pool. Singles and doubles with air-conditioning and bath for P1,320–2,200. Suites range from P2,300 to 5,800.

Standard

Sundowner Centrepoint Hotel, on Fuente Osmena. Tel: 211131, fax: 210118. Clean and attractive rooms with TVs. There is a restaurant and disco. Rooms with air-conditioning and bath for P1,250–1,560.

Cebu Hallmark Hotel, on Osmena Blvd. Tel: 77671-75, fax: 53733. Reasonable place to stay but the cheaper rooms don't have windows. P280–330 for singles with fan and bath, P420–540 for singles with air-conditioning and bath, doubles for P590–700.

Park Place Hotel, on Fuente Osmena. Tel: 211131, fax: 210118. Clean and agreeable rooms, most with windows, but not all. Singles and doubles with air-conditioning and bath for P1,200–1,700, and P1,940–2,400. They have suites for P2,900. Restaurant and coffee shop.

Hotel Esperanza, on V Gullas St. Tel: 221331-35, fax: 53733. Like a lot of the hotels in the downtown area, this one can be quite noisy at night. Otherwise very good value with a decent restaurant. Rooms with fan and bath for P330, with air-conditioning and bath for P440–750. Their suites are P1,700.

Budget

Fuente Pension House, on Don Julio Lloreno St. Tel: 214133, fax: 224365. One of the quieter downtown places with a nice coffee bar on the roof. Rooms with air-conditioning and bath for P620–730.

Ruftan's Pension, on Pelaez St. Tel: 79138. Popular with budget travellers, with rooms for P220–340. Good value.

Jovel Pension House, 24-K Uytengsu Rd. Clean and comfortable rooms with fan for P290–340, with fan and air-conditioning for P440–490.

Kukuk's Nest Pension House, 157 Gorordo Ave. Tel: 312310. Very comfortable rooms in an old Cebuano-style house. Rooms with fan for P360–420, with bath and fan for P520. Breakfast is included.

Gali Pension House, on Maria Cristina St. Tel: 213626. Clean, simple rooms at low rates. Fan-only rooms for P220, rooms with air-conditioning and bath for P440. The restaurant turns into a nightclub during the evening.

Casa Loreto Pension House, 21 Don Gil Garcia St. Tel: 52879. Good sized rooms with air-conditioning and bath for P390–460. Has a coffee shop.

Elicon House, on General Junquera St. Tel: 73653, fax: 73507. Clean, standard rooms and a friendly staff. Rooms with fan only for P180–240, singles and doubles with air-conditioning for P320–420, and P440–490. There is a good café attached.

Where to eat

When it comes to food, Cebu is one place in the Philippines where visitors are spoilt for choice. Restaurants serve what seems to be in most demand, in this case Filipino, European, Japanese, Chinese and American food.

Kukuk's Nest Garden Restaurant and Pension House, on Gorordo St. Good all-round dishes served in the garden of an old Cebu house. A nice setting.

Pete's Kitchen, on Pelaez St. Nice and cheap Filipino food.

Angel Arano's, at Fairlane Village, 29 Guadllupe. An excellent Basque restaurant run by a husband and wife team. Inky squid and basted lamb dishes are particularly good.

Alavar's Seafood House, on Gorordo Ave. Well prepared seafood dishes at reasonable prices.

Cosina sa Cebu, on Ascension St. Tasty Cebuano dishes at low cost.

Tung Yan, on Archbishop Reyes St. Expensive but has a good reputation.

Talk of the Town, on Gorordo Ave. Usually gets voted the best Chinese restaurant in Cebu. Prices to match but worth it if you fancy a splurge.

Mikado Restaurant, in the Mango Plaza, General Maxilom Ave. A good place for sashimi and tempura.

Ginza Restaurant, in the Belvic Complex, General Maxilom Ave. Good general Japanese cuisine plus some Korean dishes.

Eddie's Log Cabin, on M C Briones St. Very good Filipino and American food. Their steaks are excellent. Also popular breakfast spot.

La France, at the Park Place Hotel, Fuente Osmena. High quality French and European dishes.

Shakey's Pizza, on General Maxilom Ave. The usual pizzas plus live music.

McDonald's, on Osmena Blvd. On the ground floor of the Emsu Hotel.

Café Adriatico, on Fidel Ramos St. A lovely setting for snacks and coffee in an old colonial house. One of the trendiest places to be seen in Cebu.

Entertainment and nightlife

The tourist boom has certainly made an impact on Cebu's nightlife and entertainment industry. There are countless bars, discos, cinemas, go-go joints, and nightclubs. There are even a few straightforward pubs. Nightspots are opening and closing all the time, so don't be surprised if some of the following venues listed here have moved on, changed name or vanished altogether.

Pubs, bars and music

Kentucky Bar, in the Fuente Osmena area. Cheap beer and other low-priced drinks. Rowdy and friendly.

Kukuk's Nest, on Gorordo Ave. Popular watering hole with foreigners.

Boulevard, on Osmena Blvd. Cheap beer and a large video music screen.

Our Place, on Pelaez St. Simple, unpretentious pub. Popular with foreigners and locals alike.

The Viking, on General Maxilom Ave. Go-go bar. Vietnam War R&R ambience is probably unintentional.

Silver Dollar Bar, on Osmena Blvd. Slightly seedy girlie bar.

The Club, on General Maxilom Ave. Another boozy pub. Very reasonable rates and good selection.

Discos and nightclubs

Puerto Rico Bar, on General Maxilom Ave. A performance disco and drinks venue.

Balls, on General Maxilom Ave. A popular disco.

Bai Disco, in the Cebu Plaza Hotel. One of the most popular discos in town.

Cities Music Lounge, on Genera Maxilom Ave. A good place to have a drink and watch the latest music videos.

Cebu Casino, on Nivel Hills, Lahug. An exclusive place for well-dressed and well-heeled guests who wish to try their luck at blackjack, roulette and the like.

Shopping

Although you may not wish to buy a ukelele or guitar, these are among the best known items produced in Cebu. Other noteworthy local products include rattan and bamboo furnishings, shellcraft, and export-quality mangoes. Guitars can be bought in the workshops where they are made on Mactan Island or along Lincoln Street. There are several guitar factories in the Abuno and Manbago districts on Mactan which also make mandolins and other string instruments. If you intend taking one back home with you, it is better to buy an export model made to resist non-tropical climates. They will cost a bit more but it is worth it. You should also make sure you get a sturdy case, as many airlines, PAL included, do not allow guitars to be stored as hand luggage. Carbon Market is probably the cheapest place to buy normal souvenirs. You can also haggle here. There are many excellent department stores in Cebu. Some of the best are the Gaison Main and Metro on Colon Street, Rustan's on General Maxilom Street, and Robinson's on Fuente Osmena. Good quality handicrafts and antiques can be found at Ursula's Designs at 157 Gorordo Ave. There is a duty-free shop almost next door. There are several antique and curio shops along Magellenes Street, and General Maxilom Avenue. Copies of the magazine *What's On in Cebu* and daily newspapapers like *The Freeman* and *Sun Star*, can be picked up around town, or at the National Book Store, a big Philippine book chain. Their best branch is on General Maxilom Avenue.

Scuba diving sites

Diving is one of the island's main attractions and a factor influencing many people's choice in coming here. Although diving can occasionally be interrupted by bad weather or the approach of a typhoon, diving is nevertheless a year-round activity. Visitors usually gravitate to Moalboal Island for this, as the rates here compare favourably with almost anywhere else in the Philippines. There are also good sites with properly affiliated diving courses on Sogod and Mactan islands and elsewhere. Courses leading to the PADI International Certificate can be taken at Moalboal on the west coast for as little as US$240. Many resorts also offer diving packages which include accommodation, food, equipment and a boat. This can be a good way of saving money. If you just want to float over the coral with the minimum of equipment, you can hire a mask, snorkel and flippers from a dive shop or resort for about P150 a day, sometimes a little less. A more expensive option is to join a dive boat cruise. Dive boats have cabins for overnight accommodation and can reach many interesting coral reefs and small islets that lie between Cebu and Bohol.

Mactan Island

Mactan is the closest island to Cebu, to which it is connected by a bridge. The island stands on an ancient coral reef raised about 3m above sea level. The airport, a shipyard, oil depot, and small urban centre represent its modern commercial side, with coconut plantations, fishing villages and mangrove swamps hinting at an older Mactan. The island, particularly the area around Punta Engano, is rich in shells. Many of the island's fishermen, in fact, have turned their hands in recent years to the more lucrative shell-gathering trade. Mactan is remembered as the spot where Magellan was killed by Chief Lapu-Lapu and his men in an attack that took place in knee-deep water near Punta Engano. A statue of Lapu-Lapu, now a national hero, the first Filipino to resist Spanish rule, stands in front of the town hall. The Battle of Mactan, as it is known, is celebrated every 27 April when bancas, decorated to resemble Magellan's galleon, lead a colourful water parade to the beach where he fell. A re-enactment of the planting of the cross and the battle take place in the morning. For many foreigners especially, Mactan is synonymous with a holiday in the Philippines. For the upmarket tourist, there is nothing in the archipelago to compare with the kind of exclusive beach resorts that have been built along the island's southeast coast. The town of Lapu-Lapu, founded by Augustinian monks in 1730, is the administrative centre of the island.

Where to stay in Lapu-Lapu

Cesar's Mansion Hotel, at Pusok. Tel: 400211 13, fax: 400615. Comfortable and relaxing place with a very good restaurant. Spacious rooms with air-conditioning and bath for P1,800–2,300.

HR Tourist Hotel, also at Pusok. Tel: 400048. Not prohibitively expensive, with singles and doubles with fan and bath for P480–590, and air-conditioned rooms with bath for P700–890. There is a swimming pool and restaurant.

The resorts

Most people opt to stay on or near a beach. The following is a small selection from the many options that are offered along the resort developed east coast, between Marisondon and Punta Engano.

Marigondon

Coral Reef Hotel, at Agus. Tel: 211191, fax: 211192. A little overpriced perhaps, but it does have some good amenities. Swimming pool, restaurant, tennis court, private beach and watersports equipment. Rooms with air-conditioning and bath for P4,100–5,400, suites between P12,400 and P17,000.

Hawaiian Village Inn, between Lapu-Lapu and Marigondon. A little off the beach, so cheaper. Basic cottages with fan and bath for P500.

There are a small number of cheaper options, mostly simple beach huts, in the P250–350 range. These include the **Driftwood Beach Resort, Aga's Tienda** and the **Tongo Beach Resort**.

Maribago

Club Kontiki Resort. Tel: 400310, fax: 400306. Not much of a beach here but good for diving. Fairly basic rooms with fan and bath for P740–1,600.

Maribago Bluewater Beach Resort. Tel: 211620, fax: 5010633. Excellent amenities here. Restaurant, swimming pool, tennis court, watersports facilities and diving tuition. A lovely section of the beach. Rooms with air-conditioning and bath for P3,500. There are some roomy cottages as well with air-conditioning and bath for P6,000.

Tambuli Beach Resort, in Buyong. A classy beach resort popular with Japanese tourists. Very good watersports facilities here. Comfortable and tastefully furnished singles and doubles for P2,300–3,000.

Hadsan Beach Resort, at nearby Buyong. Tel: 72679. Rooms with fan and bath for P600–740, singles and doubles with air-conditioning and bath for P1,100–2,900. Restaurant, private beach and swimming pool. Windsurfing and diving as well.

Punta Engano

Shangri-La's Mactan Island Resort. Tel: 310288, fax: 311688. A large, deluxe hotel boasting a huge swimming pool, four restaurants, a tennis court, and all the watersports you can think of, including parasailing. Rooms with all mod-cons for P5,200–11,400. Suites for P29,500.

Mar Y Cielo Beach Resort. Tel: 212232, fax: 501 1268. If you want to check out this luxury complex, you can buy an admission ticket for the day for P250. This entitles you to a meal as well. Spacious rooms with air-conditioning and bath for P2,800–3,900. Watersports facilities, restaurant, bar and swimming pool.

Olongo Island

Also known as Santa Rosa, Olongo Island is easily reached by outrigger from Maribago. The sands here are toothpaste-white and inevitably palm-fringed. The island is surrounded by coral reef, teeming with marine life and dramatic drop-offs that will thrill divers. A lot of the coral in the south has been damaged by dynamite-happy fishermen, the scourge of Filipino environmentalists. Most people visit Olongo Island as a day trip.

A coastal circuit of Cebu
Liloan to Toledo

The highway north from Cebu City takes a course that passes through the suburb of Mandaue City, past the old lighthouse at Liloan, through the city of Danao and local beaches at Mryna and Look Beach, to Carmen. This is a pleasant provincial town worth stopping off at. There are oyster farms, caves and coral gardens in this area, and a lively Ati-Atihan festival in January. Sogod, 60km north of here, is one of the first beach resorts to have been developed in this part of the island.

Sogod

This is a popular resort with good access to other beaches and islets in the area. Capitancillo Islet can be reached in two hours from Sogod. It has a marvellous, as yet unspoilt, coral reef extending for almost 3km. Ormoc Shoal and Nunez Shoal off Calanggaman Islet can also be reached by *banca* from Sogod.

Where to stay
Cebu Club Pacific Beach Resort. Tel: 212291, fax: 314621. An excellent place to stay with good scuba-diving facilities. They also organise dive packages. Has a restaurant, swimming pool and tennis court. Comfortable cottages with air-conditioning and bath for P2,200.

Alegre Beach Resort, at Calumboyan. Tel: 311231, fax: 214345. This is the above resort's main competitor. Equally good facilities. Rooms with TV, refrigerator, air-conditioning and bath for P6,500, suites for 12,000.

Bantayan Island

The waters of Bantayan Island, 15km offshore from Cebu's northern coast, are rife with reefs and shoals, coral fish, prawns, lobsters and crabs. The island is divided into the municipalities of Santa Fe, Madridejos and Bantayan. There are some good beaches on the island, mostly in Santa Fe, Talisay and Kota. The main town of Bantayan has a picturesque plaza, a well-supported market and pleasant port area. There is a small airport a couple of kilometres from the town. If you happen to be here during Holy Week you can enjoy the town's lively festival and procession. Local handicrafts centre around shellcraft and abaca weaving. Items made in this way can be seen at the open markets in Bantayan and Santa Fe. The island is reached by boat from Hagnaya. There are also buses from Cebu City to Hagnaya and San Remedio.

Where to stay

Admiral Lodging House, on Rizal Ave. One of the cheapest options with basic fan-only rooms for P130–190.

Saint Josef Lodge, on President Osmena St. Another cheap place with quite decent rooms with fans for P70–90.

Kota Beach Resort. Tel: 225661, fax: 221701. Secluded and attractive-looking spot 1km south of Santa Fe. Simple but comfortable cottages with air-conditioning and bath for P600–900.

Santa Fe Beach Club, in Talisay. Tel: 225829. The beaches in Talisay are not as good as elsewhere, but the village itself is charming and the people friendly. Cottages at this resort go for P400 with fan and bath, and for P1,100 with air-conditioning and bath.

Toledo

Located on Cebu's west coast, Toledo was only founded in 1853. It is a major mining centre. The mainstay of the local economy, in fact, are the operations being carried out in the area by the Atlas Consolidated Mining and Development Corporation, the largest copper extractors in Asia. The effect of pumping the refuse from this operation into the sea around Toledo is likely to have adverse effects on the coral and fish life of this region in the near future. Environmentalists have already pointed out that one of the by-products of copper is cyanide. You can take a bus to Toledo from the Southern Bus Terminal in Cebu City if you are interested.

Moalboal

This west coast village and beach area is one of the most popular diving spots in the country. It offers the most competitive rates in the Philippines for people interested in obtaining the PADI diving qualification. Good value applies not only to diving courses and packages but also to accommodation and food, which are very reasonable. The village of Moalboal is quite a traveller's hangout these days with shops, restaurants and cottages and bungalows springing up on any available patch of beach. A severe typhoon practically destroyed Panagsama Beach, Moalboal's main resort beach, in 1984, so if you are not particularly interested in diving or snorkelling you might be better off spending your time at White Beach, a short distance away by outrigger. Most divers make for the area around Pescador Island which has a tremendous reputation for its marine life and largely intact coral beds. You can take a *banca* or outrigger there from what remains of Panagsama Beach. There are many dive shops along Panagsama Beach. They all offer similar rates but it is worth shopping around. Some of the most reliable are Philippine Dive & Tours, Nelson's Dive Shop, Visayan Dives and Ocean Safari Philippines. Moalboal is an all-year round diving spot.

Where to stay

Ocean Safari Lodge. A clean and friendly place with simple rooms with fan and bath for P190–240.

Moalboal Reef Club Diving Lodge. A very comfortable place. Rooms that have fans are P520, with fan and bath for P680, and with air-conditioning and bath for P1,350–1,900.

Eve's Kiosk. Basic dorm beds with fan for P140, cottages with fan and bath for P180–280. There is a restaurant and bar here as well as a disco. Popular with the budget set.

Pacita's Nipa Hut. Another popular budget hangout with nice little cottages for P380, with fan and bath for a bit more.

Pacifico's Cottages. Cottages suitable for single or double occupancy with fan and bath for P200–300.

Where to eat

In the Panagsama Beach area, the most popular restaurants are **Eve's Kiosk**, **Hannah's Place**, **Pacita's**, **Susan's Seaside Restaurant** and the more upmarket **Café Europa**. **Lucy's Restaurant** is also well spoken of. **Divina's Restaurant** and **Chief Mau's Station** are lively spots to enjoy food, margaritas at sunset and a friendly evening-to-night ambience.

Liloan and Sumilon Island

The Manureva Beach Resort in Liloan, a nicely designed house run by a Frenchman, Jean-Pierre Franck, is a good place to be based for trips to nearby Sumilon and Dako Island. The resort organises trips into the interior of Cebu to places like Kawasan Falls, and also diving trips to outlying islands and islets. Sumilon Island is especially recommended. It is a noted marine life area and diving spot. There are fine white beaches and coral gardens on its eastern and northwestern coasts. Visibility is very good in these waters and you can be assured of seeing turtles, barracuda, manta rays, sea snakes, hammerhead and even whale sharks, if you stay long enough.

Argao

South of Cebu City, facing the Bohol Strait, Argao is an old town with some vestiges of the Spanish colonial era and a few good beaches, most notably at Mahawak, Kawit and Mahayahay. It became a fashionable resort back in the 1980s when the impressive Argao Beach Club opened its doors. Neighbouring Dalaguete, known for some reason as the "Summer Capital of Cebu", has a nice beach.

Where to stay

Argao Beach Resort. Tel: 74613. The best place along this stretch of the coast. Has a swimming pool, restaurant, tennis courts and all the usual watersports amenities. Singles and doubles with air-conditioning and bath from P2,300–2,700, suites for P6,000.

Bamboo Paradise. Tel: 271. A very friendly place with a popular resturant. Good value. Rooms with fan and bath for P380–440.

Sunshine Beach Club. Good moderately priced accommodation. Rooms with fan and bath for P300–400, singles and doubles with air-conditioning and bath for 640–1100. Has a swimming pool and restaurant.

NEGROS ISLAND

Located west of Cebu and southwest of Panay, Negros is the fourth largest island in the Philippines. Negros is divided into three provinces: Negros Occidental, Negros Oriental, and Negros del Norte. For travellers island-hopping through the Visayas, Negros is a convenient and logical stopover. The island's main geographical feature is Mount Kanlaon (2,465m, 8,090ft), the highest peak in the Visayas and a popular attraction for hikers. A series of volcanic peaks running from north to south form the wide Central Cordillera. This central mountain range protects western Negros from the scouring northern trade winds, but leaves it exposed to the southwestern monsoons. The island is not as typhoon prone as other parts of the Visayas. Generally speaking the island is dry from December to May, wet from June to October. The north and west are the main lowland plains set aside for cultivation. Very few roads penetrate the interior of the island. Negros took its name from its Negrito inhabitants, but nowadays the Negrito population, made up of tribes like the Aata, Mamanwas and Ati, is much reduced. The majority of its inhabitants are of Panay extraction, and close cultural ties have been kept with this neighbouring island.

For Filipinos, Negros means sugar. The island produces over half of the country's cane. Negros began to export its sugar on a large scale in the 19th century after the opening up of Cebu and Iloilo as ports for overseas commerce. The completion of the Suez Canal in 1869 was another catalyst in the growth of the island's economy. A small number of sugar barons, largely of Spanish mestizo descent, were able to amass vast fortunes almost overnight. This wealth helped them to maintain lifestyles focused around their palatial *haciendas*, of legendary decadence. Despite blatant exploitation at the hands of the feudal land-owning class, the *sacada* (plantation workers) were able to at least make a living from the sugar boom, even though the work was seasonal. All of this changed in 1985 when the world market price for sugar slumped to such a low that it was hardly worth harvesting the cane. This caused considerable civil unrest among the poor sugar-dependent Negrenses. This simmering discontent was exacerbated by the government's inability to provide aid, and the self-serving attitude of land owners unprepared to set aside even a small percentage of their land for food staple cultivation. Many Negrenses resorted to joining the New People's Army in its ongoing guerrilla war against the government. Things seem to have improved considerably since then, and the economy, with most of its eggs in one basket, has sensibly made efforts to diversify. Fish processing is an important activity, and crops like rice, corn, fruit, vegetables and root crops are now being grown. Pottery and basketry are some of its notable handicrafts. For travellers, Negros offers a number of good beaches, Spanish colonial towns, the curious gold-rush settlement of Hiniba-an, visits to sugar plantations and refineries, and hiking trails around the slopes of Mount Kanlaon.

Sugar trains

Train buffs will love this island, as a number of old locomotives are still kept in use for transporting sugar cane. Engines that have been recently retired can still be seen in their sidings. Diesel locomotives have largely replaced these lovely old wood- and bagasse-fed boilers, but during the peak of the harvest season, usually from November to May, some of these old timers are pressed back into service. You may even be able to hitch a lift on one of them if you are lucky. Over 1,600km of narrow-gauge tracks cut through the cane-fields of Negros. It is quite a sight seeing one of these blackened locos huffing and puffing its way across a spindly bridge spanning a river bed or ravine. Some of the best working and retired steam engines can be seen near the sugar mills belonging to the Central Azucarera de la Carlota in La Carlota, Ma-ao Sugar Central in Bago, the Hawaiian-Philippine Sugar Co in Silay and at Hinoba-an, where the Insular Lumber Co has a particularly rare engine on display. All extant and retired engines are listed and described in detail in Colin Carraf's interesting book, *Iron Dinosaurs*, if you can find a copy.

Getting to and around the island

There are daily PAL flights from Manila and Cebu to Bacolod and Dumaguete. Bacolod, Dumaguete and San Carlos are the main ports of entry into Negros, although there are several other ferry points from Negros to Cebu. There are regular sea links with Manila, Mindanao, Bohol, Cebu, Panay, Siquijor and Guimaras. There are no direct bus routes through the interior of Negros. Trips across country to places like Mount Kanlaon require changes, but these can be done easily enough. Regular express buses link Bacolod, Dumaguete and San Carlos. Ceres Liner buses heading for the ferry pier at Port Danao, for the crossing to Cebu, leave Bacolod at 08.00, 09.00 and 09.45 daily. Jeepneys and minibuses cover the shorter distances and tricycles are handy for city sightseeing and ferry and airport transit.

Bacolod City

Known to Filipinos as Sugar City, Bacolod is the capital of Negros Occidental. The city sits right in the centre of the sugar plantations, and its fortunes have risen and declined with the cane. It has weathered most of the bad times and remains today a pleasant, comparatively affluent city, popular as a convention centre for visiting investors and other business people. There are few remarkable sights in the city, but it is a good starting point for excursions into the sugar-growing areas nearby. Bacolod's main plaza, not far from the sea wall, is the centre of town, a popular venue for fiestas and cultural shows, or for meetings between friends after an evening promenade. Sunday afternoon is a time of great gregariousness in the plaza. San Sabastian Cathedral is near here. The wealthy suburbs of Bacolod, with their large Spanish-style mansions, are indications of the province's former wealth. So too are its fine antique collections. Some of these are well worth seeing. The Vega Antique Collection, on Mandalagan Street, has some excellent examples of ivory and wood *santos*, period furniture and a large number of Indo-Chinese ceramic items. There are more *santos* and Chinese pottery at the Torres Antique Collection, in the Torres Compound, Airport Division. People interested in rare or exotic flowers can visit the greenhouses of the Suarez Orchid Collection on Lacson Street. Bacolod's main cultural event is the week-long MassKara Festival held in October. The festival only began in 1980, and its symbol, a smiling mask, was adopted to demonstrate the people's cheerful temperament and resignation in the face of the declining sugar industry.

Getting there
There are three daily PAL flights between Bacolod and Manila, and one flight a day to Cebu. The airport is just under 4km from the downtown area. You can take a cab from the airport or walk on to the main road outside and hail a passing jeepney. Bacolod is well connected to Manila, Cebu, Guimaras Island and other destinations. Bacolod's Banago Wharf is about 7km from the city centre. There are plenty of Ceres Liner express buses to Dumaguete and San Carlos. These buses connect with the ferries leaving San Carlos for Toledo on Cebu Island. Similar connections are made with the ferry leaving Danao and Tuburan ports in Negros Occidental for Cebu. The Northern and Southern Bus terminals are the places to go. You can catch a jeepney marked "Shopping" from the plaza area to get to the terminals.

Where to stay
Bacolod Convention Plaza Hotel, on Magsaysay Ave. Tel: 83551 59, fax: 83392. Popular with business people. Extremely comfortable rooms with refrigerators, TVs, air-conditioning and bath for P2,300–2,700. Suites for P3,900. A very good restaurant and swimming pool.

Sugarland Hotel, near the airport. Tel: 22462 69, fax: 28367. Comfortable rooms with air-conditioning and bath for P700–1,100. Has a swimming pool and restaurant.

Goldenfield Garden Hotel, in the Goldenfield Commercial Complex. Tel: 83541, fax: 22356. A deluxe hotel with very comfortable and tastefully decorated rooms. With air-conditioning and bath for P1,400, suites at P2,300–2,700.

Sea Breeze Hotel, on San Juan St. Tel: 24571. A friendly establishment: rooms with air-conditioning and bath for P640–750.

Family Pension House, on Lacson St Extension. Tel: 81211. A quiet place with comfortable rooms and a friendly management. Offers a wide budget range of accommodation. Dormitory beds with fans for P90, rooms with fan and bath for P180, and with air-conditioning and bath for P240.

Halili Inn, on Lacson St. Tel: 81548. A bit run down but popular with backpackers. Rooms with fan for P90–120, with a fan and bath for P130–190, and with air-conditioning and bath for P390.

Pension Bacolod, on 11th St. Tel: 23883. No frills rooms with fan for P90–130, with fan and bath for P160–190, and with air-conditioning and bath for P320. There is a small restaurant here.

Townhouse Bacolod, on North Drive. A quiet location with clean, pleasant rooms with fan for P140–190, and with air-conditioning and bath for P240–290.

Where to eat

Las Rocas Hotel Restaurant, Simple, inexpensive Filipino dishes.

Reming's and Sons Restaurant, in the plaza. Good local Filipino food in an unpretentious setting.

Ihaw-Ihaw, on Gatuslao St. Cheap Filipino food.

Remings Food Centre, just off the plaza. Good, cheap Filipino dishes.

Seafood Market Restaurant, in the Goldenfield Commercial Complex. More upmarket with excellent seafood dishes.

Alavar's Sea Foods House, near the Family Pension House. Another fine seafood restaurant.

Inaka Japanese Restaurant, on Galo St. Good Japanese restaurant with the usual sushi, sashima, tempura and so on.

Kong Kee Diners and Bakery, Inexpensive and well prepared Chinese and Filipino food.

Old West Steakhouse, in the Goldenfield Commercial Centre. Very good steak and Western-style dishes.

Mira's Café, on Lacson St. Has very good native-grown and blended coffee.

Roli's, near the Sea Breeze Hotel. Another good coffee shop. Popular for breakfast.

There are several cheap batchoy (noodle soup) restaurants and chicken barbecue stalls around the plaza and near the Best Inn.

Entertainment and nightlife

There are several good bars, many discos and a few folk music venues in Bacolod. Some are located in the sophisticated setting of good hotels and shopping complexes, others are to be found in the seedy after-dark haunts of Gatuslao, with its go-go bars and strip joints.

Disco 2000. A popular dance spot in the Goldenfield Commercial Complex.

Macho Disco. Another favourite along Lacson St.

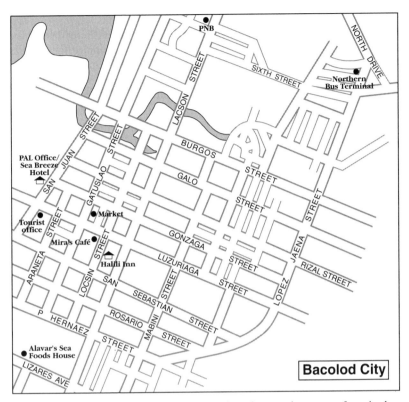

Bacolod City

Deja-vu Disco, also on Lacson St. Live bands and go-go dancers perform in the intervals between the recorded music.

Limelight Pub, in the Goldenfield Commercial Complex. A good bar with live music every night.

Music Room, on Gatuslao St. A pleasant downtown atmosphere with good music.

Negros Hot Spot, in the Goldenfield Commercial Complex. A very large live music venue.

Ang Sinugba Restaurant, on San Sebastian St. Has live folk music every night.

Super Bowling Lanes, also in the Goldenfield Commercial Complex. The largest bowling alley in the Visayas.

Macapara Golf and Country Club, within the city. Has an 18-hole course, swimming pool, tennis courts and other recreational facilities. Open to the public.

Side trips from Bacolod
There are several day or one-night trips which can be made from Bacolod. One of the most popular is to the hot sulphur springs at the **Mambucal Summer Resort**, located on the slopes of Mount Kanlaon, 32km southeast of Bacolod. The centre offers a lot more than just hot springs.

There are hiking trails, picturesque forests and woods, two spring-fed swimming pools and a small restaurant. Cabins can be rented here for P150. There is also a tourist lodge, and rooms are available at the Pagoda Inn (P200). Weekends can be very crowded and the accommodation is more expensive. Weekdays are gloriously quiet. You can get to the resort by jeepney from Libertad Street. The last jeepney back to Bacolod leaves at 16.30, but it is best to confirm this. **Mount Kanlaon National Park** begins about 5km from the outskirts of Bacolod. It is an excellent area for hiking. The slopes and lower ground can be done as a day trip, but if you want to climb the mountain properly you should allow yourself three or four days to do it comfortably. It is best to take a guide with you in either case. Guides can be organised through the Negros Mountaineering Club (tel: 23807). If you prefer, you can find your own guide in Mabucal. Some fine examples of the old "Red Dragons" as they used to be called, the brightly painted locomotives that were used on the plantations, can be seen at the Ma-ao Sugar Central, in **Ma-ao**, southeast of Bacolod, at the end of the road from Bago.

Silay City

The road north from Bacolod passes through Talisay, where the house of General Aniceto Lacson, a hero of the revolution, can be visited. Silay is an old city, much older in fact than Bacolod. Vestiges of the Spanish colonial era remain in its well-preserved colonial houses. Silay was once the foremost cultural centre of this region, a heritage evident in the superb Hofilena Art Collection, which can be found along 5th de Noviembre Street. The gallery is quite a gem, with works by Picasso, Goya, the two eminent Filipino artists Hidalgo and Luna, and other well-known names. The town is also something of a ceramic centre. You can view good quality pottery at the Maninihon Clay Products showroom. One of the biggest plantations on Negros, the Hawaiian-Philippine Sugar Company, lies just outside of Silay. This is another good place to see the old sugar trains.

Victorias

People usually stop off here to visit the Victorias Milling Company, the largest sugar mill in the world, if we are to believe the publicity blurb. Guided tours begin at the main entrance. Apart from being able to see at close range how raw cane is processed, visitors can inspect the company's venerable collection of old steam engines. Visitors who turn up in shorts, T-shirts and flip-flops, by the way, will not be admitted on the tours. The company's complex also contains the controversial "Angry Christ Mural", in its St Joseph the Worker Chapel. This extraordinary piece of religious art and psychedelia, made from broken soft-drink and beer bottles, was executed by the American artist Ade de Bethune. It is a witty and original, slightly irreverent, portrayal of Christ on the Day of Judgement, circled by saints bearing distinctly Filipino features. Tours run from 09.00 to 13.00, and from 14.30 to 16.00. There are several jeepneys daily from the

Northern Bus Terminal in Bacolod to Victorias. There is also a Rainbow minibus from Bacolod to Victorias. You then have to take another jeepney marked "VMC" to the mill.

Manapla

Another interesting free interpretation of biblical figures can be seen at the Hacienda Rosalia Chapel, a native-designed church some kilometres north of Victorias. The facade of the church has been fashioned out of wood into the shape of a salakot, a locally made hat worn by farmers to protect themselves against the sun. Christ is depicted here being crucified on a cartwheel, the kind found in this part of Negros in fact. The localisation of biblical events from the Middle East to the Philippines in general is quite extraordinary, something that travellers will notice as they move around the island. It is almost as if the whole of the New Testament were being relocated on to Philippine soil and, at times, even slightly upstaged.

Ilacaon Island

Also known as Lakawon Island, Ilacaon would make a good day trip from Manapla or Cadiz Viejo. The island is only 1km long but is blessed with a very fine white beach, palm trees and a friendly little fishing village on the island's west coast. Snorkelling on the island's coral reef is excellent. People come here at the weekend for picnics and beach life, otherwise the island is virtually empty.

Cadiz City

There is not a great deal to do in this pleasant fishing port itself, but if you happen to be there during the town's version of the Ati-Atihan festival, it would certainly be worth staying over. This is held on the fourth Sunday of January, making it possible, if you were really interested in the festival and wished to compare them, to attend the Ati-Atihan in Kalibo on the second weekend of January, the '"alternative Ati-Atihan" (see *Chapter Fifteen*) held in Ibajay the following week, and then the Cadiz one on the last weekend. It is just a thought.

San Carlos City

San Carlos is another sugar and shipping port, this one linking up with Bacolod, Dumaguete, Toledo and Cebu City. The town has a cave of some renown, the grotto of Our Lady of Lourdes, and the nearby Manit Lake and Spring. Refugio Island (also called Sipaway Island) is said to have unspoiled beaches and water with excellent visibility for snorkelling. You can hire a *banca* to take you there for about P30. You can get to San Carlos by Ceres Liner express bus from the Northern Bus Terminal in Bacolod. It takes a little over three hours. San Carlos is not an especially appealing place to stay but, if it suits, you could try the **Papal Lodge** (P150–200) on V Gustilo St, or the **Coco Grove Hotel** (P220–280) on Ylagan Street. There is also a **YMCA** near this hotel.

Dumaguete

Dumaguete City is the provincial capital and commercial centre of Negros Oriental. This city, which sits at the feet of the Cuernos de Negros Mountains, attracts a large number of students to Silliman University, a well-regarded institute founded by an American missionary, Horace B. Silliman. It is the only Protestant university in the Philippines. Its well laid-out main campus and other faculties are spread throughout the city. Its anthropology museum is well worth looking at. It has, among other things, some curious voodoo items removed from Siquijor Island. Silliman Beach and Marine Laboratory are an artificial reef made from used tyres which is not suitable for swimming, but they do have very good diving courses here twice a year. Dumaguete's market is full of life and worth a look. Other sights include the pottery workshops at nearby Daro, an old Spanish watchtower, and some moderately good beach resorts to the north at Bantayan, and at Banilad to the south.

Getting there

PAL flies twice a day to Manila and Cebu. The airport is 3.5km north of the city at Sibulan. There are regular sea links between Dumaguete, Manila, Cebu, Bohol, Mindanao and Siquijor. There are good Ceres Liner bus connections between Dumaguete and the Northern Bus Terminal in Bacolod. There are also some buses that ply the southern route between Dumaguete and Hinoba-an on the southwest coast.

Where to stay

OK Pensionne House, on Santa Rosa St. Tel: 2133. Basic but clean rooms at reasonable rates. With fan and bath for P200–260, with air-conditioning and bath for P370–440. Has a restaurant.

The Habitat, on Hibbard Ave. Tel: 3134. Friendly with clean and spacious rooms. Rooms with fan and bath for P420–550, with air-conditioning and bath for P670–800.

Plaza Inn I, on Dr V Locsin St. Friendly with a restaurant. Rooms with fan for P400, with air-conditioning and bath for P540.

Al Mar Hotel, on Rizal Blvd. Tel: 52567. A cosy and friendly place with a nice restaurant. Rooms with fan and bath for P220–330, with air-conditioning and bath for P 340–520.

Hotel de Orient, on Real St. Good rooms with fan and bath for P520, with air-conditioning and bath for P630.

South Sea Resort Hotel, in Bantayan, 2km north of town. Tel: 2857. A very comfortable place to stay with a good restaurant and swimming pool. Quite upmarket. Singles and doubles with fan and bath for P680–1,100, singles and doubles with air-conditioning, bath, TV and refrigerator for P1,140–2,450.

Panorama House and Beach Resort, on Cangmating Beach, in Sibulan. About 6km from town. Very comfortable accommodation in a spacious sea-facing house. Run by a Swiss. Singles and doubles with fan and bath for P640.

Where to eat

Baybay Restaurant, in the South Sea Resort Hotel. An excellent place for Filipino and Western food as well as seafood.

Aldea, on the corner of San Juan and Percides Sts. A nice rooftop location for reasonably priced Filipino and Chinese food.

Lab-as Seafood Restaurant, on E J Blance Rd. Native dishes and seafood at affordable prices.

Jo's Restaurant, on Percides St. Tasty chicken dishes.

Mei Yan, on the beach at Calindagan. One of the best Chinese restaurants in town.

Manson's Fastfood, on Pericles St. Good for a quick lunch.

University Cafeteria. You can stroll into the self-service cafeteria in the university if you want a quick subsidised meal.

BOHOL ISLAND

Bohol lies between Leyte and Cebu, with the Mindanao Sea washing its southern shores. Dozens more islands are attached to the province. Bohol itself is the tenth largest island in the archipelago. The island is covered in volcanic formations which have weathered into mellow, visually pleasing hills, many of which, like the famous Chocolate Hills, are covered in grass. Bohol is a major producer of coconut. Its other cash crops include abaca, sugarcane and tobacco. Grazing lands set aside for cattle and fishing are also important. The island produces steel, iron and tinplate and is said to have large deposits of manganese which is mined on the Anda Plateau. Rare shells found in the waters surrounding Bohol fetch a good price. Tagbilaran is known for its excellent seafood dishes. Dried fish (*daing*) is a local speciality. Its handicrafts, some of which are of export quality, are well known throughout the Philippines. These include shellcraft, pottery, basketry and decorative objects woven from sugar and fibres such as abaca and *buntal*. Bohol is a populous island, with almost 900,000 occupants. The Boholanos speak a Cebuano dialect which is quite distinctive. The island was settled by the Spanish as early as 1565 when Legaspi made a blood pact with the Bohol Sultan Datu Sikatuna.

Travellers are drawn to Bohol because of its splendid landscape, friendly people and good beaches. Balicasag and Cabilao are considered some of the best diving and snorkelling spots in the Philippines. Bohol is home to the world's smallest monkey, the long-tailed *tarsier.*

Getting to and around the island

PAL and Aerolift have daily flights between Manila, Cebu and Tagbilaran, the provincial capital. The airport is 3km from town and easily accessed by tricycle. The sea lanes around the island are busy with several companies operating ships between Bohol, Manila, Mindanao, Cebu and

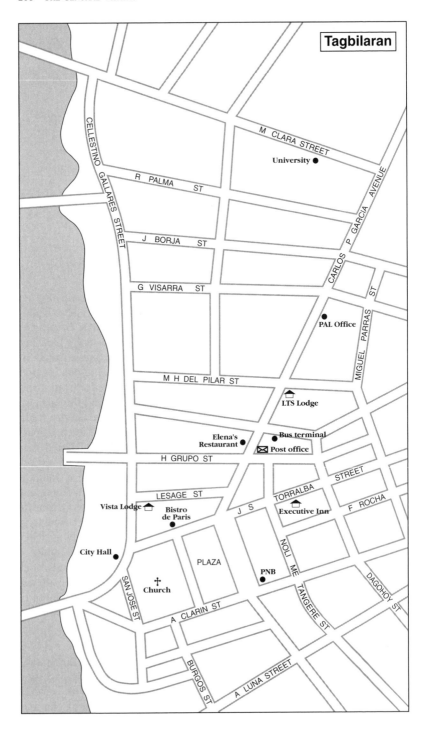

Tagbilaran

many other destinations within the Visayas. Some of the major shipping lines operating from Bohol include the William Lines, Sulpicio Lines and Sweet Lines. Tagbilaran is also the main transportation hub for land routes to Carmen, Ubat, Jagna and other major towns. Carmen, because of the Chocolate Hills, is the main destination for most visitors. Jeepneys also cover most of the main routes and provide local transport as well.

Tagbilaran City
The small provincial capital of Tagbilaran is the main commercial centre on the island and principal port of call. It is an old town with a rebuilt cathedral, lively market selling competitively priced local handicrafts, and a main plaza which is the social hub of the town. There are few sights as such to be seen, but a fine view of the town and neighbouring Panglao Island can be had from Banat-i Hill, 4km outside Tagbilaran.

Where to stay
Hotel de la Roca, on Graham Ave. Tel: 3179. Comfortable accommodation near the airport. Rooms with air-conditioning and bath for P520–840, suites for P990. Has a restaurant and swimming pool.

Matiga Lodge,Torralba St. Clean rooms in friendly guesthouse. Excellent views of the bay and Panglao Island. Rooms with fan and bath for P280–340.

Vista Lodge, on Lesage St. Tel: 3072. Simple and clean. Low rates mean that it is often full. Rooms with fan from P90–120, with fan and bath for P130–150, and with air-conditioning and bath for P260–290.

Sea Breeze Inn, on C Gallares St. Tel: 2326. Good basic but clean rooms for P190–220 with fan and bath, and for P320–440 with air-conditioning and bath. There is a restaurant here.

Executive Inn, on J S Torralba St. Good value with single and double rooms with fan for P100–130, rooms with fan and bath for P150–260, and with air-conditioning and bath for P320–440.

Bohol Tropics Resort Club, on Graham Ave. Comfortable and spacious rooms with TV, refrigerator, air-conditioning and bath for P1,100–1,640. Good amenities that include a swimming pool, fitness room, tennis court and restaurant.

Where to eat
Roberto's Bar and Restaurant, on Torralba St. Has excellent Filipino and local food. The restaurant is frequented by business people in the area. Fine views of the bay.

Horizon Restaurant, near the market. Good, inexpensive local food.

Elena's, also in the market area. Tasty Filipino and local food.

Garden Café, next door to the church. Good local dishes and some nice fruit omelettes.

The Bistro de Paris. Good for all-round European, seafood and Filipino dishes.

There are many good chicken barbecue stalls around the market and small, inexpensive seafood restaurants and stands near the wharf.

Side trips from Tagbilaran

There are various places of interest within 30 or 40km of Tagbilaran which can be reached by tricycle, jeepney or private car hire. **Mansasa**, just 2km east of the city, is the site of some interesting pre-Hispanic burial sites. Just 1km from here, **Bool** is where the blood pact between Legaspi and Sikatuna was sealed. The **Carlos P Garcia Memorial Park**, 2km from the centre of town, is a pleasant place to stroll in. It is dedicated to the Boholano who was president of the Philippines from 1957 to 1960. **Maribojoc**, 15km from town, has the famous Punta Cruz Watchtower. The Spanish built it in 1796 as a lookout post for detecting marauding pirates. The view from the top over the Visayas is excellent, especially on a clear day. **Antequera** has an interesting basketware market which is at its best on Sunday. The town is about 10km northeast of Maribojoc. **Mag-Aso Falls**, with its natural swimming pool, is only 1km from Antequera. A little northwest of Maribojoc there is an attractive church at **Loon**. The main feature of this 18th-century construction is its colourful ceiling frescoes. **Baclayon**, situated about 7km southeast of Tagbilaran, is worth visiting for its church, said to be one of the oldest in the Philippines. Built in 1595, the church is a fine building with an interesting carved altar and soaring bell tower. In the convent next door there is a small museum of religious artifacts and relics.

Panglao Island

Panglao Island is connected to Tagbilaran by two bridges, one near the City Hall, and the newer one southeast of town. Hinagdanan Cave, with a not particularly clean underground swimming pool, and caverns full of stalactites and stalagmites, is one of the main sights on the island. Most people come here for the attractive beaches and good diving and snorkelling spots. Some travellers have complained, however, that some of the more appealing beaches tend to get clogged with seaweed and seagrasses. This is particularly noticeable between December and March. The most appealing locations are Bikini Beach, Momo, Alona and Doljo beaches. There is plenty of attractive and relaxing accommodation along these beaches. The reefs found on Panglao's north and western coastline offer the best opportunities for diving and snorkelling. Panglao is a popular place to take a diving course. There are some companies running these on Alona Beach. One of the best is the Sea Quest Scuba Diving Center, where a five-day PADI Certificate course will come to US$220. The Sea Explorers Scuba Diving Centre, also on Alona Beach, is very good too. Other dive centres include the Bohol Divers Lodge, Playa Blanca and 6-Sea. The island can be reached by JG Express bus from Tagbilaran. The bus to Alona Beach takes about 90 minutes. You can also go by tricycle, but it is wise to arrange a time for the return ride as it is not easy to find one on the island later in the day.

Where to stay

Alona Beach Resort, on Alona Beach. Reputed to be the cheapest accommodation here. Simple bungalows for P200–250. Good value.

Alona Kew White Beach. Pleasant air-conditioned cottages for P600–750.

Villa Angela. Nice rooms with air-conditioning and bath for P750–900.

Swiss Bamboo House. Small place but friendly. Rooms with fan and bath for P440. Has a good restaurant and dive hire and tuition facilities.

Bohol Beach Club, 2km east of Alona. Very comfortable rooms with fan and bath for P1,600–1,850. There is a swimming pool, restaurant and diving facilities.

Hoyohoy Beach Resort, in Tawala. Comfortable cottages for P400–480.

Balicasag Island

Balicasag is an island located about 10km southwest of Panglao which can be easily reached by *banca*. The island is surrounded by a superlative coral reef which has been declared a marine sanctuary. Very few foreigners even make it here but the rewards for those who do are self-evident in the waters' rich wealth of fish, clear visibility, and in its interesting subterranean features – sunken caves, dramatic drop-offs and outstanding coral. It is possible to stay in comfortable cottages at the **Balicasag Island Dive Resort** (P1,200–1,400). You can hire equipment here and also take courses. Enquiries and reservations can be made through the Philippine Tourist Authority in the Governor's Mansion, Tagbilaran, or at the PTA on Rizal Park, Manila (tel: 599031).

Pamilacan Island

Pamilacan is another offshore gem destined before long to play host to a large number of tourists. For the time being, however, it remains a name whispered reservedly among the diving *cognoscenti*. The island's name means "Mating Place for Manta Rays". The waters are known for these giant fish, and if you are lucky you may be able to swim close to shoals of them during the breeding season. The coral, in fact, is teeming with fish of all kinds. Although some of the coral has been damaged by fishermen, there are still excellent diving sites left such as Cervera Shoal and the reefs off the north shores of Pamilacan. The island has lovely white beaches as well. It is possible to stay in a simple cottage at **Nita's Nipa Hut** for about P300. This includes meals, but you should bring your own provisions for the first night as they may not be expecting visitors.

A coastal circuit

A complete coastal circuit of the island covers 161km. This can easily be done by bus or jeepney with stopovers on the way. **Loay**, 1km east of Albuquerque, is the location for the Santa Fe Beach, a popular weekend resort with locals and people from Tagbilaran. **Loboc** is a little inland from here but worth the diversion to see its old church and monastery.

Tontonan Falls and the natural swimming pool at **Logarita Spring** are not far from here. On the road between Loay and Dimiao, **Lila** makes a good stop for the Roslaes Beach and Spring Resort. The swimming here in spring-fed pools is very refreshing. **Jagna** is an important little port for services to destinations within the Visayas. Ilihan Hill, just north of Jagna, is a well-known pilgrimage site. The beautiful Tinugdan Spring and waterfall is about 10km inland from here. **Anda** is the next town of note on the east coast. The Anda Peninsula is mined for manganese. Pre-Hispanic wooden coffins have been found in caves at nearby Candijay. There is a good beach at Anda which always seems to be empty. Bugnao Beach, south of Anda and near Candabong, is a good example of the kind of pristine, totally unspoilt beaches and bays that can still be found in the Philippines. As you progress up the east coast one of the last towns you pass through is **Ubay**, a small port where boats can be taken to Leyte Island. **Talibon** on the north coast is of a similar size and the boats that dock at its wharf sail to Cebu. It is also possible to catch a *banca* or outrigger to nearby Jao Island. Further down the west coast of Bohol, **Tubigon** has a regular ferry service to Cebu. The remainder of the road between Tubigon and Tagbilaran is dominated by the offshore islands of Inaruran, Mantatao, Pangangan, Cabilao and Sandingan, all of which offer good diving and snorkelling prospects.

The Chocolate Hills

Bohol's biggest tourist attraction certainly lives up to expectations. This extraordinary concentration of 30m-high mounds are best seen at sunrise when the declivities behind each hill swirl with sun-suffused mist, or at sunset when the formations take on a mellow character as their outlines blend. The last time I was here an innovative group of Japanese tourists were conducting a moon-viewing party with *sake* and rice-cakes. The name derives from the tonal changes that the hills undergo from green during the wetter months to a chocolate-brown at drier times, notably April and May. There are a staggering 1,268 of these limestone and shale hills in all. Geologists are not certain exactly how the mounds were formed but the most likely explanation appears to be that they were created through the interaction of clay and marine limestone, enhanced by weathering. These strange configurations are, naturally enough, the subject of numerous myths and legends. Visitors can hike through or over these hills at will. The best viewing point for photography is from the **Chocolate Hills Complex**, a youth hostel at Buenos Aires, near Carmen. Visitors are urged to stay at least one night to catch the incomparable sunsets and sunrises here. The accommodation is a bit run down, however. The swimming pool doesn't usually have any water and when it does, it often seems to go through the same colour changes as the hills. The restaurant at the complex is the only place there is to eat. Dormitory beds here are P100, rooms with bath and a balcony, with wonderfully compensating views, are P300.

Getting there

The best method is to take either an Arples Line or St Jude bus from Tagbilaran to Carmen, the main jumping-off point for the hills. It is a 2hr ride. You should tell the driver where you are going so that he can drop you off at the road that leads to the Chocolate Hills Complex. It is about a 15-minute walk to the complex from the road.

SIQUIJOR ISLAND

Siquijor is the most densely populated island in the Philippines, and yet its smallest province. The interior of this hilly limestone island, like so many others in the Visayas, is dominated by a central mountain range; the narrow deltas and floodplains around the coastal areas form fertile strips for the cultivation of crops. In the case of Siquijor, copra, rice, cassava, corn, abaca, peanuts and tobacco are important cash crops. The island is also noted for its fish and shell gathering and its mining of manganese. The Siquijodnons, as they call themselves, speak Cebuano. Travellers who make the effort to get to Siquijor will find a well-preserved environment, fine beaches and good snorkelling.

   The Spanish who first landed here in the 16th century called the island "Isla del Fuego" ("Island of Fire"). It is thought that they mistook masses of glowing fireflies, seen from the decks of their ships, for volcanic fires. Oral history holds that the island rose from the sea in a great storm that tossed up thunder and lightning bolts. The story is partly corroborated by the discovery of fossilised sea forms on the mountain interior of the island.

Beliefs and practices

Siquijor is an interesting oddity. To many Filipinos the island is synonymous with sorcery, shamanism, black magic and the excesses of voodoo. The island is certainly shrouded in its fair share of mystery. Superstition, despite centuries of Christianity, still plays a major role in the beliefs and value systems of its inhabitants. San Antonio is said to be the centre of shamanism on the island, and there are still many *mananambals,* good and malevolent witches and warlocks, active on Siquijor. Voodoo potions, incantations and agents, in the form of poisonous spiders and other venomous insects, are still employed by sorcerers in the service of clients seeking vengeance or retribution from an enemy. The whole business is very complex and, obviously, a closed door to casual visitors to the island, but sorcerers and quite legitimate herbalists can be seen during Holy Week on the island when believers and practitioners gather for the *tang-alap* ritual in San Antonio.

Getting to and around the island

Siquijor is well connected by sea with its neighbours Mindanao, Cebu, Negros and Bohol. There are daily departures from Larena to Dumaguete on Negros Oriental, and frequent ferries between Lazi and Cebu, and

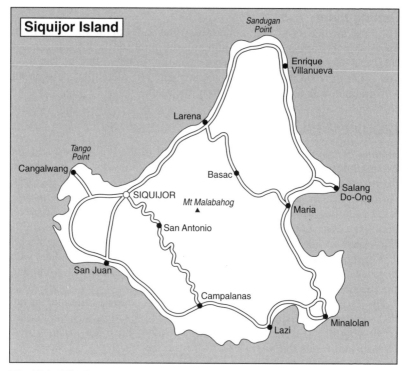

Plaridel (Mindanao) and Larena. Sweet Lines and George & Peter Lines operate a service between Larena and various destinations like Plaridel, Iligan, Cebu City and Bohol. Jeepneys and tricycles are the best way to get around the island.

Larena

Larena is really only important as a port town. A flurry of activity accompanies the arrival of a new ship. Between ships it reverts back to the pleasant, sleepy little place it normally is. There are some well-kept colonial houses worth looking at around town and an attractive bay with a good beach near Congbagsa.

Where to stay

Larena Pension House, near the wharf. Simple accommodation in rooms with fan for P120–230, or with air-conditioning for P350.

Luisa & Son's Lodge, by the wharf. There is a restaurant here and the owners are helpful people. Simple but cosy rooms for P100–120 with fan. You can also hire motorbikes or a jeep from here.

Casa de Playa, further up the coast at Sandugan. P340 for a good room with fan.

Hidden Paradise, at Bitaog, 9km north of Larena. Good value. Small cottages with baths for P200. Positioned in a well-appointed bay.

San Antonio

The small town of San Antonio is located in the mountains of the island and is known as the herbal centre of Siquijor. Many nature healers come here to learn the art, to exchange information and buy natural medicines. It's an interesting place to be during Holy Week when druid-like figures perform animist rituals, and herbalists from all over the island turn up to meet with kindred practitioners.

Siquijor

Although this is the provincial capital of the island, Siquijor is a small town noted for little more than its tasty sardines. It is a good base for visiting San Antonio and exploring the southeastern coast. There are only a few places to stay here. The **Buhisan Lodge** offers the ultimate backpacker digs with rooms for P80. The **Dondeezco Beach Resort** in Dumanhug, 2km west of Siquijor, has decent rooms with fan and bath for P330–450.

San Juan

San Juan is worth visiting for its white beach, said to be one of the best on the island. It is called Paliton Beach and there is good accommodation there at the **Coco-Grove Beach Resort**. Rooms with air-conditioning and bath are P590. They have a restaurant and you can charter an outrigger from them for trips along the coast.

Lazi

Lazi is a colonial town with an old cathedral that has some beautiful old houses. The town is better known for its Sunday cockfights and Lapac Beach, a short way out of town. The only accommodation I know of here is the **Traveller's Den**, which has clean but rather bare rooms for P200.

Salag Do-Ong

Salag Do-Ong is one of the most popular weekend beach resorts on Siquijor. The beach is not very large so it can become quite crowded at the weekends. There are good coral gardens offshore. It is located to the far north of Maria Bay, but you have to walk about 2km from the main road to reach it. Just follow the Siquijodnons.

Chapter Fifteen

Romblon and Panay

ROMBLON

Romblon Province is a mountainous region comprising about 20 islands in all, with Romblon, Tablas and Sibuyan ranking as the largest. The Spanish first visited the islands in 1582, finding them a strategically convenient stopping-off point between the Visayas and Manila. The remains of Spanish forts and watchtowers are evidence of the island's susceptibility to attacks by the Dutch and Moro pirates. The province is often called "Marble Island" by Filipinos. High quality marble is found in large quantities on Romblon, Cobrador and Alad islands, and is one of the mainstays of the economy. Other sectors include forestry, farming, fishing and cattle raising. Most Romblonanons, as they are known, speak both Ilonggo and Tagalog. There are a number of distinct regional dialects as well.

The islands offer visitors good diving and snorkelling, fine beaches and the prospect of quiet treks along the island's country roads, and over its pleasant, green hills and dales. Many visitors now include Romblon as an untaxing stopover on their way to or from Boracay and Puerta Galera.

Getting to and around the islands

PAL has flights from Manila to Tugdan Airport on Tablas, on Tuesday, Thursday and Saturday. Ferries link San Andres on Tablas with Romblon town. William Lines sails between Manila and Odiongan (Tablas) every Tuesday. Negros Navigation sails to Romblon from Manila on Mondays, and Madrigal Shipping does three runs a week between Manila and Odiongan. Several other boats arrive regularly from places like Roxas, Batangas and Lucena. Pump boats provide the main inter-island transport in this region. Jeepneys and tricycles cover an impressive amount of ground and provide links between even quite small villages. You can negotiate with tricycle-drivers to have a day's outing around the island. A circuit of Romblon Island, for example, should cost no more than P250.

Romblon Island

Romblon town is the provincial capital of the island province. Its natural harbour is one of the most sheltered in the Philippines and boats often dock here when a typhoon is brewing. The town's architecture is an interesting mixture of native, nipa-roofed houses and old Spanish buildings. Its cathedral is well worth seeing, as it has a number of valuable paintings, icons and a sumptuous Byzantine altar. The old Spanish fort of San Andres, built on a hilltop in 1640 as a defence against pirates, is now used as a weather station. There are fine views from the top. The town's lively market sells many local handicrafts including small, portable items made from marble like ashtrays, eggs and paperweights. Side trips from Romblon can be made to the lovely beach at Agnay, about 10km southwest of town, and to the so-called Marble Beach, a couple of kilometres south of here at San Pedro. Marble workshops can be visited in small villages and there are two old lighthouses out at Sabang and Apunan which can be climbed for good views of the surrounding countryside and shore.

Where to stay

Feast Inn, just behind the market. Reasonably priced rooms with fans and bath in a good location for P200–280. There is also a restaurant here.

The Agnay Tree House, 8km from town. Unusual accommodation in two side-by-side tree houses. Quite well fitted out, spacious and comfortable. Only P150 a night.

Tumanon Inn, 1.5km from town at Mapula. Popular with people who want to get away from it all. The rooms are small and simple. The daily rates (P300–450) include three square meals.

Moreno Seaside Lodge, in the harbour area. Very basic, clean rooms with fan for P90–150.

Tablas Island

Tablas is the largest of the big three islands of Romblon Province but is not as often visited as Romblon Island. Most settlements are found on the coast as most of the interior is taken up with a central spine of mountains running almost the entire length of the island. There are very few cross-island roads. There is a regular outrigger service between Romblon town and San Augustin, leaving twice daily at 08.00 and 13.00. The small airport is at Tugdan, a little north of Alcantara.

Around the towns

Santa Fe is significant only as a mooring point for pump boats arriving from Boracay and Caticlan on Panay Island. The fare to Boracay, one of the most popular beach resorts in the Philippines, is P90. You could also try hiring your own boat if there are enough of you. You can stay here at the White House, the Tourist Inn, Asis Inn and at Dolly's Place. Lodging rates range from about P200 to P300.

Looc is a small fishing port where you can also take pump boats over to Mindoro, Panay and Boracay. There are several jeepneys operating from Looc to other towns on the island like San Agustin and Odiongan. You can stay at the Plaza Inn, Tablas Pension House or at Tirol's Lodging House, all in the P100–200 range.

Odiongan is the province's largest town and its busiest port, with regular links to Manila and Batangas. The pier area is about 3km from the town centre. You can stay here at the Cabrera Lodging House, Haali Beach, Gaday's or the Shelbourne Hotel. Rates range from P200–300.

San Agustin is a cheerful little town in which to spend a night or two, and is also a good base from which to make excursions to Busal and Bitu Falls and the Cagba-a-ya ruins standing in a coconut plantation a couple of kilometres out of town. There are daily *bancas* from Romblon town to San Agustin. Tried and tested accommodation here includes the Steve Montessa Lodging House, the S& L Lodge and the Madali Lodge House, all in the P150–280 price range.

Sibuyan Island

The centre of Sibuyan Island is dominated by **Mount Guintin-guintin** (2,057m, 6,751ft), a densely forested and moss-covered peak that was first successfully ascended only in 1982. The mountain, naturally enough, is the focus of numerous myths and legends, none of them very encouraging to prospective climbers.

The main source of income for the inhabitants of the island comes from cattle raising, logging, fishing, agriculture and the weaving of tough nito vine. Sibuyan is far wilder than Romblon or Tablas, and some of its thicker forest areas have yet to be explored. The islanders are known to practise witchcraft. All things considered, Sibuyan is a pretty extraordinary place.

Magdiwang is a small town in the north of the island which serves as a dock. From there you can make a circuit of the island by jeepney. If you take the road north you can make a detour to the Kawa Kawa Waterfall where it is possible to swim. There are no lodging houses in Magdiwang. Visitors usually stay in private houses which charge about P75 per person.

Taclobo is a good springboard for making forays into the interior, the jungle-covered hills of the Cantingas River valley for example. Taclobo is situated on the southeast coast of the island. The Lagting Falls are within a short walk of Taclobo.

You can make more penetrations into Sibuyan's virgin interior from **San Fernando**. It is also possible to take a *banca* out to the nearby island of Cresta de Gallo, which is known to have excellent coral gardens. There are a small number of guesthouses in San Fernando. Among those that get the thumbs-up from travellers are Bernie's Inn and the Jenmar Lodge. Expect to pay between P90 and 150.

PANAY ISLAND

The triangular land mass of Panay Island is divided into four provinces: Aklan, Capiz, Antique and Iloilo. The Western Cordillera runs down the length of Antique Province, separating it from the other three provinces. Rugged Mount Madja (2,117m, 6,947ft) and Mount Nangtud (2,050m, 6,728ft), dominate this chain. Panay's sugar- and rice-growing plains are densely populated. The city of Iloilo, with over 300,000 residents, is the largest on the island. Livelihoods are mostly eked out from fishing, agriculture and tourism. Iloilo and Capiz are well known for their wealth of shells. Weaving is also an important, though reduced, activity. The Panay lowlands were settled in the 13th century by Bornean *datus*. According to written accounts of the event, they were greeted upon landing in San Joaquin in 1212 by Atis (Negritos), the island's dark-skinned aborigines. In exchange for purchasing a large tract of lowland plain, the newcomers gave gifts to the Atis and celebrated the agreement with a great feast, an event that forms the basis for many of the festivals that take place today on the island. With the withdrawal of the Atis to the mountains, which they continue to inhabit today, the *datus* divided the island into three *sakups,* or districts: Aklan (now Capiz and Aklan), Irong-Irong (Iloilo Province), and Hamtik (Antique). The fragments of Chinese and Siamese porcelain found in burial sites around the island are evidence of a lively overseas commerce predating the arrival of the Spanish. Legaspi occupied the island in 1569, driven there by food shortages on Cebu. The name of the island in fact comes from the Spanish *pan hay* ("there is bread"). Colonial rivals in the person of English adventurers, like the buccaneer Sir Thomas Cavendish who attacked Arevalo in 1588, and the contentious Dutch, as well as slave-seeking Moros, kept the Spanish alert until the last of the Muslim raids at the end of the 17th century. Today Panay is one of the most popular tourist destinations in the Philippines. Visitors flock to the island to attend Kalibo's extraordinary Ati-Atihan festival, to visit the elegant old colonial city of Iloilo and to spend time on Boracay Island, long regarded as one of the best beaches in Asia.

Getting to and around the island

Because of the continuing tourist boom, transport to and from Panay, like Cebu, is generally no problem. PAL has daily flights from Iloilo City and Kalibo to Cebu City, a Sunday flight from Iloilo to General Santos, and Monday, Wednesday, Thursday and Saturday flights from Iloilo City to Puerto Princesa. Boracay Air, Aerolift and Pacific Airways have daily flights to and from Manila from Iloilo City, Roxas and Kalibo.

Iloilo City is the island's foremost transportation hub for ships, but there are inter-island ports dotted all along the coastline, and many of the archipelago's sea lanes converge on Panay. There are regular boat links to Manila, Cebu, Romblon, Negros, Mindoro, Palawan, Mindanao, Leyte and other destinations. A major highway skirts the coast and there are similar routes crossing the centre of the island. These are served by numerous buses. Secondary roads, as usual, are the province of the redoubtable jeepney.

Iloilo City and Province

Iloilo is Panay's largest province and one of the country's most densely populated regions. The busy provincial capital of Iloilo is not only the commercial, transportation, educational, religious and cultural hub of this administrative division, but of the whole of the western Visayas. Rice and sugarcane, the source of the city's economic rise in the 19th century, are still trans-shipped from the harbour, and many of the fine old mansions built with the wealth they created remain in this graceful, colonial city.

Sights and events

Iloilo's post office is at the epicentre of the lively old downtown area and is a good starting point for a walking tour of the city. Alternatively, you could start at the Department of Tourism office on General Luna Street, picking up a useful town map and other information at the same time. PAL's office is on the same street (tel: 75925). So is the Philippine National Bank, one of the best places to cash travellers cheques. The waterfront is close to the post office and there is also a lighthouse and park a little further on near the mouth of the Iloilo river. This is a popular sunset promenade, and was the site of Fort San Pedro, built in 1616. The San Jose Church and Plaza Libertad are near here. J M Basa Street, a road lined with restaurants, shops, handicraft emporiums and cinemas, and the central market, is well worth a look. You can walk up from here to the Museo Iloilo, on Bonifacio Drive. The museum is called the city's "window on the past", and is an excellent introduction to the culture of Iloilo and Panay in general. Apart from its displays of Stone Age, pre-Hispanic and later items, visitors can enjoy watching video presentations highlighting the festivals and other attractions of Panay. The museum is open daily from 09.00 to 12.00, and from 13.00 to 17.00. Admission P10. If you happen to be in Iloilo City on the fourth weekend of January, you can witness the city's biggest event, the Dinagyang Festival. It is an exuberant fiesta, with a costume parade, religious processions, masses, a colourful regatta and race held in the Iloilo Strait, cockfights, and an incessant beating of drums well into the night, hinting at the pagan roots of this festival.

Where to stay

Hotel del Rio, on M H del Pilar St. Tel: 271171, fax: 70736. A very attractive hotel a short distance from the town centre. Nice location on the river. Rooms with air-conditioning and bath for P850–1,000, suites for P1,600–1,950.

Sarabia Manor Hotel, on General Luna St. Tel: 271021, fax: 79127. A first-rate hotel with swimming pool, restaurant, disco and garden. Rooms with air-conditioning, bath and TV for P840–1,000, suites from P2,900–4,200.

Castle Pensionnettes, on Bonifacio Drive, near the museum. Plain and simple rooms but clean. With fan and bath for P440–520.

The Residence Hotel, on General Luna St. Tel: 72454.

Family Pension House, on General Luna St. Tel: 27070. Popular with budget travellers. Has a good restaurant. Rooms with fan and bath for P190–220, with air-conditioning and bath for P290–640.

Eros Travellers Pensionne, on General Luna St. Tel: 71359. Basic but clean rooms for P190–240 with fan and bath, and from P260–340 with air-conditioning and bath.

Hotel Centercon, down a small lane just off of J M Basa St. Good value. Clean and reasonably sized rooms with air-conditioning and bath for P290–380.

Madia-as Hotel, on Aldeguer St. Tel: 72756-59. Comfortable rooms and a restaurant. Rooms with fan and bath for P320–360, with air-conditioning and bath for P440–520.

Where to eat
The streets around the centre of Iloilo, especially those near J M Basa St, offer a wide choice of places to eat and socialise.

Golden Salakot, in the Hotel del Rio. Not as expensive as it looks. Reasonably priced lunch and dinner buffets. Eat as much as you can.

Mansion House Restaurant, on J M Basa St. A good place for Western-style breakfasts.

The Summer House, on J M Basa St. Another good place to have breakfast, Western or Filipino style.

Oak Barrel, on Valeria St. A good eatery for trying out the western Visayas' cuisine.

Ted's Oldtimer, on Valeria St. An excellent place to try out the renowned noodle dishes of Iloilo.

Nena's Restaurant, on General Luna St. Also a good place to sample Iloilo dishes.

Lee Garden, on J M Basa St. Reasonably priced Chinese and Filipino food.

For snacks and delicacies check out the **King Ramen Restaurant** (Japanese noodles), the **Panaderia de Iloilo** and **Panaderia de Molo** on Iznart and Rizal streets for baked goodies, and the **Magnolia Icecream and Pancake House** for snacks and desserts.

Entertainment and nightlife
Tavern, on Kamalig St. A lively downtown bar.

Ihawan Garden Restaurant, on Delgado St. Has live music every night. You can just order drinks and snacks if you arrive after dinner elsewhere.

Open Air Restaurant, overlooking Fort San Pedro Drive. A popular bar.

Sugbahan Plaza. Has a number of presentations and activities including game shows, music performances and satellite video programmes.

Popular discos are the **Treasure Hunt Disco** in the Hotel del Rio, and **Base Disco** at the Sarabia Manor Hotel. Other discos worth frequenting are the **Kuweba**, **Love City Disco** and the **Bayani Super Nightclub**.

Around Iloilo

About 3km west of the city centre, visitors pass through the town of **Molo**. It is worth stopping here to have a look at the town's Gothic Renaissance church. The building is quite a feature of this area as it is made entirely from coral rock. You can also visit the Timoteo Consing Old House in the nearby plaza. It has an important collection of antiques. If you are hungry you can walk over to the Panaderia de Molo on Lopez Street. It is the oldest bakery in this part of the island and has a good selection of cakes, breads and biscuits. Another 3km further on from Molo is the residential town of **Arevalo**, with a number of well-maintained 19th-century homes. Arevalo is something of a weaving centre, locally produced and processed fibres being woven into fabrics and hand-embroidered for clothing and several other kinds of handicrafts. You can see looms functioning at Samamay Dealer on Osemena Street. The showroom where you can buy fabrics and clothes is housed in one of the town's lovely old merchant homes. **Oton**, 11km west of Iloilo, is another weaving centre. The town gained some temporary fame when a skeleton, wearing an enigmatic gold mask, and ritually surrounded by Siamese, Annamese and Chinese porcelain, was dug up in a burial site here.

Guimaras Island

This island is so close to Iloilo City that it is not necessary to overnight there, although some people like it enough to do so. It is a large island offering a lot of topographic variety and interest. Visitors come here to explore its caves, waterfalls, beaches, pleasant fishing villages and natural springs. Coral islets lie off the south and southeast coasts and there are extensive coral reefs all along the east shore. Guimaras's three municipalities are Jordan, Buenavista and Navaho Valencia. Jordan is the capital of this new province. Jordan is making a name for itself as the venue for the annual Ang Pagtaltal, a Visayan-style passion play that takes place over Good Friday. Animist beliefs and Catholicism merge in the *pangalap* ritual which is held at the Catiliran Cave in Navaho Valencia on the same day. Crowds of believers crawl on their hands and knees through the half-kilometre of caverns, chanting prayers in Latin in the hope of gaining supernatural powers and protection from evil spirits. It is quite a sight as they emerge from the gloom.

One of the more conventional sights of Guimaras is the Daliran cave near Buenavista, and Isla Nabourot, a lovely little island south of Navaho Valencia. More side-trips with a religious flavour include a visit to the Trappist monastery at Barrio San Miguel, and the 45-minute walk from Jordan to Bondulan Point. There is a huge cross on the hill here, the site of an annual re-enactment of the Crucifixion on Good

Hanging coffins near Sagada

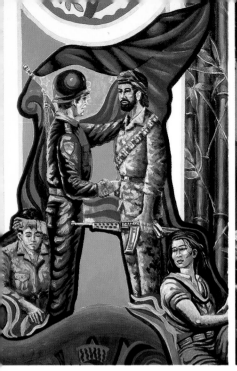

ART OF THE PHILIPPINES
Above left: *A street mural depicting an end to armed resistance*
Above right: *The land of fish and fruit*
Below: *Malaysian-style batik in Zamboanga*

Above: *Strongly associated with the Philippines, the jeepney is more than just a mode of transport*

Below: *Children on Bohol Island commandeer an abandoned car*

The sands at Boracay, where some of the finest beaches in Southeast Asia are to be found

Friday. The event attracts not only crowds of locals but a growing number of tourists. Visitors can get around the island by using jeepneys. The main routes are between Jordan and Navaho Valencia and San Isidrio, where there are boats to nearby Nagarao Island. If you want to stay on Guimaras, there is accommodation at the **Guimaras Hotel and Beach Resort**, 2km west of Jordan, the **Nagarao Island Resort**, on Nagarao Island, and at **Colmenaras Hotel and Beach Resort** in Cabalagnan.

Pan de Azucar Island

As you drive north from Iloilo City through Zarraga, Barotac Viejo and Ajuy, you will come to the market towns of Concepcion and San Dionisio. A group of attractive islands, easily reached by outrigger boat, lie within enticing visibility of these settlements. Pan de Azucar ("sugar bread") Island is the best known, and reputedly most beautiful, of the islands. Sandy white beaches, attractive landscapes, extremely friendly people and easy access would seem to be the perfect ingredients for the development of commercial tourism. From what I have seen of the island and its close neighbour, Little Agho Island, this is a very likely scenario in the near future.

Where to stay

There is no accommodation as such on the islands. Some private households are happy to put visitors up overnight, however. This is an informal arrangement and you might have to discuss things like meals. Expect to pay about P75 for the night, extra for food. In Concepcion there is the **SBS Iyang Beach Resort**. It has simple cottages with fan and bath for P280. The owners can also arrange a boat to the islands.

Sicogon Island

Continuing on the same road north, you will eventually come to Estancia, the main starting point for boats to Sicogon Island and further on to the Gigantes island group. Ceres Liner buses leave every day on the hour to Estancia from the Tanza bus terminal in Iloilo City, for the five-hour trip.

Where to stay

Pa-on Beach Resort. A little out of town. Decent rooms with fan and bath for P290–380, with air-conditioning and bath for P480–560. Has a restaurant.

The Fuentes Lodging House, on Inventor St. Very basic rooms with fan and bath for P100–190.

Terry and Em Lodge, on Cement St. Basic but clean rooms for P90–140, with fan for P130–150.

A 30-minute *banca* ride from Estancia gets you to Sicogon Island, location of the magnificent Sicogon Island Club complex. At the time of writing, the resort remains closed, but it may very well be open again by now. The forested hills around Sicigon contain wild pigs, monkeys and a host of birds. The surrounding seas are ripe with fish and lobsters, and the island's many natural springs provide cool, fresh water. The shoreline is dotted with unspoilt white beaches. You can climb Mount Bantili (335m) and take all of this in from the top.

The Gigante Islands

A two-and-a-half hour *banca* ride from Estancia will land you in one of the Gigante Islands, either Gigante Norte or Gigante Sur. The islands are wild and rugged and there is no accommodation save the hospitality of the locals, which, fortunately, is usually fairly forthcoming. There are many caves, said to be the hiding places of pirates in former times, along these shorelines. Gigante Sur has a number of interconnecting caves of which Turtle, Tiniphagan and Elephante caves are the easiest to explore. Gigante Sur has its own caves, swimming holes, and a resident population of monkeys. The Cabugao Islands, with their fine beaches and only partly unexplored caves, lie to the south of the Gigantes.

Iloilo City to San Jose de Buenavista

The route by highway from Iloilo City to Buenavista will not appeal much to beach addicts, but there are several other points of interest along this coast, and there is plenty of available transport to get there.

Guimbal

The first stretch from Iloilo City to Oton is noted for the gathering of kapis shells. Just south of Oton, Tigbauan would be a good place to stay overnight if you wanted to visit the Nadsadan Falls near Igbaras. There are two swimming holes and a resthouse there. Near Tigbauan, at Leon, there is the impressive ruin of a massive Renaissance-Romanesque style church, the biggest, apparently, in Panay.

Guimbal, a little further south, is famous for producing what are considered to be the best mangoes in Panay. It is an old town (founded in 1590) and has a yellow coral rock church to prove it. Igbaras, 11km inland from here, has another ruined church and is well known for its Santacruza Festival in May. Visitors can stay at the **Garzon Beach Resort** (P240–330) while in Guimbal.

Miagao

Completed in 1797, Miagao's famous church looks more like a Saracen fortress than a house of God. Said to be one of the finest examples of its kind in the Philippines, the church and its watchtowers were built to withstand not only attacks from marauding Moro pirates but also earthquakes, as testified by its 4m-thick walls. The facade of the church is well worth looking at, as it features a finely carved St Christopher and Infant Jesus in a tropical setting of papaya, palm and guava trees, symbols representing fertility.

San Joaquin

Another coral church, this one completely white, can be found in the town of San Joaquin. The stonework depicts scenes from the 1859 Battle of Tetuan in Morocco, in which the Moors were routed by the Spanish. On the second Saturday of January, the town celebrates Pasungay, or Festival of the Bulls, at the same time as its town fiesta. Bull, carabao and horse fights take place over the weekend. The **Talisayan Beach Resort** (P400–P500) is probably the best place to stay in San Joacquin.

Anini-y and Nogas Island

Anini-y, with its impressive old Augustinian Church of coral, is the starting point for day trips to Nogas Island. This little-known gem of an island has soft white beaches, superb diving and snorkelling potential and the appeal of few visitors. There are no regular services to the island so if you would like to go there you will have to hire a *banca* for the trip. The island is only a little way offshore so it should not cost more than about P150 for the return trip.

San Jose de Buenavista

This small town, noted for its cathedral, bamboo handicraft industry, Binirayan Festival and one or two good beaches to the north and south, is the capital of Antique Province. This rather sleepy old town is also one of Panay's gateways to Palawan and the Cuyo Islands. Visitors can stay at the **Autajay Beach Resort** (P400), the **Annavic Hotel** (P280–475) or the **Susana Guest House** (P90–130). The coastal road further north to places like Culasi and Pandan is in bad repair, so jeepneys take an inordinately long time reaching their destinations.Once you get to Pandan, there are smoother jeepney connections to places like Kalibo and Malay. There are hourly buses to and from Iloilo City. The journey takes two and a half hours.

Roxas City

This provincial capital, located at the mouth of the Panay River, is also referred to as Capiz, the name of the province. Roxas is a logical stopover between Manila and Romblon. Apart from the house and national shrine of former president Manuel Roxas, one or two Spanish watchtowers and a local handicraft industry, Roxas has little to detain the traveller. During the first week of October, however, the town hosts the exuberant Halaran Festival, a colourful carnival-like event which attracts many visitors. December 8 is also a good time to be in Roxas as the Feast of Our Lady of the Immaculate Conception is held then. Beauty pageants, cultural shows and evening, candle-lit processions are the highlights of this fiesta.

Getting there

PAL has daily flights to and from Manila. Roxas Airport (tel: 210244) is at Baybay, 4km from town. Their office is on Plaridel Street (tel: 210618).

There are weekly ships to Cebu City, Leyte, Masbate, Milagros, Palompon and other destinations. There are several Manila-bound ships every week.

There are 12 express buses every day to Iloilo City with regular buses and minibuses linking Roxas and Kalibo.

Where to stay
River Inn, on Lapu Lapu St. Tel: 809. A quiet and friendly atmosphere. Simply furnished and decorated rooms with fan for P120–140, with air-conditioning for P270.

Beehive Inn, on Roxas Ave. Tel: 418. A little run down but still good value with rooms with fan for only P90–120, with bath and fan for P130–150, and with air-conditioning and bath for P290. The Beehive also has a restaurant.

Halaran Avenue Pension, on Roxas Ave. Tel: 675. An agreeable place to stay with a restaurant. Comfortable rooms with fan for P150–190, with fan and bath for P200–240, and with air-conditioning and bath for P300–370.

Villa Patria Cottages, on Baybay Beach. Tel: 180. A pleasant and spacious place with single and double rooms for P540 and P640–800.

Where to eat
Haralan Plaza Hotel, on Rizal St. Said to be the best restaurant in town. Has a good selection of Filipino and European-style dishes at moderate prices.

Real Kitchenette. Cheap meals and snacks with live folk music during the evenings.

John's Fast Foods, near the Halaran Avenue Pension. Very cheap Filipino and Chinese dishes. A friendly atmosphere.

Halaran House Restaurant, in the guesthouse of the same name along Roxas St.

Kalibo
Kalibo is the oldest town in Aklan and the province's capital. The Aklanons, though quite closely related to the Ilonggos, speak their own very distinctive Aklanon dialect. They are well known for their dexterity in making handicrafts from rattan, bamboo and pandanus, as well as their weaving of abaca and *pina* cloth. Kalibo has three ports, a reasonable beach at Busuang, and its Museo It Aklan, which displays historical exhibits alongside contemporary local art. The Jawili Falls, 20km northwest of Kalibo near Tangalan, is well worth a visit. With its seven-tiered waterfall and swimming basins, it is one of the most beautiful spots between Kalibo and Boracay. For most of the year Kalibo is little more than a sleepy provincial backwater, a rather forgettable town travellers pass through on their way to Boracay Island. Kalibo comes alive with a vengeance during the month of January, however, when it stages its spectacular Ati-Atihan Festival.

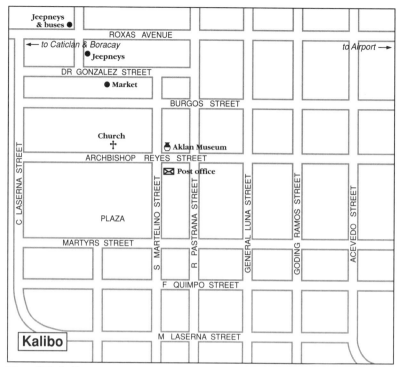

The Ati-Atihan

Variously described as the "Mardi-Gras of the Philippines", the "country's greatest party" and "the Tam-Tam Mamba of the Philippines", the extraordinary Ati-Atihan is one of the most exciting and exuberant festivals in the country, a fact attested to by the incredibly high visitor ratings over the second week of January when the event is held, and during the preceding week. The name "Ati-Atihan" means "to look like an Ati", and refers to the practice of face-blackening with soot which was first done by the early lowland settlers on the occasion of an annual festival held to renew ties with the Ati people from whom they had bought land. Spanish friars later incorporated Catholic elements into the festival by combining it with the Feast of the Santo Nino. The days preceding the festival are almost as electrifying as the main event itself, with costumes being tried on, make-up applied, dances practised and the beat of the Tam-Tam drums driving everything to a crescendo that spills out on to the streets on the Friday, when floats, parades and processions appear in full force. The climax of the festival is the Sunday when the largest procession, making its way in gloriously unrestrained fashion towards the church, is held. Many visitors join in the dancing, drinking and uninhibited revelry characterised by village groups dressed as tribes, each decked out with their own distinctive costumes, making their way along the streets to the sound of drumming and cries of *"Hala, bira!"*

Unless you enjoy festive crowds and lots of noise, the Ati-Atihan can overwhelm. Most people, however, leave having had a whale of a time. The only snag with the Ati-Atihan is finding suitable accommodation. In the end, most people settle gratefully for whatever they can get. In the days leading up to the festival, the town's lodging houses are usually full to capacity, and the tourist office, who are in charge of finding people rooms at this time, are hard pressed to accommodate visitors whose number seems to increase with every year. The only real solution, unless you can find a private household that will put you up or are prepared to pop into Kalibo two or three weeks before the event and set something up, is to book well in advance. This can be done through the Kalibo Ati-Atihan Homestay Association, c/o KAMB, Municipal Tourism Office, Kalibo, Aklan. You can also see advertisements carried by the Manila newspapers which offer excursions to the festival by ship. If you opt for this, accommodation is conveniently located aboard.

The Alternative Ati-Atihan
If you despair of ever getting accommodation but would still like to see the Ati-Atihan, make for the small town of Ibajay, equidistant from Kalibo and Caticlan, where, at least in the view of the locals, "the real thing" takes place. They may be right. The Ati-Atihan at Ibajay is just as old as the Kalibo one, more authentic in many ways and certainly far less commercialised. The festival is held on the weekend after the Kalibo one. Sunday is the climax of the event.

Getting there
There are three daily PAL flights between Kalibo and Manila. There are also four weekly flights to Cebu City. The airport is 4km from town. Boats regularly dock at Kalibo's three ports. Sulpicio Lines, Negros Navigation, Gothong Lines, William Lines and Aboitiz Lines are among the main companies whose ships dock here on their way to Manila, Cebu and other ports of call. Pump boats also connect Aklan to Mindoro and Romblon as well as a number of closer destinations like Boracay and Malay.

Obuyes Lines run regular buses between Kalibo and Roxas City, and there are also several daily Ceres Liner buses undertaking the four-hour run to Iloilo City. Look out also for buses to San Juan de Buenavista, Pandan and Caticlan. Jeepneys and tricycles, as usual, cover the in-between ground.

Where to stay
Glowmoon Hotel, on Martelino St. Tel: 3193. Cosy and clean rooms with fan for P240–330, fan and bath rooms for P400–590, and with air-conditioning and bath for P600–740.

Hibiscus Garden Club, in Andagao. A well-organised place with pleasant rooms for P380–440 with fan and for P680–770 with air-conditioning and bath. There is a restaurant and swimming pool. It doesn't cost anything for airport service both ways. Good value.

L M Plaza Lodge, Martyrs St. Very reasonably priced rooms with fan for P140, with fan and bath for P170–220, and with air-conditioning and bath for P330–440.

Gervy's Lodge, on R Pastrana St. Tel 3081. Simple but clean rooms at low cost. P80–140 with fan. There is a decent restaurant here as well. Deservedly popular with budget travellers.

Caticlan

At the northwest tip of Panay, Caticlan is the crossing point for trips to Boracay Island. Ask for the ticket counter where you have to register for the outriggers that ply the Tabon Strait between Boracay and Caticlan. If you arrive too late you can stay at the friendly and comfortable **Twin Pagoda Inn** (P200–340).

BORACAY ISLAND

For an island that is only 7km long and 1km wide at its narrowest point, comprises a mere three main villages and a number of smaller sitios, Boracay certainly carries a high profile as a tourist destination. Sadly, Boracay is no longer the Philippines' best-kept secret, and has not been for a good fifteen years or more, but the island still has one of the best beaches in Southeast Asia, as well as pretty, well-kept accommodation, friendly locals and a fine selection of restaurants. There are times, especially during the low season, when the island really does resemble a prototypical island paradise. Boracay was virtually unknown until the 1960s when the fashion for accessories made from *puka* – shells – put the island on the map. The lustre and finish of the shells found in Boracay are said to be the best in the Philippines, though their number is much depleted now. Visitors who came at that time, following the perfumed hippy trail from other parts of Southeast Asia, liked what they saw, and soon news of the delights of this idyllic island in the stream, where budget travellers could live for weeks or even months on a pittance, spread. Boracay has come a long way since then, and may now have reached the brink of overdevelopment. White Beach, Boracay's main feature, is no longer the haunt of beachcombers, solitary fishermen and unobtrusive shoestring travellers. Air-conditioned bungalows, discos, buffet lunches, bars and massage parlours have replaced the little enclaves of cheap nipa-roofed huts and the rustic restaurants lit at night by storm lamps and candles, where travellers used to repair for a simple repast of fish, salad and bottles of San Miguel. Droves of Filipinos now turn up on the island looking for work, and theft is no longer the shocking rarity it once was. Boracay may no longer be the innocent traveller's hideaway it used to be, but it remains, despite its "premier beach resort" status, an appealing and carefree place to stay for a few days or even longer. Popularity has not diminished its beauty, just made it more available. The beaches remain stubbornly beautiful, there are no ashphalted roads as yet, the water is still

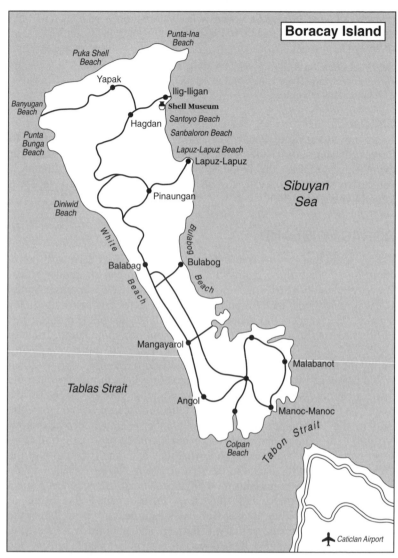

Boracay Island

Punta-Ina Beach
Puka Shell Beach
Yapak
Banyugan Beach
Ilig-Iligan
Shell Museum
Santoyo Beach
Hagdan
Sanbaloron Beach
Punta Bunga Beach
Lapuz-Lapuz Beach
Lapuz-Lapuz
Sibuyan Sea
Pinaungan
Diniwid Beach
White Beach
Bulabog Beach
Balabag
Bulabog
Mangayarol
Tablas Strait
Malabanot
Angol
Manoc-Manoc
Colpan Beach
Tabon Strait
Caticlan Airport

aquamarine, and the same balmy breezes rustle the coconut palms that line the shore. There are even several backpacker places still left, although these have been relocated behind White Beach and elsewhere. Boracay is still a relatively inexpensive place to stay.

Getting to and around the island

Aerolift has a Manila to Caticlan flight every day. In the high season, especially just before and after the Ati-Atihan Festival in Kalibo, the service is increased to three times a day. This is the quickest way there.

Pacific Airways and Boracay Air offer the same number of flights. PAL has a daily flight between Manila and Kalibo. You can take a jeepney from Kalibo to Caticlan for the crossing, or buy PAL's all-inclusive package which, for an extra P150, includes a bus connection from the airport to Caticlan and across to Boracay.

There are regular buses between Iloilo City and Caticlan, usually via Kalibo. Boat stations 1, 2 and 3 along White Beach will get you back to Caticlan. You can also arrange to hire your own *banca* or outrigger for a trip around the island or a sunset cruise. Tricycles run up and down the compacted earth road that connects Manoc-Manoc and Yapak Beach. Mountain bikes can also be hired from the Boracay Beach Club Hotel, or from Jony's Place in Balabag for about P20 a day.

Where to stay
Luxury
Fridays, at Balabag. Lovely, spacious cottages on the beach for P2,900–3,520. Reservations can be made through their Manila sales office at Romalca Hotels Inc, 8th Floor, Pacific Star Bldg, Makati. Tel: (63) 2 812 9139.

Club Panoly Resort Hotel, at Punta Bonga. Very comfortable cottages for P3,400–4,600.

Nirvana Beach Resort, in Mangayad. Good rooms in the P1,650–1,900 range.

Boracay Beach Club Hotel, in Balabag. Luxurious comfort with an excellent Spanish restaurant. Some of the rooms have real marble baths. Cottages for P1,800–2,200. Good value at this level, with breakfast thrown in.

Moderate
Lorenzo's Beach Resort, in Mangayad. Clean and spacious rooms for P780–1,200.

Red Coconut, in Balabag. Pretty cottages for P950–1,700.

Boracay Terraces, in Balabag. Cottages for P1,200–1,700.

Morimar Beach Resort, in Mangayad. Cottages in the P850–1,200 range.

Casa Pilar Cottages, also in Mangayad. Good, reasonably spacious cottages for P850–100.

Budget
Sea Breeze Cottages, in Balabag. Cottages for P250.

Serina's, also in Balabag. Cottages for P250–340.

La Isla Bonita Cottage, in Mangayad. Offers cottages for P450–740.

The Resthouse, Balabag. Very basic cottages for P260–330.

Laughing Water Cottages, in Din Iwid. Cottages on a hllside for P250–360.

Lea Homes, in Mangayad. Cottages for P400–550.

The Magic Palm, in Mangayad. Cottages for P400.

Roy's Rendevous, in Angol. Has cottages for P540–650.

Where to eat

Food is one of the great pleasures of Boracay. Lingering dinners are a good way of passing the evenings, especially if you are not enamoured of the disco or bar scene. The strip of restaurants found between Angol and Mangayad is recommended. Balabag is where the more expensive places are.

Nigi Nigi Nu Noos. If you practise it a couple of times it is easy to say. Standard Filipino food at low cost.

Boracay Garden Restaurant. A nice setting for Chinese and German food.

Casa Pilar. Good standard Filipino food.

The Green Yard. Good all-round Filipino and European dishes. Nice baked cakes. They play a lot of Chris Rea CDs here if I remember rightly.

Jony's Place. Has surprisingly authentic Mexican food.

The English Bakery and Tea Room. An excellent place for scones and the like. They used to have a special Sunday roast and Yorkshire pudding evening, quite strange fare for this tropical, saltwater island.

Red Coconut. One of the first fashionable restaurants to open on the island. Deservedly popular, with excellent European and Chinese dishes.

Chez Deparis. One of the best places for French food. There are several French places on the island.

Da Mario. The place to go for Italian dishes.

Sundown Restaurant. Good for Swiss, Austrian and German food.

Zorba. Greek food. Also some Filipino dishes.

Boracay Steak House. Probably the best charcoal-grilled steaks on Boracay.

The Hump. A good Filipino restaurant located on a hill. A lovely setting at sunset.

Entertainment and nightlife

The nightlife on Boracay can get quite heated once the sun has set and the temperature has cooled down a bit. It is surprising how animated people who spend the whole day as immobile beach lizards can become once they put their toes on a dance floor. One of the best places to step out is **Bazura's** at Mangayad, but there are plenty of choices. **The Beachcomber**, Boracay's first ever disco, is still going strong, so too are **Sharks Bar and Disco** and **Roxy Park**. **Tito's Bar** and the **Guitar Bar** are good places to hear live music. The **Sulu Bar** in Angol shows videos and has a billiards table. For a more refined evening, try the **Titay Restaurant** in Mangayad where they put on dinner buffets and cultural shows.

Island activities

A pleasantly indolent mood characterises life on Boracay, but for more purposeful travellers the island offers a number of activities to keep them busy. Although the **scuba diving** here is not as good as in other parts of the Philippines, Boracay has many diving companies that can take you out to good dive spots. Most are located along White Beach. Some of them offer courses leading to full PADI certification. Expect to pay about US$275 for a three- to five-day course, all inclusive. Some of the most reputable companies are Philippine Water Diving School, Victory Divers, Calypso Diving School, Lapuz-Lapuz Diving Safari and the Far East Scuba Diving Institute. Some of the larger beach resorts, like Fridays Boracay, Laguna de Bay and the Boracay Beach Club Hotel, also offer courses. Snorkelling is good off the eastern shore, near Lapuz-Lapuz. Masks, flippers and snorkels can be hired almost anywhere on the island for about P150 for the day. **Windsurfing** is a popular activity on Boracay, and those who have never done it before can have instruction. Tuition usually works out at about P500 an hour. **Fishing** is best done from off the side of a *banca* some way out at sea. Boats can be hired for a full day's fishing, or just plain **cruising** around the island for about P600, quite a good deal as the boats usually take up to eight people. Comfortable distances and flat terrain make **hiking** a pleasant way of getting to know the island. Particularly recommended is the hike to Puka Shell Beach on the island's northern tip. You can pass through the village of Yapak on the way. This is where puka and heishi shells were, and still are to some extent, collected. There is a small but interesting collection of sea-shells along with some other handicraft works at the **Kar-Tir Shell Museum** in Ilig-Iligan. There is a stable near Balabag where visitors can hire horses. **Horse-riding** rates are about P400 per hour, slightly cheaper by the hour if you go without a guide or for a longer period. Anyone who wishes to play **tennis** can find good courts at the Tirol-Tirol Beach Club, near the tourist office in Mangayad. It is not strictly an activity but if you would like to experience a real professional **massage**, rather than the ambiguous "massage services" found elsewhere on Boracay, try a session at the Shiatsu Centre in Mangayad. An hour's orthodox massage, or Japanese-style *shiatsu,* will cost P250.

Chapter Sixteen

Leyte and Samar

LEYTE

Leyte is broken into three administrative divisions: the province of Leyte, with its capital at Tacloban, Southern Leyte, whose capital is Maasin, and Biliran, with its provincial centre at Naval. The island is connected to neighbouring Samar by the San Juanico Bridge. The island is bisected by the Central Cordillera, a dense and rugged area of jungle slopes, rocky escarpments and forested ridges above which extinct volcanic peaks loom. A third of Leyte is said to be covered in forest. This valuable commodity, however, is gradually vanishing as the loggers move in. Some of these are blatantly illegal operations, as demonstrated in November 1991 when over 5,000 people in Ormoc died in a massive flash flood that was blamed on loggers who had reduced the forested highlands to stump and shale. Logging is an important industry and continues unabated. The wide and extensive Leyte Valley is the island's largest area of cultivated lowland. Large quantities of corn, rice, vegetables, root crops and banana are grown as staples. A certain amount of tobacco, sugarcane, abaca and coconuts are cultivated as cash crops. The Samar Sea is rich in fish.

Magellan made his first landing in the Philippines on Homonhon Island, off Samar, in 1521, before proceeding to Limasawa Island off the southern coast of Leyte. This became the site of the first Catholic mass held on Philippine soil. Most people associate Leyte with another important landing site – the return of MacArthur's liberating forces on 20 October 1944. In the subsequent fighting, much of it of the gruesome hand-to-hand variety, and often in appalling conditions, roughly 60,000 Japanese and 3,500 American soldiers perished. For today's traveller, Leyte is an interesting stepping stone on the way to or from Cebu or Mindanao.

Getting to and around the island

PAL flies daily between Tacloban and Manila, and has flights to Cebu City on Monday, Wednesday, Friday and Sunday. Tacloban is the island's main seaport, with regular connections to Manila, Cebu, Panay, Mindanao, Samar, Bohol and the Camotes Islands. There are a number of ports on the west and south coasts as well. There are regular buses and minibuses running between Tacloban and Ormoc and most of the larger towns on Leyte. There are also buses linking Tacloban with various towns on Samar. Daily Philtranco Company buses leave Tabloban for the 28-hour ride to Manila. Buses leave at 05.30 and 16.00. Jeepneys do a sterling job linking up villages off the main roads. Tricycles are the easiest mode of transport for sightseeing around towns.

Tacloban

As the provincial capital of Leyte Province, Tacloban is also its commercial, cultural and educational centre and a major transportation point. Its deepwater harbour is said to be one of the best in the Visayas. Most of the city's 140,000 Taclobanons are Warays. Numbering among their more famous public figures is Imelda Marcos, a member of the wealthy and powerful Romualdez family, who hail from Tolosa, just a few kilometres south of Tacloban. Tacloban's sights are packed into a relatively small central area easily covered on foot. Starting at the busy wharves, you can walk up a little to T Claudio Street, where the house President Osmena occupied during the liberation of the island can be viewed. Near the Plaza Libertad and Trece Martires Street, there are several stalls selling local handicrafts at knockdown prices. The mural on the wall of the provincial capital building here depicts the island's two most important events: Magellan's first mass and MacArthur's landing at Red Beach. The Tacloban Tourist Office is just in front of the Capitol if you need information or a free local map. If you enter the nearby University of the Philippines Botanical Garden, you can get a commanding view of the bay and Samar across the water divide. There is a small park near the gardens which has a statue called the Maria Kannon, which was donated by Japan as a token of peace. If you proceed to the Plaza Real you can enter the famous Santo Nino Church. It is actually the diminutive ivory statue of the Infant Jesus which attracts most interest, not the church itself. An annual city fiesta is held on 30 June to celebrate the disappearance and miraculous recovery of the statue in 1889. The adjoining Heritage Museum on Real Street has some interesting religious and ethnographic items on display. It is next door to the People's Center and Library, with a good collection of books on Leyte and Samar and some dioramas depicting ethnic tribes and some of the island's historical events. A couple of blocks from here, on Justice Romualez Street, visitors can enter the Governor's Guesthouse, formerly known as the Price Mansion after the American businessman who built it in 1910. Like many grand buildings in the Philippines, this one has a chequered history having been used, among other things, as an officer's club by the Japanese, and as MacArthur's headquarters during the liberation of Leyte and Samar. The Divine Word University is just opposite the house and is interesting to visit as it has a small museum relating the history of the island from the Stone Age right up to the 1944 landing.

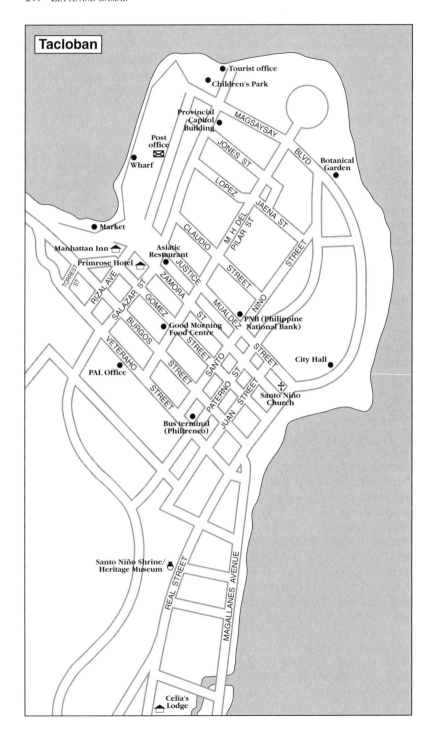

Tacloban

- Tourist office
- Children's Park
- Provincial Capitol Building
- MAGSAYSAY BLVD
- JONES ST
- Post office
- Wharf
- Botanical Garden
- LOPEZ
- JAENA ST
- Market
- CLAUDIO
- M H DEL PILAR ST
- Manhattan Inn
- Asiatic Restaurant
- Primrose Hotel
- JUSTICE ST
- ZAMORA ST
- TORREST ST
- RIZAL AVE
- SALAZAR ST
- GOMEZ ST
- MUALDEZ
- NIÑO STREET
- PNB (Philippine National Bank)
- BURGOS
- Good Morning Food Centre
- SANTO STREET
- STREET
- City Hall
- VETERAHO STREET
- PAL Office
- STREET
- PATERNO
- JUAN STREET
- ST
- Santo Niño Church
- Bus terminal (Philtrenco)
- Santo Niño Shrine/ Heritage Museum
- REAL STREET
- MAGALLANES AVENUE
- Celia's Lodge

Where to stay

The Manhattan Inn, on Rizal Ave. Tel: 4170. A popular hotel with a good restaurant. Rooms with air-conditioning and bath for P500–620, suites for P700.

Primrose Hotel, on Salazar St. Tel: 2248. Comfortable rooms with fan and bath for P240–300, with air-conditioning, bath and TV for P480–600.

Manabo Lodge, on Zamora St. Tel: 3727. Friendly establishment with clean, basic rooms for P190–280 with fan, and for P220–350 with fan and bath.

Leyte State College House, on Paterno St. Tel: 3175. Simple rooms with fan and bath for P220, and rooms with air-conditioning and bath for P240–350. Has a tearoom and canteen.

Cecilia's Lodge, on Paterno St. Tel: 2851. Simply furnished but cosy. Rooms with fan for P130–190, with fan and bath for P160–290, and with air-conditioning and bath for P320–480.

Where to eat

Agus Restaurant, near the Sagkahan fish market. Leyte is noted for its excellent seafood. This is one of the best places to sample it

Asiatic Restaurant, on Zamora St. Good Filipino and Chinese food.

Seabreeze Canteen, near the Children's Park. A nice setting with superb views of the city. Serves simple Filipino-style dishes and beer.

Good Morning Food Centre, on P Zamora St. Reasonably priced Filipino and Chinese food.

Sunburst Fried Chicken, on Burgos St. Good chicken dishes in this popular chain.

Rovic Restaurant, on Zamora St. A good place for European and American style dishes.

Felisa's is a very good place for breakfast.

Side trips from Tacloban

Red Beach, the site where American forces landed on the island, is located 12km south of Tacloban, near the town of Palo. There is a special Liberation Day ceremony held here on 20 October, which is a large well-attended event. Palo's cathedral was requisitioned as a hospital and shelter during the reoccupation. Japanese foxholes, bunkers and pillboxes can be seen on the climb up to Guinhangdan Hill behind the cathedral. The famous statue of MacArthur, General Carlos P Romulo and President Sergio Osmena wading ashore here can be seen in the Imelda Park which overlooks Red Beach. The 2km-long **San Juan Bridge**, spanning the shores of Leyte and Samar, is an impressive construction worth stopping to have a look at. It is said to be the longest bridge in Southeast Asia. It is also one of its most beautiful. It may remind travellers of another graceful construction, the cantilevered bridge that connects Butterworth with Georgetown on Penang Island, Malaysia. **Busay Falls**, 33km north of Tacloban, is a lovely setting for a half or full day's excursion. The seven-tiered falls have several natural swimming pools, an observation tower and a fish farm. The setting, amid tropical vegetation and wild orchids, is very pleasant.

Tacloban to Biliran

The highway west of Tacloban soon splits off in a northwesterly direction for Biliran Island. The island, which is connected by bridge to Leyte, became an independent province in 1992. Naval is the provincial capital. A circular road connects the main coastal towns of Almeria, Kawayan, Culaba, Caibiran and Biliran with Naval. The island's mountainous interior is covered in lush tropical forests and jungle. Biliran Volcano (1,200m, 3,938ft) can be climbed with a guide from Caibiran, but few people show much inclination to do so. The island has some quite good beaches, most notably those at Banderrahan, Naval, Agta and Sambawan. The east coast of Biliran has some excellent waterfalls and springs. The best, perhaps, are at San Bernardino, an idyllic location with lush tropical vegetation and a spring-fed pool near a beach. Mainit Spring, 30 minutes from Caibaran, is known for its curative waters. Racquiza and Libtong springs are alternative hot sulphur springs in the same area. Tumalistis Falls can be reached by *banca* from Caibiran. Locals claim that the falls have the world's sweetest water, a view endorsed, naturally, by all the island's tourist offices. You may never have a better chance of visiting Maripipi Island than when you are staying on Biliran, as this is the closest and most convenient departure point for this astonishingly beautiful and largely undeveloped island. It takes about two hours by *banca* to reach the island from Naval. Its well-preserved coral gardens and tranquil beaches are perfect for snorkelling and relaxation. One of the best beaches can be found at Napo Cove, a secluded stretch of sand on the north coast. The water here is spotlessly clear. The setting of the island, with its untouched beaches, and an extinct jungle-covered volcano at its centre, is, like several other such remote places in the Visayas and elsewhere in the Philippines, marvellously redolent of a lost world. As if to confirm the impression, visitors will find that on Maripipi there are no telephones or TVs. In fact, there is no electricity. Unfortunately for visitors, there is also no listed accommodation on the island, so if you want to stay you will have to approach one of the friendly local people and negotiate with them for a roof for the night.

Getting there

EGV Lines buses leave the wharf at Tacloban at 04.00, 05.00,12.00 and again at 15.00 for the five-hour trip to Naval. There is a bus for Caibiran as well which leaves sometime after 09.00. There are also daily buses from Ormoc to Naval and Caibiran.

Where to stay

Rosevic Executive Lodge, on Vicentillo St., in Naval. This guesthouse has reasonable rooms with fan for P120–200, with fan and bath for P240, and with air-conditioning and bath for P360.

LM Lodge, in Naval. Basic accommodation but clean. Rooms with fan only for P220.

Agta Beach Resort, at Almeria. Probably the best place to stay at present. Simple but clean rooms with fan for P120–180, with fan and bath for P140–300, and with air-conditioning and bath for P400. There is a restaurant.

Ormoc

Ormoc is a busy port connecting Leyte's west coast with Cebu. It is a lively commercial centre but has few sights worth looking at. The market and wharf area are always bustling with activity. The Philippine-Japan Peace Memorial on Carlota Hills and the remnants of an old Spanish bridge are the city's main points of interest. The Camotes Islands, which are part of Cebu Province, can be easily reached from here. Tongonan Hot Spring National Park can be reached by jeepney from Ormoc. The park is quite small, only about 3km², but there is a lot concentrated into the area, including a warm pool whose waters are said to contain curative properties, a geyser that erupts every hour, and a number of wild deer, monkeys and birds. The park is situated in the midst of forested hills at an elevation of 2,000 metres, making it pleasantly cool. The start of the Lake Danao National Park can be found at the west end of the Leyte Mountain Trail, a challenging hiking course. Lake Danao is surrounded by densely forested hills that are home to a number of wild pigs, monkeys, deer and birds.

Getting there

There are hourly buses from Ormoc to Tacloban which start at 04.00. JD Bus Lines, PEBL and Philtranco buses have a non-stop service which cuts down on time. There are also buses to Naval, Maasin and Baybay. Air-conditioned Philtranco buses leave daily for Manila at 06.45. It is better to reserve seats in advance.

Where to stay

Hotel Don Felipe, on Bonifacio St. Tel: 2460, fax: 2160. The best choice in Ormoc. Has a restaurant. Clean and comfortable rooms with fan and bath for P160–220, with air-conditioning and bath for P440–850, and P500–1,340 for suites.

Eddies Inn, on Bonifacio St. Budget accommodation with rooms with fan and bath for P120–190.

Pongo's Hotel, on Bonifacio St. Tel: 2211. A hospitable place. Also manages Pongos Lodging House. Rooms with fan and bath for P170–300, with air-conditioning and bath for P320–390. Suites are P550.

Gutierrez Guest House, on Bonifacio St. Another low-cost backpacker place. Rooms with fan for P120.

Baybay

The highway south of Tacloban hugs the Leyte Gulf, passing through the towns of Palo and Abuyog before reaching Tolosa, Imelda Marcos's hometown. As the road runs inland from Dulag, you pass the site of some major battlefields from the Second World War. There is a large Japanese war cemetery at San Diego. Another point of interest before the road reaches Baybay is the Mahagnao Volcano National Park near La Paz. The volcanic cone of Mount Mahagnao sits at the centre of the park, whose other attractions are its lake, hot sulphur springs and a lagoon. Trails lead through forests with wild orchids. Baybay is a busy little export port which also has ferries to Cebu and other points around the Visayas. An old Spanish church is the town's main feature.

Where to stay
Travellers Inn, near the pier. Basic rooms for P100.

Ellan's Lodging House, also near the pier. Habitable rooms for P100–140.

Visayan State College of Agriculture, 7km north of Baybay. The college has a guesthouse attached where it is possible to stay.

Enzian Beach Resort, at Caridad, 18km north of Baybay. A pleasant place with a restaurant and swimming pool. Comfortable rooms for P800.

Maasin
The capital of Southern Leyte Province is a port and trading centre. There are regular connections by ship from here with Cebu, Mindanao and Bohol. The town's Spanish cathedral is its main feature of interest. There are nearby beaches at Pugaling, Ibarra and Canturing, and waterfalls at Busay and Cacao.

Getting there
It takes about three hours from Tacloban to Maasin. There are several buses plying this route every day.

Where to stay
Ampil Pensione, on Abugao St. Basic rooms with fan and bath for P120–180.

Sky View Lodging House, on Garces St. Reasonable rooms with fan for P90–130.

Verano Pension House, in Matahan. Friendly and comfortable place. Nice rooms with fan for P140–190.

Liloan and Limasawa Island
People generally go to Liloan, on Panaon Island, for the diving and snorkelling. It is only a short distance by ferry from Surigao in Mindanao to Liloan. It is only a 45-minute ride by *banca* from Padre Burgos on the tip of Southern Leyte to the island of Limasawa. This is now a national shrine, containing Magellan's Cross. The spot where the navigator planted the cross, and also the grave of Rajah Kolambu, the leader who received Magellan, are well marked.

SAMAR ISLAND

The island of Samar is divided into three provinces: Eastern, Northern and Western Samar, with its coastlines facing the San Bernardino Strait, the Samar Sea and the Pacific Ocean. Samar is the second largest island in the Visayas. Lying between South Luzon and Leyte, the island is surrounded by some 180 other small islands and islets. The hills and escarpments of the island are thickly forested, plains forming a coastal strip around the island which only widens into a large area of flat cultivable land in the north. The island's main crops are rice, abaca, sweet potatoes and maize. Eastern Samar is a major producer of copra. Samar's climate is quite distinct from other parts of the Philippines. Dry spells are infrequent, rain being widespread, though rarely heavy, throughout the year. October to December sees the arrival of ferocious typhoons. May to September is generally considered to be the best time to visit Samar.

Homonhon is the small island in the Samar group where Ferdinand Magellan first landed on 16 March 1521. Surprisingly, Samar has not attracted that many visitors in the centuries since Magellan's discovery of the island. The few travellers who come here are drawn by Samar's biggest attraction, the Sohoton National Park, its reputation for good beaches, idyllic waterfalls, hot springs, remote yet-to-be-spoilt offshore islands, and its reputation as the home of the much-prized golden cowrie and other rare shells. Tourism is still in its early stages on Samar.

Getting to and around the island

PAL has flights between Calbayog and Manila every day of the week except Wednesday and Sunday. There are also Tuesday, Thursday, Friday and Sunday flights from Catarman to Manila. There are regular ferries between Samar and Manila and other points in southern Luzon as well as the other islands of the Visayas, most notably Cebu, Leyte and Masbate. The 2km long San Juan Bridge connects Leyte with Samar. There are daily air-conditioned Inland Trailways and Philtranco buses leaving Catarman for Manila. Philtranco buses originating from Mindanao also stop off at Catbalogan and Calbayog on their way to Manila, but you may find that they are full. The journey to Manila, including ferry crossings, takes between 24 and 26 hours. Jeepneys connect local villages and cover some of the shorter inland routes. Tricycles are useful for shorter runs around or in the vicinity of towns.

Allen

Allen is a small port with a busy little wharf that has ferries that go to Matnog on Luzon. You can also find boats bound for the Dalupi and Capul islands. Buenos Aires Beach, a short way out of town, is a pleasant place to kill time while you are waiting for a bus or ferry.

Where to stay
Bicolana Lodging House, near the wharf. Very basic but clean rooms for P50–90. It has a restaurant.

El Canto Lodging House. Has basic rooms for P50–100.

Buenos Aires Beach Cottages, 3km south of town. Simple cottage accommodation for P100–150.

The Balicuatro Islands
Bani and Biri islands in the Balicuatro group are considered by the diving *cognoscenti* to be among the most alluring diving spots in this area of the Visayas. The islands can be reached by boat from San Jose. The boats sail to the village of Biri, on Biri Island, and San Antonio on Tingyao. The coral gardens here are in excellent condition and the beaches, dotted at random around the craggy shores of the islands, are also well worth visiting. Large parts of the Balicuatro Islands are due to be declared as marine sanctuaries. San Antonio is an attractive little village where it is possible to stay overnight. This can be organised through the **House Schiefelbein**, a lodging house in Geratag near San Jose.

Catarman
The old Spanish port and university town of Catarman is the capital of Northern Samar Province. It is the commercial centre of the region and a trans-shipment centre for abaca. There are several quite good beaches in the vicinity of the town, the best being Calayag, Tamburosan and White Beach. Boats can be taken up the Catarman for fascinating Conradian cruises into the interior. Side trips can also be made from Catarman to Loang, the Pinipisakan Falls and scenic Batag Island.

Getting there
PAL flies five times a week between Catarman and Manila. The airport is only half a kilometre from the town centre. PAL's offices are at the airport and on Bonifacio Street.

Where to stay
Pahuwayan Lodging House, on Bonifacio St. Basic rooms with or without fan for P60–110.

Joni's Lodging House, in the market. Reasonable rooms with fan but not much else for P100–180.

J&V Hotel, at White Beach in Cawayan. Has good clean rooms for P60–100. There is a restaurant.

Calbayog City
Calbayog City is an important commercial, industrial and fishing port as well as a trans-shipment point for abaca and copra. The coastal road from Allen to Calbayog is regarded as one of the most beautiful in the

Philippines. It is particularly attractive around the village of Viriato, where all the scenic features of this route (offshore islets, colourful boats moored in picturesque bays, forested mountains, sheer cliffs and little indented coves) come together. Side trips can be made from Calbayog to nearby Darosdos Falls, Panas Falls, Ginogo-An Cave and Mapaso Spring. The Blanca Aurora Falls, 50km southeast of Calbayog, are a little off the beaten track but are considered to be the most beautiful on Samar.

Getting there
PAL has five flights a week between Calbayog and Manila. PAL's office is on Navarro Street. Buses and jeepneys regularly ply the routes between Calbayog, Allen, Catarman and Ormoc on Leyte Island. There are also weekly ships between Calbayog and Masbate.

Where to stay
Wayside Lodging House, in the centre of town. P120 for basic rooms with fan.

San Joaquin Inn, on Orquin St. Tel: 387. Very basic rooms with fan for P120–200, and with fan and bath for P220–300. Has a restaurant.

Calbayog Hotel, on the seafront, 1km from the centre. Simple but clean rooms with fan for P90–140.

Seaside Drive Inn, in Rawis. Tel: 234. The nicest place to stay in Calbayog. Clean and tidy rooms for P100–190, with fan and bath for P220, and with air-conditioning and bath for P390.

Catbalogan
Although Catbalogan is the capital of Western Samar Province, and the island's foremost commercial centre, there really is not that much reason to dally here. Most travellers who stay here are heading either towards Tacloban on Leyte Island or south towards the Sohoton National Park.

Getting there
Philippine Eagle and other bus companies serve the main bus routes from Vatbalogan to Allen, Calbayog and Catarman. There are several buses to Tacloban every day but it is more scenic to take the ferry across the San Juanico Strait. Boats drop in at Catbalogan from Manila en route to Tacloban. There is also a weekly ferry to Mindanao, and more frequent voyages to Cebu.

Where to stay
Santo Rosario Pensione, in the district of Ubanon. A simple but welcoming place with rooms for P90.

Kikay's Hotel, on Curry Ave. Tel: 664. Clean rooms with fan for P90–160, with air-conditioning and bath for P280. Has a restaurant.

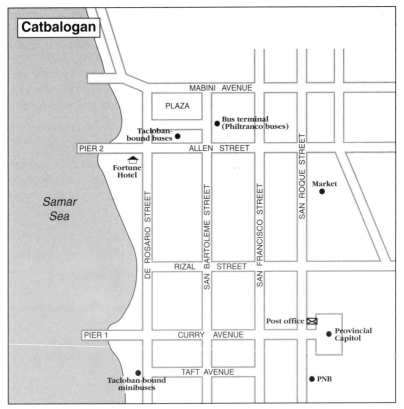

The Hotel Saint Bartholomew, on San Bartolome St. Reasonably good rooms with fan for P120–220, with fan and bath for P180–290, and with air-conditioning and bath for P390. There is a restaurant.

Fortune Hotel, on Del Rosario St. Tel: 680. A clean and well-run place. Simple rooms with fan for P120–190, with fan and bath for P240, and with air-conditioning and bath for P400. Has a restaurant.

Sohoton National Park

It takes a bit of effort getting there but no one who is on either Samar or Leyte islands should pass up the chance to visit the park. Tacloban on Leyte is actually far closer to the park than Catbalogan, and it can be done as a day trip. Either way, you should take a jeepney which is heading for the town of Basey. Once there, you will need a permit to visit the park by river. These, as well as boats, can be obtained from the local guides there. The trip upriver to the park takes just under two hours. The journey is little short of fabulous. The park is famous not only as a reserve for wild animals and as a natural beauty spot with waterfalls, forests and jungle, but for its spectacular limestone caves. The best known are Panhulugan, Bugasan and Sohoton. Aside from the predictable clusters of stalactites and stalagmites, many of the caves have crystal-encrusted walls, earning the more notable ones the name "wonder caves". Your boatman or the park ranger who lives near the entrance to the main caves will guide you through this labyrinth of caverns and underwater rivers. You will need a strong lamp for this. If you are doing the park as a day trip, it is important to start early in the morning as the last jeepney is supposed to leave around 15.00. Ideally you should aim to catch the 07.00 jeepney from Taloban. It is possible to stay overnight at the ranger's lodge but you should bring your own food and other provisions with you.

Borongan City

It is obvious from the moment that you approach Borongan that the area is a major copra centre. Coconut plantations and forests surround this former Spanish garrison, now capital of Eastern Samar. Copra, rattan and bamboo are the main trading goods of Borongan, but its handicrafts, made from *buri*, pineapple fibre, abaca and coconut husks, are also well known. Few travellers, however, actually stay here. Those who do usually end up at the Domsower Lodging House on Real Street, where comfortable rooms can be had for P130–240.

Guiuan

Guiuan is a pleasant little town to idle away a few hours in. It is located along the northeast coast of Leyte Gulf. The 16th-century church here, with its hand-carved altar and collection of *santos* , is said to be one of the finest in the eastern Visayas. There are boats from here to Tacloban every two days. Dumpao and Sapao beaches can be reached from town by tricycle. On the way to the beaches you will pass the old US naval base, now abandoned, that played quite a key role in the liberation of the island. It is possible to reach Homonhon Island, where Magellan made history, by *banca* from Guiuan. Its takes about two hours.

Where to stay

Bluestar Lodging House, on Concepcion St. Good, basic rooms for P70–120, with fan for P130–150.

Arcenos Boarding House, on Managantan St. Standard rooms for P70–110, with fan for P90–140.

Villa Rosario Lodging House, on Concepcion St. Simple accommodation but quite comfortable. Dormitory beds with fan for P70, rooms for P90–120, and with fan for P120–170.

Chapter Seventeen

Mindanao

Mindanao is a vast region, its 22 provinces covering over one-third of the archipelago's entire land mass. Its topography is varied, always surprising the traveller, with near-inaccessible mountain ranges, volcanic cones, undulating plateaux, flat plains, rivers, lakes and dense mysterious jungle and forest. Its highest peak, Mount Apo (2,954m,) is found near the city of Davao. The island is split into four administrative divisions: Western, Northern, Southern and Central Mindanao. The island's main revenue comes from agriculture. There are large banana groves and pineapple plantations in the south and in the vicinity of Cagayan de Oro. Although large tracts of the island have been cleared and exploited for their forest, mineral and energy resources, most of Mindanao's natural resources have not even begun to be developed. Migrants from Luzon and the Visayas are often drawn by the island's promise of wealth and opportunity, turning parts of Mindanao into frontier regions not unlike the American West in the last century. The occasional report in the national papers of a lucky strike by a lone prospector in the mountains of Mindanao has even been known to trigger the odd gold rush or two.

Although archaeological findings suggest that the island was settled as early as 4,000 years ago, Mindanao today is a predominantly Muslim region of the Philippines. Broadly speaking, there are three main cultural groups co-existing on the island: islanders who converted to Islam before the arrival of the Spanish, Christian migrants from other parts of the archipelago, and the tribal minorities known as "cultural communities". Problems have arisen in the past between indigenous Muslims and large numbers of Christians and lowlanders who have come to settle in areas Muslims regard as their spiritual homeland.

Getting to and around the island

PAL has numerous daily flights from a number of airports around the island, as well as international flights from Indonesia and Borneo. Cagayan de Oro, Zamboanga and Davao are major airports in Mindanao. Several ships coming from Cebu and other islands in the Visayas dock at Mindanao's northern ports, and its southern ports at Cotabata, General

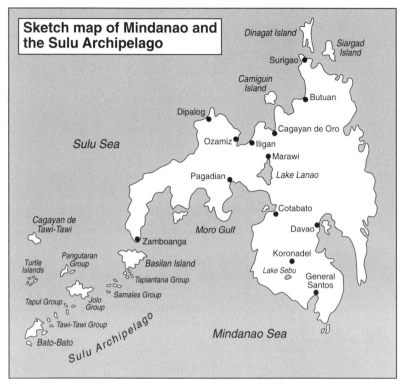

Sketch map of Mindanao and the Sulu Archipelago

Dinagat Island
Siargad Island
Surigao
Camiguin Island
Butuan
Dipalog
Cagayan de Oro
Sulu Sea
Ozamiz
Iligan
Marawi
Pagadian
Lake Lanao
Cagayan de Tawi-Tawi
Cotabato
Moro Gulf
Davao
Zamboanga
Koronadel
Pangutaran Group
Turtle Islands
Basilan Island
Lake Sebu
General Santos
Tapiantana Group
Samales Group
Tapul Group
Jolo Group
Tawi-Tawi Group
Sulu Archipelago
Mindanao Sea
Bato-Bato

Santos, Davao and Zamboanga also receive ships from the Visayas and Manila. Buses connect up with the Visayas via ferries, and it is also possible, though time consuming, to travel all the way from Manila to Davao by bus. Buses rarely travel at night internally, so dawn departures are the norm if you intend to travel a long distance within Mindanao. Everyone hopes that the entente cordial achieved back in 1996 between the government and the Moro National Liberation Front (MNLF) will continue, but should this not be the case, it would be wise to check the security situation in the area you intend to pass through before booking your seat. Minibuses and jeepneys cover shorter distances. There are also coastal launches which run from port to port. This is a good way of getting around but the boats are often subject to delays so you should allow plenty of time if you intend to use this means of transport.

CAMIGUIN ISLAND

Camiguin, a volcanic island located in the Mindanao Sea, lies about 7km from the northern mainland. There are seven volcanoes in all on Camiguin, the best known being Hibok-Hibok (1,250m, 4,102ft), which last erupted in 1951. Its rich volcanic soil supports large quantities of rice, corn, bananas, coconuts and root vegetables. Fishing is also an important activity here. The

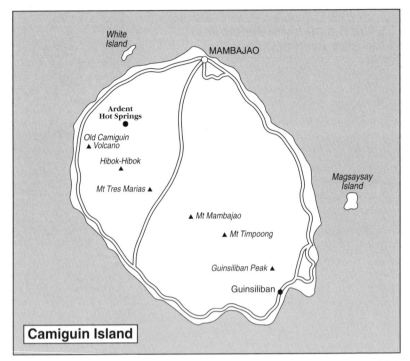

Camiguin Island

island's best-known products are sweet *lanzones,* a fruit which is plentiful, especially in October when the town of Mambajao hosts the Lanzones Festival. Easter is also a fascinating time to be on Camiguin, with its passion plays, and its Good Friday procession of impressive, life-sized *santos.*

In many people's eyes, Camiguin qualifies as another one of those Philippine island paradises. It is not difficult to see why. The island and its offshore islets are dotted with white sands, hot and cold springs, waterfalls, and picturesque villages, built on stilts over mangrove swamps, that are decorated with bougainvillaea and orchids. The Camiguenos themselves are known for their unforced friendliness and hospitality. Most travellers who visit Camiguin vow to return.

Getting to and around the island

There are PAL flights from Mambajao to Cebu City on Monday and Saturday. There are sometimes delays and cancellations as this is not a profitable run. There are more reliable ships and ferries connecting Camiguin to Mindanao, Cebu, Leyte and other parts of the Visayas. *Bancas* can also be chartered for inter-island trips. The port of entry to Camiguin is at Benoni wharf, about 17km from Mambajao. There is also a daily ferry connecting Cagayan de Oro to Guinsiliban.

It is not possible to make a complete circuit of the island in only one vehicle. You will need to combine buses, jeepneys and tricycles (called *motorellas* here). Vehicle departures and arrivals between major towns are usually set to coincide with ferry departures. You can ask around about motorbike rentals. There are no agencies here but private owners and beach resorts may be able to help you out. Providing that they are in a decent condition, this is one of the best ways of seeing the island.

Mambajao

As the provincial capital of Camiguin Province, the quiet little town of Mambajao makes a good base for exploring the island. Camiguin, though little visited, is not as remote as it sounds. In Mambajao for example, there is a tourist office, located in the Capitol Building, and it is even possible to change travellers cheques at the local branch of the PNB. The town's lively market has a good selection of basketry and locally made handicrafts, and there are some well-preserved colonial houses and an old Spanish church. The town shuts down fairly early as the electricity supply is generally cut off at around 23.00.

Where to stay

Shoreline Cottages. Well-built bungalows with fans for P320.

Tia's Beach Cottages, in Tapon, not far from the town centre. Reasonable accommodation in cottages. P300 with fan.

The Tree House, at Bolok-Bolok, 1km northwest of town. The tree houses can accommodate two people. P300. There is a restaurant, tennis court, and some watersports amenities, too, as the tree houses are located right on the waterfront. You can hire mountain bikes here too.

Gue's Guesthouse, on Cabua-an Beach, a little southeast of town. Basic rooms with fan for P250.

Island sights
Katibawasan Falls

The falls are only a kilometre or so from town by tricycle, although you will have to walk the remaining 2km from the track at the end of Pandan village to reach them. The falls are 50m high and the water very cold. If you bathe at noon it is not so chilling. It is possible to stay at the resthouse near the falls, but if you would like to do this you must make a reservation with the tourist office in Mambajao.

Ardent Hot Spring

The opposite applies to this small hot spring whose temperature is 40°C. The best time to bathe here is when it has just rained or in the very early morning when the water is not so scalding. Again, you will have to combine a short tricycle ride from Mambajao with a 1.5km walk from the church in Kuguita village. Ask locally for directions if your driver doesn't know the right path to take. There are dormitory beds (P75) and cottages (P250) if you wish to stay on.

White Island

This island, located about 2km offshore from Agoho in the north of Camiguin, boasts a wonderful white beach and excellent snorkelling opportunities. There are fine views of Hibok-Hibok to be had from here. It would be a marvellous place to set up a tent for the night, providing that you had brought enough provisions with you. It only takes 15 minutes by *banca* from Agoho.

Hibok-Hibok

The most active volcano on Camiguin, Hibok-Hibok has been responsible not only for the death of over 2,000 people on the occasion of its last major eruption in 1951, but for the exodus of over 30,000 worried islanders since then. The volcano can be climbed comfortably within four hours from Esperanza. It's an interesting climb over grass, scree and lava rock formations to the top where there is a fine view of the lake at the heart of the cone. It is possible to climb down to the crater lake. It is advisable to hire a guide from the tourist office in Mambajao before setting out.

Tangub Hot Springs

About 3km southwest of the town of Naasag are the Tangub Hot Springs, sometimes called the Mainit Hot Springs. The thermal pools here are interesting because they are positioned right next to the sea. You can sit in a pool and enjoy the bucolic mingling of salt and sulphur water, while gazing out over the sea. There are some good snorkelling spots nearby as well. You will have to pay the tricycle driver a bit extra to go here, usually something in the region of P70.

Bonbon

This half-ruined town can easily be reached on foot from Tangub Hot Springs. Much of the original town was destroyed by a lava flow after the eruption of Vulcan Daan in 1871. Part of the town, including its cemetery, is submerged. Until recently, gravestones were still visible at low tide.

Catarman

A little further down the coast, Catarman is where the Spanish relocated after the destruction of Bonbon. It is now the island's second largest town. There is a small museum in the town. The two cascades at Tuwasan Falls and the Santo Nino Cold Springs are both within access of the town. There is no accommodation in Catarman but it is possible to put up at the high school. Some local families are prepared to accept boarders too.

Benoni

This is the island's main port with ferries to and from Mindanao and elsewhere. While you are here you can visit Taguines Lagoon, an attractive artificial lake about 2km south of Benoni. A good place to stay here is the **Travel Lodge** (P200), which serves superb food, including fish they have bred themselves. The cottages here are built over a network of bamboo bridges.

THE MINDANAO MAINLAND
Surigao City
The trading centre and capital of small Surigao Province has a population of about 185,000 people. The town was already a busy commercial centre even before the arrival of the Spanish. The Casa Real, or Governor's Residence, is a reminder of the colonial era. So too is the town's main plaza, a busy place at all times. The waterfront market also attracts a lot of activity. For travellers, Surigao is a convenient jumping-off point for trips to the Siargao and Dinagat islands, and as a starting point for a descent of Mindanao from the north. Visitors can also spend time on Mabua Beach, where the swimming is reputed to be excellent. Day-asan, a floating village about 5km from Surigao, makes an interesting half-day side trip. There are over 300 houses in the village, all of them built on stilts over a mangrove swamp. Early December to the end of January can be wet in the north of Mindanao. April to June are the optimum months for fine weather.

Getting there
There is a PAL flight between Surigao and Cebu City once a day. Aerolift has direct flights every day between Surigao and Manila. Escano Lines, Sweet Lines, Negros Navigation and Abolitiz Lines have regular weekly or twice weekly ships between Surigao and Manila. When the weather allows, there are also large *bancas* plying the route between Surigao and Pintayan on Panoan Island. There are several express buses connecting Surigao to Butuan City, Cagayan de Oro and Davao.

Where to stay
Fredden Hotel, on Borromeo St. Inexpensive, basic rooms with fan for P230.

Tavern Hotel, on Borromeo St. Tel: 87300. The No 1 place in town. Rooms with fan for P90–120, with fan and bath for P120–220, and with air-conditioning and bath for P380–600. Has a restaurant.

Litang Hotel, on Borromeo St. Simple but clean rooms with fan for P260.

Flourish Lodge, also on Borromeo St. Basic and clean. Rooms with fans for P90–120.

Garcia Hotel, on San Nicolas St. Tel: 658. A reasonably good place. Rooms with fan for P90–140, with air-conditioning and bath for P240–300.

Where to eat
Daddings Refreshments, next to the market. A good line in cheap Filipino dishes. Popular with the locals.

Cherry Blossom Restaurant, on San Nicolas St. A good selection of Filipino and other dishes. Has live music in the evenings.

New Perlas Kitchen, near the plaza. Inexpensive dishes in a friendly atmosphere.

Tavern Hotel, on Borromeo St. A nice setting near the waterfront.

Rimon's Food Shop, on the outskirts of town. A good place for inexpensive Chinese and Filipino dishes.

Offshore islands
There are numerous offshore islands and islets east of Surigao where the sands are white and the sailing good. Islands like Nonoc, Hikdop, Dinagat, Bayagnan and Sibale are easy enough to get to by *banca* but, despite their scenic beauty, few travellers seem inspired to go there. Most foreigners head for Siargao Island, the largest of the offshore islands. Dapa is its largest town but most travellers make for General Luna. Union, a village set in a bay with an outstanding beach, is easily reached from here. It is also possible to visit the attractive islands of Anahawan, Daco, Guyam, La Janoza and others from here. You can also hire bancas from Pilar and Del Carmen to explore nearby mangrove swamps. Siargao can be reached by launch from Surigao to either Del Carmen or Dapa.

Where to stay
Pisangan Beach Resort, in General Luna. Basic rooms for P220, but it includes three meals. Unbeatable value.

Lucing's Carenderia, Juan Luna St, in Dapa. Clean rooms for P50–80, with fan for P90–120.

Butuan
Butuan is the provincial capital of Agustan del Norte, and a busy commercial and passenger port with links to many destinations in the Visayas. Some historians claim that Butuan is the cradle of human settlement in the Philippines, a view partly corroborated by the discovery in 1976 of a thousand-year-old outrigger. This can be seen on display at Ambangan, near the airport. The Northern Mindanao Regional Museum, near the City Hall, displays a number of other interesting ethnological and archaeological items. The other main point of interest in Butuan is its lively and colourful market where local handicrafts and fruit are sold.

Where to stay
Butuan Lodge, on Lopez Jaena. Clean rooms with fan for P200–240.

Embassy Hotel, on Montilla Blvd. Tel: 3737. Friendly place with quiet rooms. There is a restaurant here. Rooms with air-conditioning and bath for P430–500.

Hensonly Plaza Hotel, on San Francisco St. Tel: 3196. Adequate rooms with fan for P90–120, with air-conditioning and bath for P240–300.

New Narra Hotel, on R Calo St, a little way from the centre. Tel: 3145. Clean and comfortable. Rooms with fan and bath for P150–190, with air-conditioning and bath for P240–320. Has a restaurant.

Almont Hotel, on San Jose St. Tel: 3332. The most upmarket establishment in Butuan. Nice rooms with air-conditioning and bath for P380–640. Has a good restaurant.

A & Z Lowcost Lodging House, on Langihan Rd. Clean and friendly place. Rooms for P50–70, with fan for P60–90. They have another branch on San Francisco St.

Where to eat
Bahay ni Aling Cora, on R Calo Street. A large selection of dishes to choose from.

Golden Dragon Restaurant, on Concepcion St. One of the best Chinese restaurants in town. Dishes and set meals at low cost.

Punta Engano Restaurant, in the Almont Hotel on San Jose St. A good selection of international dishes.

Jet's Sinugba, on Villanueva St. Good quality seafood at affordable prices.

Embassy Hotel, on Montilla Blvd. Good European, American and Filipino dishes.

Cagayan de Oro
The capital and commercial centre of Misamis Oriental is a large, modern university city that gives the impression of being relatively affluent. The city supports a population of over 400,000 people. The Spanish changed the name Cagayan to Cagayan de Oro, after the discovery of modest amounts of gold in the area. Although there is not a great deal to do in the city itself, day excursions can be made to San Pedro and Raagas Beach, and Macahambus Cave, which lies about 14km south of town. Just over the Cayagan River, the Huluga Caves were the site of a number of interesting discoveries of early stone and metal tools, skeletons and fragments of Ming pottery. There is an extensive pineapple plantation at Camp Phillips, some 30km or so from Cagayan. You can catch a minibus there from Cagayan. The plantations sometimes run tours. The canning factory of the famous Del Monte brand of pineapple is at Bugo, about 15km east of Cagayan. Less exertion is needed to visit the Lawndale Spring Resort at Taguanao, 7km south of Cayagan. It is a relaxing place with spring-fed swimming pools. You can reach it by taking a jeepney from Cogon Market. For more information on side trips like this, enquire at the tourist office (tel: 3340) in the Pelaez Sports Complex on Valez St.

Getting there
There are two PAL flights a day between Manila and Cagayan, and three weekly ones from Cebu to Cagayan. There are also thrice-weekly runs

between Davao and Cagayan. PAL offices can be found at the airport, and at 21 Tirso Neri St (tel: 3701). Macabalan Wharf, 3km from the town centre, sees the arrival of several ships every week from various ports in the Visayas and Manila. There are several daily Ceres Liner and Bachelor Express buses running to and from Butuan, and Davao. There are also numerous Diamond Express, Bachelor Express and Fortune Express buses connecting Cayagan de Oro with Malaybalay, Kolambugan, Pagadian, Surigao, Zamboanga and other major towns and cities.

Where to stay
Excelsior Hotel, on A Valez St. Comfortable rooms with air-conditioning and bath from P670–840.

Diner's Lodging, on Yacapin St. Simple rooms in clean surroundings. Rooms with fan for P200–250.

Parkview Lodge, on Tirso Neri St. Tel: 5869. Quiet situation near a pleasant park. Comfortable rooms for P180–220 with fan, P300 with fan and bath, and P400 with air-conditioning and bath.

Philtown Hotel, on Makahambus St. Tel: 726295, fax: 723089. Comfortable rooms in a hotel with a restaurant and disco. Rooms with air-conditioning, bath and TVs for P900–1,240.

Oro United Inn, on Gomez St. Tel: 4884. Straightforward rooms with fan and bath for P180, and with air-conditioning and bath for P270–340.

VIP Hotel, on J R Borja St. Tel: 3629, fax: 6441. A comfortable place with a restaurant. Rooms with air-conditioning and bath for P680–950. Some have TVs. Suites for P980–1,250.

Where to eat
La Taberna Café and Restaurant, on Mabini St. Popular with foreigners. A good selection of all-round dishes.

Roxy's All American Diner, on C. Taal St. Good for steaks, burgers and Budweisers.

Paolo's Pizza, on Victoria St. Good homemade pizzas. Not particularly cheap though.

Imperial Palace, on C Taal St. A good place for Chinese food.

Amakan Restaurant, on Pabayo St. Good, affordable Filipino food. *Inihaw* is a speciality here.

Ice Cream Palace, on C Taal St. Ice-creams and hot dishes too.

Consuelo Restaurant, on Gaerlan St. Good American and Italian style dishes.

Persimmon Fastfoods & Bakeshoppe, on Valez St. Good for cheap sandwiches, self-service Filipino dishes.

There are several stalls in **Cogon Market** that are good for cheap Filipino savouries and meals.

Malaybalay

The capital of landlocked Bukidnon Province is located along a tributary of the Pulangi River. It is a small town considering its designation, but on the first week of September it hosts an important tribal event, the extraordinary Kaamulan Festival. The function of the festival is to reaffirm ties between the eight tribal groups that inhabit the area, as well as to promote understanding between the indigenous ethnic groups and the region's lowland settlers. The highland minorities troop down from the hills in the full splendour of their costumes to participate in three days of parades, dance, music, song, tribal games and ritual. It is one of the most colourful and dramatic events in Mindanao's cultural calendar, and highly recommended if it coincides with your itinerary. At the time of writing, the only place visitors can stay is the **Haus Malibu**, along Bonifacio Drive (tel: 5714). You could try asking private households if they would be prepared to take in a lodger.

Getting there

There are daily Ceres Lines and Bachelor Express buses plying the two-hour route between Cagayan de Oro and Malaybalay. They usually leave on the hour.

ILIGAN TO ZAMBOANGA

Iligan City

Iligan, the provincial capital of Lanao del Norte, is an important port and industrial area that is also the gateway to the Muslim heartland of Marawi and Lake Lanao. The area itself is unprepossessing, surrounded as it is by steelworks, chemical plants and paper mills. Iligan's major event is the Ang Sinulog, a festival honouring the city's patron saint, San Miguel the Archangel, which is held on 29 September. Nearby Maria Cristina Falls are no longer the scenic spot they were before 1952, when a hydroelectric plant was built there. You can still look down on to the falls from a bridge but it can hardly be the same. The Timoga Springs, about 1km from the Maria Cristina Falls, make a better side trip. These unspoilt waterfalls have a natural swimming pool whose water is cool and refreshing. It is easy enough to get to. Just take a jeepney bound for Marawi and get off at the Agus Bridge. There is a turning behind the bridge which can be followed for 1.5km to the waterfall. There are one or two passable beaches near Iligan. The best are Kanaway, Dalipuga and Tag-ibo beaches.

Getting there

PAL has daily flights between Cotabato and Iligan. PAL has an office at the airport and one on Quezon Avenue. (tel: 2037). Iligan is served by ships from Manila, Cebu, Panay, Siquijor and Batan. Fortune Express, Diamond Express and Bachelor Express buses have a regular timetable of routes between Iligan and Cagayan de Oro, Davao City, Kolambugan,

Pagadian and Zamboanga. Buses for the longer stretches may leave as early as 04.30, so it is wise to pre-plan the trip.

Where to stay

Crystal Inn, on Tibanga Highway. A clean lodging house, with modest rooms for P250–300.

Maria Cristina Hotel, on Mabini St. Tel: 20645. The best hotel in town. It has a good restaurant. Rooms with air-conditioning and bath for P600–750, suites for P1,300.

MC Tourist Inn, on Tibanga Highway. Tel: 5194. Good value. Rooms with fan for P160, larger rooms with fan and bath for P280, and rooms with air-conditioning and bath for P390.

Iligan Day Inn, on Benito Ong St. Reasonable, clean rooms with fan and bath for P240.

Iligan Village Hotel, near Pala-o. Tel: 21752. One of the most comfortable and pleasant hotels in the region. There is an orchid garden here. Nice rooms with air-conditioning and bath for P750–900, suites for P1600.

Where to eat

Café Hermoso, on Badelles St. Said to be one of the best Filipino and regional restaurants in Iligan. A popular breakfast venue too. Try the local coffee and papaya set.

Coconut Palace Lutong. Almost as popular as the Café Hermoso, and on the same street.

Bahayan Restaurant, on Luna St. Inexpensive Filipino food.

Canton Restaurant, on Quezon Ave. Good Chinese and Filipino food.

Patio Alejandra, on San Miguel St. A wide selection of Filipino and other dishes, including extensive seafood choice.

Enrico's Restaurant, next door to the PAL office on Quezon Ave. Tasty food in a friendly setting.

Nightspots with food, snacks and beer include the **Pacific Crossing Beer Gardens**, the **Ang Kusina Folkhouse** and **Snowland** where you can watch videos.

Marawi and Lake Lanao Area

As you drive from Iligan to Marawi, or the Islamic City of Marawi as it is officially known, there is a certain point where you realise that you have crossed a clear, though unmarked, cultural borderline. The resemblance to parts of Indonesia or Malaysia is striking as the Catholic Filipino lowlands give way to a Muslim domain in which women in dazzling *malongs* discreetly avert their eyes from strangers, and men congregate in cafés, as they do all over the Islamic world, to smoke and drink strong, aromatic local coffee. Spires have been replaced by the outlines of domes and pencil-thin minarets, crosses with crescent moons.

The market town of Marawi is the provincial capital of Lanao del Sur, and is located at the eastern end of Lake Lanao, the second largest lake in the Philippines. There are 25 settlements built around the lake, connected to Marawi by launch and road. The town and lake are the cultural and spiritual centre for Islam in the Philippines. The faith is embodied not only in the number of mosques visitors see dotted around the lake but in several religious schools, or *madrasas,* the observance of Islamic holidays like Ramadan, and the presence of the Mindanao State University (MSU). The Muslim-run institute includes the King Faisal Mosque and the Aga Khan Museum of Islamic Arts. The museum contains an interesting number of Muslim, Maranao and minority tribal objects and textiles, as well as Chinese ceramics and a natural history section. The museum closes at the weekend but is open from Monday to Thursday, 09.00 to 11.30, 13.00 to 17.00, and from 09.00 to 10.30, and 13.30 to 17.00 on Friday. The tourist office is located inside the Marawi Resort Hotel which is located near the museum, within the MSU campus itself. The town has a lively market selling local textiles, brassware, and Indonesian-style fabrics like batik, though these imitations pale against the originals. Brassware is of high quality throughout Mindanao, however. If you want to see how it is made, you can take a launch to the brassware centre of the Maranao in Tugaya, on the west shore of the lake. Everybody in the town seems to be involved at some level in the manufacture of brassware objects, so there is a vast selection to choose from.

Getting there
The easiest way to get to Marawi is by jeepney from Iligan. You can find them at the Marawi Terminal. It only takes 45 minutes to reach the MSU campus where they stop.

Where to stay
The Marawi Resort Hotel, located on the MSU campus. A comfortable set-up with a swimming pool, tennis court, golf course and restaurant. The views from the hill on which the resort stands are excellent. Rooms with bath for P470–550, cottages with bath for P390–470.

Budget travellers may be able to find a bed in the university dormitory or at the guesthouse run by **Dansalan College**. As a last resort, there is also the possibility of a **homestay** with a family.

Ozamiz City
The largest port and commercial centre of Misamis Occidental, Ozamiz was originally a fortified Spanish town. Fort Santiago, also known as Kota, like so many similar buildings throughout the archipelago, was requisitioned as a garrison by the Japanese in the Second World War. Other points of interest in and around the town include its cathedral, and a national park located around the slopes of Mount Malindang, about 25km west of Ozamiz.

Getting there
Daily Lilian Liner buses between Ozamiz, Dipolog, Oroquieta and Pagadian are plentiful. Fortune Liner and Bachelor Express buses serve the route from Ozamiz to Kolambugan and Pagadian. There are also hourly ferries connecting Ozamiz and Kolambugan.

Where to stay
Country Lodge, on Ledesma St Extension. Decent rooms with fan and bath for P200–280, with air-conditioning and bath for P300–380.

Surigao Pension House, on Mabini St Extension. Tel: 21114. A good location in a clean and quiet guesthouse. Rooms with fan and bath for P100–140, with air-conditioning and bath for P200–300.

Cebuana Lodge, on Port Rd. Basic but clean rooms with fan for P90–120.

Holiday Tourist Inn, on Blumentritt St. Tel: 20073. A cosy guesthouse with nice rooms with fan and bath for P170–230, and with bath and air-conditioning for P320–380.

Other accommodation in the centre of town includes the **Grand Hotel** (P150–250), the **Soriano Tourist Inn** (P140–200), **Minerva Inn** (P100–180), and **Hilbon Lodge** (P220–330).

Oroquieta City
The capital of Misamis Occidental is a small city situated in the midst of a coconut-growing region. As a trading and commercial centre it is overshadowed by Ozamiz. Its main industry is limited to coconut processing. The main points of interest in the area are the Sibukai Hot Spring and the Punta Blanca Resort. There are daily Lilian Liner buses between Ozamiz and Oroquieta and Dipolog.

Where to stay
Beach Resort Elvira, on Orbita St. A comfortable place located on the beach 20km away at Plaridel. Dormtory beds (P100) and rooms with fans (P280) are available.

Joy Lodge, in the centre of town. Plain and simple rooms with fan for P90–140, with air-conditioning and bath for P220–340.

Dapitan City
The old Spanish trading centre and harbour at Dapitan is a pleasant place to stroll around. A Jesuit mission was established here in 1629 but Dapitan is best known as the town where Jose Rizal was exiled by the Spanish between 1892 and 1896. He actually lived in Talisay, 4km from Dapitan. The tireless doctor busied himself during this enforced period by constructing the town's waterworks system, practising medicine and dabbling in a little cartography. His house is now the Rizal Shrine. The small museum is open daily from 08.00 to 17.00. Rizal also lived in the Casa Real, an administrative building that can also be visited. Saint James

Church, where he attended mass, is near the town plaza where you can see the large relief map of Mindanao which he made. There is no listed accommodation in Dapitan. Homestays can be made with **Paterno Bajamunde** and **Thaddeus Hamoy** near the beach, for about P275, which includes breakfast and dinner.

Dipolog City

Dipolog City, the capital of Zamboanga del Norte, is another old Spanish settlement which now serves as an important commercial centre for the region. A beautiful coral reef and beach can be visited at Aliguay Island, a 45-minute ride by outrigger from Dipolog. There are other, though not so fine, beaches outside the city at Gals, Olingan and Surg.

Getting there

There are daily PAL flights between Manila, Cebu, Zamboanga and Dipolog. The PAL offices are in the airport and on Rizal Avenue. (tel: 2171). The airport is 3km from the town centre. Aerolift flies the same schedule but only four times a week. Sulpicio Line has a weekly Manila-bound ship which stops off at Dipolog. Trans-Asia sails to Dipolog from Cebu on Tuesdays. There is also a William Lines Iligan to Dipolog boat every Saturday. Lilian Liner buses run daily between Dipolog and Pagadian, taking in Ozamiz and Oroquieta on the way. Fortune Liner and Almirabte buses cover the Zamboanga to Dipolog route.

Where to stay

CL Inn, on Rizal Ave. Tel: 3491. Generally regarded as the finest hotel in town. Very comfortable rooms with air-conditioning and bath for P350–500. Their spacious suites are P850.

Ranillo's Pension House, on Bonifacio St. Tel: 3030. Clean rooms with fan for P100–120, fan and bath for P240–290, and with air-conditioning and bath for P300–360.

Ramos Hotel, on Magsaysay St. Tel: 3299. Decent rooms with fan and bath for P150–280, with air-conditioning and bath for P400–550.

Village Hotel, at Scayab, 3km from town. Tel: 56154. A quiet place with comfortable rooms and a friendly staff. Rooms with fan and bath for P240, with air-conditioning and bath for P450.

Other accommodation in and around town includes the **Hotel Arocha, San Lorenzo Travellers Inn**, **Elizabeth Hotel**, **Gonzales Inn** and the **Dakak Park and Beach Resort**.

Pagadian City

The first thing visitors notice about the commercial centre of Pagadian is what an ethnic mixture it is. Residents include early settlers from Luzon and the Visayas, Christians and Muslims from other parts of Mindanao, Chinese merchants and several local ethnic minorities, like the Tausug,

Subanon, Maranao, Tiruray and Sibubong. Weaving and other local crafts can be seen in the market and elsewhere. Side trips from Pagadian can be made to Tukuran Beach, Lake Dasay, the Pulacan Falls and to the nearby island of Dao-Dao.

Getting there
PAL flies between Cebu and Pagadian every day, and also has Zamboanga to Pagadian daily flights. PAL has an office in the airport and in the Peninsula Hotel, on Jamisola Street (tel: 199). Aerolift flies between Manila and Pagadian three times a week. The airport is 5km from town. SKT Shipping Lines run three boats a week between Zamboanga and Pagadian. Several Almirante and Fortune Liner buses leave every day from Zamboanga to Pagadian. Lilian Liner buses run between Ozamiz and Pagadian, and there are Fortune Liner and Bachelor Express buses covering the Iligan to Pagadian run.

Where to stay
Pagadian City Hotel, on Rizal Ave. Tel: 285. Clean and comfortable rooms with air-conditioning and bath for P400–500.

Peninsula Hotel, on Jamisola St. Tel: 52115. Quite spacious and comfortable rooms with fan and bath for P180–230, with air-conditioning and bath for P390–460.

Guillermo Hotel, on Rizal Ave. Tel: 42062. Very good place with comfortable rooms and a restaurant. Probably the best in town. Rooms with air-conditioning and bath for P600–720, more expensive rooms with TV, fridge, air-conditioning and bath for P900–1,050.

Other places around town include the **Zamboanga Hotel**, the **Sea View Hotel** on the National Highway, and **Roxanne Hotel** on F S Pajares Ave.

Zamboanga
For years before I even visited the Philippines, the 'z', 'bo' and 'ga' of Zamboanga, evocative of destinations like Zanzibar, Borneo and Tonga, promised an exotic, slightly seedy, turn-of-the-century trading port, where adventure and a colourful bunch of native and expatriate characters, easily sought out in the cafés, crumbling trading houses and Oriental markets, would abound as in the novels of Conrad and Maugham. Zamboanga in fact is a rather modern and brisk city, not quite the mysterious "pearl of the southern Philippines" the travel literature put out by the tourist office would have us believe, though it can still, with its glittering, aquamarine seas and views of palm-strewn offshore islands, lay claim to being a little exotic. Its other epithet, "City of Flowers", may very well have come from the Malay word *jambangan* ("land of flowers"). The unromantic Spaniards who developed the port in the 17th century were clearly unimpressed, pragmatically dubbing the settlement Samboangan, or "Docking Point". Zamboanga was one of Spain's fortified settlements, used in their campaigns against the Muslims, and a significant naval battle

Zamboanga City

in which the Moros were defeated took place near by at Punta de Flechas. The Spanish left quite a strong linguistic legacy in this area. The verbs and vocabulary of Chavacano, the main dialect spoken in this region of Mindanao, are said to be 70% Spanish. You will also hear Tausug, Samal, standard Filipino and English being used by the linguistically gifted Chavacanos, as the people here are called.

Justice R T Lim Boulevard is the city's main thoroughfare, an avenue that neatly bisects the town and provides the route for an interesting walk past the city's cafés, restaurants and bars and down to its lively port area. On the east side of the waterfront, Fort Pilar is worth a visit. The Spanish completed the fort in 1635. Its ramparts saw plenty of action over the years as it defended the city against Dutch, English, Portuguese and Moro attacks. You can also see some interesting exhibits at the Marine Life Museum while you are here. The museum is open every day except Saturday, from 09.00 to 12.00, and from 14.00 to 17.00. The shrine of the city's patron saint, Nuestra Senora del Pilar, can be seen outside the fort's east wall. It's an interesting place to visit, especially on evenings during the weekend when people come here to light candles and offer prayers. If you walk a little way from the fort you will come across a wooden bridge leading to the floating village of Rio Hondo, a conglomeration of three

Muslim villages, the other two being Campo Muslim and Sahaya. Although the settlement might be termed a slum, it is still a fascinating, genuinely exotic place, at least in comparison with the rather functional style of architecture found elsewhere in Zamboanga. You can cross over the causeways that form the village streets and get a good view of the settlement and the dome of Campo Muslim's mosque, by standing on the bridge that connects Rio Hondo with the mainland. There are some interesting shopping venues in Zamboanga. The spacious Alta Mall Building in the suburb of Tetuan has a large number of handicrafts on display from all over Mindanao. Zamboanga has a number of shell shops and stalls near the waterfront which make and sell decent souvenirs. There are a number of intriguing cubby-hole shops in the area between J S Alano Street and the fish market, which are fun to explore.

Getting there

There are daily PAL flights between Manila and Zamboanga as well as links between the city and destinations on Mindanao such as Davao, Dipolog, Pagadian and Cotabato. The PAL office is at the airport. Several shipping companies have routes operating between Zamboanga and other important ports on Mindanao, such as Davao, Cotabato, Pagadian and General Santos. There are medium-to-long-distance Bachelor Express, Fortune and Lilian Express buses running daily between Zamboanga and Cagayan de Oro, Pagadian, Iligan, Dipolog and other departure points.

Where to stay

Atilano's Pension House, on Mayor Jaldon St. Not as good as it used to be according to travellers who stayed there a few years ago, but still excellent value and friendly. Rooms with fans for P160–200.

Zamboanga Hermosa Hotel, on Mayor Jaldon St. Tel: 9912040-42. Comfortable rooms and a good location. Rooms with air-conditioning and bath for P360–440.

Kao Pi Hung Hotel, on General Lim Ave. Has a karaoke bar, and restaurant. Run by friendly Chinese people. Rooms with air-conditioning and bath for P240–420.

Garden Orchid Hotel, on Governor Camins Rd. Tel: 9910031, fax: 9910035. Unquestionably the best hotel in town. Comfortable and tastefully furnished rooms with air-conditioning and bath for P1,300–1,560. Has a nice restaurant. Airport transfer.

Lantaka Hotel, on Valderroza St. Tel: 9912033-36, fax: 9911626. A pleasant sea-facing location with a pool and restaurant. Nice rooms with air-conditioning and bath for P880–1,000, suites for P1,600.

Hotel Marcian Garden, on Governor Camins Rd. Tel: 9912519-21, fax: 9911874. Clean rooms, a convenient location near the airport, and a restaurant. Rooms with air-conditioning and bath for P430–550.

Hotel Paradise, on R. Reyes St. Not quite paradise but good enough for one or two nights, and centrally located. Rooms with air-conditioning and bath for P390–480. Has a restaurant.

Imperial Hotel, on Campaner St. Tel: 9911648. Simple rooms with fan for P100–140, with fan and bath for P180–220, and with air-conditioning and bath for P260–340.

Other accommodation that passes muster includes the **New Astoria Hotel** on Mayor Jaldon St, **Unique Hotel**, on Corcuera St, **New Pasonanca Hotel**, on Almonte St, **Mag-V Royal Hotel**, on San Jose Road, and the **Hotel Presiosa**, on Mayor Climaco Ave.

Where to eat

Alavar's Seafoods House, on R T Lim Blvd. A good place for fish dishes. Zamboanga is renowned for its seafood. This is a good chance to sample curacha, a delicious shellfish speciality associated with this city.

Antonio's, on Pasonanca Rd. A diner for cheap Filipino food.

Lantaka Hotel, on Valderroza St. One of the more upmarket restaurants in town. The breakfasts here are excellent and affordable. International menu for lunch and dinner.

La Patissiere, on Pilar St. Another upmarket eatery, popular with the Zamboanga business community and others who can afford it.

Café Blanca, in the Platinum 21 Pension House along Barcelona St. Affordable Filipino and Western-style food.

Abalone Restaurant, on Mayor Climaco Ave. Another good seafood restaurant.

Other restaurants offering good value include the **Sunburst Fried Chicken** outlet on Corcuera St, **Palmeras**, the **Tropical Cuisine**, and **Village** in the downtown area.

Entertainment and nightlife

Zamboanga's entertainment scene is fairly tame compared to many other major cities in the Philippines but it is steadily improving. If the peace pact between the MNLF and the government proves to be lasting, the good citizens of Zamboanga may feel more inclined to stay out later at night.

Talisay Bar, in the Lantaka Hotel. A popular travellers' hang-out.

Lutong Pinoy, near the airport. An open-air restaurant that has a bar and live music.

Kao Pi Hung Hotel, on Governor Lim Ave. The best karaoke bar in town.

Village Zamboanga, near the airport. A good nightspot for drinkers.

Shinjuku Bar, on La Purisima St. Another night haunt for drinkers and bar people.

There are several discos located in and on the outskirts of town. Some of the most popular are the **Casa de Oro**, on Justice Lim Blvd, **King's Palace Disco**, on Tomas Claudio St, the **Love City Disco**, near the airport, and the **Latin Quarter Disco** just up the road from there.

Side trips from Zamboanga

Great and Little **Santa Cruz Islands** are a popular day trip for the people of Zamboanga. The islands form part of a national park and there are some fine beaches and coral reefs to be enjoyed here. On Great Santa Cruz Island there is a Muslim village located in a mangrove lagoon, and a Samal cemetery. About 7km west of Zamboanga there are a number of Yakan families who are engaged in weaving. The fabrics they produce are quite striking. There are a number of good beaches worth stopping off at on the way to the village. About 15km north of town, **Pasananca Park** makes a relaxing excursion. The park is famed for its flowers which bloom in great profusion. The 58h park is quite popular at the weekends as there are a number of attractions there, such as swimmings pools, a tree house and an amphitheatre. While you are here you can also visit nearby **Climaco Freedom Park**. From the top of the park's highest rise, **Holy Hill**, there is a magnificent view of Zamboanga, the Basilan Strait and several offshore islands.

BASILAN ISLAND

It only takes an hour and a half from Zamboanga to the island province of Basilan. About one-third of the inhabitants on Basilan, and the numerous small islands and islets that surround it, are members of the Yakan, an ethnic minority that, with a few exceptions, is only found on Basilan. The Yakan, who are predominantly engaged in farming, are known for their lively festivals, colourful Muslim ceremonies and their hospitality towards strangers. The remainder of Basilan's quarter million residents are made up of the Chavacano, Tausug, Samal, Badjao and Visayan peoples.

Basilan's little-known interior is a rugged, hilly and rather daunting place, but the climate is kind to visitors with few dramatic extremes. Rain falls throughout the year, with moderately dry months between November and April. Basilan is a producer of high quality rubber and copper. Noted cash crops include abaca, African oil (a palm extract), pepper, cocoa and coffee. The seas surrounding the island yield generous amounts of fish, crustaceans and seaweed, much of it for trans-shipment to other parts of the archipelago.

Getting there

There are daily ferries between Zamboanga and Basilan. The first boat leaves at 07.00, the last at 16.00. It only takes 90 minutes. There is also a slightly shorter run between Lamitan and Zamboanga, leaving from Basilan daily at 08.00.

Isabela

The small provincial capital is easily negotiated on foot. The approach to the town by boat from Zamboanga is interesting as it sails through a channel surrounded on both sides by mangroves and small hamlets and villages that stand on stilts. The sights of Isabela are easily seen within a morning. These include its modest cathedral, market, wharf area, and Claretcraft, a showroom for locally made native handicrafts. There are some Muslim teahouses near the wharf. There is a latex plant 4km outside of town: the Menzi processing plant, which is interesting if you have never seen how rubber is manufactured. *Bancas* can also be taken from the wharf to nearby Malamawi Island. There is a Samal village on stilts here, a duck sanctuary, Muslim cemeteries, and a quaint little fishing village at Panigayan. White Beach is a well known beauty spot but, strangely, no one ever seems to go there. There is a tourist office in the Capitol building.

Where to stay/eat
New Basilan Hotel, on J S Alano St. Very reasonably priced rooms and a good restaurant. P100–180 for rooms with fan, P190–300 for rooms with fan and bath.

Selecta Hotel, also on J S Alano St. Rooms with fan and bath for P120–240. Basic but clean.

The Bistro, a restaurant near the wharf, has excellent food. Try sticking to seafood on Basilan as this is a speciality. The **Queen Bee** opposite the New Basilan Hotel is also very good. The **New International Restaurant**, and **Awin's Icecream House** on Valderossa St are also recommended. You can eat well at the restaurant in the **New Basilan Hotel**, but it is not as cheap as the others.

Cotabato
There isn't a great deal for the visitor to see or do in Cotabato, but it is a pleasant enough place to stroll around or break the journey between Zamboanga and Davao City. The ambience is strongly Muslim, though in fact there are said to be more Christians living in the town than Muslims. Islam came to Cotabato as early as the 14th century, predating the Spanish conquest of the Philippines and getting a considerable headstart on Jesuit zealots who only arrived here in 1872.

Getting there
PAL flies between Cotabato and Zamboanga every day except Wednesday and Saturday. There are also PAL flights on the same days between Cotabato and Cagayan de Oro. PAL has an office in the airport (tel: 2086) and one on Don Roma Vilo Street. There are several daily J D Express and Maguindanao Express buses running between Cotabato and Koronadel. Mintranco buses are the main carriers between Davao City and Cotabato.

Where to stay
El Corazon Inn, on Makakua St. Pleasant rooms with fan and bath for P260–320, and with air-conditioning and bath for P360–440. Suites go for P750–850.

Padama Pension House, on Quezon Ave. Standard rooms with fan for P120–140, with fan and bath for P160–200.

Hotel Filipino, on Sinsuat Ave. Quite good value. Spacious rooms with fan and bath for P240–320, with air-conditioning and bath for P360–480.

Koronadel

Like Cotabato, there are few sights to delay the visitor in Koronadel. Most travellers find Koronadel a convenient base for visiting the Lake Sebu area. Koronadel, also known as Marbel, is the capital of South Cotabato Province. Cotabato is home to the native B'laan and Maguindanao.

Getting there

There are plenty of daily Yellow Bus Company vehicles plying the Davao City to Koronadel route. They go via General Santos. There are also several minibuses every day from General Santos to Koronadel.

Where to stay

Rosamar Hotel, on Alunan St. Simple, basic rooms for P90–120.

Alababo's Home, on Rizal St. Clean and basic rooms with fan and bath for P140–220, with air-conditioning and bath for P300–360.

Dizon Place, on Alunan St. Plain and simple rooms for P90–110. Good value.

Samahang Nayon Home, on Roxas St. Tel: 272. A comfortable old place with a friendly staff. Rooms with fan and bath for P140–220, with air-conditioning and bath for P240–300.

Surallah

The Alah Valley town of Surallah is ideally placed for trips to Lake Sebu. There are several mini side trips which can be made from Surallah. Lake Buluang is a swampland which is home to a number of interesting birds, some of which are indigenous to the Philippines. The area can be reached by taking a jeepney to Buluang. The lovely Seven Falls are located in the middle of a tropical rainforest 15km from Surallah. You will have to walk for about an hour along a jungle path to reach the falls. A jeepney or tricycle will drop you off at the trail which leads off of the Surallah road to Lake Sebu road.

Lake Sebu

One of the most beautiful inland stretches of water in the Philippines, Lake Sebu is the geographical homeland of the T'boli people and culture. There is a lively T'boli market held on the lakeside every Saturday morning which should not be missed. It is not only a good chance to get a glimpse of these reclusive and timid people, but also to inspect the accomplished textiles, brassware and other handicrafts they produce. Horse-fights are sometimes held near the market. In the event that you cannot attend the market, there is a good cross-section of T'boli handicrafts on display at the giftshop in the Santa Cruz Mission building. The T'boli hold an interesting harvest festival in September which features a torch procession at night. The Lake Sebu Village Festival, held in November, is also well worth attending as there are traditional ceremonies, dance and music performances rarely seen at other times of the year. Sadly, like many other extraordinary ethnic cultures of Southeast Asia, the T'boli traditions and customs are vanishing far too quickly.

Getting there
There are regular jeepneys from the market in Surallah to Lake Sebu. The journey takes about one hour.

Where to stay
Hillside View Park and Tourist Lodge, on the lake. A very scenic setting right on the lake shore. Simple but pleasant rooms for P75–100.

Santa Cruz Mission, on the lake. A cheap option with rooms going for only P50–90. There is a kitchen here too which guests are welcome to use if they wish to do their own self-catering.

Municipal Guesthouse, on a hill near the lake. Another attractive setting. The rooms are tastefully decorated in a traditional native way using natural materials. Rooms for P380–440.

Ba-ay Village Inn, also on the lake. A friendly place run by a T'boli tribesman who speaks English. Simple unpretentious rooms for P60–100.

General Santos
The old name of Dadiangas is also used for this modern city. The town is named after General Paulino Santos who led a number of pioneers from Luzon to develop the site of the present city in 1939. The city is a fairly uninspiring place occasionally accessed by travellers as a waystation between Lake Sebu and Davao City. The city's patron saint, Our Lady of Peace and Good Voyage is honoured in a festival which takes place every January in the third week of the month.

Getting there
PAL has two flights a day between General Santos and Manila. The airport at Buayan is about 8km from the city. There are weekly sailings to and from Manila, Cebu, Zamboanga and other destinations. Yellow Bus and Bachelor Express buses connect General Santos, Davao and Koronadel. There are also minibuses between Davao, Koronadela and General Santos.

Where to stay
South Sea Lodge 1, on Pioneer Ave. Basic rooms with fan for P240, and with air-conditioning for P390.

Fisherman's Inn, on Veteran St. Clean rooms with fan for P120–170.

Phela Grande Hotel, on Magsaysay Ave. Tel: 2950. Nicely decorated rooms with air-conditioning and bath for P600–780, suites for P1,600.

Pioneer Hotel, on Pioneer Ave. Tel: 2422. A comfortable hotel with a coffee shop and restaurant. Rooms with fan and bath for P340–390, with air-conditioning and bath for P400–450. Suites go for P800.

Reasonable accommodation can also be found at the **Concrete Lodge** on Pioneer Ave, the **Tierra Verde Hotel** and **Pietro's Hotel**, both on the National Highway, and the **Mututum Hotel** along P Archaron Blvd.

DAVAO CITY

Davao City is a major transportation, commercial and industrial hub, educational centre with two universities and several colleges, gateway to the region's main attractions, international port and also something of a boom town. Davao is said to be the fastest-growing city in the Philippines after Manila. Although the downtown area known as "City Town" is not forbiddingly large, the precincts of the city are extensive. Many of the orchid farms and banana plantations surrounding the city are actually within the municipal boundaries of Davao. Most Davaoenos are of Visayan extraction, speaking a fairly standard Cebuano, but there are also substantial numbers of Chinese and Muslims. There is even a Chinatown district just off Magsaysay Avenue. The interesting Lon Wa Temple on the road to the airport is the biggest Buddhist temple on Mindanao. The city is noted as something of a handicraft centre and there are many shops and emporiums that sell good quality textiles like dagmay cloth, shellcraft, brassware, antiques and locally made batik. Some of the city's major festivals are the Araw Ng Dabaw, a foundation-day event held in March and featuring processions, carnivals, sports events and beauty contests. Lengthy passion plays are held over Easter Friday, and the feast day of San Pedro, the city's patron saint, takes place at the end of June. The Kadayawan sa Dabaw Festival is an interesting event as it attracts many highland tribal members who appear in full costume. The festival features a number of their dances, songs, horse-fighting contests and ritual performances. A fruit and orchid festival is held at the same time. People interested to know more about the cultures of ethnic groups living in the Davao area can visit the Dabaw Museum near the airport. The museum is open from Tuesday to Sunday from 09.00 to 17.00. The staff at the tourist office in the Apo View Hotel along J Camus Street are very obliging with information and maps of the city.

Getting there

Davao City is well served by air, sea and land. PAL flies twice daily between Manila and Davao, once a day from Cebu, and three times a week from Zamboanga and Cayagan de Oro. It is also possible to fly between Davao, Borneo and Indonesia. There are weekly sailings between Davao and Manila, Zamboanga, and Cebu. There are regular Bachelor Express buses from Surigao, Mintranco buses from Cotabato, Yellow Bus vehicles from General Santos, and Bachelor Express, Ceres Liner and St Benedict Lines buses to and from Butuan.

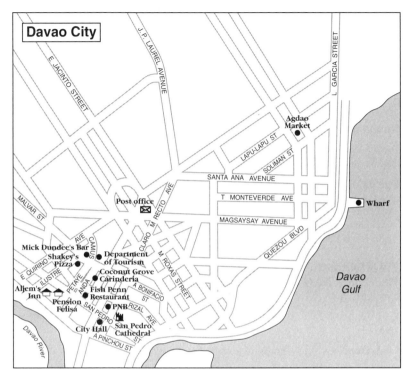

Where to stay

Le Mirage Family Lodge, on San Pedro St. Tel: 63811. Good standard rooms with fan for P110, with fan and bath for P180–220, and rooms with air-conditioning and bath for P280–350.

El Gusto Family Lodge, on A Pichon St. Tel: 73662. A very pleasant place with its own little garden. Rooms with fan for P120–240, with fan and bath for P160–280, and with air-conditioning and bath for P300–380.

Hotel Maguindanao, on Claro M Recto Ave. Tel: 78401, fax: 2212894. A comfortable place with TVs in all the rooms. Also has a restaurant. Rooms with air-conditioning and bath for P900–1,250.

Manor Pension House, on A Pichon St. Tel: 2212511. A clean and well-run place with a restaurant. Has rooms with air-conditioning and bath for P640–750.

Insular Hotel Davao, at Lanang, near the airport. Tel: 76051, fax: 62959. Very good facilities here with a swimming pool, tennis and squash courts, no less than three restaurants and a lovely garden. Superb views of Samal Island and the Davao Gulf.

Royale House, on Claro M Recto Ave. Tel: 73630. Well-kept rooms and a restaurant. P170–260 with fan, and P360–480 with air-conditioning and bath.

Other accommodation that can be recommended includes **Aljem's Inn** on Ilustre St, the **Pension Felisa** on Pichon St, the **Tourist Lodge** along MacArthur Highway, **El Mimar Tourist Lodge** on Pelayo St, and the slightly upmarket **Marina Azul Resort Hotel** on Times Beach.

Where to eat

Molave, on Reyes St. A popular chicken place.

Coconut Grove Carinderia, on Anda St. Good, inexpensive self-service Filipino food.

Davao Insular Hotel's restaurant. More upmarket than the downtown places.

Zugba Restaurant, in the Apo View Hotel. Another upmarket eatery.

Kusina Dabaw, on San Pedro St. Good Chinese and Filipino dishes.

Davao Majestic Restaurant, on Bonifacio St. Very popular for Chinese food. Can be quite crowded in the evenings.

Dunkin' Donuts and **Shakey's Pizza** are on Malvar St, and there is a Jollibee outlet along Rizal St. The food stalls near the wharf are good for local specialities like *kilaw-ni*, a marinated raw fish dish, and for those who like tropical fruits such as rambutans, star fruit and durian, the large **Bankerohan Public Market** and the **Anda-Rizal Fruit Centre** will delight.

Entertainment and nightlife

Vinta Bar, at the Davao Insular Hotel. Popular with local business people and travellers.

Casa Blanca Bar (and Restaurant), on Laurel Ave. A lively nightspot watering hole.

Mick Dundee's, on J Camus. A friendly bar run by an Englishman and his Filipina wife.

The city's dance flashpoints include **Electric Dreams** and **Curves & Faces**, on San Pedro St, the **Bodega Disco** on E. Quirino Ave, **Spam's Disco** in the Apo View Hotel, and **Bronco** on Rizal St, which also has live music. **Fish Penn** is a good place to have a drink, eat and watch videos, while the **Horizon Folk Theatre** is a good place to enjoy live folk acts.

Side trips from Davao

There are a great many interesting excursions possible from Davao. There are several beaches located along the 20km or so of black sandy coastline that stretches southwest of the city. **Times Beach** is the nearest to Davao, although the water may not be as clean as you would like. Serious divers and travellers looking for clear waters and good coral usually head for **Samal** and **Talikud Islands**. There are some sunken Japanese ships off of the western coast of Samal which add interest to any dive in that area. There is a **Japanese Peace Memorial** and cemetery at Mintal, south of Davao. The **Yuhico Orchid Farm** is near there. Just 3km south of town visitors can watch durian fruit being processed into sweets and jam at the **Mindanao Industrial Confectionery** and **Loal Abon's Durian Factory**. Those who have never smelt durian before should be prepared to find the odour overpowering. The **Philippine Eagle and Nature Research Center** in Malagos, about 35km northwest of Davao, makes a fascinating trip for anyone interested not only in birds but in nature in general. Also called the

Malagos Gardens, the research centre here is attempting to study and breed the Philippine eagle, only a tiny number of which still exist. The aviaries at the gardens contain a number of other bird species as well. The centre can be reached by taking a jeepney from Davao to Calinan and then transferring to a tricycle for the remainder of the trip. Mount Apo (2,954m, 9,695ft), the highest peak in the Philippines, is situated about 40km southwest of Davao. The mountain and the area around it comprise the **Mount Apo National Park**. Apo is a dormant volcano. The area is ideal for nature lovers, covered as it is with hiking trails, virgin rainforest and rare species of falcon, mynah, Philippine eagles and other bird and wildlife. Its lakes, waterfalls, thermal pools and hot springs course, bubble and hiss around the feet of the mountain, lending some credence to its native name "Mountain of Sulphur". For those who want to climb the mountain there are several routes available. March to May are considered the optimum months for climbing, although this is an all-year-round activity. Even for people in pretty good shape, three to four days should be allowed for the ascent. Proper preparation, the right equipment and provisions and an experienced guide are essential. Try and get hold of the informative, locally available, *First Guide to Climbing Mt. Apo*, by Reynaldo G Sorongon, if you can. A trip to the tourist office in Davao for the latest information on climbing in this region is also highly recommended.

Chapter Eighteen

The Sulu Archipelago

For travellers, the Sulu Islands, in more than one meaning of the word, are the Philippines' last frontier. Located at the southernmost tip of the archipelago, this is just about as far as you can go without spilling into Borneo. As a travel destination it remains one of the least visited areas of the country. The islands, in fact, were closed to foreigners for many years because of the ongoing security problem between the MNLF and government troops stationed here. Even now, visitors would be wise to confirm that the agreements signed and sealed by both parties are still being honoured. Hopefully peace has come to the Sulu Archipelago and the islands will start to come into their own as an out-of-the-way but safe destination.

The two provinces of Sulu and Tawi-Tawi and their capitals, Jolo and Bongao, are the administrative centres of a cluster of islands, the main groups of which are Pangutaran, Samales, Tapul, Tawi-Tawi, Sulu, Sibutu, Cagayan de Tawi-Tawi and Tapiantana. Basilan Island in the far north of the chain is also included as one of the Sulu Islands. Over 90% of the islanders are Muslim, though there is a small Christian community found mainly in the towns. The dominant ethnic group are the Tausug, though there is a sizeable Samal minority. The Badjao are another significant minority. Those of the Badjao who have not adopted the ways of landlubbers like the Tausug are sea gypsies, floating around the archipelago at will. The highest concentration of the animist worshipping Badjao, however, are found in and around the waters of Sibutu and Tawi-Tawi. The Sulu and Celebes seas are notorious for being pirate-infested waters. Boats are routinely boarded and stripped of valuables. Whole crews have even been annihilated by these aggressive sea dogs. There are many inter-island and circumnavigational routes which boat operators from the mainland and even Jolo are reluctant to sail.

Getting to and around the islands

The main gateway to the Sulu Islands is from Mindanao. PAL has daily flights between Zamboanga, Jolo and Tawi-Tawi. Boats leave daily for the 12hr journey between Zamboanga and Jolo. Enquire at the Ever Lines, SKT, Sampaguita and Magnolia offices in Zamboanga or direct at the wharf. There are also irregular numbers of boats between Basilan and the other islands. Jeepneys and tricycles come into their own on the main islands.

JOLO ISLAND

The island and its main town are both called Jolo, pronounced more like "Ho-lo". Local people refer to the island as Sug, and the town as Tijanggi. The interior of Jolo is a rugged, densely wooded region, pockmarked with a chain of mountains and volcanic peaks and crater lakes. Although there is a certain amount of agriculture on Jolo, the main source of income for the islanders comes from fishing. Seaweed farming, cattle raising, logging, the cultivation of coconut, cassava basketry, and other handicraft activities and trading are the mainstay of the Sulu economy in general.

The town

Jolo is the only place within this archipelago where the Spanish succeeded in making any impact, albeit a small one. The 53,000-strong provincial capital was originally the hereditary domain of the sultans of Sulu. The Spanish managed to build a settlement here but not until 1878. The walls of the old settlement and a watchtower still exist. Parts of Jolo were devastated by fighting which took place in the town itself in February 1974. Today, Jolo continues to be a brisk trading port for a wide range of both legal and contraband goods destined for other parts of the Philippines, as well as overseas destinations like Singapore and Sabah. Jolo's Barter Trade Market is the place to see what's going on.

The town's public market is also worth a visit, especially if you like seafood and fruit. The Sulu Ethnological Museum, a private collection which can be visited at the Notre Dame of Jolo College, provides a good introduction to the culture, trading history and folklore of the islands. Hand weaving can be observed at the Nacida Shop within the college campus. You can buy well-made handicrafts here, including tightly woven mats, textiles, bags and the colourful headclothes worn around the islands. Other points of interest in Jolo include the impressive Masjid Jami mosque, a nearby village on stilts, the Moorish-style Capitol building, and several good beaches within a few kilometres of the town, the finest perhaps being Maubuh Beach at Lambayong. Quezon Beach, 3km from Jolo, also has excellent sand. Walk or catch a tricycle up to Brigade Camp for a fine view of the town and its surroundings.

Where to stay and eat

Helen's Lodge, on Buyon St. Tel: 104. Simple but clean place with rooms for P90–140 with fan, and for P160–280 with fan and bath. There is a restaurant.

The **Unique Hotel** (P140) and the **Maharajah Hotel** (P150) are other places travellers can stay. There is not a great deal to choose from when it comes to eating, but the **Plaza Panciteria** has good Chinese dishes, the **Alvar**

Restaurant serves local food and seafood, and **Bee Gees** along Sachez St, serves inexpensive Filipino dishes. Coffee shops are good places to soak up the local atmosphere.

BONGAO

Both Bongao Island and town, as in the case of Jolo, have a single designation. Bongao is the largest and most important town in the Tawi-Tawi group. There are two harbours and a small airport near by on Sanga Sanga Island which is connected to Bongao by bridge. There is a Tawi-Tawi Ethnological Museum here at the MSU-Sulu College of Technology and Oceanology which is worth seeing. The large Capitol building is also worth walking up to for the views it affords of the town and coast. Some of the offshore islands and islets in this area are said to be excellent for snorkelling. The best view of the surrounding area and interior can be had from Mount Bongao (314m, 1,030ft) which stands behind town. It only takes an hour to reach the top. The mountain is sacred to both Muslims and Christians, so visitors should be on their best behaviour when ascending its slopes. The graves of two high-ranking Muslims are found on the mountain. There is quite a lot of wildlife on Mount Bongao's slopes, including wild monkeys and a large colony of well-camouflaged snakes, so be careful to stick to the man trails and not to touch any vegetation before inspecting it. The mountain gets quite crowded in October when there is a big festival held there.

Getting there

PAL has ten flights a week between Zaboanga and Tawi-Tawi. You can use a tricycle or jeepney from the airport on Sanga Sanga to Bongao. There are ships passing through Bongao from Jolo and Zamboanga almost every day. There are also smaller boats sailing between Bongao and the islands of Manuk, Simunul, Bilatan and elsewhere.

Where to stay

Sarah's, near the wharf. Basic but clean rooms in a friendly lodging house. Rooms with fan for P130.

Southern Inn, on Datu Halun St. Simple rooms for P270, with fan and bath for P380.

SITANGKAI

Sitangkai, a fascinating island only 40km from Borneo, is where the Philippines end. Depending on the situation when you arrive, you may have to present yourself to the local military people who will record your presence and check your passport. Passengers and freight have to be carried to the shore in smaller boats as the water on the massive reef that surrounds the island is too shallow to moor in. Sitangkai is often described as "the Venice of the Far East" on account of the large number of floating villages found in the area. Most of Sitangkai's 10,000 or so inhabitants in fact live in houses built on stilts. Most of the island's residents are Badjao who have struck a nice compromise by continuing to live above the water but without having to drift around on their boats. Some water nomads still remain in the area though. Seaweed, sea cucumbers and fishing provide the main income for the Badjao. *Bancas* can be hired for trips out to some of the more remote floating villages like the one at Tong Tong, for about P400–600 a day.

Where to stay
Yusuf Pension House, run by the very hospitable Hadji Yusof Abdulganih. The verandah of the pension is a good place to watch the boats going past and catch one of those glorious southern sunsets. Any other accommodation available will be in private houses, in which case you can approach the mayor for a recommendation.

OUTER ISLANDS

The 75 islands of the Siasi-Tapul group are spread out between Jolo and the Tawi-Tawi islands. Siasi, Tapul, Lugus and Lapac are well-populated islands. There are boats almost every day plying the 4hr route between Jolo and the important fishing port of Siasi, as well as other smaller islands. Siasi is well known for its jewellery, pottery and woodcarving. The **Samales**, a group of 20 or so islands scattered between Jolo and Basilan, and the **Pangutaran** group to the northwest of Jolo, might be accessible but you would have to charter a *banca* for the trip and take plenty of provisions as there is no accommodation as such on the island. More geographically remote but more populous are the group of islands known as **Cagayan de Tawi-Tawi**, located about equidistant between Palawan and the Sulu Archipelago. The inhabitants of this group are mainly Jama Mapun natives who appear to be both practising Muslims and animists. The islands can be reached by boat from Zamoanga, and simple accommodation on Cagayan is available at the **Yarrada Beach House** on Long Beach in Ungus Mataha, along the north coast. South of these islands, closer to Borneo, are the Turtle Islands. Turtles come ashore every year and lay eggs on the islands' beaches. There is a turtle sanctuary on Lihiman Island. The scuba diving and snorkelling potential of these and other outlying islands in the Sulu Archipelago is said to be phenomenal, but with the waters still teeming with pirates and other unsavoury freebooters, it may be some time before these wild and lawless frontier areas classify as one of the peripheral destinations of mainstream tourism in the Philippines.

Chapter Nineteen

Palawan Island

The name Palawan appears to originate from the Chinese, "Pa-lao-Yu", land of beautiful and safe harbours. More than 1,760 islands and islets account for the province of Palawan, giving the impression at times of an archipelago within an archipelago. The largest province in the Philippines, Palawan is situated in isolated splendour from the rest of the country, surrounded as it is by the South China Sea to the west, the Mindoro Strait to the north, the Sulu Sea to the east, and the Balabac Strait in the south separating it from Borneo. The major island groups that form a part of the province are the Dumara-Cuyo islands, the Calamians, Coron, Culion, and the Balabac group to the southwest.

Administratively, the island is regarded as part of Luzon, geographically it is closer to the Visayas and Mindanao, while geologically, ethnically, zoologically and botanically it is more closely connected to Borneo than the Philippines. Mountains averaging 1,100m in elevation run a north–south course through the island, forming a rugged spine covered in many places with dense forest and jungle. A great deal of Palawan is still almost virgin territory, with wildernesses of rainforest, mangrove swamp, marshland, unexplored caves, deserted beaches and bays, primitive tribes and untrammelled coral gardens.

Palawan's transitional location between the Philippines and Borneo has endowed it with a rich and exotic flora and fauna. Land bridges connected the island with Borneo aeons ago, allowing not only for now-extinct animals such as elephas and stegodons to migrate across the isthmus, but also plants. Rare animal species like Palawan mongooses, leopard cats, flying lemurs, armadillos and over 600 species of butterfly inhabit a world of hardwood trees, indigenous orchids and, as more modern forms of agricultural and logging technology are introduced to the islands, increasingly threatened tracts of almost virgin rainforest. Rice and coconuts are Palawan's main crops, but cassava, cashew nuts, vegetables, corn, bananas and a wide range of other fruits are grown on the island's limited strips of cultivable land. Palawan's waters supply over 60% of the country's fish catch. The seas northwest of Palawan are rich in gas and oil reserves,

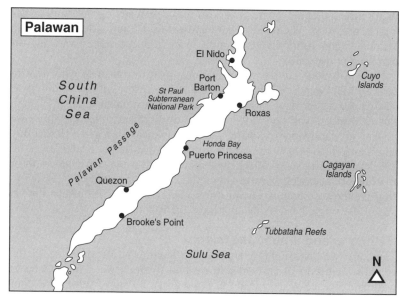

while the island boasts quantities of untapped copper, manganese, chromite and other mineral resources.

Although the Spanish established an *encomienda* here in 1591, and friars founded churches and settlements throughout the 17th century, the colonial rulers of Palawan had very little real impact on the culture of the island. Palawan is scarcely populated. Native Palawenos like the Pala'wan and Batak are ethnically closer to the people of Borneo than the Philippines, descended as they are from primitive groups of proto-Malays. Muslims and people of Chinese extraction constitute two significant minority groups, with Tagalogs, settlers from the western Visayas, and several tribal minorities like the Taganua, Kalamians and Tau't Batu making up the rest of the population.

For travellers, the allure of what may sound like an aquatic Eden is qualified by a large incidence of malaria. The presence of malaria-carrying mosquitoes on the island is a serious consideration when planning a trip to Palawan. A course of malaria pills is vital, but a strong insect repellent and a mosquito net are helpful precautions. If you do think you may have contracted malaria, you should make straight away for the main hospital in Puerto Princesa where the staff are familiar with such cases. Outside of the capital, medical facilities are generally fairly inadequate.

SNORKELLING AND DIVE SITES

Diving and snorkelling are becoming popular activities on Palawan. With over 60% of the country's coral found in its waters, the choice is vast. Many of Palawan's coral reefs have not even begun to be exploited for their tourist potential. Coral is best off the eastern and northeastern coasts which are more sheltered. The marine life all around the island is abundant, and pearl diving, though much reduced these days, is still practised in the south.

There is a wide choice of destinations open to travellers who wish to take a PADI course or just find a comfortable resort with good diving to stay in for a few days or weeks. El Nido is the most popular, though Puerto Princesa can be a good base for dive cruises, most of which are booked in Manila, private charters, and for tours to places like Honda Bay and Table Head which can be organised by dive shops. Island Divers at 371 Rizal St, has an excellent reputation. The Busuanga Islands north of El Nido are also well known. Diving is an all-year activity but March to June are the best months. Diving aficionados claim that Tubbataha Reef is one of the single best diving spots near the island.

Getting to and around the island

There are two PAL flights a day between Manila and Puerto Princesa, the island's main port of entry. There are two flights a week from Cebu as well, and a twice-weekly flight to Iloilo City on Panay. Aerolift has four flights a week between Manila and Busuanga, as well as daily flights to El Nido during the tourist season. Air Link also has three flights a week from Manila to Busuanga, and Pacific Airways operate twice-weekly flights between Cuyo and Manila. William Lines has a direct route between Manila and Puerto Princesa once a week. Viva Shipping Lines, Asuncion Shipping Lines and numerous smaller companies operate between Puerta Princesa and other ports on Palawan and various

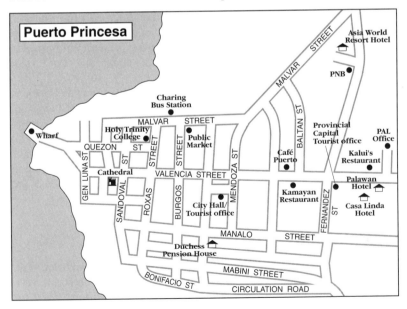

destinations on Luzon. Puerta Princesa in Central Palawan is the main transportation hub for overland travel. Buses and jeepneys strike out from here in most directions, but the poor condition of the roads and the obstacle of geography limit the number of routes and affect the reliability of schedules. Bad weather and frequent breakdowns are other factors impeding smooth overland travel. If you have to charter your own jeepney or a tricycle for some of the poorer inland roads, it can end up being very expensive. The dry months from November to June are the best time to move around the island. There is a very useful boat service between Coron and El Nido which has facilitated travel to the north of the island. Boat cruises from two or three days up to a couple of weeks are an interesting and surprisingly inexpensive way of getting around the islands. These are proving quite popular with travellers, as the tours include full-board and meals as well as travel. A typical cruise on a comfortable and well-equipped outrigger or catamaran might cost about US$40–50 a day.

CENTRAL PALAWAN
Puerto Princesa
The provincial capital, situated on a sheltered, deepwater harbour along the island's east coast, is Palawan's main commercial and transportation centre. Civic pride is high in Puerto Princesa, which must rank as one of the most strikingly clean cities in the Philippines. The Spanish founded the city in 1872 but there are few reminders of their presence. Hotel- and restaurant-lined Rizal Street is the city's main boulevard, connecting the airport to the east with the wharf to the west. The few sights the city has include its twin-spired cathedral, a fascinating public market with an excellent fish section, a busy wharf area and several beautiful old stone buildings which stand in marked contrast to the wooden huts you see built over the water near the wharf. The city's main celebrations are its Foundation Day fiesta held on 4 March, and its annual Our Lady of the Immaculate Conception festival which takes place on 8 December, a colourful event featuring processions, beauty contests and concerts in the park. There are two tourist offices, one at the airport and another along Rizal Street. There is also a Provincial Tourist Office on Rizal Avenue. Visitors can change travellers cheques and US dollars at the PNB, Metrobank and at A S Money Changer. This is definitely the place to do it, as there are virtually no money-changing facilities outside of Puerto Princesa.

Where to stay
Palawan Hotel, on Rizal Ave. Tel: 2326. Pleasant rooms near the airport. Singles and doubles with air-conditioning and bath for P500–620.

Badjao Inn, on Rizal Ave. Tel: 2761, fax: 2180. A well-managed place with a large garden and restaurant. Rooms with fan and bath for P220–300, with air-conditioning and bath for P490–700. Some rooms have TVs and refrigerators.

Yayen's Pension, on Manalo St Extension. Tel: 2261. A friendly place with a garden and coffee shop. Pleasant rooms with fan and bath for P100–200, with air-conditioning and bath for P420.

Casa Linda, on Trinidad Rd. Friendly and helpful people run this popular inn and restaurant. Room with fan and bath for P340–390, with air-conditioning and bath for P470–540.

Bavaria House, on National Rd. Basic cottages with fan and bath for P290–340. Run by a German.

Emerald Hotel, on Malvar St. Tel: 2611. A comfortable place to stay with a swimming pool and restaurant. Rooms with air-conditioning and bath for P550–700, suites for P900.

Greenwood Country Traveller's Resthouse, on Rizal Ave Ext. Has a coffee shop, pool and restaurant. Rooms with air-conditioning and bath for P500–750.

Aberlardo's Pensione, on Manga St. Tel: 2049. Basic rooms with fan for P170–220, and with air-conditioning and bath for P480.

Where to eat

Casa Linda's, on Trinidad Rd. An excellent restaurant in a pleasant garden setting. Don't forget to spray yourself liberally with insect repellent though.

Edwin's Food Palace, on Valencia St. Good Chinese and Filipino food.

Kalui's Restaurant, near the Badjao Inn on Rizal Ave. One of the best places in town. Palawan is renowned for its seafood and this is a good place to sample it. Apart from the food there is an excellent library of books on Palawan and other subjects here, so it is all very civilised.

Ignacio Restaurant, on Quezon St. Inexpensive and tasty Filipino dishes.

Café Puerto, on Rizal Ave. Very good French dishes.

Rumble Bumble Noodle House, on Rizal St. Good for a quick cheap bowl of steaming noodles.

Sonne Gasthaus, on Manalo St Extension. Good for breakfast. Also has German and Filipino dishes.

Trattoria Terrace, on Rizal Ave. European pasta dishes and well-cooked steaks.

Entertainment and nightlife

The Kamayan Folkhouse & Restaurant, on Rizal St. Has folk singers at night.

Café Puerto, on Rizal Ave, features live guitar music and folk singers.

Café Nostalgia. As the name suggests, the café serenades its customers with old favourites.

Prism Disco, in the Asiaworld Resort Hotel Palawan. A smart dance club.

Bang Bang Disco, on Valencia St. Also has live music.

Edwin's Food Palace & Disco, also on Valencia St. Has films showing in the daytime, and then becomes a disco at night.

Side trips from Puerta Princesa

White Beach is actually in the city itself, on its eastern side. Also towards the airport you may notice the conspicuous **Vietnamese Refugee Centre** which is easily reached by tricycle. The attraction here for most visitors is a good Vietnamese restaurant called Phoo which is located near its gate. **Iwahig Penal Colony** is one of the largest open prisons in in the world. Visitors come here as there is a souvenir shop where handicrafts made by the inmates can be bought. The prison is a commendable showcase for the country's generally progressive penal system. It's a lively institute with prisoners engaged in a number of different activities from rice cultivation and fishing to making handicrafts. You can catch a jeepney from Valencia Street to the colony at 09.30 daily. It's about 25km from town. On the way back from the prison you can stop off at the Irawan **Crocodile Farming Institute**, where work is going on to protect the endangered Philippine crocodile from extinction. Admission to the centre is free. It is open from Monday to Friday, 13.00–16.00, and on Saturday from 08.00 to 12.00. **Honda Bay** and the islands that can be reached from its beach or wharf are popular with locals at the weekend and with divers and snorkellers throughout the year. *Bancas* can be hired to visit Snake, Starfish and Pandan Islands. Tagburos, 12km from Puerto Princesa, is the main gateway to the area. There are good beaches and coral reefs here. Serious divers can hire a banca and sail 6km west of the bay to an almost perfect coral reef that lies between Pandan and Canon islands. It is possible to stay overnight at the very pleasant **Meara Marine Island Resort** on Meara Island. There are jeepneys and buses heading in this direction from the market in Puerto Princesa. **Santa Lucia Hot Springs** makes an interesting excursion from the capital, but in order to reach them you will have to hike for 7km after being dropped off by jeepney or boat at Santa Lucia. Weekends can be crowded, as many locals undertake the hike then. On Mondays the springs are closed for cleaning. **Turtle Cove** is along the Santa Lucia coastline. There is a popular dive spot near there called Putol na Ilog, which has an extensive coral reef easily accessed by *banca* from Santa Lucia.

NORTHERN PALAWAN
St Paul Subterranean River National Park

If Palawan is one of the last great destinations for the ecotourist in the Philippines, then the Underground River, as it is better known, is a unique and spectacular part of what the island has to offer anyone even mildly interested in the country's natural wonders. The park covers 39km^2 of tropical forest, caves, soft beaches, marble mountains and the famous underground river itself, said to be the longest in the world. The park's wildlife is diverse, with monkeys, lizards, snakes and over 60 species of birds. Among the rarer forms of birdlife identified in the park are the Philippine cockatoo, Tabon birds, the white-bellied sea eagle and Pacific reef egrets.

The Underground River is entered through a hole in the rock of a scenic lagoon on Palawan's west coast. The network of caves and caverns extend for over 8km through corridors of stalagmites and stalactites, echoing chambers and Hansel-and-Gretel-like caverns supported by tapering and fluted columns and piped walls. Between caverns the river follows an unbroken faultline which has formed a pitch-black, at times low, tunnel through which bats swoop continuously overhead. The river is explored by boats provided by the park authorities and a guide equipped with a strong kerosene lamp.

The park can be reached as a day trip from San Vicente and Port Barton, or by outrigger from Macarascas and Baheli, but the easiest way of getting there is from Sabang. The Park Ranger Station can be reached on foot by following the beach at Sabang in an easterly direction for about 2km. It is another 2km along a jungle track, or a path known as the "monkey trail", before you reach the entrance of the cave. An admission fee of P150 is charged for the permit to the cave. This includes the paddle boat and guide who will take you along the river. It is also possible to go by boat from Sabang to the cave for about P350. Very basic accommodation is available at the ranger's station, but you will have to bring your own food if you intend to stay overnight, There is no electricity there, but lamps are supplied. A little discomfort is a small price to pay for the experience of staying over in this beautiful, untamed part of the island. Trips can also be made from Sabang to a more recently discovered cave called Ren-Pat Cave, to a lovely waterfall that cascades into the sea west of Sabang, and to Cabayugan, a village south of Sabang that is located in a spectacular setting of karst and marble mountains. From Cabayugan it is a short distance to the Kawali and Lion Caves.

Where to stay

Villa Sabang. Has comfortable though simple cottages for P200–240. There are also cheaper dormitory beds for P100. There is a restaurant here and the villa staff can organise mountain trekking day trips with a guide.

Robert's Beach and Cottages. Comfortable cottages for P200, with bath for P240. Conveniently located next to the friendly Coco Grove Canteen.

Mary's Cottages, near the entrance to the national park. Small and comfortable cottages for P240–280. Has a restaurant.

Bambua Jungle Cottages. It is about a 1km walk to the cottages but well worth it as the setting, in a jungle clearing surrounded by mountains, is stunning. Nicely designed cottages for P100–300. The restaurant here is one of the best in the area.

San Rafael

A night or two in this small coastal village can be exceedingly relaxing. The atmosphere in and around San Rafael is soothing, though there are possibilities for exertion in the form of swimming, snorkelling, jungle hikes to waterfalls, and a trek to nearby Batak tribes, if required. Buses leave from Puerto Princesa for San Rafael in the early morning. There are plenty of jeepneys as well which leave from the terminus near the market in Puerto Princesa.

Where to stay
Tipanan sa Palawan Resort, on Tanabag Beach, a little east of San Rafael. Small but clean cottages with fan and bath for P275. There is a restaurant.

Duchess Beachside Cottages. Run by the same people who manage the Duchess Pension House in Puerto Princesa, the cottages here are right on the beach. There is a restaurant. P150–200.

Port Barton
Because of its well-appointed beach, excellent dive spots and the natural beauty of its setting, Port Barton has been transformed from a sleepy little village into one of the top beach destinations in the country. The spartan but friendly locally run inns of a few years ago are now in competition with new beach resorts opened by foreigners and investors from Manila. The area is still exceptionally beautiful, though, and the bay facing Port Barton is well endowed with dazzling white beaches and coral gardens. Side trips can be made from here to the Underground River when the weather allows. On average, boatmen charge about P150 for a half-day snorkelling expedition into the bay, P2,000 per person for a two-day excursion to the Underground River, and P2,750pp for a three-day trip by outrigger to El Nido. In the case of these last two options, the weather should be studied very carefully before committing yourself.

Getting there
Jeepneys leave from the market in Puerto Princesa for Port Barton between 07.00 and 09.00 daily. Jeepneys can also be taken from the market in Roxas throughout the morning. A jeepney in the other direction, heading for Puerto Princesa, departs from Port Barton at 06.00. There are also Rozas-bound jeepneys later in the morning.

Where to stay
Summer Homes. Simple frame cottages for P250.

Shangri-la Scandinavian Resort. Basic cottages for P200, with bath for P300–400. Good diving amenities here and a restaurant.

Allsan's Cottages. Basic accommodation but clean. Cottages for P250.

Elsa's Place. A popular complex with a nice restaurant. Rooms for P140–190, cottages with bath for P300–350.

Manta Ray Island Resort, on Capsalay Island, sometimes known as the Three Sisters Island. A very attractive place with a lovely garden and well-decorated cottages. Under Italian management. Cottages are P1,800, which includes meals. The food is very good.

Roxas

Roxas is a small, relatively unimportant port and regional trading centre with a lively fruit and fish market. It is a waystation for travellers heading north or south. There are several interesting islands scattered around the bay near Roxas which might profitably detain the traveller. Stanlake Island is a nesting site for tabon birds and a silica sand extraction area. Green Island has an extensive reef good for snorkelling. Coco Loco Island (its real name is Reef Island) is probably the most beautiful coral island in the area and also offers comfortable accommodation for visitors.

Getting there

There are daily Puerto Royale buses leaving from the market in Puerto Princesa every morning. The first one is at 03.00. Morning jeepneys also undertake the 5hr run. There are regular boats from Reef Island to Roxas. The Coco-Loco Island Resort's own boat runs twice daily between Roxas and Reef Island.

Taytay

The little fishing port of Taytay was founded by the Spanish in 1622, and served as the provincial capital of Palawan for some years. It was also an important military base. Ruins of its old stone fort and a Spanish church still remain. *Bancas* can be hired from Taytay to visit nearby islands like Elefante Island with its clear lagoon. Paly Island is interesting, as giant turtles come ashore from November to December to lay their eggs. Flower Island is an idyllic place which has a good dive resort run by a Frenchman. Pabellones Island is noted as a place where birds' nests, destined to be made into bird's nest soup, are gathered. Interesting side trips can be made from here down a river lined with mangroves to Malampaya Sound, Tabuan and Liminangcong. There is also a beautiful lake surrounded by forest and jungle called Lake Danao, which can be reached by jeepney in under 30 minutes.

Getting there

It takes about nine hours by Puerto Royale bus from the market in Puerto Princesa to Taytay. The bus, therefore, leaves early, at 05.00. In the opposite direction, the bus bound for Puerto Princesa leaves even earlier, at 03.00.

Where to stay

Pension House, along Taytay Bay. Reasonable rooms with fans for P70–100 and cottages with fans and bath for P140–550. There is a nice restaurant here.

Publico's International Guesthouse. Pleasant rooms for P140. There is also a restaurant here.

Government Resthouse, beside Lake Danao. Basic accommodation (P120) arranged through the park ranger there.

Flowers Island Beach Resort, about 50km northeast of Taytay. Tastefully decorated cottages offering full board for P700pp. You can check at Pem's Pension House in Taytay for information on availability of cottages, as they are in short supply.

El Nido

The small town of El Nido, its immediate setting and the islands of the Bacuit Archipelago which face it, are fast gaining a reputation as one of the most beautiful natural regions of the Philippines, a superb resort option and diving spot. Swiftlets build their nests in the caves and crags of the towering limestone cliffs that dominate the area. Their nests are the main ingredient of nido soup, more commonly known as bird's nest soup, an expensive dish much coveted by the Chinese. You will have to go to Hong Kong or Manila, though, to try it. If you are lucky you might be able to observe gatherers climbing over their elaborate framework of bamboo scaffolding to collect the precious nests. Resorts around the area offer facilities for scuba diving, snorkelling, waterskiing, canoeing and windsurfing. You can easily join groups of people renting a *banca* to the outlying islands and islets of the archipelago, or enjoy a cruise on a glass-bottomed boat. Other excursions include the black marble Pinasil Cave at Bigan, flora and fauna at the marine turtle sanctuary at Intalula, a day trip to the extraordinary Calauit Game Reserve where African animals are bred and kept, and the dramatic rock formations at Dilumacad, which are best seen at dawn. The impressive Malingay Falls and the Makalimot hot springs also make good excursions from El Nido. The area is fairly remote, especially for people coming overland, so travellers often end up staying for at least a few days to make the effort of getting there worth their while. Many people, including large numbers of Japanese enthusiasts, come here for the diving. The coral is breathtaking out in the archipelago and the visibility excellent. The diving season runs from November to June.

The increasing popularity of the area, and its reputation as one of the last great unspoilt wildernesses of the Philippines, has led to the creation of some very comfortable accommodation, particularly on scenic Miniloc Island, location of the world-class El Nido Resort. New accommodation is being built on Pangalussain, Matinloc, Pinsail and Turtle Islands.

Getting there

Chartered planes fly from Manila to the small airstrip located near El Nido, where passengers bound for the El Nido Resort board outriggers for the remaining 45-minute stretch to town. Most people arrive by land. There is an early morning jeepney from Puerto Princesa which undertakes the 10hr trip, and there is also a Puerto Royale bus which leaves at 05.00 for Taytay, where it is possible to transfer to a jeepney for the final stretch to El Nido. There may be other bus options from Puerto Princesa by now, so check at the market. There is one boat a week between Manila and El Nido and several *bancas* run between Liminancong and El Nido. It is possible to charter a *banca* for the three-day voyage from Port Barton to El Nido, but extreme care should be taken to check out prevailing and expected weather conditions. If you have a good stomach and a level head, this is one of the most challenging adventures that can be undertaken in the Philippines.

Where to stay

Mr Ellis Lim's. An inexpensive guesthouse. Mr Lim himself is a mine of information about the area. Decent rooms with fan for P200–250.

Marina Garden Beach Cottages. A peaceful location on the beach. Cosy rooms for P80–140, and cottages for P240–350.

Lally and Abet Beach Cottages. Another quiet location at the end of the bay. Pleasant rooms from P280, and cottages with bath for P450. There is a restaurant.

Bay View Inn. Pleasant place with a balcony restaurant. P100–130 for simple but clean rooms.

Austria's Guest House. Has a nice restaurant and pretty garden. Rooms for P60–80, and with fan for P90–120.

Malapacao Island Resort, on Malapacao Island. A real island retreat run by an Australian woman and a Filipino who like to keep animals and grow all sorts of interesting plants. It's definitely not your standard beach resort but if you like nature and tranquillity, this is the place to stay. Dormitory beds for P440, rooms for P600–950, and cottages with bath for P700–1,350. These rates include three meals a day.

El Nido Resort, on Miniloc Island. The best-known accommodation in the area. Full board in excellent, tastefully decorated cottages for US$220–340 a day. The meals are buffet style and excellent. The rates also include full use of diving gear and diving excursions organised by the resort. Reservations can be made through the company called Ten Knots Philippines (tel: 818 2640).

Other good places to stay in and around El Nido are the **Gloria Fernandez Beach Cottages**, **El Nido Cliffside Cottages**, **Tandikan Cottages**, **Lualhati's Cottage** near Corong-Corong, and the **Pangalusian Resort**, on Pangalusian Island, where beautiful, very upmarket cottages can be rented for US$220–330.

Where to eat

Countryside Restaurant. A nice selection of local food and seafood dishes.

Tia Bodin Restaurant. Good Filipino and local dishes. Sometimes has live music.

Vicenta's Eatery. Inexpensive Filipino and other food.

Elm's Café. Well-prepared dishes at affordable prices.

THE CALAMIAN GROUP

For those who are prepared to make the effort to reach them, the Calamian Group, sometimes referred to as the Calamianes, is a remote region of untamed beauty. The three main islands of Busuanga, Culion and Coron are large forested and mountainous terrains, while the smaller islands and coral islets in the group offer divers the challenge of a lifetime in waters which have barely been tested yet. There are innumerable Second World War shipwrecks listing in the shallow waters of these islands, particularly in the Coron Bay area, which add extra interest for serious divers. There is a diminutive airport at Busuanga served by PAL, Air Link and Aerolift. There are also shipping lines that include the Calamian Group in their schedules.

Busuanga Island and town

The two main settlements on the island are Busuanga town and Coron. During the dive season there are daily Aerolift flights to Busuanga. The town is a good base from which to explore the other parts of the island and some of its special sights like the Calawit National Park, an interesting wildlife sanctuary. Pinnacle Rock, off the northwest coast of the island, is a popular spot for snorkelling, with shallow drop-offs and countless shoals of fish. You can hire *bancas* in Busuanga and sail up to Malajon Island as well, the nearest large land mass to the rock. Nearer to Busuanga, the Simlayan Waterfall and a number of caves can be visited.

Concepcion, a village between Busuanga and Coron, is an interesting little area. Concepcion Falls are a popular weekend spot for locals, but there is also a pearl culture farm close to here. Near to the farm, divers occasionally swim out to the wreck of a Japanese cargo ship which was torpedoed here in 1944. Part of the ship is visible above the water line. Divers should be very careful exploring the muddy waters around the wreck, however, as there is still live ordnance aboard.

Where to stay
Busuanga
Las Hamacas Resort. A good atmosphere in this cottage complex run by a Filipina woman and her French husband. Comfortable cottages for P1,800–2,800 a day, including three meals.

Concepcion
Pier House Lodging. Another foreigner, an Englishmen this time, runs this place. Cottages with fan and bath for P120–150. Has a nice restaurant and diving trips can be arranged.

Sea Side Highway Lodging House. Basic but clean rooms for P80–140. Can also organise boat tours for the day.

Coron Island

Coron Island is situated across the water from Coron town on Busuanga Island. Coron Island is a scarcely populated island of lakes, limestone rock hills and forests. Fishing, logging, mining and shellcraft are the island's main activities. One of the main attractions on the island is the Makinit Hot Springs, said to be one of the finest in the Philippines. It is possible to soak in pools here which are only a few metres from the beach. Visits can also be made to Lake Abuyok and the nearby Siete Pescados Islands. Delian and Guintungauan islands, both noted for their excellent coral, shells and marine life, can also be visited by *banca* from Coron.

Where to stay
L&M Lodging House. The rooms are very small here but their location, built on stilts over the water, is novel, and each has a small veranda where, mosquitoes permitting, you can sit out. There is a restaurant, and diving options are offered too. Rooms with fan for P90–180, with fan and bath for P240.

Kokosnuss Resort. A comfortable place with a swimming pool, restaurant and nice garden. Standard cottages for P250, cottages with bath for P550.

Bert Lim Lodging House. More like a homestay set-up, as this is a private house where guests take three meals a day. Friendly establishment with rooms for P320.

Sea Breeze Coron Lodging House. A friendly and cosy place with rooms for P90–160 with fan, P240 with fan and bath.

Culion Island
Known in the Philippines as Leprosy Island, on account of the 600 or so lepers who live in the colony here, the area around the settlement of Halsey is the home of several members of the Kalamian ethnic minority. Off of the southeast coast of Culion, there are a series of excellent coral reefs, where divers and snorkellers can see a fine cross-section of marine life, including turtles, giant clams and the occasional barracuda. The area further south, called Tres Reyes, offers even better snorkelling and diving prospects.

THE CUYO ISLANDS

Though administratively part of Palawan Province, the two main islands of Cuyo and Agutaya, and the 40 or more other islands in this group, sit to the north of the Sulu Sea in rich fishing grounds fractionally closer to Panay Island than they are to Palawan. So far, the islands have hardly been affected by tourism and their environment remains relatively unspoilt, at least for the time being. Many of the islands in this group are formed entirely of coral, and the clear waters of this region offer stunning visibility and marine diversity.

Getting there
At present there are two ships serving the Cuyo Islands, both out of Puerto Princesa. There is also a Cardinal ferry which stops off every fortnight at Cuyo on its way between Puerto Princesa and San Jose de Buenavista on

Panay Island. There may be some unscheduled stopovers by other companies going further afield as well. It would be worth while checking there to see if any plans exist to lay on further services to the islands. Jeepneys and tricycles are extremely rare on the island. The only viable way of getting around is from port to port by privately chartered boat, a rather expensive way of doing things.

Cuyo Island and town

Cuyo is an attractive little town with neat and tidy streets, an old Spanish fort completed in 1677 as a defence against Moro pirates, a number of old stone houses, and the more distinctive bamboo variety favoured by the locals. Cuyo must be one of the cheapest places in the Philippines to eat cashew nuts, which are grown here in abundance. Most foreigners who ever make it to Cuyo come for the snorkelling as much as the peace and quiet of nature. Snorkellers usually charter *bancas* to visit places like Gosong Rock and the coral-rich areas to the south and west of Canipo, or a little further on to the marine abundant southern coast of Taganayan Island.

Agutaya Island

The small wooded island of Agutaya was the site of an old Spanish fort, but is better known these days for its offshore coral and the impressive Sua Caves. Another set of caves further north, the Baluarte Caves, can be visited by banca. It takes longer to visit the Halog Island Bird Sanctuary but it is a couple of hours at sea well spent. Agutaya's offshore islets like Manamoc and Oco are beloved of adventure snorkellers.

SOUTHERN PALAWAN

Quezon

Quezon is a pleasant but rather inactive little west coast fishing town which few travellers would bother to pause in were it not for the Tabon Caves. To be fair, there is quite a good beach at Quezon, and a small underground river which can be partially explored. The offshore island of Tamlagun can be reached in one hour by *banca* from Quezon. It is another beautiful Philippine island that has all the usual adjuncts of paradise – a dazzling white beach, friendly natives and superb offshore coral. There is even accommodation on Tamlagun, in the form of basic nipa huts run by a German who lives on the island.

The Tabon Caves, which are now part of a national park, were first excavated by Dr Robert Fox in 1962. Fox discovered tools, the fossilised bones of various kinds of birds and bats and, most significantly, a woman's skullcap which was dated to about 22,000BC. The caves were used as both residence and burial site. Only a small number of the 200 or more caves at Tabon have been explored so there may be more finds to come. There is not actually a great deal to see in the caves but they are

atmospheric and the archaeological importance attached to them gives
them a certain aura. If you want to visit the caves you have to go to
Quezon's National Museum first, to pick up a guide.

Getting there

There are several daily Charing Bus Lines buses running to and from
Puerto Princesa and Quezon. There are also plenty of jeepneys plying this
route during the mornings.

Where to stay

Villa Esperanza, near the bus terminal. A well-organised place with a
restaurant. Basic rooms with fan for P100, with fan and bath for P340–400.

New Bayside Lodging House, near the wharf. A friendly and obliging place.
Simple rooms with fan for P120, with fan and bath for P150.

Tabon Village Resort, 4km northeast of Quezon on Tabon Beach. A nice
bayside location with comfortable accommodation. P100–140 for rooms, and
P240–350 for cottages with baths.

Brooke's Point

This very English-sounding town, with its navigational watchtower, takes
its name from the explorer Sir James Brooke who, for some reason that
has never been explained, placed his services and energy at the disposal of
the area's early settlers. Apart from the watchtower which he built, some
of the points of interest in the area are the offshore dive sites around
Tagalinog Island, the Sabsaban Waterfalls and the sulphur springs at
Mainit, 12km northwest of Brooke's Point.

Getting there

Princess Transport, Mic Mac Trail and Puerto Royale buses have daily
departures from Puerto Princesa to Brooke's Point. Look out also for
jeepneys that undertake the same route.

Where to stay

Silayan Lodge. A friendly place with simple but clean and serviceable rooms.
P70–120 for rooms with fan, P180 with fan and bath, and P350 with air-
conditioning and bath.

Sunset Travel Lodge and Garden. Has a restaurant and disco. Rooms with fan
and bath for P240, with air-conditioning and bath for P380.

Cristina Beach Resort, along Tagusao Shore, 7km northeast of town. Although
the beach is not up to much, the resort is run by friendly and obliging people
and there is a decent restaurant.

Rio Tuba

Road and boat links connect Brooke's Point with the small fishing village
of Rio Tuba, where the road swerves west before snaking up the coast
back to Quezon and beyond. The port was known as the gateway to Ursula

Island, a former bird sanctuary of some importance. Before hunters and egg-gatherers devastated the island, ornithologists from around the world would make the pilgrimage to the island to observe species like terns, imperial pigeons and rare doves. Sadly, few of the estimated 150,000 birds that used to inhabit the island remain. Ursula's only remaining assets are its sandy white beach and its offshore coral. What happened on Ursula Island is something that is being replicated in one form or the other all over the Philippines. Travellers bear just as much responsibility as the Philippine people themselves in making sure that the natural wonders of these islands are cherished and venerated, not ravished.

The protected Philippine eagle (Pithecophaga jeffreyi) *is the national bird of the Philippines.*

ASIA PACIFIC
BUSINESS TRAVEL GUIDE
1997/8

Covering the countries of the Pacific Asia Travel Association: Australia, Bangladesh, Cambodia, China, Fiji, Hawaii,
Hong Kong, India, Indonesia, Japan, Korea, Laos, Macau, Malaysia, Nepal, New Zealand, The Pacific Islands,
Pakistan, Papua New Guinea, The Philippines, Singapore, Sri Lanka, Taiwan, Thailand and Vietnam

Asia-Pacific Business Travel Guide 1997/98

The business and independent travellers's essential guide to the 36 countries of the Pacific-Asia area.

Doing Business, Etiquette, Tourism Update, What to See, Key Facts, Useful Addresses, over 1000 hotels from Karachi to Honolulu.

"Any business traveller heading east for the first time can be confident with this in his briefcase" - Executive Travel, London

"The most comprehensive, yet compact, Far East guide on the market" - Lloyds List, London

"A fund of information" - Check-In Magazine, Munich

*"**The** Book on business travel"* - Recommend Magazine, USA

328 pages, full colour paperback ISBN 1-871985-25-0   £9.95

(Also now available on the Internet under **http://travel.cm-net.com/pata**)

PRIORY
PUBLICATIONS LTD

SYRESHAM, BRACKLEY
NORTHANTS NN13 5HH
TEL 01280 850603/850218
FAX 01280 850576
E-MAIL priory@dial.pipex.com

Appendix One

Language

Filipinos claim that their country is the third largest English-speaking nation in the world after the USA and Britain. Certainly there are enough competent speakers of the language for visitors to get by without having to utter a word of Filipino or any of the other official languages and dialects of the islands, but it does raise an appreciative smile if you can express yourself with even the most rudimentary phrase, especially in provincial areas.

Numbers

1	*Isa*
2	*Dalawa*
3	*Tatlo*
4	*Apat*
5	*Lima*
6	*Anim*
7	*Pito*
8	*Walo*
9	*Siyam*
10	*Sampu*
11-19	*Labing isa, labing dalawa, etc*
20	*Dalawampu*
21	*Dalawampu isa, etc*
30	*Tatlumpu*
40	*Apatnapu*
50	*Limampu*
60	*Animnapu*
70	*Pitumpu*
80	*Walampu*
90	*Siyamnapu*
100	*Isang daan*
101	*Isang dan at isa, etc*
200	*Dalawang daan*
1000	*Isang libo*
1,000,000	*Isang milyon*

Days of the week
Notice the similiarity to Spanish.

Monday	*Lunes*
Tuesday	*Martes*
Wednesday	*Miyerkoles*
Thursday	*Huwebes*
Friday	*Biyernes*
Saturday	*Sabado*
Sunday	*Linggo*

Months

January	*Enero*
February	*Pebrero*
March	*Marso*
April	*Abril*
May	*Mayo*
June	*Hunyo*
July	*Hulyo*
August	*Agosto*
September	*Septyembre*
October	*Octubre*
November	*Nobyembre*
December	*Disyembre*

Phrases and basic vocabulary

Hello	*Mabuhay*
Good morning	*Magandang umaga*
How are you?	*Kumusta ka?*
Goodbye	*Palaam na*
Thank you	*Salamat*
What is your name?	*Ano ang pangalan mo?*
How much is this?	*Magkano ito?*
What time is it?	*Anong oras na ba?*
It's too expensive	*Ang mahal naman*
Do you have…	*Mayroon ba kayong*
Where is…?	*Saan naroon ang… ?*
I don't have any time	*Wala akong panahon*
Where can I catch the (bus)?	*Saan ang sasakay ng* (bus)?
How many km is it to…?	*Ilan ang kilometro hanggang?*
The bill, please	*Akina ang kuwenta ko*
Good/bad	*Mabuti/masama*
Delicious	*Masarap*
Shop	*Tindahan*
Restaurant	*Restauran/kainan* (eating place)
Chemist	*Botika*
Church	*Simbahan*
Train station	*Himpilan* ng tren
Road	*Daan*
Room/bathroom	*Kuwarto/banyo*
Food	*Pagkain*
Rice	*Kanin*
Bread	*Tinapay*
Tea/coffee	*Tsa/kape*

Appendix Two

Further Reading

Agoncillo, Teodoro, *A Short History of the Philippines*, Mentor Pocketbook, Manila, 1975.

Alejandro, Reynaldo G, *Philippine Dance, Mainstream and Crosscurrents,* Vera-Reyes, Manila, 1978.

Carunungan, Celso Al, *Filipiniana,* Makiling Publishing House, Quezon City, 1968.

Casal, Gabriel S, *T'boli Art*, Filipinas Foundation Inc, Manila, 1978.

Costa, Horacio de la, *Readings in Philippine History*, Bookmark, Manila, 1965.

Fernando, Gilda Cordero, *The Culinary Culture of the Philippines*, Bancom Audiovision Corporation, 1978.

Fernandez, Doreen G, and Alegre, Edilberto N, *Sarap*, Mr and Ms Publishing Co, Manila, 1988.

Gironniere, Paul de la, *Adventures of a Frenchman in the Philippines*, Rarebook Enterprises, Caloocan City, 1972.

Gonzales, C Pedro and Rees, P Colin, *Birds of the Philippines*, The Haribon Foundation for the Conservation of Natural Resources, Manila, 1988.

Goodno, James B, *The Philippines: Land of Broken Promises*, Zed Books, London, 1991.

Hamilton-Paterson, James, *Ghosts of Manila, Vintage,* 1995.

Huke, Robert E, *Shadows on the Land – An Economic Geography of the Philippines*, Bookmark, Manila, 1963.

Jackson, Jack, *The Dive Sites of the Philippines*, New Holland, London, 1996.

Jagor, Fedor, *Travels in the Philippines*, London, 1873.

Joaquin, Nick, *The Aquinos of Tarlac*, Cacho Hermanos Inc, Manila.

Joaquin, Nick, *A Question of Heroes*, Ayala Museum, Manila, 1977.

Licauco, Jaime T, *The Truth behind Faith Healing in the Philippines*, National Bookstore, Manila, 1981.

Mijares, Primitivo, *The Conjugal Dictatorship of Fernando and Imelda Marcos*, Union Square Publications, San Francisco, 1986.

Patanne, E P, *The Philippines in the World of Southeast Asia*, Enterprise Publications, Manila, 1972.

Pedrosa, Carmen Navarro, *Imelda Marcos*, St Martin's Press, New York, 1986.

Robertson, Dorothy Lewis, *Fairy Tales from the Philippines*, Dodd, Mead, New York, 1971.

Roces, Alfredo, *Filipino Heritage*, Lahing Pilipino Publishing, Manila, 1978.

Seagrave, Sterling, *The Marcos Dynasty*, Harper & Row, New York, 1988.

Smith, David and Westlake, Michael, *The Diver's Guide to the Philippines*, Unicorn Books, Hong Kong, 1982.

Steinburg, David Joel, *The Philippines: A Singular and a Plural Place*, Westview Press, Boulder, Colorado, 1982.

White, Alan, *Philippine Coral Reefs*, New Day Publishing.

Zaide, Gregorio F, *The Pageant of Philippine History*, Philippine Education Company, Manila, 1979.

STANFORDS MAPS CHARTS BOOKS

over 30,000 titles

·Maps·Travel Guides·Atlases·Charts & Travel Writing for all corners of the World·

**Flagship Store
12-14 Long Acre
Covent Garden
London WC2E 9LP**

**rapid delivery
international mail order service
Phone 0171-836 1321 or Fax 0171-836 0189**

THE WORLD'S FINEST MAP & TRAVEL BOOKSHOPS

Bradt Publications

Guides for adventurous travellers

Bradt gets there first!

☑ First for country guides

Albania: A guide and illustrated
   journal
Belize, Guide to
Brazil, Guide to: Amazon, Pantanal,
   Coastal Regions (August 1997)
Burma, Guide to
Cuba, Guide to
Eritrea, Guide to
Estonia, Guide to
Ethiopia, Guide to
Ivory Coast
Laos & Cambodia, Guide to
Latvia, Guide to
Lebanon, Guide to
Lithuania, Guide to
Madagascar, Guide to
Malawi, Guide to

Maldives, Guide to
Mauritius, Guide to
Mozambique, Guide to (July 1997)
Namibia & Botswana, Guide to
North Cyprus, Guide to
Philippines, Guide to
Senegal
South Africa, Guide to
Spitsbergen, Guide to
Tanzania, Guide to
Uganda, Guide to
Venezuela, Guide to
Vietnam, Guide to
Zambia, Guide to
Zanzibar, Guide to
Zimbabwe & Botswana, Guide to

☑ First for backpacking and hiking guides

Africa, Backpacker's (East &
   Southern)
Central America, Backpacking in
Chile & Argentina, Backpacking in
Ecuador, Climbing & Hiking in
Mexico, Backpacking in

Peru & Bolivia, Backpacking &
   Trekking in
Poland & Ukraine, Hiking Guide to
Romania, Hiking Guide to
South America Ski Guide

☑ First for rail guides

Australia & New Zealand by Rail
Eastern Europe by Rail
Greece by Rail, with major ferry routes
India by Rail
Russia by Rail, with Belarus & Ukraine

Spain & Portugal by Rail
Sri Lanka by Rail
Switzerland by Rail
USA by Rail

☑ First for wildlife guides

Antarctica: A Guide to the Wildlife
Madagascar Wildlife

☑ First for road guides

Africa by Road
Central & South America by Road

Russia & Central Asia by Road
   (November 1997)

For a fast and friendly mail order service contact
Bradt Publications, 41 Nortoft Road, Chalfont St. Peter, Bucks SL9 0LA
Tel/Fax: +44 1494 873478

Bradt

MEASUREMENTS AND CONVERSIONS

To convert	Multiply by
Inches to centimetres	2.54
Centimetres to inches	0.3937
Feet to metres	0.3048
Metres to feet	3.281
Yards to metres	0.9144
Metres to yards	1.094
Miles to kilometres	1.609
Kilometres to miles	0.6214
Acres to hectares	0.4047
Hectares to acres	2.471
Imperial gallons to litres	4.546
Litres to imperial gallons	0.22
US gallons to litres	3.785
Litres to US gallons	0.264
Ounces to grams	28.35
Grams to ounces	0.03527
Pounds to grams	453.6
Grams to pounds	0.002205
Pounds to kilograms	0.4536
Kilograms to pounds	2.205
British tons to kilograms	1016.0
Kilograms to British tons	0.0009812
US tons to kilograms	907.0
Kilograms to US tons	0.000907

5 imperial gallons are equal to 6 US gallons
A British ton is 2,240 lbs. A US ton is 2,000 lbs.

Temperature conversion table

The bold figures in the central columns can be read as either centigrade or fahrenheit.

Centigrade		Fahrenheit	Centigrade		Fahrenheit
−18	**0**	32	10	**50**	122
−15	**5**	41	13	**55**	131
−12	**10**	50	16	**60**	140
−9	**15**	59	18	**65**	149
−7	**20**	68	21	**70**	158
−4	**25**	77	24	**75**	167
−1	**30**	86	27	**80**	176
2	**35**	95	32	**90**	194
4	**40**	104	38	**100**	212
7	**45**	113	40	**104**	

INDEX